THE RISING
Ireland: Easter 1916

Fearghal McGarry is Senior Lecturer in History at Queen's University, Belfast. He is the author of a number of books on Irish history in the twentieth century, including *Irish Politics and the Spanish Civil War* (1999), and *Eoin O'Duffy: A Self-Made Hero* (2005), which is also published by Oxford University Press.

Praise for *The Rising*

'A vivid and compelling narrative that explores the thoughts, fears, and motivations of the revolutionaries in this seminal event...a poignant mosaic of idealism, bravery, and humanity'

The Boston Globe

'Seamlessly weaves together these richly evocative witnesses with current historiography and narrative.'

America

'A very readable, yet historically important book that will appeal to general readers and to experts.'

The Irish Times

'The Rising not only provides a lucid explanation of what happened in 1916, it also gives us the best account yet of what it was like to be there: with Pearse and Connolly in the GPO, under de Valera's command defending Mount Street Bridge, or just suffering through it all as a helpless civilian. Fearghal McGarry has a keen biographer's eye for human detail and uses it here to weave together the myriad stories of the Easter rebellion.'

Peter Hart, author of *The I.R.A. at War*

'The finest account yet of the 1916 Rising.'

Irish Economic and Social History

'Indispensable . . . a study with which all commentators will have to engage seriously if they themselves are to be taken seriously.'

Irish Historical Studies

'This enormously engaging book is 1916 from the bottom up, as experienced by the ordinary men and women who took part in it . . . McGarry's exceptionally clear account of the pre-war contours of militant Irish nationalism is perhaps as good as we are going to get . . . superbly readable . . . an excellent book.'

History Ireland

'An absorbing study and a rich contribution to the research, development and legacy of Irish contemporary history.'

Literary Review

'A gripping narrative . . . McGarry has triumphantly succeeded in establishing the experience of the Rising at street level.'

Saothar: Journal of the Irish Labour History Society

'An exceptionally balanced, indispensable account of the Rising'

Irish Catholic

THE RISING

IRELAND: EASTER 1916

FEARGHAL McGARRY

OXFORD
UNIVERSITY PRESS

OXFORD
UNIVERSITY PRESS

Great Clarendon Street, Oxford OX2 6DP

Oxford University Press is a department of the University of Oxford.
It furthers the University's objective of excellence in research, scholarship,
and education by publishing worldwide in

Oxford New York

Auckland Cape Town Dar es Salaam Hong Kong Karachi
Kuala Lumpur Madrid Melbourne Mexico City Nairobi
New Delhi Shanghai Taipei Toronto

With offices in

Argentina Austria Brazil Chile Czech Republic France Greece
Guatemala Hungary Italy Japan Poland Portugal Singapore
South Korea Switzerland Thailand Turkey Ukraine Vietnam

Oxford is a registered trade mark of Oxford University Press
in the UK and in certain other countries

Published in the United States
by Oxford University Press Inc., New York

British Library Cataloguing in Publication Data
Data available

Library of Congress Control Number.

2009939952

Typeset by SPI Publisher Services, Pondicherry, India
Printed in Great Britain
on acid-free paper by
Clays Ltd, St Ives plc

ISBN 978-0-19-280186-9(Hbk.)
ISBN 978-0-19-960597-2(Pbk.)

2 4 6 8 10 9 7 5 3 1

Acknowledgements

I would like to thank the staff of the (Irish) Military Archives, particularly Commandant Victor Laing, and the National Archives of Ireland for access to the witness statements of the Bureau of Military History. Patrick Maume and Peter Hart read an early draft of this book, providing generous advice and saving me from many errors. Eve Morrison read the manuscript and shared her unsurpassed knowledge of the Bureau. Máirín Garrett compiled the index. I am grateful also to Lorcan Collins, David Fitzpatrick, Tommy Graham, Margaret Hogan (RTÉ), James McConnel, Sandra McDermott (NLI), Will Murphy, and Colette O'Daly (NLI). I have benefited from the expertise of Matthew Cotton and the staff of OUP, series adviser Richard Evans, and the anonymous readers. Thanks to all who offered advice, encouragement, or assistance along the way, particularly my colleagues and undergraduate and postgraduate students at the School of History and Anthropology, Queen's University Belfast.

This book is dedicated to the girls in my life—Selina, Sofia, and Ava—not least for putting up with the writing of it.

F McG

Who is Ireland's Enemy?

Who is Ireland's enemy?
Not Germany, nor Spain,
Not Russia, France nor Austria;
They forged for her no chains,
Nor quenched her hearths,
Nor razed her homes,
Nor laid her altars low,
Nor sent her sons to tramp the hills
Amid the winter snow.

Who spiked the heads of Irish priests
On Dublin Castle's gate?
Who butchered helpless Irish babes,
A lust for blood to sate?

* * * * *

O God! that we should ever fail
To pay those devils back.
Who slew the three in Manchester,
One grim November dawn,
While 'round them howled sadistically
The Devil's cruel spawn?

Who shattered many Fenian minds
In dungeons o'er the foam,
And broke the loyal Fenian hearts
That pined for them at home?
Who shot down Clarke and Connolly
And Pearse at dawn of day,
And Plunkett and MacDiarmada,
And all who died as they?

Brian O'Higgins

Contents

List of Plates and Maps

Plates

Maps

List of Abbreviations

AOH	Ancient Order of Hibernians
DMP	Dublin Metropolitan Police
GAA	Gaelic Athletic Association
GOC	General Officer Commanding
GPO	General Post Office
ICA	Irish Citizen Army
IPP	Irish Parliamentary Party
IRA	Irish Republican Army
IRB	Irish Republican Brotherhood
OTC	Officer Training Corps
RAMC	Royal Army Medical Corps
RIC	Royal Irish Constabulary
UIL	United Irish League
UVF	Ulster Volunteer Force

Chronology

1798	23 May: United Irishmen rebellion, resulting in thirty thousand dead
1801	1 January: Ireland becomes part of the United Kingdom under Act of Union
1803	23 July: Robert Emmet's rebellion in Dublin
1829	13 April: Catholic Emancipation Act
1845–51	Great Famine, resulting in one million dead and mass emigration
1858	17 March: Formation of Irish Republican Brotherhood in Dublin
1867	5 March: IRB (Fenian) rebellion
1870	19 May: Home Rule movement founded by Isaac Butt
1879–81	Land War hastens land reform in Ireland
1880	17 May: C. S. Parnell elected chairman of Irish Parliamentary Party
1884	1 November: Gaelic Athletic Association established
1886	8 June: W. E. Gladstone's Home Rule Bill defeated in House of Commons
1890–91	November 1890–February 1891: Irish Party splits following O'Shea divorce scandal
1891	6 October: Death of Parnell
1893	31 July: Formation of Gaelic League
	2 September: Gladstone's second Home Rule Bill defeated by House of Lords
1900	30 January: John Redmond reunites Irish Parliamentary Party
1905	28 November: National Council Convention adopts Sinn Féin policy
1907	5 September: Sinn Féin formed
1909	30 November: Lloyd George's 'People's Budget' rejected by Lords
1911	18 August: Parliament Act revokes Lords' power of absolute veto
1912	11 April: Government of Ireland (Third Home Rule) Bill introduced in Commons
	28 September: Ulster Solemn League and Covenant signed by unionists on 'Ulster Day'
1913	31 January: Ulster Volunteer Force formed
	26 August: ITGWU strike, leading to lock-out, begins

1919   21 January: Dáil Éireann (Irish parliament) convened in Dublin
        Irish Volunteers at Soloheadbeg ambush kill two policemen
1920   23 December: Government of Ireland Act partitions Ireland and devolves
        power to Northern Ireland state
1921   11 July: War of Independence ended by truce
        6 December: Anglo-Irish Treaty signed in London
1922   7 January: Dáil Éireann approves Treaty by 64 to 57 votes
        28 June: Irish Civil War begins with fighting in Dublin
1923   24 May: Civil War ends in defeat for anti-treaty IRA forces
1949   18 April: Southern Ireland becomes a republic on Easter Monday
1998   22 May: Electorate of both Irish states endorse Belfast Agreement's new
        constitutional framework for Northern Ireland, north/south, and Irish/
        British relations

Ireland

Introduction

At ten minutes past midday on Easter Monday, 24 April 1916, thirty members of James Connolly's Irish Citizen Army approached Dublin Castle, the imposing complex of buildings that housed the Irish executive and functioned as the administrative heart of British rule in Ireland. Despite their assortment of pistols, rifles, and shotguns, some onlookers did not regard them as much of a threat, mocking their military pretensions by shouting 'pop guns' as they passed.[1] Nor apparently did Constable James O'Brien, a veteran of the Dublin Metropolitan Police in his mid-forties, who stood alone, unarmed, as he manned the public entrance to the Castle. As the uniformed rebels made to push their way through the main gate, he stretched out his arm, blocking their entrance. From a ground floor window, close by the gate, Constable Peter Folan watched in disbelief as Seán Connolly, a well-known amateur actor who was normally to be found working as a clerk in the nearby City Hall, raised his rifle, shooting O'Brien in the head at point blank range. The first victim of the Easter Rising remained on his feet for several seconds, before falling quietly to the ground. The raiding party hesitated, perhaps shocked, before rushing through the gate towards the Upper Castle yard. A soldier caught in the open fled for cover as the advancing rebels fired their shotguns towards the window of a nearby guardroom where six sentries had gathered around a pot of stew.

The rebels quickly overwhelmed the soldiers, who they had unnerved by throwing an unexploded home-made bomb into the guardroom, and tied them up with their own puttees. Less than twenty-five yards away, the Under-Secretary for Ireland, Sir Matthew Nathan, had just begun a meeting with the army's chief intelligence officer, Major Ivon Price, and the Secretary of the Post Office, Arthur Norway, to discuss the suppression of the Volunteer movement, following the discovery of a German

attempt to smuggle rifles into Kerry. Hearing the shots, Price instantly
grasped their significance: 'They have commenced'.[2] Drawing his revolver,
he bolted towards the Castle yard, firing in the direction of 'half a dozen
Volunteers in green coats, dashing about'. Remarkably, Price—soon to
become a Companion of the Distinguished Service Order as a result of his
valiant efforts—appears to have been the only armed soldier within
Dublin Castle at that moment: the sentries had not been equipped with
live ammunition for their rifles, while the nearest reinforcements consisted
of a small force of twenty-five soldiers in the nearby Ship Street barracks
on the other side of the Castle buildings.

What happened next remains unclear although almost everyone
involved agreed that the Castle should have fallen: 'They could have done
it as easily as possible', Price told the commission of inquiry into the
Rising.[3] 'The Volunteers could have easily taken the Castle', Constable
Folan confirmed, 'there was not a gun in it, and any ammunition to be
found was blank'.[4] The *Irish Times* attributed the Castle's survival to the
quick reactions of a plucky sentry who had promptly closed the heavy iron
gates to the Castle yard.[5] Others suggested that the rebels chose to retreat
despite having breached the Castle's defences. J. J. Foley, a postal clerk
who watched the rebels enter the Castle yard, believed that they were
startled by the loud bang of a slammed door.[6] Helena Molony, one of two
women among the Citizen Army raiders, blamed their failure on the
confusion within their own ranks:

> it appeared that the men behind Connolly did not really know they were to
> go through...there was hesitation on the part of the followers. Sean
> Connolly shouted 'Get in, get in'. On the flash, the gates were closed. The
> sentry went into his box and began firing. It breaks my heart—and all our
> hearts—that we did not get in.[7]

Whatever the reason, the Castle survived but it endured the ignominy of
remaining besieged by the rebel raiding party which occupied the City
Hall and *Daily Express* buildings overlooking the Castle gate. Although
two hundred soldiers from the Royal Irish Regiment and Royal Dublin
Fusiliers were immediately despatched to relieve the Castle, they failed to
dislodge the rebels who had barricaded the surrounding buildings and
streets. It was not until almost two hours after the initial attack, when
soldiers finally gained entry to the Castle grounds through the Ship Street
entrance, that the seat of British power in Ireland was secured.

The raid on the Castle encapsulates much of the drama, horror, and confusion of a week that would culminate in the destruction of much of central Dublin. Like the Rising, it exemplified both the remarkable audacity—or absurdity—of the rebels' ambitions and what many would come to regard as the complacent ineptitude of the British administration. The notion that a tiny band of poorly armed rebels could penetrate the heart of the British establishment in Ireland must have seemed unthinkable, to supporters and opponents of the union alike, until they actually did so. Indeed, the most likely reason why the Castle did not fall was that the rebels (who had orders to occupy City Hall rather than the Castle) had not considered it a realistic possibility; after breaching the Castle's defences, they appeared unsure what to do next. We don't know for certain why the organizers of the rebellion did not make more of an effort to capture the most valuable strategic and symbolic target in the country, but in this respect the attack also exemplified the wider Rising which prioritized heroic gestures over practical objectives and was beset by a string of missed opportunities and unforeseen disasters.

It was not only in its audacity that the attack represented a shocking assault on the establishment. The working-class rebels who attacked the Castle belonged to a revolutionary socialist militia, dedicated to the overthrow not merely of British rule but the capitalist order; even more unsettling for some, their numbers included two female combatants, symbolizing the Citizen Army's rejection of the prevailing social as well as economic values. Perhaps most shocking of all, they were prepared to kill their own compatriots to achieve their aims. Although the Easter Rising is usually seen as a chivalrous affair, particularly in contrast to the ruthless guerrilla war that followed, Constable O'Brien—like other men, women, and at least one child who were deliberately shot that day—was unarmed. Like many of those killed by republicans in the struggle for independence, he was an Irishman and probably a Catholic and a nationalist.

The assault on the Castle also demonstrated the tremendous power of political violence, even when deployed on a small scale in a militarily ineffective way by an unrepresentative minority. Arthur Norway, a persistent critic of his administration's reluctance to suppress the separatist movement, had few doubts about the significance of what he had witnessed that afternoon. Describing Britain's humiliating failure to prevent the Rising as an episode 'more disgraceful than can easily be found in its great history', he placed the blame squarely on the Irish

Chief Secretary, Augustine Birrell, and his subordinate, Nathan, whose credibility had been as thoroughly shattered as the Castle's aura of invincibility. Nor were they the principal political casualties of the rebellion. Norway later recalled how, as he observed the 'strange and awful scene' from the darkness of the Castle yard amidst the awesome roar of rifles, machine guns, and bombs as British army soldiers fought to retake City Hall, he had

> turned to the Attorney General, and said, 'This seems to be the death knell of Home Rule'. Now he was a sane and moderate Nationalist. But he said thoughtfully, 'Upon my soul, I don't know are we fit for it after all'. And then, after a little interval, 'The man I am sorry for is John Redmond'.[8]

The raid on Dublin Castle is famous, as are many of the pivotal events of Easter week which have formed the subject of movies, fiction, ballads, poems, school-lessons, commemorations, and endless public and political controversy: few events in Irish history have been so remembered, re-enacted, and re-imagined. Biographies have been devoted to the leading figures, and the rebellion has formed the subject of political, military, diplomatic, and local studies, including Charles Townshend's recent and authoritative *Easter 1916: The Irish Rebellion*. The focus of this book, however, is different. It tells the story of the Rising from within and below, describing the events of this period from the perspective of those who lived through it, particularly the men and women from ordinary backgrounds who have remained unknown figures. It draws on a vast range of first-person narratives, many previously unpublished, to convey the experience of revolution—what it actually felt like—and to address a range of basic questions which continue to divide historians. What led people from ordinary backgrounds to fight for Irish freedom? What did they think they could achieve given the strength of the forces arrayed against them? What kind of a republic were they willing to kill and die for?

Only recently, with the release of the records of the Bureau of Military History, whose vast collection of witness statements form the spine of this study, has it become possible to address these questions in any great detail. Comprising over seventeen hundred first-person accounts detailing the revolutionary experiences of members of Sinn Féin, the Irish Republican Brotherhood, Cumann na mBan, and the Irish Volunteers, the Bureau forms one of the richest and—in relative terms—most comprehensive oral history archives devoted to any modern revolution. While the witness statements do not, for the most part, fundamentally alter our knowledge of what occurred, they enhance our understanding of the motivations, mentality, and experiences of the revolutionary generation, preserving something of the texture and complexity of the past rarely recorded by conventional sources. The statements do not, for example, explain why the raid on Dublin Castle failed—Molony was mistaken in her recollection of a sentry firing shots while Constable Folan prudently chose to return to his work in the Castle library (pasting reports about separatists into books of press cuttings) after he was fired on—but they do tell us a great deal about the events that led up to the attack, what it felt like to be involved in it, and the atmosphere in the Castle and the General Post Office (GPO) in the days that followed.[9] Although the statements were made long after the Rising, they illuminate the thinking of separatists before 1916, a period in which British rule or, at best, Home Rule within the union appeared to represent the only realistic futures and a popular revolution seemed a hopeless pipe dream. The Bureau's witness statements will settle few arguments. Individually, they are inconclusive, contradictory, and fragmentary; but, collectively, they offer an unrivalled insight into the process by which a nation and society was transformed by revolutionary violence.

Given its centrality to this study, a few points about the source—and the use made of it—are necessary. Established in 1947 by the Irish government, in collaboration with a committee of professional historians and former Irish Volunteers, the Bureau of Military History's investigators (predominantly senior army officers) were tasked with compiling detailed witness statements from participants in the Irish revolution. In some cases, these were written by the witnesses but, more frequently, they were formed into a coherent statement by the investigators before being submitted to the witness for verification and signed approval.[10] By the time the Bureau was wound down a decade later, it had accumulated 1,773 witness statements (ranging widely in terms of length, accuracy, detail, and interest), 36,000 pages of evidence, and over 150,000 documents (not consulted for this study). In March 1959, to the dismay of the historians who had cooperated with the project, the collection was placed in eighty-three steel boxes in the strong room of government buildings, where it remained unavailable for public or scholarly scrutiny until its release, following the death of the last recipient of a military service pension, in March 2003.

Given their provenance, the statements of the Bureau of Military History form a problematic source. Many veterans—including Eamon de Valera, the head of the government that established the Bureau and the most prominent living rebel leader by the 1940s—refused to provide statements. Some chose not to participate because of their opposition to the State, others because of their unwillingness to betray confidences, their desire to forget the past, or (as perhaps in the case of de Valera) their reluctance to formally detail their role in it; others refused because of their distrust of the project or the government responsible for establishing it.[11] Many of those who did provide statements were selectively chosen. Relatively few female participants were interviewed, while constitutional nationalists, British officials, and unionists were generally (but not entirely) excluded from the Bureau's remit to record 'the history of the movement for Independence'.[12] Witnesses, who were subject to many pressures, discussed some aspects of the past less frankly than others. They were provided with questionnaires which effectively encouraged them to focus on particular aspects of the revolution while avoiding others, most notably the Irish Civil War of 1922–3. The statements describe not the events of 1913–21 but the witnesses' flawed memories of them from a remove of several decades; their recollections were inevitably distorted by subjectivity, the passage of time, the accumulation of subsequent knowledge, and the impact of later events including, most problematically, the Civil War which bitterly divided Irish revolutionaries for decades or, in many cases, lifetimes.

The Bureau's statements represent a heavily mediated form of oral history, recording those aspects of the past that interviewees were able or willing to recall, reflected through the lens of a state-sponsored historical project. Historians tend to regard oral sources either as a particularly suspect form of empirical evidence, which is nonetheless deemed capable of yielding valuable objective evidence when combined with supposedly more reliable sources such as state archives, or—more radically—as a unique form of source that can provide distinctive insights into mentalities and perceptions rather than objective realities.[13] As oral historians point out, what is thought to have happened is often more significant than what actually occurred, while, for those who study historical memory, the selective nature of oral testimony—its distortions, confusions, and omissions—is more valuable than its accuracy.

Both methods have been applied to these sources. On some issues, the statements provide just as reliable an insight as conventional sources such as police and press reports, which are obviously subject to their own particular distortions. In the absence of any substantial written records of the military plans for the Rising or the inner workings of the Irish Republican Brotherhood, the witness statements constitute some of the most useful evidence we have. But they also provide a valuable, if necessarily subjective, guide to mentalities. Although the reality of the separatist perceptions of Ireland under the union outlined in this book might justifiably be disputed by historians, these perceptions nonetheless constituted the basis for their politicization and actions. While conscious of both the problems and opportunities posed by oral sources, I have generally not drawn attention to them in the narrative that follows. Despite occasionally highlighting inaccurate, implausible, or illogical assertions and, more often, silently discarding unreliable evidence, my aim has been to use this unique source to allow those who fought for a new Ireland to tell their story in their own words.

I

The Rising Generation
Separatism in Ireland

Between 1913 and 1923 a political revolution occurred in Ireland. The violent events of this decade—which included international war, rebellion, guerrilla warfare, partition, secession, and civil war—shaped modern-day Ireland. At the heart of this process was the Easter Rising: before it, the great majority of Irish Catholics backed the moderate constitutional nationalism of the Irish Parliamentary Party; after it, popular support shifted decisively towards Sinn Féin and its more radical goal of a republic. The outcome of the insurrectionary struggle for independence was dominion government for the twenty-six southern counties, and devolved British rule in the north-east of the country, a settlement which armed republican groups continue to contest to this day. Almost a century later, there is general agreement about the events of this revolution but still little consensus on their interpretation. The Easter Rising, the most controversial event in Ireland's modern history, remains central to arguments about the nature and legitimacy of the struggle for independence.

Even now, there is a remarkable degree of uncertainty about fundamental aspects of the Rising. Did the rebels think they had any chance of success? Were they trying to seize power or engaging in a symbolic act of blood sacrifice? What sort of republic did they wish to bring about? The wider impact of the Rising also provokes debate: why did the actions of a small number of unrepresentative individuals have such a profound influence? Fewer than two thousand separatists fought in the rebellion, which most Irish people initially regarded as a reckless fiasco. Yet, by January 1919, a revolutionary government had secured a democratic mandate to establish the republic that the rebels had died to proclaim.

The Easter Rising's place in the broader context of Irish history is no less disputed. Did it represent an unpredictable deviation from the course of Irish politics since the Act of Union? Since its emergence in the 1820s, Irish nationalism had been dominated by constitutional politicians. In contrast, the separatist tradition, while sometimes enjoying a good deal of public sympathy (particularly in retrospect), consistently failed to mobilize support in an effective military or political form. Moreover, by the early twentieth century, Ireland was becoming a more modern, prosperous, and stable society as the historic grievances of nationalists—the demands for religious equality, land ownership, and self-government—were gradually redressed. In 1885, when W. E. Gladstone, the Liberal Prime Minister, announced his conversion to Home Rule, many nationalists assumed that they would see peaceful self-government within their own lifetimes. Although Home Rule for Ireland was enacted at Westminster in September 1914, that alternative future was destroyed—along with much of the centre of Dublin—in April 1916.

The impact of the Easter Rising on subsequent political events remains equally controversial. How responsible were the rebels for the violence which would become such an enduring feature of Irish political life throughout the twentieth century? Since 1916, every republican movement—including the War of Independence-era Volunteers, the anti-treaty IRA of the Civil War, the Provisional IRA during the Troubles, and present-day dissident paramilitaries—have justified their violence by recourse to the spiritual and ideological legacy of the Easter Rising.

I

This book will address all of these questions from an unusual angle: the ideas and experiences of the largely unknown individuals who participated in the Irish revolution at its grassroots. Before doing so, it is necessary to sketch out the broader historical context. Where does the history of the struggle for Irish independence begin? For traditional republicans, like the nineteenth-century revolutionary John O'Leary, the story of Irish freedom stretches back over eight hundred years to Strongbow's invasion of Ireland in 1169: 'If the English had not come to Ireland, and if they had not stayed there and done all the evil so many of them now allow they have been doing all along, then there would have been no Fenianism'.[1]

Although the English Crown's formal authority within Ireland can be dated to King Henry II's expedition in 1171–2 (undertaken in response to Strongbow's success), few historians would take such claims seriously, both because there was as yet no real concept of an Irish national identity in the twelfth century, and because the Anglo-Norman invasion formed part of a much longer and more complex history of mutual interaction and colonization between the hybrid peoples of the two islands and continental Europe. The story of Ireland as a centuries-long struggle for the freedom of a Gaelic, Catholic people from English oppression was a later construct, rooted in the emergence of modern forms of nationalism in the eighteenth and nineteenth centuries, a reality that did nothing to undermine the appeal of this compelling narrative, as exemplified by the ballad which prefaces this book, for modern nationalists.[2]

For many nationalists, the formative era in the struggle for Irish freedom was the sixteenth- and seventeenth-century period of Reformation, plantation, and Counter-Reformation: a brutal and catastrophic era of colonization, dispossession, repression, and exile.[3] The historical basis for seeing this period as the point of origin for centuries of subsequent conflict between both Ireland and England and Catholic and Protestant communities within Ireland is considerably stronger. The late fifteenth century witnessed efforts by King Henry VII to secure the English State's incomplete control over Ireland, most notably Poynings' Law (1494), which subordinated the Irish parliament to English authority in order to better secure the English Crown against rival claimants. The Reformation, which divided sixteenth-century Europe into rival Protestant and Catholic states, had a profound impact on Ireland due to the failure of Protestantism to root itself in Ireland as successfully as it had in England. Although Henry VIII was declared supreme head of the Church of Ireland in 1536 and king of Ireland in 1541, the Gaelic Irish and Old English population remained largely Catholic. The failure of the Reformation in Ireland would become inextricably bound up with the subsequent development of modern Irish nationalism.

The Elizabethan era saw greater efforts to consolidate Protestantism and English rule, and further rebellions by the Gaelic aristocracy (which won international support from the Catholic kingdom of Spain). The policy of plantation, begun under Tudor rule and intensified during the reign of James I (1603–25), would leave a lasting mark on Ireland: the colonization of the native Irish population and the appropriation of its land by

English and Scottish Protestant settlers was intended to reinforce English domination, convert the Catholic population, and bring the benefits of Protestant civilization to the barbarous natives, enriching the colonizers and stimulating economic growth in the process. However, the vulnerability of the plantations was demonstrated in 1641 when the Gaelic Irish and Old English rebelled, resulting in the sectarian massacre of four thousand Protestant settlers and counter-reprisals against Catholics. The rebellion marked the beginning of an extended period of civil war in Ireland, a conflict bound up with wider violent struggles within Britain and continental Europe.

The suppression of the Confederate Catholics of Ireland (who established a provisional executive in Kilkenny in 1642 to assert their rights as subjects of Charles I) during Oliver Cromwell's notorious nine-month campaign was characterized by unprecedented ruthlessness: war, famine, and disease killed around one-fifth of the Irish population during the Cromwellian reconquest of 1649–52.[4] It also resulted in a transformation in Irish landownership which would persist into the late nineteenth century.[5] Although many individual plantations failed, the lasting legacy of the policy was the creation of a permanent population of lowland Scottish Protestants in Ulster. Throughout this traumatic period of conflict, it was religion—rather than nationality or ethnicity—that provided the vital context, even if the subsequent collective memory of this period would come to form an essential part of the story of Ireland for later nationalists and unionists. In the late seventeenth century, the politics of religion would again provide the impetus for violent conflict, most notably at the iconic Battle of the Boyne in 1690 (commemorated to this day by Northern Irish unionists) when William III defeated the deposed Catholic monarch James II. The outcome of the Williamite War confirmed the Protestant dominance of Irish society established by the Restoration.[6]

Although a tradition of sectarian conflict can be traced back to the early modern period, the vital context for modern Irish separatism was provided by the 1798 rebellion and the Act of Union that followed. The 1790s, as Thomas Bartlett has observed, formed 'the crucible of modern Ireland when separatism, republicanism, unionism and Orangeism captured the Irish political agenda for generations to come'.[7] While Ireland had become a more stable political entity in the eighteenth century, its stability rested on inequality, as was illustrated by the infamous penal laws which (however sporadically and selectively) repressed Catholic worship and excluded Catholics from political and administrative offices, land ownership, education, and professions such as the law and army. In response to the growing power of propertied Catholics, the military demands of the State, and more relaxed Protestant attitudes, a series of Catholic Relief Acts had begun to dismantle the penal laws by the end of the century but the Catholic majority continued to be denied political equality by the Irish parliament. Despite this, later nationalists would regard 'Grattan's parliament' (1782–1800) as a kind of golden age of self-government, largely due to their admiration of its supposed achievements of legislative independence and protectionist prosperity, and their perception that it had come about as a result of agitation by a largely Protestant patriot Volunteer force. In reality, the parliament was an exclusively Protestant assembly whose independence from Britain was illusory: its legislation could be vetoed from London and real power continued to reside in the British-appointed Irish executive at Dublin Castle, which was accountable to the British government rather than the Irish parliament.

Partly in response to these limitations, the Society of United Irishmen was founded in Belfast in 1791 by William Drennan, a physician and poet; Wolfe Tone, a Trinity College-educated barrister; and Thomas Russell, librarian of Belfast's radical Linen Hall Library, to campaign for parliamentary reform and an end to English control of Irish affairs. The formation of the United Irishmen is regarded as the birth of modern Irish republicanism, and later generations of republicans would make much of the fact that its Belfast membership was dominated by Presbyterians who, like Catholics, were excluded from patronage and power. In Dublin, the movement attracted middle-class Catholics and Protestants in roughly equal numbers. Influenced by the democratic and republican ideals of the American and French revolutions, the United Irishmen developed in an increasingly radical direction, demanding universal male suffrage and Catholic emancipation (even if some of its leading figures remained privately concerned by the prospect). Following its suppression by the authorities, the society reorganized itself as a secret oath-bound organization dedicated to achieving an Irish republic by armed insurrection. Up to fifty thousand rebels rose in 1798 in a series of uprisings which were ruthlessly crushed by the authorities, resulting in the death of around thirty thousand people. A further abortive rebellion, led by Robert Emmet, occurred in Dublin in 1803.

For later separatists, the achievement of a movement of Catholics, Protestants, and Presbyterians in uniting against British rule in the progressive cause of a democratic, secular, republic would remain an essential corner-stone of Irish republicanism. The stirring rhetoric of Wolfe Tone would inspire republicans throughout the next two centuries:

> To subvert the tyranny of our execrable government, to break the connec-tion with England, the never-failing source of all our political evils, and to assert the independence of my country—these were my objects. To unite the whole people of Ireland, to abolish the memory of all past dissensions, and to substitute the common name of Irishman in place of the denomina-tions of Protestant, Catholic and Dissenter—these were my means.[8]

But, as ever, the reality was rather more complex. The 1798 rebellion was the result of an uneasy alliance between an enlightened middle-class movement and the Defenders, an agrarian secret society whose Catholic membership was more attuned to social and economic grievances and sectarian communal animosities than progressive political ideology. Consequently, the insurrection of 1798 resulted not only in fighting between the Crown forces (aided by loyalist yeomanry) and rebels, but sectarian massacres such as the burning of over a hundred Protestants in a barn in Scullabogue in County Wexford. Such atrocities, and the publicity they received, hastened the decline of the Protestant patriot tradition and radical Presbyterian support for republicanism.

The insurrection resulted in the Act of Union, which came into effect on 1 January 1801, as the British government moved decisively to secure its grip over an assertive, unstable, and politically discredited dependency at a time of international crisis. The act created a new state: the United Kingdom of Great Britain and Ireland. The Irish Commons and Lords were replaced by the presence of one hundred Irish MPs and thirty-two peers at Westminster. The Anglican Churches of England and Ireland were united, the latter remaining the established church of a predomi-nantly Catholic country, and taxation and financial harmony gradually followed. Despite the Act of Union, the geographical, religious, economic, and political distinctiveness of Ireland (which, in 1800, contained a popu-lation half that of Great Britain) ensured that genuine unity remained elusive, a reality reflected by the continued existence of a directly appointed Irish executive at Dublin Castle.

Perhaps most important was the measure excluded from the Act of Union. Underpinning the logic of the union was the belief (encouraged by the British government) that it would allow for a resolution of the

Catholic question. While an Irish parliament controlled by a Protestant ascendancy was unlikely to support full political rights for Catholics (who had won the right to vote and hold most civil and military offices in 1793), the incorporation of the Catholic majority of Ireland as a permanent minority in the United Kingdom would permit such equality without endangering the Protestant constitution of the State. Indeed, alongside patriot sentiment, the fear that Westminster could not be trusted to maintain the Protestant supremacy in Ireland accounted for much Protestant hostility to the union (and the support of many educated Catholics for the measure). However, the failure of William Pitt (in the face of the determined opposition of George III) and subsequent British prime ministers to introduce Catholic emancipation alienated many Irish people from the union.

The extent of Catholic support for—and Protestant opposition to—the union illustrates the openness and unpredictability of Ireland's political future in the early nineteenth century.[9] Moreover, as in earlier centuries, it was religion rather than nationalism that continued to provide the vital driving force for political developments. The skilful harnessing of the demand for Catholic emancipation in the 1820s by the charismatic, belligerent barrister Daniel O'Connell—created the first mass movement in Irish political history (and one of the earliest forms of the phenomenon anywhere). O'Connell's campaign—which skirted the limits of legality—resulted not only in the enactment of Catholic emancipation in 1829 but the emergence of modern Irish nationalism as 'the liberator' turned his attention to the repeal of the Act of Union in the 1830s. That O'Connell's rise was inextricably bound up with the politics of sectarian grievance would profoundly influence the nature of the constitutional nationalist tradition. The perception that British politicians had conceded emancipation not as the just demand which they knew it to be, but as a result of O'Connell's successful exploitation of brinksmanship and the implicit threat of force would also prove significant.

Throughout much of the century that followed, Irish politics remained both highly local and closely integrated within wider British party politics: most Irish MPs were elected as members of the principal British parties until well into the second half of the century. From the mid-1880s, however, when Irish politics polarized over the national question, the majority of Irish MPs were elected as either supporters of Home Rule or (principally in Ulster) as unionists. Nationalist political culture, which grew in confidence and organizational strength over the course of this century, was characterized by two seemingly opposed traditions: moderate constitutional nationalism and militant physical-force separatism. Constitutional nationalists sought self-government within the union by peaceful methods: O'Connell's campaign for repeal was followed by the formation of Isaac Butt's Home Government Association (1870), and Charles Stewart Parnell's more effective Irish Parliamentary Party (1882), which persuaded the Liberal Party to support Home Rule in 1886. In contrast, republicans—most notably Young Ireland (responsible for the farcical 1848 rising) and the Irish Republican Brotherhood (IRB) which rose in 1867—sought the goal of a republic to be achieved, if necessary, by force.

Underpinning these differences over means and ends were divergent ideologies and mentalities. Republican revolutionaries (who drew on mid-nineteenth-century romantic nationalism and the example of revolutionary movements elsewhere in Europe) placed more emphasis on Ireland's distinctive culture as a justification for independence, and they stressed the importance of non-sectarian, egalitarian, and secular ideology. Constitutional nationalist politicians, a more pragmatic and utilitarian breed, were more attuned to the sectarian realities of Irish society, and tended to base arguments for self-government more on principles of democracy and good government than essentialist criteria such as language, cultural identity, or the soul of the nation (although they were far from immune to the appeal of these). Constitutional nationalists, whose ambitions for self-government were dependent on securing the agreement of their allies within the British political system they formed part of, tended to attribute English opposition to their demands to fear or ignorance. Republican rhetoric, as exemplified at its most extreme by John Mitchel who popularized the idea of the mid-nineteenth-century Famine as English genocide and much of the later anglophobic discourse of Fenianism, more often depicted England as an intrinsically evil entity, motivated by ill-will towards Ireland, and their more moderate nationalist rivals as self-serving and morally corrupt.

But it is also important not to exaggerate the differences between these two political traditions, particularly in the decades before the Rising. It was in the interest of Fenians to exaggerate their distrust of parliamentary politics and rejection of constitutional politics in a way that obscured the significance of the movement's interventions in Irish politics, most notably its support for the Parnellite party during the Land War in the early 1880s.

Where republicans proposed a crude dichotomy between the spirit of Fenianism (signifying authentic nationalism) and constitutional nationalist politics (compromise and betrayal), historians detect a more complex spectrum of shifting loyalties. Irish politics under the union did not allow for clear boundaries between these intertwined political traditions. Daniel O'Connell is believed to have been a member of the United Irishmen in his youth; Parnell, who may well have taken the Fenian oath, achieved political dominance in Ireland following a complex and uneasy alliance with the IRB, and even John Redmond—the most moderate (or, his detractors would allege, imperial) of the great constitutional nationalist leaders found himself at the head of Ireland's largest (and largely Fenian-controlled) paramilitary force in 1914.[10] Similarly, some Fenians became prominent parliamentarians in later life, in some cases even accepting high office and royal honours elsewhere in the British Empire.

The constitutional ties that bound Britain and Ireland would form the vital context shaping the major political developments that followed over the next two centuries including, most recently, the Belfast Agreement of 1998. There is little more consensus over the nature of the union now than there was in the nineteenth century when it meant different things to different people. For unionists—who coalesced as a distinctive, coherent, Protestant, political movement in their campaign against Home Rule in the mid-1880s—the union embodied civil, religious, and political liberty. The spectacular industrial growth in the Protestant-dominated north-east of Ulster, which underpinned the economic strength of the movement, was also attributed to the union: 'Look at Belfast', the belligerent Presbyterian minister Henry Cooke famously declared, 'and be a repealer—if you can'.[11] Just as unionists attributed Ulster's prosperity to the union, nationalists blamed the shortcomings of nineteenth-century Irish society— sectarian discrimination, poverty, emigration, and famine—on precisely the same political structure.

While historians believe that social and economic developments in Ireland were only partially influenced by the political structure of the state in which they occurred, they differ as to the effectiveness and legitimacy of the union. To the consternation of republicans, the union proved sufficiently adaptable to resolve many of the outstanding grievances of the Catholic majority by the late nineteenth century. In particular, the emergence of a politically radical but socially conservative popular nationalism, in the form of Parnell's Irish Party which threw its weight behind the

Fenian-backed Land War (1879–81), resulted in a series of acts which would grant most Irish tenants ownership of the land they farmed. Just as land reform diluted the economic power of the Protestant elite, which had retained considerable influence in the administration of Ireland after the Act of Union, the reform of local government in 1898 undermined its political authority, placing local bodies in nationalist hands throughout all but Protestant-dominated Ulster.

Despite such reforms, many Irish nationalists came to regard the union as a source of oppression, lacking in political legitimacy. Archbishop Croke for example, writing in the 1870s, believed that 'the great bulk of our Irish Catholic people are Fenian in heart or sympathy'.[12] Although Ireland formed an integral part of the United Kingdom (and Irish MPs were actually overrepresented at Westminster after the 1884 Reform Act), republicans regarded Ireland's relationship with Britain as one of imperialist subjugation. The union was a product of English political and security interests rather than Irish aspirations, and it was preserved by the threat of force despite the clearly expressed wishes of an Irish majority for self-government. The essential problem with the union (as with the Northern Ireland State for later generations of republicans) was that it was designed to frustrate nationalist aspirations for independence. As Arthur Griffith, the founder of Sinn Féin, put it: '103 Irishmen in the House of Commons are faced with 567 foreigners... [on a] battleground... chosen and filled by Ireland's enemies'.[13]

The truth lies somewhere in between: the complex and ambiguous nature of Ireland's relationship with Britain embodied aspects of democracy (such as it was understood and practiced in this period) and imperialist domination, a reality reflected by the ambivalence of Irish nationalist attitudes towards Britain. There was a colonial dimension to the Irish State under the union (as exemplified by its unaccountable executive and paramilitary police force), but Ireland differed from other imperial colonies in forming an integral part of the United Kingdom with all the rights, freedoms, and privileges which that entailed.[14] Moreover, many of its problems—most notably the Great Famine which resulted in the death of one million people and the emigration of a further two million—were a consequence of poverty and social and economic underdevelopment as well as misgovernment. The legitimacy of the union remains a crucial, irresolvable, issue on which much turns. If Ireland is viewed as forming an integral part of an imperfect but flexible and increasingly democratic constitutional arrangement, the actions of the Easter rebels appear unreasonable and reprehensible. Alternatively, for those who regarded the union as an imperialist façade underpinned by the threat of military force, the rebellion represented a justifiable and admirable assertion of national sovereignty.[15]

Such questions remain central to any understanding of the outlook of nationalists born in the late nineteenth century, the generation responsible for the Irish revolution whose experiences the rest of this chapter focuses on. The Ireland in which they were born was a country where the republican tradition appeared to be a dying anachronism. The IRB, which at its mid-Victorian peak, numbered forty thousand members, was moribund by 1910: 'a home for old Fenians'.[16] By 1914, the leaders of the Irish Party considered themselves the government of the Irish nation in waiting and were treated as such by the British administration at Dublin Castle. This has led many historians to argue that the violent events which followed represented an unpredictable aberration 'from a familiar and stable path of constitutional democracy'.[17]

There are two principal interpretations that seek to explain how 1916 came about and why it had such a decisive impact. The first attributes the success of the Rising to the profound cultural and political changes that occurred between the fall of Parnell (following a divorce scandal) in 1890 and the Great War. The demise of Parnell—a steely, charismatic, yet reserved figure who infused constitutional nationalism with a dignity that appealed even to militant nationalists—and the resulting split within the Irish Party poisoned Irish political life, divesting it of idealism and integrity. The generation which reached adulthood after the fall of Parnell turned away from conventional politics, devoting its energy to the cultural nationalist movements which flourished at the turn of the century. By promoting an awareness of the importance of national identity and the baleful impact of 'anglicization', organizations like the Gaelic League and the Gaelic Athletic Association (GAA) created a more assertive form of nationalism that ultimately led many to question the idea that Home Rule represented the attainment of genuine independence. Although few in number, the Easter martyrs awakened the Irish people to this new spirit whose appeal transcended that of John Redmond's aging party, tainted by its identification with British imperialism and the politics of compromise.

Despite being endorsed by many of those who lived through the period, and given eloquent expression by W. B. Yeats, who grasped the opportunity to write himself into the national narrative, it is an interpretation which has been rejected by many historians. Although the Irish Party was shattered by the split, it reunited under John Redmond in 1900, absorbing potential rivals such as the United Irish League and the Ancient Order of Hibernians, and dominating Irish politics until after the outbreak of the Great War. In contrast, advanced nationalists failed to win a single parliamentary seat throughout this period. Although the Irish–Ireland movement played an important role in shaping ideas about national identity, most of those who joined cultural nationalist movements continued to support Home Rule. Given the lack of evidence to suggest that the Irish Party was anything other than the representative voice of Irish nationalism, most historians focus on the impact of the crises brought about by Ulster's opposition to Home Rule from 1913 and Redmond's support for the Great War to explain the collapse of the Irish Party.

The first part of this book seeks to reconcile these contrasting interpretations by drawing on the testimony of hundreds of cultural nationalists, political activists, and revolutionaries who lived through this period. The second and third chapters outline how the crises of 1913–14 revived separatism, creating an unexpected opportunity for insurrection. The book begins by surveying separatist politics before the Home Rule crisis to explore the appeal and significance of republicanism during a period of apparent failure. In particular, it focuses on the politicization of the 'rising generation', those men and women born around the time of the fall of Parnell who would bring about the Irish revolution between 1913 and 1921.

II

At the turn of the century, Irish separatism remained a marginal and divided political force. The most enduring and important separatist organization was the Irish Republican Brotherhood which, since its formation in 1858, had dedicated itself to achieving an Irish republic through the use of physical force. Following the failed Rising of 1867, the IRB adopted a new constitution in 1873, resolving to 'await the decision of the Irish nation, as expressed by a majority of the Irish people, as to the fit hour of inaugurating a war against England'.[18] This paved the way for its involvement in agrarian and constitutional politics. At its most politically influential, following the 'new departure' in the late 1870s, the IRB became an important force within the Land League and the popular nationalist movement underpinning the Irish Parliamentary Party. However, the growing strength of constitutional nationalism ultimately undermined support for the physical-force variety, as did the determined infiltration of Fenianism by British security forces, and public disapproval of the IRB's involvement in violent outrages within Ireland and Britain. Fear of prosecution—or, for some, excommunication—led to further fragmentation and decline. The IRB remained influential within the Parnellite wing of the divided Irish Party but this proved double-edged, providing the Fenians with a focus for political activity, but offering another avenue for their absorption into parliamentary politics. The reunification of the Irish Party in 1900 further marginalized Fenianism as the IPP's leader, John Redmond, came to embrace a moderate, imperial form of Home Rule. By 1900, the IRB no longer posed a meaningful threat to either constitutional nationalism or British rule in Ireland.

What did it mean to be a Fenian during these years of failure? Although an oath-bound hierarchical fraternity, the IRB's internal structures were democratic, as were its objectives.[19] Fenians were (theoretically at least) organized in 'circles' of up to a hundred members led by 'centres', who were further represented at county, district, and divisional level; members of the latter formed the supreme council which represented the four provinces of Ireland and Britain and regarded itself as the legitimate government of the Irish Republic. The IRB's principal purpose was to promote republican values among the Irish people and to safeguard its own existence until the next revolutionary opportunity arose. Consequently, it prioritized recruitment and propaganda; although a secret society, it was often a highly visible presence in Irish society. Not unlike present-day radicals, its members attended meetings, paid subscriptions, organized demonstrations, and initiated public campaigns; they circulated leaflets, wrote pamphlets, and even published newspapers. One of its most important public roles was the organization of commemorative activities, such as the annual pilgrimage to Wolfe Tone's grave in Bodenstown.

As well as infiltrating more popular cultural nationalist bodies such as the Gaelic League and the Gaelic Athletic Association, Fenians founded dramatic, literary, and debating societies, pipers' bands, choirs, youth clubs, sports teams, dance halls, and even a cinema to recruit members and promote their revolutionary message. From trade unions to abstinence associations, there were few societies that Fenians would not subvert in an effort 'to instil patriotism in the members'.[20] IRB circles disguised themselves as any number of innocuous organizations to avoid police attention. 'We met in Parnell Square every month', a member of the Lord Edward circle recalled, 'we would say "Tonight is our sodality night" '.[21] In Dundalk, the IRB used coursing meetings as a cover—'All prominent men were encouraged to take an interest in dogs and usually kept one'—while tobacco shops played an important role as meeting places in Dublin.[22] The result was a revolutionary underground, extending throughout Ireland to Britain, America, Australasia, and every major global destination for mass Irish emigration after the Famine.

But none of this activism stemmed the movement's sharp decline. The IRB's falling membership resulted, in part, from a concern to build the organization 'by good men or none': potential recruits were closely vetted for ideological and moral shortcomings. The Catholic Church's opposition to oath-bound societies also deterred many recruits and prompted others to leave. But the IRB's lack of appeal, as one supreme council member conceded, was largely due to the popularity of constitutional nationalist politics: 'in those days of denationalisation there may not have been in a whole district a single man imbued with republican ideas'.[23] In Macroom, Co. Cork, for example, the IRB slowly died out as 'most of the members were suspended, one by one, for taking part in politics'.[24] The experiences of Robert Kelly, the IRB centre in Newry, Co. Down, were typical of many provincial Fenians in this period. Despite successfully infiltrating the Gaelic League and GAA, establishing branches of the Irish Ireland Society and Cumann na nGaedheal, subverting the local trades council, and promoting campaigns against British army recruitment, foreign imports, and imperialism, he was unable to sustain an organized separatist presence in the town. Like many IRB organizers, he concluded that his town 'was from the separatist viewpoint rotten'.[25]

Aside from apathy, the IRB faced a number of problems. Most Fenian activity was distinctly non-revolutionary. Liam Walsh's circle in Waterford met only twice a year: 'we used to discuss ways and means of contacting Irish-Ireland organisations with a view to swearing in likely candidates, so that when a favourable opportunity arose an armed rising would be started in Ireland'.[26] 'The principal business transacted' at the quarterly meetings that Séamus Connell attended 'was to listen to Tomás O'Loughlin's appeal to make ready for the fight against British rule'.[27]

Meetings of the supreme council, according to one of its members, 'were largely devoted to reports on the state of the organisation in the several divisions, on finance, on publications; on such events as the Wolfe Tone and Emmet commemorations; on possibilities for the advancement of the Irish republican doctrine and . . . to defeat denationalising schemes'.[28] Revolution was not on the agenda, prompting influential nationalists—such as the acerbic journalist D. P. Moran—to ridicule Fenians as 'prating mock rebels'.

In some parts of the impoverished rural west, the IRB was involved in violence but the extent to which the shooting of bailiffs, policemen, or landlords reflected patriotic rather than social impulses was questionable. In theory, the IRB opposed agrarian violence, arguing that social problems could not be resolved before independence; nor, in reality, was it in its interests to see the resolution of grievances which fuelled resentment of British rule. However, in practice, IRB leaders did support agrarian violence where it resulted in local support.[29] Although the movement was consequently often identified with social radicalism—and its rejection of the traditional deference shown to landlords, magistrates, and priests formed much of its appeal to its predominantly lower-class membership—it remained committed to political independence rather than any particular social order.

It has been argued that the widespread popularity of mid-Victorian Fenianism was due less to its revolutionary purpose than its role in offering young men a place in the world through 'fraternal association and communal self-expression'.[30] Although turn of the century Fenianism was a far more exclusive fraternity, some of its own members expressed similar doubts as to its revolutionary intent. Denis McCullough, one of a younger generation of activists (who would become president of the IRB's supreme council shortly before the insurrection), recalled the depressing circumstances of his induction in a Belfast pub: 'I was duly sworn in by a large, obese man, a tailor by trade . . . I was disappointed and shocked by the whole surrounds of this, to me, very important event and by the type of men I found controlling the Organisation; they were mostly effete and many of them addicted to drink'.[31]

Even sympathetic observers regarded the movement as anachronistic: 'every sizable town possessed a tiny sprinkling of diehard separatists . . . they were respected as idealists, living in a world and an age to which they did not belong'.[32] Augustine Ingoldsby was one of many disillusioned Fenians during this period: 'I had not a very high opinion of the IRB and I did not think they were men of ability'.[33] By the eve of the Home Rule crisis, the Brotherhood remained a marginal force lacking popular support and credibility—'little more than a tiny committee struggling to stay alive'—but its very survival would ultimately prove significant, as would the seizure of its leadership by a younger, more determined, generation of activists in 1912.[34] For much of this period, however, it was cultural and political developments rather than revolutionary Fenianism that provided the most significant challenge to constitutional nationalism and British rule.

III

For many of the generation born around the time of the fall of Parnell, the formative experience of their social and political lives was provided by involvement in cultural nationalist organizations. The Gaelic Athletic Association and the Gaelic League, founded in the late nineteenth century to revive Gaelic culture and reverse the perceived anglicization of Irish society, were the most significant of these. Dedicated to the moral and spiritual (rather than political) regeneration of the nation, both organizations proved immensely popular. By 1908, at the height of the popularity of the cultural nationalist revival, there were 800 GAA clubs and 671 Gaelic League branches in Ireland, with hundreds more based among expatriate communities abroad.[35]

Although both organizations were formally non-political, and attracted the great majority of their members as a result of their social appeal, their objectives of Gaelic revival and 'de-anglicization' were implicitly political. Prominent Fenians were involved in the GAA from its formation, while the Gaelic League fell under the IRB's direct control in 1915. Cultural nationalism also contributed to the radicalization of nationalism in more subtle and profound ways, by changing the way Irish people thought about national identity. The ideas it popularized presented a potential challenge to constitutional nationalism: what was the point of Home Rule if the Irish people became increasingly indistinguishable from the English? Its success in promoting the notion of a distinctive Irish culture, entirely separate to that of Britain, could not but strengthen the position of those who believed that real independence necessitated a separate state rather than a limited form of devolution within the United Kingdom.

As with other essentialist movements that emphasized the importance of ethnic, linguistic, and cultural aspects of the national community that emerged elsewhere in late nineteenth-century Europe, this ostensibly regressive phenomenon was largely a consequence of modernity. The formation of the GAA in 1884, for example, was a product of the same factors—more leisure time, greater prosperity, the growth of the popular press, better transport, and the desire to codify and centralize associational activity—that had resulted in the founding of the Football Association in England two decades earlier.[36] The seemingly distinctive ethos underlying the values that the GAA successfully promoted—strength of character, virility, and patriotism—represented a gaelicized form of the imperialistic values associated with British team sports such as cricket and rugby. However, their avowed aim of de-anglicization—and the long frustration of nationalist aspirations in Ireland—gave organizations like the GAA a political significance lacking in their British counterparts.

Despite the aspirations of figures like Douglas Hyde, the Protestant founder of the Gaelic League who believed in the potential for culture to reconcile sectarian divisions, the Irish-Ireland movement brought about a more narrow sense of national identity. The ideal of the Gael became intertwined with an ethnic conception of identity based on the notion of the pre-Plantation Catholic Irish as the authentic Irish people. Such a worldview—exemplified at its most extreme by the influential rhetoric of D. P. Moran who spoke of Irish Protestants as 'resident aliens' in 'a Catholic nation'—was a product of the discrimination and humiliation experienced by generations of disempowered Catholics. Cultural nationalism exerted a powerful psychological appeal by asserting the achievements of Ireland's historic civilization, which Gaels contrasted with the coarse materialism of contemporary England. It appealed particularly to the rapidly expanding class above the masses: educated, urban youth seeking their way in a society lacking in opportunity.

Although relatively few members succeeded in learning the language, this did not prevent them from enjoying the League's concerts, lectures, debates, céilithe (dances), and feiseanna (festivals) or, for a minority, experiencing its radicalizing influences. P. S. O'Hegarty, an IRB supreme council member, recalled the impact of the Munster Feis he attended in 1902: 'Something in the songs...something in the music...something in the atmosphere gripped me and I seemed to be put in touch with something far back in the race...for the first time I saw the whole of Ireland'.[37]

Although many members recalled that 'there were no politics spoken' at Gaelic League meetings, some branches were more militant than others, and there were many ways in which cultural activism could lead to politicization. In Clonmel, James Ryan's branch learned not only Gaelic but Irish history, patriotic songs, and dances under the suspicious gaze of the police.[38] Tom Harris was introduced to the IRB's newspaper, *Irish Freedom*, during his Irish lessons: 'we became more absorbed in political discussion than in our pursuit of the language'.[39] Similar influences permeated the GAA. In Belfast, Thomas McNally recalled that his team 'had an old military hut as a club room and here I learned something of nationality— seannachí [story-telling] and celidhes were held and national songs were sung and our own dances performed so that I can say the idea of nationalism was taking root'.[40]

For the most committed Gaels, cultural nationalism became more a way of life than a pastime, encompassing a moral as well as cultural dimension: 'there was a sort of honour among the fellows', Augustine Ingoldsby believed, 'We advocated general good conduct, respect for women . . . I never saw the sign of drink on anyone at any of our céilidhes'.[41] Gaels spurned foreign influences in as many aspects of their lives as practicable, even their dress: 'It became evidence of your political opinions to be seen wearing Irish tweed garments . . . to appear at any function in the regulation evening suit was to arouse lively suspicions of your political opinions'.[42] Unsurprisingly, cultural nationalist organizations provided an ideal recruiting ground for the IRB. Padraig O'Kelly believed that his generation experienced 'a kind of natural graduation' from cultural nationalism to separatist violence:

> One usually began by playing Gaelic Football or Hurling; from that the next step was to the Gaelic League; from that again to the Sinn Féin movement and later to the Irish Volunteers. For relaxation we attended céilithe and the Abbey Theatre. We bought nothing but the Irish-made goods . . . With that background it was rather a natural progression to participation in the Rising.[43]

Such accounts provide a valuable insight into the process of radicalization for a zealous minority but a misleading impression of the impact of cultural nationalism generally. Hundreds of thousands of people passed through the GAA and Gaelic League but only a tiny proportion became separatists before 1916, and only a small minority of these participated in the Rising. Most Irish people had no difficulty in reconciling participation in the Irish-Ireland movement with support for constitutional nationalism. The Irish Party, for its part, regarded cultural nationalism not as an insurmountable challenge to its authority but as yet another interest group to be conciliated or absorbed. Rather than representing a powerful movement inexorably radicalizing the masses, the Gaelic League actually experienced a sharp decline in the years before the Rising. Nonetheless, for separatists like Augustine Ingoldsby, cultural nationalism was crucial in reviving 'the spirit of nationality in the country'. How these two important strands of thought—the separatist and the cultural nationalist—converged is considered next.

IV

The IRB faced a dilemma: an insurrection without popular support was futile but conventional politics was seen as not only ineffective but corrupting. Fenianism, however, did not have a monopoly on militant nationalism; the emergence of new forms of political activism, which would coalesce in the creation of Sinn Féin in 1907, provided the most important political development of the first decade of twentieth-century Ireland. Sinn Féin can be seen as both an attempt to resolve the impracticability of republicanism and a convergence of the two most active strands of nationalist activism—the cultural and the separatist—beyond the control of the Irish Party.

The emergence of Sinn Féin was a convoluted process, hindered by the fractious culture of separatism. An umbrella protest group rather than a conventional party, it drew together activists from Cumann na nGaedheal, the National Council, and the Dungannon Clubs. Emerging during a burst of activism prompted by the centenary of the 1798 rebellion, pro-Boer fervour, and opposition to the royal visits of 1900 and 1903, these organizations shared a common ethos and overlapping membership. They represented a politicization of the cultural nationalist agenda, a source of inspiration evident from their protectionist policies and membership of enthusiastic Gaels. But although radical nationalists were united in opposition to the Irish Party, they remained divided between republicans (or separatists)—who sought complete independence from Britain (an objective that necessitated the use of violence)—and 'advanced nationalists' who, more pragmatically, were willing to accept some form of link with Britain in return for essential independence.

These divisions had been surmounted by 1907, partly due to pressure from Irish-America where it was thought 'absurd to have three small organisations in Ireland all advocating the Sinn Féin policy'.[44] The dominant ideological influence behind this new departure was Arthur Griffith. A supporter of the Parnellite and Fenian traditions in his youth, Griffith had spent several years in South Africa running his own newspaper, before returning to Ireland to establish the *United Irishman* newspaper in 1899. In his influential tract, *The Resurrection of Hungary: A Parallel for Ireland*, published in 1904, Griffith drew on a historically dubious but empowering interpretation of the formation of the Austro-Hungarian dual monarchy to argue that it was possible for Irish nationalists to undo the union without recourse to violence. An equally questionable reading of Irish history led him to argue that the repeal of the Act of Union—leading to a return to the 1782 constitution of the King, Lords, and Commons of Ireland—could provide a basis for genuine independence.

In essence, Griffith preached a gospel of self-reliance (as the name Sinn Féin—'ourselves'—suggests). He argued that by taking over local government bodies, contesting parliamentary elections but abstaining from Westminster, and withdrawing cooperation from British institutions while asserting Irish autonomy in every sphere of life, nationalists could build a counter-state. In contrast to many separatists, he emphasized economic revival as much as political regeneration, arguing that protectionism would bring about a modern industrial state of twenty millions. Although republicans disliked Griffith's idea of a monarchic link to Britain, his 'Hungarian policy' offered a pragmatic basis for cooperation between advanced nationalists and republicans. As one Fenian admitted: 'Outside the IRB there were few republicans and Griffith knew it and so did we'.[45] Moreover, Sinn Féin's programme did not require a commitment to what many saw as the unattainable ideal of a republic nor to the risky and morally questionable use of violence. The proposal to sit on local bodies offered a rationale for engaging in electoral politics, while the strategy of abstentionism offered protection from the corrupting influences of constitutional politics.

Griffith was an effective propagandist, as the Ulster Protestant Ernest Blythe testified: 'I became converted to Sinn Féin on the night I sat up reading my first copy of the *United Irishman*'.[46] '*Sinn Féin* was a magical voice to us young people', Denis Madden recalled, 'It seemed to bring back, to the more intelligent young people, a call which had been heard long ago'.[47] But, in conventional terms, Griffith was a mediocre politician, lacking charisma and personal ambition. A combative autodidact, many colleagues found him impossible to work with: 'He did not appear to want co-operation, but obedience'.[48] Patrick Pearse described Griffith as 'too hard, too obstinate, too intolerant, too headstrong', characteristics that may account for the success of many of his ideas despite the opposition they provoked from republicans and Home Rulers alike. Established during a demoralizing period when the Liberal Party had dismayed nationalists by offering only the extension of local government, Sinn Féin initially won the support of two Home Rule MPs. Although it established 115 branches, and held 13 seats on Dublin Corporation, the party fell into decline after losing a by-election in 1908. Despite its ineffectiveness, the 1909 Land Act helped to restore flagging nationalist confidence in John Redmond, while the general election of 1910, which left the Liberals reliant on his party's support at Westminster, further galvanized the campaign for Home Rule.

Sinn Féin had missed its opportunity. Kevin O'Shiel, who arrived in Dublin to study law in 1910, recalled that his fellow students regarded its supporters as 'either idealistic idiots, baying for the moon, or designing mischief-makers, paid and employed by the Castle to subvert and destroy the Home Rule movement'.[49] A Sinn Féin activist in Dundalk in County Louth—one of only twenty in the town—felt they 'were looked upon as cranks and dreamers, whose ideals were hopeless and impossible of fulfilment'.[50] Aside from apathy, derision, or hostility, Sinn Féiners faced overwhelming obstacles: police harassment, dismissal from employment, exclusion from patronage or advancement, and even assault by Irish Party supporters who objected to physical force as a rival ideology rather than a method of dealing with political competitors. By the eve of Home Rule, 'the words "Sinn Fein" generated ridicule rather than admiration or fear'.[51]

V

Given its failure to mount an effective challenge to the Irish Party, what significance can Sinn Féin and the many other small radical organizations of this period claim? What impact did they have on the politicization of the minority who fought in 1916 and the wider generation who followed their lead? Sinn Féin was more important for what it represented—an attempt to harness the energy and idealism of cultural nationalism in a more tangible political form—than what it achieved. Although unsuccessful in conventional terms, the separatist revival radicalized a determined activist core, which developed in an increasingly militant and militaristic direction, a trend exemplified by two neglected organizations, Inghinidhe na hÉireann (the Daughters of Erin) and Na Fianna Éireann (Warriors of Ireland).

Emerging as a protest against 'the orgy of flunkeyism' generated by Queen Victoria's visit to Ireland in 1900, Inghinidhe (affectionately known as 'the ninnies') demonstrated how advanced nationalists sought to radicalize those previously excluded from political activism, including women, children, and the working class. Its objectives reflected its broader milieu: it aimed to revive Ireland's language, literature, music, dancing, history, customs, games, and industries, while also advocating violence to achieve 'the complete separation of Ireland from England'. The ninnies sought to politicize the children of Dublin's poor, providing free classes in areas where 'the British army got its most valuable recruits', organizing excursions to the graves of republican martyrs, and encouraging its young members to distribute seditious literature and attack symbols of British imperialism.[52]

Inghinidhe's moralistic ethos was equally characteristic of the wider cultural nationalist milieu. One popular activity was to prevent fraternization between Irish girls and British soldiers: 'thousands of innocent young country girls, up in Dublin, at domestic service mostly, were dazzled by these handsome and brilliant uniforms', Helena Molony recalled, 'These young girls had not the faintest idea of the moral, social, or political implications of their associations with the "red-coats" '.[53] This campaign met with some success when soldiers were confined to one side of the capital's main street: 'A decent girl could not walk down the Post Office side without being molested. Then such girls got the name of a "soldier's totty" '.[54] Such minor triumphs demonstrated how separatists could harness moral concerns, shared by many nationalists and the Catholic Church, in support of more overtly political objectives, such as opposition to the British army, which otherwise generated less support. Separatists rarely drew distinctions between moral, cultural, and political values and considered themselves more virtuous than their constitutional rivals. Although it included many feminists among its membership,

Inghinidhe was also typical of separatist organizations in prioritizing national over sectional concerns such as women's suffrage.

Despite its small membership, Inghinidhe's energetic activism, propaganda, and innovative publicity stunts made a considerable impact. Although its claim to have attracted thirty thousand children to the 'patriotic children's treat' (a picnic to reward those who had not attended the celebrations for Queen Victoria's visit) was a dubious one, the event undermined the authorities' efforts to cultivate popular support for the monarchy and contributed to the subsequent emergence of Sinn Féin.[55] The organization also published its own newspaper, described by its editor, Helena Molony, as 'a funny hotch-potch of blood and thunder, high thinking, and home-made bread'. *Bean na hÉireann*, Molony noted, was the only newspaper in Ireland to support the physical-force tradition between 1908 and the IRB's launch of *Irish Freedom* in 1910.

Inghinidhe's influence was also demonstrated by the role of one of its leading members, Countess Markievicz, in founding (along with the ubiquitous Bulmer Hobson, a leading IRB, GAA, and Sinn Féin activist from Ulster) Na Fianna Éireann in 1909. Born into the Gore-Booths of Lissadell estate in County Sligo, Markievicz's Ascendancy background was as unconventional for a republican as her behaviour was for a woman. 'Madame was in our minds a truly strange lady. Some of us might think she was forward—even her smoking in our presence often shocked', one of her young protégés recalled, 'some of the boys were not even pleased at her wearing our uniform'.[56] Intense, energetic, childlike in her exuberance, Markievicz opened her 'big generous heart' and large Rathmines house to her boys: 'The rooms of her home were simply littered with treasures', Seán Prendergast enthused, 'Seldom a night passed without its quota of Fianna boys showing up for a sing-song or other form of revelry'.[57] 'She loved "her boys"—boasted of it', he recalled, 'Her happiest moments were when she was showering her solicitude on one of our sick members or encouraging Andy Dunne, who had a sweet soft tenor voice, to take lessons in singing. She even wrote songs for him'. Hobson's interest in the movement was more utilitarian: he believed children were easier to convert to the gospel of physical force.

Open to boys (and, reluctantly, girls) between eight and eighteen, regardless of 'class or creed or party', the Fianna played an important role as a link between the separatist revival of the early twentieth century and the Volunteering phenomenon of the Home Rule era. By 1912 twenty-two branches had been established, mainly in the cities and larger towns. Like Inghinidhe, the organization reflected the spirit of its times: it aimed to win independence through 'the training of the youth of Ireland, mentally and physically ... by teaching scouting and military exercises, Irish history, and the Irish language'.[58] Although a republican body, the ideological influence of the Irish-Ireland movement is more evident from its members' recollections. 'I soon found myself moving towards everything that was Irish-Ireland', a leading member recalled, 'We were taught to be aggressive to the RIC, and the boys in Camden Street would avail of every opportunity to attack the Protestant Church Boys Brigade, who at that time were strong and would carry the Union Jack'.[59] 'Paddy Hegarty would give lectures on Ireland's glorious past', Liam Brady recalled, 'He told us of Finn McCoole and the daring exploits of the Fianna; of the coming of the English and their destruction of our Irish industries, and the methods they had been using for almost seven hundred and fifty years to destroy our Irish language and culture'.[60]

Such accounts demonstrate how traditional republican ideology was superseded by Catholic and cultural nationalist influences in the early twentieth century. Con Colbert, in many respects an archetypal Fianna officer, was widely admired as 'the very personification of the Gael ... everything about him was Irish'.[61] Describing him as a 'total abstainer' who was 'enthusiastic about everything Irish', his sister recalled that his favourite phrase was 'for my God and my country'.[62] The account of one young Cork member illustrates how the Irish language provided a weapon for the powerless against the powerful, reinforcing a perception of heroic communal struggle against unjust oppression:

On one occasion, at Ballincollig, the boys were preparing a meal after field exercises on what appeared to be a bit of waste ground. Suddenly, out from some trees that screened the place, came a man on horseback with hunting crop and riding boots. He was typical of the tyrants of the land war days. 'Who gave you permission to camp here', he said in a stern voice. Tomás MacCurtain ... answered in the native tongue. It could easily be seen that he was hostile to everything Irish ... He threatened to call the police. This only brought more retorts in Irish, to our great delight. He was one of those who expected people to bow before him. He could not understand his orders being disobeyed, he, a Justice of the Peace.[63]

Despite regarding itself as a distinctively Irish force, the Fianna was a gaelicized version of the Baden-Powell movement that it had been

established to counteract. It promoted the same values of citizenship, discipline, and manliness but in a nationalist rather than imperial context, and it
was a product of the same public concerns about moral and physical degen-
eration that had produced similar cults of militarism elsewhere in Europe.
The movement's uniforms, military training, and guns lay at the heart of its
appeal. As Helena Molony observed: 'The boys loved playing at soldiers'.[64]
Séamus Reader defected from the Baden-Powell scouts when he discovered
that the Fianna had better uniforms and swords.[65] The Fianna's French bayonets, another boy recalled, 'enhanced our status and made us feel like the real
thing'.[66] At one of their weekend camps, Gary Holohan (who would later
kill one of the first victims of the Rising) remembered 'getting a real gun in
my hands for the first time while on sentry duty. It was a great sensation'.[67]

But the Fianna were doing more than playing at soldiers. The movement represented a potent source of radicalization: 'here was instilled into
our youthful minds the hatred of the Sassenach . . . we longed for the day
when we too might join in the fight against the common enemy'.[68] 'In the
Fianna', another boy recalled, 'I was taught that Ireland had never got
anything and never could expect to get anything from England except by
physical force'.[69] Inevitably, the organization fell under the control of the
IRB, and by 1913 most of its leading officers were sworn Fenians. As a
result, the movement's rhetoric and activities became increasingly militaristic. As Patrick Pearse, schoolmaster, Gaelic League activist, and Volunteer leader, declared in 1914:

> The object of Na Fianna Eireann is to train the boys of Ireland to fight
> Ireland's battle when they are men . . . we hope to train Irish boys from their
> earliest years to be soldiers, not only to know the trade of a soldier—drilling,
> marching, camping, signalling, scouting, and (when they are old enough)
> shooting—but also, what is far more important, to understand and prize
> military discipline and to have a MILITARY SPIRIT.[70]

As with the Fianna's ideological trajectory, this militarization of separatism was a sign of things to come. It was, one member claimed, 'the
beginning of the military history of recent times. Previous to that, nothing
whatever was being done by any organisation in a military way'.[71] If the
Fianna had not been founded, Pearse argued, 'the Volunteers of 1913
would never have arisen'. Like Sinn Féin, the movement's importance lay
in its radicalizing influence on a determined minority like Gary Holohan:
'my outlook on life was completely changed. The Fianna was no longer a

mere pastime or social function. It became a sacred duty, and I started to bend my every effort towards the freeing of Ireland'.[72] Its most important achievement was the politicization of a cadre of similarly zealous boys— including Con Colbert, Liam Mellows, and Seán Heuston—who would later play a leading role in the Easter Rising.

VI

The importance of political organizations, cultural movements, and ideology is easily exaggerated. Separatist organizations did not have much of a presence outside the cities, even if their newspapers occasionally did. The ideological disputes of such importance to separatist activists did not interest most nationalists; they tell us very little about how ordinary people viewed their world, and why this particular generation would come to embrace a more radical form of nationalism than previous ones. Although the witness statements of the Bureau of Military History must be carefully evaluated for the reasons outlined in the Introduction, they provide a remarkable new source for understanding the motivations and experiences that politicized this generation.

What were the most important radicalizing influences? No one was born a revolutionary, but many were born into revolutionary families. Separatists emphasized the importance of having parents who 'always preached Fenianism', of coming from families with 'strong national tendencies', or being raised in 'a good Irish home atmosphere'.[73] These formative influences were reinforced by family memories, real or imagined, which (as in the case of Tomás Ó Cléirigh) could extend over several generations: 'I had no use for England as my mother told me that they exiled her great-grandfather from the country. My father was a member of the Fenian Brotherhood and his great-grandfather...had his land taken away from him'.[74] Seán Boylan, a future revolutionary, recalled:

> My ancestors took a prominent part in the '98 Rebellion and also in the Fenian Rising. Some of them were transported to Van Diemen's Land. My parents told me this and infused a patriotic spirit into me from my earliest days. My father often said to me that nothing good ever came from England. 'Even the wind', he would say, 'that blows from there is a foul one'...My uncle took a particular pride in asserting that during his life, which was a long one, that he never spoke to a policeman.[75]

Many could cite specific grievances: parents, relatives, or grandparents who were prosecuted, beaten, imprisoned, exiled, or dispossessed.

Conversely, however, it was not that unusual for parents to warn their children of the dangers of separatism: 'My father was associated with the Fenian movement but it was not through him I inherited my rebel tendencies as he tried to impress on me to have nothing to do with such movement'.[76] The theme of intergenerational conflict frequently recurs in the statements: although many of the parents of the rising generation had a radical background dating back to the Land War, by the early twentieth century they were overwhelmingly committed to the parliamentary methods that their children would come to disdain.[77] Similar intergenerational tensions existed within the separatist movement, as was demonstrated by Denis McCullough's expulsion of his own father from the IRB, and the overthrow of the organization's aging leadership: 'the conflict was the recurring one between an older generation who wished to go slowly and quietly and the younger generation eager to get things done'.[78]

Many separatists regarded their education as a radicalizing experience: 'It was the Presentation nuns who made a rebel of me'; 'I think the first of whatever bit of nationality was in me came from an old Jesuit'; 'Brother Collins...explained Irish history to us and made us study it. Through him and my parents I grew up a rebel'.[79] Like many republicans, Eamon Price attributed his politicization to the Irish Christian Brothers 'who with such devotion showed the young people of this nation how Irishmen should live and die for the country'.[80] The Christian Brothers—described with a hint of ambivalence by one pupil as 'violently patriotic'—were particularly influential, having spurned the State curriculum for one that placed more emphasis on Catholic nationalist values. By promoting a romanticized 'faith and fatherland' history, the Gaelic language, and Irish sports, and by extending secondary education to bright children beyond the middle classes, the Christian Brothers educated a disproportionate number of rebels (including seven of the fourteen men executed in Dublin after the Rising). As Peter Hart has observed: 'in teaching patriotism, the Christian Brothers created gunmen'.[81]

As the role played by the Christian Brothers indicates, the political influence of the Catholic Church was more complex than some anti-clerical Fenians would allow. Although the hierarchy was hostile to the IRB, and willing to exploit the advantages resulting from Ireland's position within the British Empire, not all bishops admired the Irish Party or its long-standing alliance with the non-conformist-backed Liberal Party. Younger priests, in particular, were often enthusiastic about the Irish-Ireland movement and the new nationalism which espoused congenial moralistic and anti-materialist values. Min Ryan recalled that her family became interested in separatism through the influence of her brother who attended the national seminary: 'Maynooth was leader of young opinion, especially regarding the language, and afterwards regarding Sinn Féin'.[82]

The neglect of Irish history and Gaelic within the curriculum devised by the Commissioners of National Education, which had initially sought to inculcate British rather than Irish patriotism, failed to deter many children from absorbing a nationalist ethos at school. Like other belated concessions by the State, the introduction of a choice between Irish or British history in the primary school curriculum and state-funding for Gaelic lessons outside regular school hours by the early twentieth century did not prevent some children from experiencing a sense of grievance. Future Volunteer Denis Madden was taught by 'a good Irishman' at his school: 'I remember he told us that we should be ashamed if we did not know *Who fears to speak of Ninety Eight*...he would give us lessons in Irish *after* school hours if we stayed on. The British did not allow Irish to be taught during school hours'.[83] Schoolteachers—well-educated, underpaid, and economically dependent on Church and State—represented an important source of radicalism.[84] National school principal and future revolutionary Thomas Ashe represented an extreme version of the archetype: 'In the school when children marched out to recreation', his sister recalled, 'he used to get them to march over a Union Jack'.[85]

Whether absorbed at school or at home, separatists like Peadar Bracken frequently claimed that it 'was a study of the history of my country and the stories told to me by the old people that gave me a national outlook'.[86] Patrick Kelly recalled: 'When I was about eight years old I began to take a keen interest in books and stories of Ireland's fight for freedom, and particularly the treatment of the people by the British garrison. I began to hate everything English, but what really made a rebel of me was a book called *Croppies Lie Down*...I vowed that if ever there was an Irish army I would join it and help beat the British out of Ireland'.[87] Elizabeth Bloxham, a Protestant from a unionist background who embraced republicanism in her youth, was struck by the importance of history in the lives of ordinary Catholics in the rural west:

The poorest and least educated Catholics had their symbols of nationality. At that time you rarely entered a house that had not a picture of Wolfe Tone and Robert Emmet. *Speeches from the Dock*, in its green paper cover, was well thumbed by some members of the family. There was talk of the Land War and of 'old unhappy far off things and battles long ago' and there was the telling of folk tales. The Protestant mind had no such hinterland.[88]

The history of Ireland—the story of centuries of heroic Catholic defiance of English oppression culminating in the Famine, Land War, and ongoing struggle for independence—provided a powerful lens through which nationalists viewed the world. What made this narrative of grievance particularly potent was that it was not necessarily produced by, or for, the separatist minority. Many of the popular works of history cited as politicizing influences by these future rebels were written by constitutional nationalists for mass consumption. Irish Party politicians also eulogized the separatist heroes of the past, arguing merely that the physical-force tradition had been superseded by the party's more effective if prosaic methods.

The power of this historical narrative derived also from the fact that it was disseminated not only through books but every conceivable medium of popular culture including ballads, poems, novels, pictures, and the stories told around the fireside, both within and beyond Ireland. Raised in Glasgow, Séamus Reader remembered: 'In my home and the homes of my companions were pictures of Robert Emmet and of the Irish Brigade at Fonteney'.[89] Eithne Carbery's poems, Gary Holohan claimed, 'did much to fan the fires of patriotism to white heat'.[90] 'Thanks to my mother's great fund of Irish songs and ballads', Seán Whelan recalled, 'I was familiar with Ireland's struggle for independence long before I could read or write'.[91] Social memory, even the very landscape, could reinforce a sense of political identity; Eamon Price remembered how 'my father on Sunday around Dublin would lead me to the historic spots and relate the deeds of glory of the past and so the seed was sown'.[92]

A remarkably diverse range of cultural influences could inculcate a patriotic mindset from early childhood. 'In my young days', Thomas Reidy recalled,

> the old men at social gatherings clasped hands and sang Irish songs together. In the winter times dances were held regularly in our townland. Patriotic songs like *Michael Dwyer* and *The Bold Fenian Men* were sung at these gatherings. I heard stories of the Fenians and so became aware of Ireland's struggle

for her freedom. In addition, I read all the books on Ireland I could lay my hands on. Amongst the books I read were A. M. Sullivan's *History of Ireland*.[93]

A burgeoning industry of newspapers, magazines, reading rooms, pamphlets, postal retail services, and publishing initiatives sprung up to meet the growing consumer demand for 'faith and fatherland' history.[94] Much of the literature produced by the separatist revival—such as the poetry of Carbery—was new, but its impact was heightened by its reliance on a widely understood frame of reference constructed by earlier nationalist writers. Its emotional and intellectual force, moreover, was rooted in the lived experiences of the Catholic community, its ability to offer an explanation for past grievances and an empowering narrative for their imminent resolution.

The history of Ireland was ritualistically re-enacted by nationalists of all varieties keen to harness its emotional appeal to their own political projects. Many people were politicized by the impact of commemorative events, particularly the 1798 centenary which, Joseph O'Connor recalled, 'occupied all our minds' attention. The newspapers and periodicals were literally filled with accounts of the battles of that time and with poems and songs about that period'.[95] The 1798 procession, Marie Perolz remembered, 'thrilled my heart, which nearly burst with joy at the sight of the flags'.[96] The impact of the war in South Africa was also emphasized by many separatists. Britain's difficulty in suppressing the Boers raised the hope that armed resistance to imperial might was not necessarily a futile gesture. Augustine Ingoldsby believed that 'it was only after the Boer War that militant nationalists created an impression that there was little or no hope of Ireland gaining her freedom unless they armed themselves'. He recalled participating in a tableau vivant—a popular form of recreation at the time—'showing dead British soldiers in uniform with Boer soldiers of the Irish Brigade standing over them...I fired some blank cartridges from a six-chamber revolver and frightened the life out of all the women'.[97]

Whether expressed through a personal identification with the history of the nation, the Gaelic language, or some other dimension of Irish culture, these accounts illustrate a resentment of British culture and an underlying rejection of the legitimacy of British rule. For separatists, these sentiments were sharpened by anxieties about deracination. P. J. Murphy was appalled by the 'displays of loyalty to England' in '"Rotten Cork" and "Khaki Cork"—names which made every honest nationalist in the city blush with shame'.[98] 'I was disappointed in Waterford', Denis Madden similarly recalled, 'It was a right seóinín [pro-British] town. The Ascendancy class seemed to dominate everything'.[99] Separatists drew strength not only from Irish culture but from their resentment of British cultural imperialism and its impact on Irish national identity; these grievances were stoked by petty slights such as the prosecution of tradesmen for displaying their name in Gaelic or the feelings of humiliation engendered by popular enthusiasm for royal visits and jubilees.

For the minority that embraced separatism before 1916, a stance that required intellectual independence and moral courage, their very marginalization reinforced their commitment. Thomas Courtney, who came to regard Galway as 'the most shoneen town in Ireland', attributed his politicization to a chance meeting in Eyre Square addressed by Arthur Griffith:

> On this occasion, the evening of a fair day, he was telling the crowd to buy nothing but Irish goods even if it were only a box of matches. The police method was staring into the faces of the people who drifted away until there was one man and three boys, including myself, left...I remember distinctly the RIC sergeant saying to the man who was speaking 'Why are you staying, there is nobody to listen to you', and his answer: 'while there is one I won't go'. This was my first clash with the RIC as, when I was told to move, I refused. They spoke to me as I was a telegraph messenger and likely to obey...For this the police tried to get me dismissed.[100]

Other politicizing factors cited in the witness statements include family or local involvement in agrarian agitation, particularly in the congested west of Ireland, and sectarian tensions, almost invariably in Ulster. But in light of the acknowledged importance of land and religion in Ireland, it is striking how seldom these factors are mentioned. Class conflict is also generally absent from the narratives, even from many of those who joined James Connolly's socialist Irish Citizen Army. While the importance of trade union militancy and the hardships endured during the 1913 Lockout features in some narratives, class tensions are rarely cited as an explicitly radicalizing factor. Similarly, resentment of social injustice rarely features: the only two witnesses to explicitly identify it as integral to their politicization were women, one of whom came from a wealthy and conservative family background.[101] In contrast, other witnesses went to great efforts to deny the importance of class politics: 'the separatist movement was essentially a movement of the plain Irish people—the common man—and remained so. It was not markedly Labour or Social in its inspiration, though the rank and file came mainly from the working classes'.[102]

The radicalization of Irish nationalists, most historians agree, was significantly influenced by social, economic, and communal tensions but few separatists explained—or perhaps even perceived—their politicization in terms other than the cause of Irish freedom. Perhaps it is unsurprising that most individuals attributed their politicization to exclusively patriotic motivations, even if a minority expressed some regret about the lack of social change brought about by independence. Separatist organizations like the IRB were reluctant to get drawn into socially divisive questions, while all nationalist parties, including Sinn Féin, prioritized national over sectional causes (as was demonstrated by Arthur Griffith's opposition to the workers during the 1913 Lockout).[103] The Catholic Church, the most important social and cultural force in Ireland, was explicitly opposed to class politics. Also, because most separatists believed that the union was primarily responsible for the poverty and injustice of Irish society, they tended to assume that the attainment of independence would in itself result in a better and fairer society.

One interesting feature of the statements was how many of the witnesses could identify a particular moment—a clash with an authority figure, a grievance, or humiliation—which led to a politicizing awareness of Ireland's subordination to Britain. However, this may well be a consequence of how memory retrospectively creates a sense of meaning in the narrative of one's own life, as the statements also indicate that few people were politicized by particular factors in isolation to others. Séamus Robinson—a participant in the Soloheadbeg ambush (widely regarded as the opening clash of the War of Independence)—exemplifies the multitude of influences that contributed to the politicization of his generation. He was born into a family with 'a national tradition' in the year of Parnell's fall: 'My paternal grandfather, a Fenian, escaped to France in 1867 . . . he swore he'd never shave again till Ireland was free—he had a luxurious beard when I saw him last'.[104] Formative childhood experiences included his education by the Christian Brothers in Belfast, his involvement in sectarian rioting with 'the orange boys', and the influence of an older Fianna brother: 'Joe himself was prepared for a life of hardship and excitement with a hangman's rope likely at the end . . . he told me in so positive, cool, matter-of-fact way that a fight would come off, not only in our time, but very shortly that I believed him'. Politicized during the turn of the century separatist revival, both boys came to regard their generation as superior to that of their parents:

> They had also become convinced that the British Empire was invincible. They had all the arguments against us young people. Then the '98 centenary celebrations set us youngsters agog and enquiring. We wanted to prepare for another fight but we were told not to be so foolish... I think it was Joe, my brother, who first pointed out to me that we should be ashamed of our father's generation. They were the first generation of Irishmen who had not struck a blow for Ireland.

Influenced by thrilling accounts of the Boer War—'Bonfires in the streets on the news of a Boer victory... The Irish Boer Brigade! How we wished we were old enough to be with them'—Robinson made his 'first definite contact with the national movement' when he joined one of Bulmer Hobson's hurling clubs. Despite his family's move to Glasgow, he remained immersed in separatism, embracing the militaristic spirit of Na Fianna with a youthful intensity:

> I prepared myself mentally and physically. I trained myself to be supple and not muscle-bound... I learned to jump my own height... I learned to sprint with all my clothes on in short bursts of 20 to 30 yards. I learned to shoot... I took every opportunity of practice at circus and show grounds and at rifle ranges.

While it is easy to dismiss such childlike enthusiasm, the political ideals and cultural forces that influenced Robinson were no childish fantasy. Swearing the Fenian oath in February 1916, he returned to Ireland with several of his friends to play his part in the Easter Rising.

VII

What do such accounts tell us about the politicization of the revolutionary generation? Historians of the revolution have analysed the structure of society in an attempt to delineate the geography of Irish nationalism. After the Rising, Sinn Féin flourished in the most rural and most Catholic counties, attracting greater support from small farmers than urban workers. The geography of violence has proven more resistant to statistical analysis but the presence of a tradition of late-nineteenth-century agrarian 'outrages' and Irish-teaching national schools form two of the most reliable predictors of IRA violence during the revolution.[105] Social background (skilled workers and the lower middle class were disproportionately prominent), urban environments, lack of emigration opportunities, and police ineffectiveness also contributed to IRA activity. Complementing such research, the witness statements illustrate how Irish revolutionaries—an unrepresentative minority—perceived their own politicization, enabling us to identify some of the social, cultural, and psychological causes of their radicalization.

Collectively, they indicate some of the factors that made youths like Séamus Robinson the rising generation, including the importance of family background, social memory, local communal influences, education, the expansion of print culture, and the growth of associational activity. While much has been made of the impact of the literary revival (not least by some of its leading figures), the influence of low-brow but vastly more popular fare, much of it generated by constitutional nationalists, is much more apparent.[106] The importance of childhood influences is striking, as is the presence of overlapping networks of cultural and separatist organizations in the cities. Conversely, there is remarkably little discussion of ideology: few revolutionaries mention the appeal of Arthur Griffith's dual monarchy, Connolly's socialism, or the attractions of a republican form of government. For many ordinary people, politicization amounted to hostility to Britain, resentment of the many everyday grievances that could be attributed to British rule, devotion to Irish culture, and a commitment to an abstract ideal of Irish freedom.[107]

The emphasis by historians on the radicalizing impact of Ulster's opposition to Home Rule and the Great War is understandable—separatism may well have failed without these crises—but the formative experiences of this generation are also important. The reinvigoration of a stale Fenian tradition by the cultural revival created a new form of politics, which developed in an increasingly militant and militaristic direction. Only a small minority joined radical bodies, and an even smaller number fought in 1916, but the speed with which their actions were endorsed by a majority of nationalists suggests that their ideals were much more widely shared. The rapid transformation of opinion after the Rising remains puzzling only if constitutional nationalism and separatism are regarded as separate traditions rather than a spectrum of shifting opinion, drawing on shared cultural influences: 'Physical-force separatism was stronger than is often supposed, and the extent to which it had a common discourse with constitutionalism is underestimated'.[108]

Irish Party politicians praised the idealism of previous generations of separatists and, as became evident in 1914, remained willing to use the threat of physical force in pursuit of their own objectives. Despite the electoral dominance of the Irish Party, the pragmatic rhetoric of Redmondism—with its message of faith in Westminster, conciliation with unionism, and compromise rather than idealism—rubbed more against the grain of popular nationalist culture than Fenianism. One recent study has also demonstrated that, in contrast to the Redmondite leadership, the rhetoric of party activists in provincial Ireland remained steeped in 'Catholicity, sense of victimhood, glorification of struggle, identification of enemies, and antipathy to England'.[109] Many nationalists opposed the impracticability of Fenianism rather than its ideals. Describing Fenianism as 'the central influence in an Irish nationalist culture that was deeply embedded in the texture of Irish identity', another recent study has argued that 'home rule did not achieve the same level of emotional resonance with the Irish people'.[110]

That these experiences were those of a specific generation was also important.[111] As early as 1905, one unionist writer warned of the radicalization of 'the generation of Irish nationalists who were children during the Parnellite and Gladstonian epoch'.[112] Separatists like Tom Clarke also spoke in similar terms: 'The tide is running strongly in our direction. We have the rising generation'.[113] What made this generation so distinctive? It was the first to grow to adulthood after the development of a powerful nationalist movement and culture, and the first to regard Home Rule not as a distant aspiration but a minimal demand, one that had been unjustly denied throughout their lifetimes. It was a generation emboldened rather than placated by the social, economic, and political reforms which it had benefited from, whose grievances were sharpened by the discrimination and humiliation—real and imagined—that formed part of everyday life in Ireland under the union.

Despite this, it would be a mistake to exaggerate the radicalization of this generation or the inevitability of its consequences. Before the Home Rule crisis, few contemporaries believed Ireland was on the verge of revolutionary change, and some of those who did worried more about the threat posed by socialists or suffragettes than republicans. Although the emergence of the Irish-Ireland and new nationalist movements created a more assertive nationalism, few people took separatism seriously because it remained difficult to see how its aims could be realized. The lives of the people whose voices feature in this book were shaped by social and political forces beyond their control, but they were also determined by their responses to these wider forces. The emergence of volunteer militias—which weakened British authority and transformed Irish politics after 1913—created revolutionary possibilities that could not have been foreseen. As in the earlier periods of instability and violence outlined in the first section of this chapter, Irish politics did not occur within a vacuum: international factors—including the rise of more assertive forms of ethnic nationalism and the weakening of multiethnic empires in the face of democratization and growing demands for national self-determination—challenged the great imperial powers, heightening the expectations and aspirations of subject peoples throughout pre-war Europe.

2

Arms in Irish Hands

Volunteering

Irish separatism remained a marginal force at the end of the first decade of the twentieth century. By the summer of 1914, however, the politics of Ireland had radically shifted, bringing closer the long-awaited revolutionary moment. It was, ironically, the imminent success of the Irish Parliamentary Party's long campaign for Home Rule which presented Irish separatists with this opportunity. What would become known as the Home Rule crisis originated within British rather than Irish politics. In August 1911, a two-year conflict between Herbert Asquith's Liberal government and the House of Lords over the 'People's Budget' was brought to a decisive conclusion by the Parliament Act which abolished the Lords' absolute power of veto (reducing it to the ability to delay legislation for two years). The government rewarded John Redmond's Irish Party for its crucial support at Westminster by introducing the Third Home Rule Bill the following April. In contrast to earlier attempts in 1886 and 1893, there was no longer any constitutional obstacle blocking Home Rule for Ireland.

In response, the unionists of Ulster, backed by powerful allies in southern Ireland and Britain, mobilized against Home Rule. In the best tradition of Irish political movements, their campaign embraced both constitutional means and the threat of physical force. In September 1912 the charismatic, highly strung leader of unionism, Sir Edward Carson, ably supported by the more stolid Belfast stockbroker James Craig orchestrated the signing of the Ulster Solemn League and Covenant in Belfast by almost a quarter of a million men. The following January the Ulster Volunteer Force (UVF), a paramilitary organization which would recruit one hundred thousand Protestant men to its ranks, was formed; by September 1913, a provisional government, prepared to use violence to secede from a Home Rule Ireland, had been formally launched in Ulster.[1] The political transformation set in motion by the radicalization of Ulster would seriously weaken both British authority in Ireland and the Irish Party's grip on nationalist politics. The formation of the Irish Volunteers, a nationalist response to the UVF, in November 1913 provided the first indication that popular nationalism was edging beyond the Irish Party's control.

I

Who established the Irish Volunteers and why? What kind of people joined the organization and for what reasons? From its very inception, these were not straightforward questions. The public inspiration behind the formation of the paramilitary force that would ultimately evolve into the Irish Republican Army was a rather unlikely figure: Eoin MacNeill, a professor of early and medieval history at University College Dublin and vice-president of the Gaelic League. MacNeill was not a republican but he reflected an increasingly vocal constituency which had become sufficiently concerned by events in Ulster to question the Irish Party's complacent dependence on the British constitutional process. MacNeill's article calling for a nationalist version of the UVF created a sensation, leading to the formation of the Irish Volunteers.

As with other historic initiatives (such as the founding of the GAA), the hidden hand of the Irish Republican Brotherhood had played a crucial role behind the scenes, even if—as one leading IRB man observed—'the idea was in the air and everybody was talking about it'.[2] Leading Fenian Bulmer Hobson characteristically claimed the credit for founding the Volunteers, recalling that he had resisted the temptation to launch the organization immediately after the formation of the UVF, waiting until the autumn when he judged the time more opportune. The IRB, which had been 'quietly suggesting and directing various developments' during the weeks before MacNeill's announcement, saw the advantage of having respect-able and moderate figures—'harmless nationalists'—at the head of the movement.[3] Despite this condescending attitude, it would later become clear that MacNeill was no dupe.

'On the formation of the Volunteers', one Dublin Fenian recalled, 'we were instructed by the IRB to join and to do everything possible to get hold of the key positions'.[4] Fenians with military training—IRB men who had belonged to or been drilled by the Fianna—'were soon picked out to fill the key positions'.[5] The IRB engaged in similar string-pulling in Cork where Tomás MacCurtain, a Fenian and Irish-Ireland activist, played the leading role in establishing the Volunteers. Some leading Volunteers regarded the involvement of prominent activists from other cultural nationalist bodies (including the GAA and Gaelic League) as a cunning ploy rather than evidence of the movement's non-political status: 'I suspect that the IRB men in these bodies were the prime movers in starting the Volunteers in Cork. They brought in men well known to them in the existing organisations to make it look representative, men such as J. J. Walsh, then chairman of the Cork county board, GAA'.[6] The IRB centre for Cork confirmed that 'they endeavoured to make the committee representative while retaining control...there was a conscious intention to keep the control of the Volunteers in the hands of members of the IRB'.[7] Although 'there was an election of a committee later, the nominations were arranged', another Volunteer noted, 'The IRB had effective control and exercised it in all appointments to Volunteer positions'.[8] As a result, 'practically all the officers were IRB men, and this gave effective control'.[9]

Volunteers described a similar process in many other areas. In Belfast, according to one member of the city's executive committee, 'the IRB had virtual control of both the Volunteer committees and was able to exercise control in matters of policy without question from the Volunteers who were non-members'.[10] 'The IRB circle was the driving force in the organisation of the Volunteers in Sligo'.[11] 'Around my part of the country', a Tyrone Volunteer recalled, 'the IRB were the driving force behind the organisation of the Volunteers'.[12] In County Tipperary, the IRB county centre was instructed by Seán MacDermott to establish the Volunteers in Clonmel but, as elsewhere, not to 'take too prominent a part, or show their hands completely'.[13] In County Wexford, Fenians were behind the organization of the Volunteers in Wexford town, Ferns, and Enniscorthy. IRB members were also prominent in the formation of Volunteer companies in England (in Liverpool and London) and Scotland (in Paisley, Glasgow, Govan, and Maryhill).

In the many towns and villages where the IRB was isolated or moribund, Fenians adopted a more subtle strategy. Kerry centre (and income-tax collector) Austin Stack told one Fenian who sought to establish the Volunteers in Tralee that a group of Irish language activists 'were taking steps to call a meeting for the formation of the Volunteers locally, that we would let that go ahead and see how it developed'.[14] These activists succeeded, where the local IRB could not have, in winning the support of the GAA, Gaelic League, and other non-separatist organizations for the new movement (which Stack then came to lead in Kerry). The IRB proceeded to selectively recruit members from the more popular Volunteer movement, gradually expanding its influence as the latter grew in numbers. The same policy was adopted in Killarney. In cities such as Dublin and Cork, where the IRB had taken the lead in forming the Volunteers, the challenge was to retain control of the organization; in those areas where it had been too weak to do so, the IRB faced the task of secretly gaining control of it.

From its very inception, the organization encompassed a spectrum of competing political factions, as separatists, advanced nationalists, and Home Rulers jostled for influence and, ultimately, control of the militia. However, all factions understood that the Volunteers should be presented to the public as a national organization, above politics and factionalism. When the organizing committee first met in Dublin, one member recalled, it was apparent that 'all those present were broadly speaking of the one school of thought i.e. Sinn Féin, Gaelic League, IRB, and it was agreed by all that the basis of the provisional committee should be widened and suitable people known as supporters of the Irish Parliamentary Party, should be asked to join'.[15] For the same reason, Arthur Griffith, one of Redmond's sharpest critics, was excluded from the organizing committee. Over the next weeks, the initial committee of twelve was expanded to thirty, placing the organization beyond the direct control of the IRB by the time it was publicly launched at Dublin's Rotunda Rink on 25 November.

Despite the organizers' fears, the meeting proved a resounding success as over three thousand men spontaneously enlisted. But what was the purpose of the organization? A provisional constitution (belatedly issued in February 1914) identified three objectives:

1) To secure and maintain the rights and liberties common to all the people of Ireland;

2) To train, discipline, arm, and equip a body of Irish Volunteers for the above purpose

3) To unite for this purpose Irishmen of every creed and of every party and class.[16]

The manifesto of the Irish Volunteers, declaimed by Eoin MacNeill at the Rotunda, provided a more detailed agenda. It identified its opposition to the campaign against Home Rule as the principal reason for its existence, the success of which would render the Irish 'the most degraded population in Europe, and no longer worthy of the name Nation'. However, 'the menace of armed violence' which threatened to subvert Home Rule was attributed to the Tory party and its supporters in the conservative press rather than the unionists of Ulster who were not mentioned. Denouncing the 'long series of repressive statutes' which had 'deprived the Irish nation of the power to direct its own course' since the Act of Union, the Volunteer manifesto preached a gospel of self-reliance. The right—and duty—'of able-bodied Irishmen without distinction of creed, politics or social grade' to form an armed militia, not merely to win Home Rule but to guarantee the civic and national liberties of the people formed the key theme, emphasized by the identification of volunteering with 'manly citizenship', 'dignity', and 'discipline', and a failure to assert these rights with degradation, serfdom, and cowardice.

The rhetoric of volunteering drew on several important political traditions. Although it is often seen as a response to the formation of the Ulster Volunteers and the broader context of the militarization occurring throughout pre-war Europe, the organization's name deliberately recalled the earlier Volunteer movement which had secured legislative independence from Britain for Grattan's Parliament in 1782. The importance of this episode in Irish history had long been emphasized by Arthur Griffith's Sinn Féin and the IRB-backed Dungannon Clubs. Volunteering also drew on a broader republican tradition of armed citizenship. Since its emergence in the late eighteenth century, European republicanism, and its equally revolutionary Irish variant, had emphasized the link between manliness, armed citizenship, and self-government. Regardless of the new organization's formal apolitical status, the rhetoric of Volunteering reflected a well-established Fenian discourse concerning the necessity for an armed national force and the inadequacy of relying on parliamentary methods to win genuine independence.[17]

Despite the rhetoric of armed citizenship and resistance to tyranny, the limits of Volunteer radicalism were also defined: 'Their duties will be defensive and protective, and they will not contemplate either aggression or domination'.[18] The manifesto reflected what has been described as Eoin MacNeill's 'constitutional separatism', a term which simultaneously conveys a preference for constitutional means, an underlying desire for a greater degree of independence than that offered by Home Rule, and an acceptance of the potential necessity for physical force in certain circumstances. The purpose of the Irish Volunteers, as MacNeill saw it, was to counter the threat posed by the Ulster Volunteers—thereby ensuring against any English betrayal of the Irish Party—but not to act as an insurrectionary force. As Patrick Pearse, whose own position would subsequently harden, explained on the formation of the movement in Galway: 'Ireland armed would be able to make a better bargain with the Empire than Ireland unarmed'.[19] Notwithstanding the organization's militant tone, there was nothing in the manifesto explicitly critical of Redmond's Irish Party or its goal of Home Rule.

Despite his prominence in the IRB, Bulmer Hobson's position differed little from that of MacNeill. The Volunteers provided the solution to a problem which had long troubled him—'the complete impracticability of insurrections on the model of 1798' in the modern age—by facilitating an alternative strategy to 'win independence by a condition of passive resistance and by guerrilla warfare if the opportunity arose'. 'The policy of the Irish Volunteer executive', Hobson insisted, 'was to prepare for a defensive struggle using guerrilla tactics, and the military training in the Volunteer paper and in the companies was directed to this end'.[20] In contrast, the more militant section of the IRB (led by Tom Clarke and Seán MacDermott) saw the Volunteers as a potential insurrectionary force which, if properly trained and led, could orchestrate precisely the sort of rebellion which Hobson dismissed as impracticable. Diarmuid Lynch, a leading IRB man, provided a more assertive, if subtle, interpretation of the Volunteers' objectives in line with this faction's aspirations: 'The "rights and liberties" mentioned were never defined, nor were the means whereby they might be "secured"'. While many had taken this to mean the defence of Home Rule, IRB insurrectionists interpreted it as 'the right of Ireland to national independence as a republican state, and to secure that right through an insurrection in arms'.[21]

What was the Volunteers' attitude to the Ulster Volunteer Force? In hindsight, it was obviously Ulster unionism rather than the Tory Party which formed the key obstacle to securing Home Rule for the entire country. However, few nationalists were willing—or perhaps even able—to acknowledge this. Regarding the Irish nation—geographically, culturally, and politically—as indivisible from the island of Ireland, few nationalists were prepared to concede that a large majority in one part of the country had as much right to remain part of the British State as they had to secede from it (even if constitutional nationalists, in 1914, and republicans, in 1921, would reluctantly accept partition in return for southern self-government).

As a result, many nationalists did not take unionism seriously, proposing a range of implausible theories to dismiss the troubling phenomenon. Whether seen as ridiculous or sinister, the Ulster Volunteers were widely dismissed as bluffers. As one Volunteer put it: 'the rank and file of the movement knew that they could never be called upon to oppose the Crown forces, that the mere fact of their organising would achieve the political objects of the leaders, and that incidentally they would be left with a powerful organisation for the domination of those of their fellow-countrymen who differed from them in their political faith'.[22] That many separatists continued to regard Home Rule as an inevitability (with some even welcoming it) partly accounted for the delay in the emergence of the nationalist counterforce. Declaring that he did not contemplate any conflict with the Ulster Volunteers, MacNeill naïvely emphasized how that force was descended from those responsible for American independence, the patriot Volunteer movement of 1782, and the United Irishmen of 1798.[23] Attributing its opposition to Home Rule to the force's manipulation by English Conservatives, MacNeill depicted the Ulster Volunteers as an empowering model for Irish nationalism:

> The action of the Ulster Volunteers, interpret it as you will, is the very essence of nationalism. They show that, whatever English parties may say, they are going to have their own way in their own country, and when you whom I am addressing come forward and show that you too are going to have your own way, we will command the respect, not only of every English political party, but of the whole civilized world. 'The North began, the North held on, God bless the Northern land'.[24]

Many separatists shared this unduly optimistic interpretation. As one IRB man, observing an armed UVF parade, remarked: 'The first lot of Irishmen to tramp the king's highway armed against a statute of the British parliament since the Fenians. More power to them!'[25] Taking this stance to its logical, if absurd, conclusion, the Tyrone republican Dr Pat McCartan reportedly loaned his car to local Ulster Volunteers during their Larne gun-running operation.

However, many northern nationalists were less inclined than southerners to share such naïve attitudes. Elizabeth Bloxham, a Protestant republican, recalled a conversation with Seán Treacy (who would later become a leading IRA gunman during the War of Independence):

> He was full of enquiries about the Ulster people. He felt sure that, at heart, they must be national. He was sure there was fine stuff in them and if only they were not kept in the dark about the history of their country they would feel as we did...I hadn't the heart to disillusion him...I mentally contrasted his outlook with what I had been familiar with in the north. Seán wanted to hear good of them but, with rare exceptions, they only wanted to hear such things of the south as would justify their prejudices and confirm their belief that Protestants lived in fear of persecution.[26]

The inadequacy of nationalist interpretations of unionism would become painfully evident over the next decade and century. In reality, the emergence of military drilling in Ulster represented more of a spontaneous reaction than staged political theatre. The Ulster Unionist political leadership—rather like the Irish Party (which first ignored and only reluctantly asserted its dominance over the Irish Volunteers as its popularity grew)—was not responsible for the emergence of loyalist paramilitarism which developed independently of 'the respectable leadership of the Orange Order and Unionist Clubs'.[27] Nationalists were slow to grasp that the formation of the Ulster Volunteers reflected a heightened grassroots militancy (one that actually predated the Third Home Rule crisis) and a genuine radicalization of unionism.[28] A similar complacency about drilling was expressed by the Chief Secretary, Augustine Birrell, who disregarded the RIC's warnings of growing unionist militancy.[29] Only slowly did it become clear that the emergence of the UVF and, crucially, the Liberal government's failure to suppress it, had created a new political context, one that left British authority in Ireland in a vulnerable position.

The political response in Britain contributed to the unfolding crisis. British Tories, bitterly opposed to what they regarded as the Parliament Act's unconstitutional usurpation of the power of the peers, recklessly seized on the Home Rule Bill as an opportunity to destroy what they perceived as a dangerously radical government.[30] The Tory leader, Andrew Bonar Law—speaking at Blenheim Palace in July 1912—openly alluded to the threat of civil war, describing the government 'as a revolutionary committee which has seized by fraud upon despotic power', and declaring his intention to support Ulster's unionists in using 'all means in their power, including force' to prevent Home Rule.[31] Nor was this mere posturing: leading Tories—including Walter Long and possibly even Bonar Law—were closely involved with the financing and running of guns into Ulster for use against their own government.[32] Whether Bonar Law's militancy was motivated by a desire to consolidate his own leadership and undermine the Liberal government rather than fervent loyalism remains a matter of debate, but the militancy and effectiveness of the unionist campaign produced far-reaching and unintended results.[33] Its success, which demonstrated the effectiveness of the threat of force, and derailed the Irish Party's campaign for all-Ireland Home Rule, created a crisis subsequently embraced by separatists.

There was then a pragmatic reason for separatist admiration of the unionist force: 'It was only under cover of a movement like the Ulster Volunteer movement that the National Volunteer movement became possible'.[34] The Ulster Volunteers represented not only a troubling adversary but, for the IRB, a providential role model, 'a chance to do openly what we had previously to do in secret'.[35] The emergence of the militias, which also reflected popular attitudes in society, was welcomed by many outside the IRB. Patrick Pearse's (subsequently much-ridiculed) response to the new movement was merely an extreme expression of a widely shared romantic militarism:

> I am glad that the Orangemen have armed, for it is a goodly thing to see arms in Irish hands... I should like to see any and every body of Irish citizens armed. We must accustom ourselves to the thought of arms, to the sight of arms, to the use of arms. We may make mistakes in the beginning and shoot the wrong people; but bloodshed is a cleansing and a sanctifying thing, and the nation which regards it as the final horror has lost its manhood.[36]

II

Other cities were quick to follow Dublin's lead. The meeting in the capital, one Cork Volunteer recalled, 'electrified all Gaelic League and Irish-Ireland circles in Cork'.[37] The idea was already 'in the minds of many people', another member stated, 'The Ulster Volunteers and the Citizen Army were in existence... The men in Cork immediately fell in with the spirit of the time'.[38] The influence of small, overlapping circles of cultural nationalists was pivotal in the formation of the Volunteers. 'The whole Volunteer movement in Cork', Patrick Higgins claimed, 'grew out of the activities of a relatively small group of men and women who had been working in different ways to promote one or other of the various aspects of the Irish-Ireland movement'.[39]

Despite the IRB's intrigues, the Volunteer organization in Cork and elsewhere was not simply a Fenian front: it was also a genuine product of the Irish-Ireland revival. 'The whole movement for national revival in Cork between 1900 and the organisation of the Volunteers started with, and depended upon, the activities of from twelve to twenty families', Cornelius Murphy insisted: 'They went into everything that looked like being national—the Gaelic League, the GAA, the Fianna, the Celtic Literary Society, the Industrial Development Association and the AOH American Alliance'.[40] 'There was an able and active group of nationalists who had been working together in various organisations for years', Patrick O'Sullivan observed, 'It was perfectly natural that they should take the initiative and leadership of the movement should fall to them'.[41] At the heart of the city's Irish-Ireland network was *An Dún*, the Gaelic League's meeting place, whose rooms were used by a diverse range of cultural and separatist organizations for meetings, debates, concerts, and ceilís. The Volunteers were not the first initiative to emerge from this milieu—Irish-Ireland activists had formed a 'vigilance committee' to protest against King George V's address to the city's corporation in 1911—but it was by far the most popular. The ostensibly non-political nature of the Volunteers allowed it to exert a much broader appeal than earlier initiatives, attracting influential Irish-Ireland activists such as Terence MacSwiney who, for ethical or ideological reasons, had been unwilling to join the IRB or Sinn Féin.

Volunteers throughout the county testified to the importance of the role played by the Gaelic League (and, to a lesser extent, the GAA) in the emergence of the new movement. Dubliner Liam O'Flaherty, a member of the Craobh an Chliabhraigh branch of the Gaelic League, believed that 'nearly every male member of the branch was an active Volunteer, while many of the cailíní [girls] were in Cumann na mBan. Practically every man and boy in the branch took part in the 1916 Rising'.[42] The account of a Volunteer in rural Cork indicated a blurring of the boundaries between both movements in some areas: 'Nearly all the members of the unit were members of Lyre Gaelic League', he recalled, 'we organised feiseanna and Irish-Ireland concerts throughout the area during the years from 1914 onwards. The proceeds of these functions were used mainly to purchase arms and equipment for the members of the company'.[43] In some places, such as London, it was the GAA rather than the Gaelic League which provided 'the driving force behind the revolutionary spirit in the Volunteers'.[44] In other areas, it was both: Dubliner John Shouldice estimated that half his Volunteer company 'were members of the Gaelic League and about one third were members of the GAA'.[45]

But although numerous Volunteers emerged from the ranks of the Irish-Ireland movement, many cultural nationalists did not immediately support the movement. As one Gaelic League activist noted: 'All branches had members who favoured the Volunteer movement and participated in it from the start. They also had members who did not take a physical force movement seriously. Individual members held different views and were free to hold them'.[46] Cornelius Murphy made much the same point:

> Members of these bodies were not, generally speaking, revolutionaries. Ninety per cent of the GAA was just GAA, the other 10% was good. I belonged to two GAA clubs when the Volunteers started, and I was the only member of either of the two clubs who joined the Volunteers. With the exception of the O'Growney branch, the Gaelic League branches in Cork were interested in the revival of the Irish language and nothing more.[47]

There were parishes, such as Kilnamartyra in County Cork, where 'the Gaelic League had no influence on the start of the Volunteers. Neither had the GAA'.[48] Similarly, in Mourne Abbey (also in Cork), the GAA and the Gaelic League 'contributed nothing to the start of the Volunteers, none of its members joining up'. The formation of Volunteer companies here, as in many other villages and towns, was attributed by its members to the fact that 'people in the district had sound national ideas, and were ready to support a vigorous national movement'.[49]

Beyond Dublin, the Volunteers were not an overnight success. In Galway, in a pattern widely repeated elsewhere, few of the six hundred men who spontaneously enrolled in the organization on its formation in that city became active Volunteers.[50] In Cork city, only nine men turned up for the first drill session in *An Dún*.[51] During the first six months in Cork, J. J. Walsh recalled, 'we had a large number of men enrolled but poor and irregular attendance at drill'.[52] The greatest obstacle was the Irish Party whose grassroots organizations, the UIL and AOH, were often hostile to the new movement, regarding it as a separatist challenge to their authority. In Cork, the AOH broke up the Volunteers' inaugural meeting in the City Hall, and their first public parades, in April 1914, were attacked

by mobs: 'bottles and other missiles were thrown at us'.[53] In Cobh, where
the AOH refused to allow the Volunteers to meet in the rooms used by
the Gaelic League, a 'large crowd looked and jeered' at the twenty-five
men who drilled in a field.[54] Employers, both unionist and Redmondite,
often discouraged volunteering, as did the RIC. More demoralizing than
such overt opposition was the apathy and ridicule of the general public.
The unfortunately named Patrick Looney recalled: 'I went to Beeing and
put up notices and gave out leaflets explaining the objects of the Volunteers. A number of men joined nominally, but the people generally thought
us mad...the politicians gave the advice—"Take no notice of him, he's
mad"'. When Looney sent membership forms to Volunteers in Kilmartain
and Bauracharing, they 'returned them some weeks later without the
name of a single recruit; they said it was useless—no one would join'. By
May 1914, his Donoughmore company had managed to recruit thirty
members but progress elsewhere remained slow: 'I called a meeting for
New Tipperary but no one turned up. I felt like giving them up for
ever'.[55]

One of the most potentially serious obstacles facing the new movement
was the attitude of the Catholic Church, not only because of its moral
authority but because the presence of priests was expected in nationalist
organizations. The Catholic hierarchy, which tended to support the Irish
Party and was hostile to separatism, shared John Redmond's lack of enthusiasm for the new movement. In contrast to their attitude to the IRB,
however, the bishops did not denounce the Irish Volunteers as it was not
a secret or subversive organization.[56] Consequently, the position adopted
by local priests was important, particularly as companies were often
formed at meetings which took place after Sunday Mass. Although not
particularly supportive of the new movement, most priests were not
openly hostile. As one west Cork Volunteer put it: 'The clergy took no
strong line against us'.[57]

Although Volunteers were more likely to recall those priests who
supported rather than opposed them, many individual priests clearly did
sympathize with the aims of the organization. Some offered their moral
support. The local curate in Carriganima, Co. Cork, 'agreed to support
the movement and arrangements were made for a public meeting after
Mass', one Volunteer recalled: 'At Mass on that Sunday Father Casey
appealed strongly to the young men to join'.[58] Others signalled their
approval by allowing church door collections to be held after Mass.[59]

In Cork city, Felix O'Doherty was despatched to seek the approval of the parish priest of Cornmarket: ' "What is the object of the Volunteers?", he asked. "Well, Canon", I replied, "it's to drive the British out of Ireland." "Wouldn't it be great if we could do it," said he, "by all means hold the collection." '[60] A minority, such as Father Wall, a curate in west Limerick, were sufficiently enthused to form their own company.[61] In County Tyrone, Fr James O'Daly and Fr Eugene Coyle attended IRB and Volunteer meetings, the latter explaining: 'I was not an official member of the organisation; my priestly calling would not allow my joining an oath-bound secret society. I attended these meetings and in this way I hoped to give the country boys the feeling that they were working on the right lines by organising, arming and training for the defence of our country'.[62]

Some priests offered more hands-on support. 'Father Matthew used to be out with us at night during training exercises', an Inchicore Volunteer recalled, 'but he was not a Volunteer'.[63] Equally enthusiastic was Fr Henry Feeney, the curate at Clarenbridge, Co. Galway, who 'threw himself wholeheartedly into the advancement of the Volunteers and did everything in his power to encourage us. Meetings of the officers were held in his house, and even bombs were manufactured there'.[64] In the same county, the curate at Kinvara recruited Michael Hynes into the movement: 'Father O'Meehan was our inspiration. He supplied us every week with papers like *Scissors and Paste* and *Nationality* free of charge'.[65] In Ferns, Co. Wexford, Father Murphy sat on the controlling committee of the Volunteers, raising funds for the company through chapel gate collections, and lending the men his car to transport rifles.[66] In Ringsend, Fr Paddy Flanagan set up his own militia to train the young men of his parish:

> He took the Fianna, on winter's evenings, through the history of the Boer War, and showed us how that war had been imposed on a peaceful people by a bullying empire. He told us how the Boers fought and how they could have won. He understood guerrilla warfare and passed his knowledge on to us...He borrowed .22 rifles from all quarters so that we could march.[67]

Such clerics were obviously atypical: Flanagan was the only priest in Dublin imprisoned after the Rising. 'He was not the ordinary type of popular curate', one of his young protégés conceded, 'Would it be indiscreet to mention that that he was the inventor of the sawn-off shot gun?' In contrast, many Catholic priests saw their role in the Volunteers in the same light as their involvement in other nationalist organizations: to ensure clerical influence, moderate any extremism, and prevent violence. As the RIC inspector general observed, the clergy was generally not opposed to the Volunteers so long as it was led by responsible people.[68]

The slow growth of the movement in County Cork was preceded by months of hard graft. In theory, any group of men could come together and call themselves a Volunteer company; in practice, it was difficult for a handful of isolated separatists in a village or small town to credibly do so. Consequently, the role of outside organizers was important, and the movement tended to extend from the cities, or other centres of strength, into less organized areas. Tom Hales, captain of Ballinadee Company, one of the strongest units in west Cork, claimed that his men 'took the lead in building up and developing other Volunteer companies in neighbouring districts, and their example and leadership were mainly responsible for the formation of many companies'.[69] The most popular method of encouraging the formation of new companies was for existing ones to parade to nearby towns and villages. Volunteer officers targeted—or were contacted by activists in—quieter areas, organizing parades, drilling, or public meetings to promote the new movement. The impressive and exciting sight of uniformed Volunteer companies, often trailed by RIC men, enlivened many a country village after Mass on a Sunday.

What factors accounted for the emergence of companies in some areas, while the same appeals fell on deaf ears in others? The success or failure of the movement tended to reflect local circumstances. Although ostensibly non-political, Volunteer companies often failed to transcend local political or factional divisions. In the County Dublin village of Lusk, two companies were founded in order to accommodate local rivalries: 'One company was started by the Rooneys and had its origin in the hurling and football club, and the other club was started by the Taylors and Murtaghs'.[70] Limerick city's rival battalions were divided on class and political lines. Where companies were felt to be dominated by a particular faction, it was not unusual for its rivals to remain aloof.

Many Volunteers, like Matthew Murphy in County Cork, emphasized the importance of a local tradition of resistance to authority such as Fenianism or agrarianism: 'There was an old tradition of Fenianism in the Kilmurray district, and the spirit it inspired never entirely died out'.[71] Elsewhere in rural Cork, Tom Hales similarly attributed the strength of Ballinadee Company to the area's strong Fenian and Land League traditions.[72]

In the west of Ireland, despite successive agrarian campaigns which resulted in increasing numbers of tenants purchasing their own farms, large numbers of smallholders remained on farms that were either too small or unproductive to provide a decent standard of living. The resulting agrarian tensions initially provided much of the impetus behind the Volunteer movement in the west. The RIC complained that the organization in Galway and Clare was 'permeated by dangerous secret societies' and recruited 'from the very class with whom the police have frequently come into collision during agrarian disturbance'.[73] In east Galway, where a strong tradition of resistance to police and landlords extended back to the Land War, the strength of the Volunteer movement (as well as Sinn Féin and the IRB) rested on an agrarian secret society run by the Craughwell blacksmith, Tom Kenny.[74] Similarly, Peter Howley observed that he had little difficulty recruiting men from the Ardrahan district as 'there was a continuous war being waged against the landlords and the RIC in county Galway, right up to the formation of the Volunteers'.[75]

These local traditions were reinforced by the important role of small numbers of influential families. In Ballinadee 'the traditional Fenian spirit and doctrine', Tom Hales claimed, 'had been handed down to us by my father, Robert Hales'. It was largely the influence of the Hales family and their neighbours, the O'Donoghues, that created the largest and most active company in west Cork: 'Together, these two families made up almost a third of the founding members of the company'.[76] In Dunmanway, an elderly circle of Fenians based around the McCarthy family 'gave help and guidance to a younger generation' of Volunteers, even handing over their funds, saved for over forty years, to purchase rifles.[77] In Kilnamartyra, it was the influence of 'a few members of the old IRB organisation', the nephew of one of them recalled, 'that encouraged many of the young men locally to join the movement'.[78] Nor was this only the case in rural Ireland; much of Edward O'Neill's Dublin company was drawn from 'five families, all related to each other'.[79]

Such local traditions of resistance survived because they were rooted in tangible social and economic realities as much as any abstract notion of patriotism or historical memory of past grievances. The land question was paramount in rural areas but it was bound up (as the account of Patrick Crowley from rural Cork illustrates) with broader social and political struggles: 'My family had been evicted out of our land in 1890 and were out of it for seventeen years. We were hostile to everything British and the police were always watching us...We had a family tradition reaching back to 1798'.[80] Tom Hales attributed the strength of the Volunteers in Ballinadee, in part, to its recent history of agrarian violence. Recalling a well-coordinated attack by ash-plant-wielding local men on twenty policemen who had impounded his father's cattle on behalf of a local landlord in 1907, Hales noted that all of those involved 'were afterwards the leading men in the Ballinadee Company'.[81]

Agrarian conflict was sometimes bound up with sectarian tensions between the declining Protestant gentry, who had owned much of the land, and their Catholic tenants who were in the process of acquiring it. The two issues were conflated in Patrick Crowley's recollections:

> Bandon and its neighbourhood were strongly Protestant and they were much against the Catholics. The landlord, Frank Beamish, served a notice to quit on my father, Jeremiah Crowley, in 1886...In 1904 I was bound to the peace for two years for knocking down the man who was minding the land for the landlord.

Another organizer similarly attributed the Volunteers' difficulties in the Bandon area to the 'anti-national influence exercised by the descendents of the Elizabethan usurpers who controlled the social and economic life of the district'.[82] Despite its ambition to recruit Irishmen of every creed, the membership of the Volunteers was almost entirely Catholic, even in southern Ireland where sectarian tensions were far less significant than in the north.[83]

In Ulster, where the UVF's radicalizing impact was most apparent, sectarianism rather than agrarianism spurred the movement on in its early months. The mid-Ulster religious borderlands, where Catholic and Protestant numbers were finely balanced, and armed men on the ground remained likely to contest the shape of any partition settlement, witnessed the heaviest concentrations of both Irish and Ulster Volunteers in the country.[84] Catholic priests were also more prominent in the Irish Volunteers (and the IRB) in Ulster than in other provinces. In Rockcorry, Fr Laurence O'Ceiran founded one of the first Volunteer companies in County Monaghan.[85] In Fintona, in rural Tyrone, the purchase of sixty rifles by Fr Eugene Coyle for his parishioners prompted the formation of a company:

> Sir Edward Carson's Ulster Volunteers were well organised in Fintona and paraded the town carrying arms two or three times a week. Fintona is a Catholic town and I felt that the arming of the Ulster Volunteers was a great

danger to the safety of the Catholic population... Sixty young Fintona Volunteers paraded on the streets of our town all armed with serviceable rifles, each rifle having attached a fixed bayonet. At the time we got the rifles, the Unionist Volunteers had only forty rifles in Fintona and they had no bayonets for them, so they ceased parading on the streets.[86]

In terms of class, the Volunteers appealed to a broad cross-section of society. Liam Tannam's Dublin company 'had all kinds of people from doctors to labourers'.[87] 'The rank and file', another Volunteer noted, 'were of the Dublin artisan class, with many clerks, shopmen, civil servants and students'.[88] Most urban Volunteers were working class, artisans, or lower middle class: particular occupations—such as grocers, barmen, and civil servants—were over-represented in some companies. Rural Volunteers were similarly drawn from the lower middle and labouring classes: an analysis of 211 Volunteers in east Galway found that 60% were (mostly small) farmers or the sons of farmers, 18% tradesmen, and 13% agricultural labourers. Only 4% were professionals, and almost all were young, unmarried, and literate.[89] However, rural companies were often led by more prosperous farmers. For example, the Hales and O'Donoghue families who ran the Ballinadee Company were large farmers and major local employers.[90]

The movement received less support from the wealthy and, possibly because of the financial and other sacrifices involved, the very poor. During an era when a majority of people remained disenfranchised, and nationalist politics tended to be led by larger farmers, professionals, and businessmen, the new movement was widely viewed as an unwelcome challenge to the status quo. Describing the rank and file of the movement as 'farmers' sons, shop assistants, and servant boys', the RIC inspector general dismissed them as 'persons of no importance' and 'men of no position in the country'.[91] John Regan, a senior RIC officer, believed that the modest social status of the Volunteers led the authorities to underestimate the threat posed by the movement: 'no organisation was regarded in some places as being of any real consequence unless it was led by what were termed "people of importance" '.[92]

The appeal of volunteering was not confined to young men. A leading Cork Volunteer insisted that 'women were a big factor in influencing the slow swing over of national opinion to the Volunteers'.[93] The Volunteer manifesto had, rather vaguely, stated that there would 'be work for women to do' and, at the inaugural meeting, MacNeill had suggested that their female supporters form an auxiliary organization, just 'as the Ulster Women's Council was organised to help the Ulster Volunteers'.[94] The result was Cumann na mBan, founded in Wynn's Hotel on 2 April 1914 'to assist in arming and equipping a body of Irishmen for the defence of Ireland'.[95] Prior to its formation there was some disagreement about its status: should women form an independent Volunteer-style organization or merely support the men in a subordinate capacity? This was never fully resolved. Nancy Wyse-Power, a leading member, noted: 'The promoters may have had in mind an auxiliary association of women acting under the general instructions of the Volunteer executive but the organisation immediately declared itself to be an independent organisation of women determined to make its own decisions'.[96] However, Min Ryan's assessment was more accurate: 'People...used to maintain that we were not an auxiliary to the Volunteers, but an independent body; but the fact of the matter was that our activities consisted of service to the Volunteers...we were not formed as an auxiliary, but we looked on ourselves as much'.[97] As a member from Tralee explained: 'We worked on our own initiative trying to do the best we could to help the Volunteers in every way possible'.[98] This was an approach that irritated some of the organization's more feminist-minded membership: 'At that first meeting one of the women present, Miss Agnes O'Farrell, suggested that we should start making puttees for the Volunteers. I was disgusted'.[99]

Like the Volunteers, Cumann na mBan was established throughout Ireland and among the larger expatriate communities in Britain. There were forty-three branches in existence before the Rising but it appealed to a narrower constituency than the Volunteers. Regardless of its subordinate status, for some women the decision to join such a movement demanded considerable independence of mind. Working women and mothers were also less likely than men to enjoy the leisure time necessary for activism. Consequently, its membership was disproportionately drawn from better-off, well-educated, or otherwise independent women, and the sisters, daughters, and wives of committed republicans. Máire Fitzpatrick from Enniscorthy was an example of the latter; she recalled how, as a child, she had envied her Fianna brothers: 'I was allowed to help with the organising, but Liam Mellows wouldn't let a girl join. Seán got the loan of a revolver and I was allowed to use it, until one day I shot a hen belonging to Mum'. When her father and brothers joined the Volunteers, she set up a local branch of Cumann na mBan.[100] The Ballinadee branch, in a pattern widely repeated elsewhere, was formed by the sisters of the Hales brothers who ran the Volunteer company.[101]

III

After six months of steady if unspectacular growth, the Volunteers had established itself as a significant presence with a membership of 27,000 by April 1914. But in the early summer, against a background of mounting political crisis, the popularity of the movement exploded. Its member-ship increased from 50,000 in late May, to 100,000 in mid-June, to 150,000 in July, finally peaking at a remarkable 190,000 in September 1914.[102] Why did the volunteering phenomenon come to appeal to such a wide cross-section of society, transcending boundaries of class, gender, and politics?

Few Volunteers felt it necessary to explain why they joined the move-ment, but those who did cited patriotism as the key factor. This was particularly the case for those who joined before the Volunteers became a mass movement in the summer of 1914. 'When I joined the Irish Volun-teers I had no particular affiliations with any political party or association with any cultural or social organization', Dubliner Henry Murray insisted, 'I had always believed in my country's right to complete independence and considered that the extent to which that right could be secured depended on the amount of force that the men of the country were prepared to exert'.[103] The Volunteers benefited from growing nationalist concerns about the methods and, increasingly, the objectives of the Irish Party. Eamon Morkan 'felt that a more active policy would be needed if anything was to be achieved in the line of independence for the country'.[104] For others, it was not merely the Irish Party but its electorate that was a cause of concern: 'the whole Irish people seemed to have become English and nationality was reduced to a mere thread that was ready to break and plunge Ireland into an abyss of slavery'.[105] Elizabeth and Nell Corr joined Cumann na mBan because they 'were so disgusted with the pro-British feeling in Belfast'.[106] For those who were already politicized, volunteering offered a more virile alternative to constitutional politics. Bernard McAl-lister joined Fingal Company 'because I had seen a chance in them of doing something to attain the freedom of our country and breaking the connection with England'.[107] Another member of the same company felt 'that there was a chance here of doing something to burst the English domination'.[108]

However, by the time the Volunteers had become a mass movement in the summer of 1914, the vast majority of its members were neither republicans nor advocates of insurrection (even if many of their Fenian officers were). The movement's appeal to ordinary nationalists, people who were supporters rather than opponents of the Irish Party, suggests that its attractions were not primarily ideological. In Ireland, as elsewhere in Europe, the appeal of such organizations was rooted in an admiration of military values and an idealization of the soldier shared by people of diverse political outlooks. The prominent Home Rule activist Tom Kettle described volunteering as part of a strange reversion to the gospel of force sweeping the world, the product not of 'logic' but a 'sudden illumination'.[109] The Irish Volunteers were merely the most successful of a remarkable array of militaristic organizations which included the Boy Scouts, the Fianna, the Ulster Volunteers, and Irish Citizen Army (the socialist militia formed by James Connolly to defend striking workers from the police during the Dublin Lockout of 1913). By 1914, an astonishing 250,000 men—representing about one in three Ulster Protestant men and one in five Catholic Irishmen—were enrolled in paramilitary organizations.[110]

The militaristic appeals of volunteering were many: camaraderie, training, discipline, uniforms, and—above all—guns. 'In business houses, workshops, offices and various professions, a feeling of comradeship which never previously existed sprung up', Laurence Nugent recalled, 'Men who had only a nodding acquaintance shook hands when they met in the street. The young men clicked their heels when they met their pals and actually hugged and pulled each other around: all were joining up'.[111] Volunteering allowed men to acquire and display the attributes of the soldier: discipline, virility, and self-respect; 'we were no longer a mob', Nugent insisted: 'We were Volunteers'. For Liam Brady who, as a child, had marched behind the British army's recruiting parades, attempting 'to keep step with the band as if obeying orders from some officer whom I highly respected', the excitement of drilling was contagious: 'the sound of marching feet could be heard all over the land. Companies were formed in various parts of Derry and soon hundreds of able bodied men were drilling openly...My youthful heart was filled with excitement and the old flame of wanting to drill and parade was once more burning fiercely within my breast'.[112]

For many, politics was a less important consideration than the thrill of
wearing a uniform, drilling, or firing a gun. 'One of my pals had already
joined a company', one Dublin Volunteer recalled, 'He told me about the
marching men and the orders of Captain Condron...I was the first Volunteer to wear a uniform'.[113] Liam Tannam testified to the glamour of a
military uniform, recalling how he would change into his 'for swank...
to meet my girl'.[114] And it was not only the ladies who were impressed by
men in uniforms. J. J. Walsh recalled the impression he made on Volunteers in Skibbereen when he appeared in a uniform which he had commissioned from a local tailor: 'the new garment created something of a
sensation'.[115] The commandant of a rival nationalist militia, the Hibernian
Rifles, attributed the decline of his force to the fact that their competitors
were 'more attractive as they had uniforms'.[116] As in other respects, the
Fianna had led the way here; its uniforms had provided one of its strongest
attractions for its young members, many of whom could recall every detail
of their outfits. Different branches had adopted their own shirts, hats, and
shorts, while the movement had even split following a row about hats.[117]

Above all, guns were central to the appeal of volunteering. Every
Volunteer 'loves a rifle', the *Irish Volunteer* acknowledged: 'a man who has
once handled a rifle and is not smitten with a desire to own one is not an
Irishman'.[118] Manliness, guns, and independence were inextricably linked
in Volunteer discourse: 'A man is not fully a man, nor is a nation a nation
without the power to direct a policy', Joseph Plunkett declared, 'The
whole nation must bear arms'.[119] Nationhood, Patrick Pearse asserted, 'is
not achieved otherwise than in arms'. Guns, and the romantic notion of
fighting for one's country, attracted many young men to the movement.
An Enniscorthy Volunteer recalled the first time he held his 'long Lee
Enfield': 'I brought my prize home and fondled and caressed it, as a lover
would his bride'.[120] A pupil at St Enda's school, where practical patriotism
formed an important part of Pearse's curriculum, recalled his 'lovely long
Lee Enfield' which the boys kept at the head of their beds: 'It was, to me,
a lovely weapon and perfectly new and I took great pride in keeping it
well-oiled and free from rust'.[121] The very sight of arms was sufficient to
recruit members. Patrick Twomey joined the movement after attending a
concert at Cork's Opera House:

> A lady gave a recitation, standing in front of the curtain. I remember the
> part of it, 'the men who died for Ireland, who will stand and take their

place?' The curtain went up showing a party of twenty or thirty Irish Volunteers on the stage with their rifles at the slope. I decided that this was my party.[122]

Conversely, lack of arms exposed Volunteers, reduced to drilling with wooden sticks, to public ridicule; the purchase of only two rifles, the founder of one Kerry unit noted, 'were a help in keeping the company together'.[123]

The appeal of volunteering was not confined to the men. As well as engaging in such gender-appropriate activities as first aid, fundraising, organizing dances, catering, learning Gaelic, sewing uniforms, and making bandoliers, sleeping bags, bandages, and badges for the men, members of Cumann na mBan learned how to parade and drill. In Belfast and Dublin, but apparently not elsewhere, women were even taught how to handle guns: 'we learned to clean, cool and load rifles and revolvers. The idea in teaching us', Molly Reynolds recalled, 'was not that we would use arms, but that we could assist the men by being able to carry out these duties'.[124] Many men and women remained opposed to the notion of female combatants. Despite being taught how to shoot, Elizabeth Corr's Belfast branch failed to assert its right to fight:

> Nora Connolly announced that at the next meeting she would ask the members to decide whether or not they would actually fight if it became necessary. After the meeting Nell and I told Nora that we did not need to wait—we were prepared to fight, and that was our reason for joining Cumann na mBan. However, at the next meeting Nora said that she had been advised not to press the matter.[125]

Maeve Cavanagh, a leading Cumann na mBan member, 'got tired' of the organization 'as they were only collecting money and such like activities', joining Connolly's Citizen Army (where women were trained to shoot) in the hope that she could play a military role in the fight to come.[126] However, even the revolutionary socialist ICA did not fully transcend the gender assumptions of the era. Although there was no formal distinction between male and female members, most of the latter served in the 'Ambulance Corps' of the ICA, which was referred to by some as the 'Women's Section'.[127]

Volunteering, like mid-Victorian Fenianism, offered many enjoyable activities, particularly in rural Ireland where there wasn't always much else for young people to do. This was also true for women for whom it offered greater independence, something which provoked disapproval from parents and authority figures. Molly Reynolds recalled 'getting into trouble at home for being out late at night', while the Belfast members struggled to obtain a meeting place 'as our organisation was not popular and not considered respectable'.[128] Young people also welcomed the opportunity to socialize beyond the prying eyes of parents and priests. Bridget Lyons swooned over Ned Daly—'I was thrilled with him and felt that although he was quiet he was very forceful'—and Peadar Clancy: 'He was fascinating and epitomised for me all the attractive heroes in Irish history'.[129] Lily Cooney was smitten by Con Colbert who presented her with his portrait: 'I was charmed because, to tell the truth, I thought an awful lot of him and, of course, he must have known it. He was not, however, at all interested in girls; he was entirely engrossed in his work for Ireland and devoted all his time to it'.[130] Romance there may have been, but love of nation came first for these earnest young patriots. They were, Marie Perolz insisted, a chaste bunch: 'we did not think about sex or anything else. We were all soldiers and I was only bothered about what I could do for Kate Houlihan'.[131]

Given the myriad attractions of volunteering, it seems likely that many people did not require a compelling reason to join the movement. Recent research on the post-1916 Irish Volunteers has emphasized that ideology was a less important recruiting factor than peer pressure and other collective factors: 'for the majority of Volunteers, the decision to join was a collective rather than an individual one, rooted more in local communities and networks than in ideology or formal political loyalties. Young men tended to join the organization together with, or following, members of their families and friendship groups'.[132] When the Hales and O'Donoghue brothers decided to commit themselves to the Volunteers, they 'delivered the young men of Ballinadee *en bloc* by recruiting friends, neighbours, cousins, work- and team-mates'.[133] Given that, at its peak in 1914, the Irish Volunteers was a much larger and far less militant force than the later IRA, non-ideological factors must have played an even more important role. The crucial issue, then, was what happened after they joined the movement.

IV

What did it mean to be a Volunteer? What did they actually do? Was the organization, as it claimed, a highly organized, well-trained nationwide force? And if so, under whose control and for what purpose? Volunteers emphasized the commitment involved in membership. The 'sacrifices made at the time, both by officers and men, were very great', one Dublin Volunteer explained:

> The men had to pay three pence a week towards the cost of rent and light. They had to pay for the ammunition they used in practice. They had to pay for their own rifle ammunition and equipment. In addition to that, the companies had to form a company fund to provide themselves with such things as first aid, field dressings, stretchers, signalling flags and lamps and a reserve of ammunition and, where possible, training tools.[134]

The time and effort required was equally demanding: 'I devoted all my time to Larkfield, between drilling and training and all. I put my heart and soul into it'.[135] Typically, a Volunteer company met three times a week: twice on weeknights for drill or parades and once at weekends for route marches or other exercises. Some met more frequently: 'Parades were held two nights a week for each group, but drilling went on every night'.[136] Training camps were held throughout the year. Cork city Volunteer Diarmuid O'Donneabhain 'camped out for two nights, carrying out exercises in sham-battles, scouting, skirmishing, and so on'.[137] Elaborate exercises, intended to encourage solidarity within companies and competition between units, were held. One Volunteer recalled the activities at a gathering at Pearse's school in Rathfarnham:

> 'D' Company obtained third place... We staged a display of company and section ordinary drill and extended movements. We gave a bayonet charge that was very realistic and had arranged for one man with a French bayonet to cover himself with sheep's blood. We had to prevent doctors from interfering, it was so realistic, in order to allow our men to carry out first aid. Tents were erected within a minute and communication was opened up by ordinary telegraphy, visual and audible, and by semaphore and Morse.[138]

Training was conducted by ex-British army instructors. Some were paid, while others volunteered their services: an Enniscorthy Volunteer recalled how his drill instructor, an ex-British army recruiting sergeant named Darcy, 'was delighted to be drilling us; he thought in his own mind he was preparing us for the British army; but we members of the IRB used him for our own use'.[139] An elaborate administrative structure, at least on paper, was established. Volunteer headquarters even developed its own postal service, complete with signed time sheets, to prevent Dublin

Castle from monitoring its despatches.[140] Railway workers, train drivers, newspaper sellers, postal workers, civil servants, and government employees provided logistical and intelligence support. Training courses were held for officers at battalion level. Examinations were held and certificates awarded; successful candidates were appointed instructors, returning to their companies to teach the syllabus to their own men.[141] Officers were expected to pass such examinations to retain their commissions, and successful candidates were gazetted in the *Irish Volunteer* newspaper. Weekly lectures were held for officers at the Volunteer headquarters on Kildare Street. The curriculum was ambitious if not necessarily practical. 'MacDonagh was a very good lecturer', one Volunteer remembered, 'He started, I think, at the campaign of Xerxes and went on to the South African War'.[142] An IRB man recalled one of MacDonagh's lectures on field supplies: 'According to him, one could live indefinitely and work hard on a diet of nothing but onions, and he urged all and sundry to sow plenty of onions without delay. What a funny idea, we thought'.[143]

One of the most striking aspects of Volunteer training was its indebtedness not only to the British army's instructors but to its methods: 'the official British infantry training manual was our textbook', one Volunteer recalled, 'we followed that model in every detail of organisation and drill'.[144] Most companies 'worked more or less on the lines of normal British army training—extended lines and that—and we did use all the British army books'.[145] Thomas Meldon, an enterprising Dublin Brigade musketry officer, took courses on semaphore and Morse code run by army personnel at the College of Science.[146] Volunteers joined rifle clubs which had been set up by the British authorities to promote arms training in anticipation of the war in Europe.[147] The Volunteers' highly conventional training programme provided a striking example of the extent to which nationalists mimicked their opponents: close order drill, parading, and signalling were useful neither for insurrectionary or defensive guerrilla warfare. There was little emphasis on the two forms of combat—rural 'hedge-fighting' and urban street-fighting—that would give the Volunteers a comparative edge over conventional British forces.

Many young nationalists admired the professionalism of the British army, another example of the tendency, shared by nationalists elsewhere, 'to emulate the national enemy against which one reacts and sets oneself'.[148] Their desire to outdo their opponents was also demonstrated by the often friendly rivalry between both forces:

The Second Battalion O/C, Tom Hunter, was marching in front with his adjutant and second in command, and on nearing the British party, gave orders to the pipers to strike up a quick march tune which they did with such effect as to throw the British out of step with their own band. I felt a thrill of delight when this happened. I should have mentioned that we were with full equipment on the parade and I was proud of my short Lee Enfield which was the latest pattern.[149]

The influence of British militarism on Irish separatists was not surprising given the highly visible (and disproportionately large) presence of soldiers stationed in Ireland, and the way in which soldiering had long been glamorized by military displays at home and involvement in colonial wars abroad. The Fianna had also led the way in this respect: many of the Volunteers' officers had been recruited from the youth movement. As a leading Fianna organizer explained: 'the military knowledge of its officers was self-acquired. The senior officers were obliged to and did studiously cull from the British Army Manuals'.[150] As a result, the Fianna's notion of the ideal officer tended to reflect the stereotypical image of the British officer. Leading Fianna officer Micheál Lonergan was widely admired by the other boys because of his ability to emulate this persona: 'Micheál had the figure and walk—the dapper style of dress, the typical crisp voice of command and all the mannerisms, without the slightest sign of embarrassment, which add to the making of the perfect officer'.[151] 'He was a very active dashing type of character, especially when he was dressed in his neat and evenly fitting uniform—so distinctive, so elegant, so truly military', another boy gushed, 'A fine genuine, manly type'.[152] The cultural confusion which arose from the resulting conflation of anglophile and anglophobe values was expressed by the admiration of one Cumann na mBan member for the Volunteer officers of the First Battalion: 'they were the nearest approach to British officers in appearance and inspired us girls with feelings of enthusiasm and caused us many heart throbs'.[153]

Despite the enthusiasm that might be expected of a volunteer army, the Volunteers were not, as some liked to believe, 'better trained than the soldiers of the British army'.[154] The RIC did not regard it as a serious military force, particularly when compared with the better-trained and armed UVF which was led by senior British army officers. Nor did many nationalists. A member of Cork's brigade council conceded that 'Volunteering was a bit of a joke at first'.[155] The most obvious problem was lack of arms: Volunteers trained with staves, pitchforks, shovel handles, and wooden guns: 'Our absolute deficiency in arms made our efforts at training seem unreal and not worth the effort'.[156] The real benefit of training was the sense of purpose inculcated among Volunteers and the undermining of old habits of deference: 'We could hold our heads up; we could drill; we could march. We were taught what discipline meant and we knew how to obey orders', one Volunteer recalled, 'discipline became a matter of honour with every man'.[157] A sense of discipline distinct from that of a conventional army was forged. Leaders were often idealized by their men: 'Although we were well-disciplined we nearly always used Christian names and very rarely names of ranks. Tomás MacCurtain and Terence MacSwiney were in a way like lovable dictators that we followed enthusiastically, having complete confidence in them'.[158] Training exercises, such as route marches, provided the movement with enjoyable activities and publicized its existence: 'We looked upon them as good days out, enjoyed ourselves and were amused by the way people thronged to the doors and windows to stare at us as we marched by'.[159]

Although its leaders were 'most particular that the Volunteers should be identified as soldiers', cultural activities also played an important role in the everyday life of the movement.[160] Volunteering, like Fenianism, blurred the boundaries between military, political, and cultural activity: 'Scarcely a Sunday passed...that there was not a muster of Volunteers for some parade, exercise, or to attend a football match or *aeriocht* [concert]. Generally these were followed by a ceilí', Joseph Lawless recollected, 'We did not mind how far we cycled for such entertainment; and we sang and danced all night to the music of a lone violin'.[161] Independently, or under the auspices of GAA clubs and Gaelic League branches, Volunteers organized feiseanna, concerts, and other Irish-Ireland activities. A Donoughmore Volunteer described the preliminaries before the military exercises at a gathering of Cork companies: 'Cathal Brugha and Liam Mellows were there that day. Cathal Brugha sang the first verse of *Ninety Eight* and gave a short address. I danced a hornpipe with Freddie Murray'.[162] Concerts and festivals provided practical and political benefits: 'On almost every Sunday aeridheachta or concerts were held for the purpose of raising funds for arms and equipment. They were also availed of to spread the gospel of physical force, as the only way of winning back our country from England'.[163] They provided an opportunity to demonstrate the growing strength of the movement. One Volunteer described an oireachtas [festival] held in Killarney in 1914 as 'the greatest week of music, song, and Volunteer parades ever seen in Kerry':

> About sixteen bands, brass, fife and drum, and pipers, supplied music for thousands of Volunteers marching through the decorated streets of Killarney... The thousands that lined the streets simply went mad when the Killarney Company marched out of An Dún... fully armed with rifles, bayonets and ammunition led by Captain Michael Spillane, the son of an old Fenian. The twelve RIC men at the Market Cross got dumbfounded and could not move.[164]

Gaelic language, music, and dancing formed part of the movement's appeal. Songs, in particular, provided an effective means of propaganda for a movement that regarded itself above party politics. Although the organization discouraged party-political discussions, Volunteers marched in step to such songs as *Ireland Boys Hurrah, God Save Ireland, The Felons of our Land*, and *Wrap the Green Flag*. Implausibly, it was the Protestant choirmaster of St John's Church in Sandymount, Cecil Grange MacDowell, who composed the music for many of the most popular propaganda verses (including such topical numbers as *The Rocky Road to Berlin* and *Pop goes the Peeler*) on the church organ.[165] He was also responsible for the musical arrangement of *The Soldier's Song*, a song which countless Volunteers could remember where they first heard it, and the powerful impact that it had: 'in a few days' time', one recalled, 'every Volunteer in Dublin was whistling or singing it'.

Peter Hart has argued that it was the act of joining and the experiences which followed rather than any prior ideological convictions which distinguished War of Independence-era Volunteers from their nationalist peers: 'people did not join the Volunteers because they were radical. They became radicalized because they joined the Volunteers'.[166] The Irish Volunteers became the most popular movement in the country in 1914: did this mean that Irish nationalism was undergoing an unprecedented radicalization? Did the organization, as its Fenian sponsors hoped, inculcate the gospel of physical force among its members, reviving the moribund separatist movement? The IRB leader Tom Clarke thought so, as his letter to an American supporter demonstrates:

> Joe, it is worth living in Ireland these times—there is an awakening—the slow, silent plodding and the open preaching is at last showing results... the prospect today—from the national point of view is brighter than it has been in many a long year... hundreds of young fellows who could not be interested in the National Movement, even on the milk and water side, are in

these volunteers and are saying things which proves that the right spot has
been touched in them by the volunteering. Wait till they get their fist
clutching the steel barrel of a business rifle and the Irish instincts and Irish
manhood can be relied upon.[167]

Some Volunteers agreed. 'Their earnestness and enthusiasm spread a new
spirit in the countryside', one Cork separatist claimed, 'papers like the *Irish
Volunteer, Irish Freedom* and *The Spark* were introduced into many homes
and the principles and policies they advocated became subjects of discussion
and comment'.[168] Volunteering certainly instilled a militaristic outlook in
tens of thousands of young men, undermining the conciliatory mood music
of Redmondism, but it did not create a republican army. The IRB's influence over the leadership of the Volunteers was a secret one which most
ordinary members were unaware of and to which they would have objected.
J. J. O'Connell, the Volunteer's Chief of Inspection, and Bulmer Hobson,
its Quartermaster General, regarded the Fianna as a far more militant force
than the Volunteers.[169] Nor was the conflict between Redmondism and
separatism the only source of ideological tension within the movement: the
leadership was also deeply influenced by those who 'believed in the ideals
of the "Irish-Ireland" movement, not the republicanism of the old IRB'.[170]
Despite Tom Clarke's optimism, the split which would occur in the summer
of 1914 revealed that the influence of both these factions over the rank and
file was marginal compared to that of the Irish Party.

V

Who controlled the Volunteers? Following the 1914 convention, the
movement was led by a thirty-one-member provisional committee
known as the Volunteer executive. Thirteen of these were IRB men,
eight were Redmondites, and four were Sinn Féiners; the remainder were
unaligned but several—including Patrick Pearse, Thomas MacDonagh,
and Joseph Plunkett—subsequently committed themselves to the IRB,
reinforcing Fenian influence over the leadership. Authority was exercised
by a general council and a general staff known as GHQ; both bodies were
headed by Eoin MacNeill, as Volunteer president and chief of staff, but
they were dominated by IRB men. Throughout the country, Volunteer
units were initially controlled by appointed or elected executive committees but increasingly came under the authority of military staffs led by

commandants who were directly responsible to GHQ in Dublin: these were often IRB men. At a lower level of the organization, the IRB also tended to dominate the officer ranks in many areas.

However, this picture of pervasive Fenian control is complicated by the fact that the IRB itself was divided on fundamental issues such as the purpose of the Volunteers. The division between IRB men who saw the Volunteers as a potential insurrectionary force and those who adopted a more moderate position, such as Bulmer Hobson, was arguably more important than that between members and non-members of the IRB. The tension between these factions, never resolved before the Easter Rising, was first brought to a head by the spectacular expansion of the Volunteers in the early summer of 1914. This sudden growth owed much to the radicalizing impact of the Curragh 'mutiny' in March (when the Secretary for War and the army command appeared to acquiesce in the refusal of a section of its officer corps to impose Home Rule on Ulster), and the UVF's illegal importation of 25,000 German rifles the following month.[171] Kevin O'Shiel, then a student in Dublin, described the mood at the time:

> It seemed then to us young nationalists, as our pristine childlike faith in Liberal promises began to weaken and dissolve, that, after all, it was but the old, old game all over again…the effect of the Curragh mutiny on Irish nationalism was terrific…but it was mild compared with that of the Larne gun-running; and particularly so, on young nationalists. It created in us a deep mental and psychological reaction, and violently shook our faith in constitutionalism.[172]

Moderate nationalists who—following the lead of the Irish Party—had previously remained aloof began to flood into the movement. For separatists, there were obvious drawbacks to this sudden popularity: 'AOH men were coming into the Volunteers in large numbers, and the threat that they would swamp the movement was becoming very real'.[173] In addition, the Irish Party reversed its policy, moving, as it had on previous occasions, to absorb its more dynamic rival. The results were dramatic. In Belfast, the Volunteers increased from 300 to 3,000 within weeks.[174] Cork city's membership jumped from 400 to 2,000 men in June.[175] Elsewhere, rival, larger Redmondite companies were formed, overshadowing the original Volunteer companies.[176]

Redmond now moved to take control of the organization, initially by means of secret discussions with Eoin MacNeill, and then by issuing a

public ultimatum demanding the appointment of twenty-five of his nominees to the executive. Although appalled by the revelation of these discussions, the IRB militants felt even more betrayed by Bulmer Hobson's
support for Redmond's proposal.

> I was with Tom [Clarke] when the news came and to say he was astounded
> is understating it. I never saw him so moved. He regarded it from the begin-
> ning as cold-blooded and contemplated treachery likely to bring about the
> destruction of the only movement in a century which brought promise of
> the fulfilment of all his hopes.[177]

In reality, MacNeill and Hobson's reluctant acceptance of Redmond's
demand was based on their desire to avoid a fatal rupture. Any such split,
Hobson argued, would weaken Redmond's position against unionism just
as the Home Rule Bill was approaching a Commons vote, and provide
him with a scapegoat should he fail at Westminster.[178] As only a minority
of the executive opposed Redmond's demand, the insurrectionist faction
was forced to concede the issue but 'the position between Tom Clarke,
Seán MacDermott and Bulmer Hobson was never the same'.[179] Interestingly, Hobson's logic was subsequently accepted by at least one of the IRB
men who voted against him at the time:

> thinking back, I have often wondered what would have happened had
> Hobson's view been rejected. There is, in my opinion, no doubt that the
> organisation would have been split from top to bottom throughout the
> country. I agree that the split was inevitable, but I cannot share the view
> that when it came it was only after irreparable harm had been done by the
> acceptance of Redmond's ultimatum. We have to ask ourselves: could this
> young organisation—only eight months after its birth—have withstood the
> shock of a split at that date and upon that issue alone?... when the split did
> occur it was on a more vital issue—one which was to favour and in time
> greatly strengthen the Sinn Féin element in the Volunteers and in the same
> time was to almost completely wipe out the Redmondite faction which had
> carried on as a separate Volunteer body after the split.[180]

The Redmondite takeover created a mass movement, 'bringing into the
Volunteers', Hobson noted, 'all sorts of people who had never touched the
national movement before'.[181] It brought money, influence, and respecta-
bility: 'wealthy men, some of the Lords...and quite a few ex-British
officers who were apparently opposed to the Orange Volunteers, joined
up'.[182] But despite the influx of Irish Party supporters, the hostile takeover

represented something of a gamble for Redmond: 'It is not yet known what party will govern the movement, and it would at this stage be premature to say what controlling influence will be exercised by the persons of position', the inspector general warned, 'so far they have taken no part in drill or discipline'.[183] In Cork, the IRB continued to dominate the leadership and officer ranks of the Volunteers, while in Belfast the 'executive committee remained soundly republican'.[184]

Opinions differ as to the impact of the takeover at the grassroots. When it came to 'actual training, no political opinions were expressed and training went on smoothly', Laurence Nugent insisted, 'The ordinary Volunteer knew little of the squabbles that were going on at the top, but they hoped for the best'.[185] In contrast, J. J. Walsh, having completed an organizing tour of County Cork, described a movement sundered by factionalism:

> At Bantry there was the unique spectacle of no less than three potential armies. At the entrance we met and addressed the O'Brienites. In the middle of the great square were a few Sinn Féiners, while at the other end we addressed the Redmondites. These groups would not work together as one body, and it was the same in many parts of the county.[186]

Others feared the takeover was calculated to divest the movement of its radicalism. Describing it as 'an unholy alliance', one militant Volunteer complained that the 'Redmondites had no intention of building up a strong effective military force'.[187] In Belfast, separatists complained, 'training practices developed into mere parades, to open air meetings, where we were addressed by Joe Devlin and some MPs', and drill was switched to Sundays to boost attendance at the matches of Belfast Celtic (owned by supporters of the AOH). The AOH's importation of obsolete Italian rifles, dubbed 'gas-pipes' by their critics, was viewed as a cynical gesture.[188]

The Irish Party's bold move reasserted its dominance of popular nationalism but at a cost. At Westminster and at home, Redmond had come to represent a particular vision of Irish nationalism: moderate, conciliatory, and committed to constitutional means, a reputation that had been bolstered by Carson's defiance of parliament. Redmond's embrace of the Volunteers muddied the waters, undermining his earlier assurances that the Liberal alliance was sufficient to win Home Rule, and further radicalizing Irish politics. As Michael Wheatley has argued, the party had been forced to act because it had found itself in the unusual position of swimming against the tide of nationalist opinion, but its traditional response of infusing itself with the lifeblood of its rivals had not proven as successful a tactic as on previous occasions. Following the take-over, the Volunteer movement—still largely under the control of enemies of the party—remained vigorous while grassroots party activism continued to slump.[189]

One of the first indications of the problems Redmond could expect, having commandeered a militia that he only partially controlled, occurred on 26 July 1914 when the Irish Volunteers succeeded in smuggling nine hundred German rifles into the seaside town of Howth. Emulating the audacity of the UVF, Hobson brought 'the guns in in daylight, in the most open manner and as near to Dublin as possible'.[190] As one leading Volunteer explained: 'The Howth landing was deliberately organised in a spectacular way to win the utmost publicity for the Volunteers to wake up the country'.[191] The police's response played into their hands. Acting without proper authority, Assistant Commissioner William Harrel instructed the DMP to disarm the Volunteers. The double standard involved in this decision, only months after the police had failed to prevent the landing of arms at Larne, was sufficient to provoke around a dozen of the hundred policemen on the scene to disobey his orders, a revealing indication of the fragility of British authority in Ireland.[192] Patrick Bermingham, a DMP constable, recalled the resentment that he and his DMP colleague Andy O'Neil, felt: '"If they are trying to rush us against the Nationalist Volunteers here is one who will have nothing to do with it." I replied "I am with you in that."' RIC constables such as J. J. McConnell also testified to the 'demoralising effect' of this incident.[193] Nationalist sentiment was further inflamed when, on the same day, British army soldiers opened fire on a truculent crowd at Bachelor's Walk on the Dublin quays, killing three. Compounding this public relations debacle, Harrel and the commissioner of the DMP were forced to resign following an inquiry into the affair.

For Redmond, whose nominees on the Volunteer executive had known nothing of the plan to import arms, the operation was an embarrassment which revealed the weakness of his authority over the movement. For militant Volunteers, Howth was a publicity and financial coup: 'after the gun-running we never had any serious financial worries'.[194] The response of ordinary Volunteers to this first, successful, defiance of

British authority on the streets of Dublin was euphoric. A young Fianna boy recalled his excitement while unloading the *Asgard*'s precious cargo: 'rifles, rifles, and still more rifles. Oh the thrill of it! We were gun-running...We were frantic, hysterical with joy at the drama that was being enacted at that moment...Some men cheered, some wept with joy; some others too overcome by emotion went pale with excitement'.[195] Another recalled:

> You would think the fellows would go mad. They started wringing each other's hands and shouting—they were wild with delight. We marched home, every man with a rifle...On our way back we were cheered on all sides. A priest—standing bareheaded on a tram-car—with tears in his eyes—shouted 'Go on now, I have given you an old man's blessing'.[196]

For some Volunteers, Howth marked the beginning of the revolution: 'it was on that day that shots were first fired in anger in the streets of Dublin by British forces in a conflict which did not end for seven years'.[197] Liam Tobin (who would become the IRA's director of intelligence) joined the Volunteers, along with a group of his friends, shortly afterwards: 'Previous to that I had been rather critical of the Irish Volunteers...That incident convinced us that the Volunteers meant business'.[198] Oscar Traynor, another future IRA leader, joined the day after Howth: 'I saw that there was something serious pending'.[199] Joseph Kenny, a Fenian officer in Bray's beleaguered Volunteer company recalled: 'We began with 10 members amidst a hostile populace and carried on until July 1914 when, as a result of the gun-running in Howth, we were swamped by the influx of new members, most of whom were associated with the AOH'.[200] The reaction in Belfast, as one Volunteer organizer reported, was equally dramatic:

> there certainly must have been thirty or forty thousand people there. I have never seen such enthusiasm...It seemed profoundly pathetic to see the joy of these poor folk at thinking they were to receive arms...So many recruits came in that it was nearly impossible to keep pace with them; the parade ground and the drill halls would hardly hold them.[201]

The Volunteers further exploited popular sentiments by staging a public funeral for the victims of the army, the sight of armed men openly parading creating further excitement.

Hobson's coup revealed—ironically considering his later opposition to the Rising—just how successfully the Volunteers could be manipulated by a conspiratorial elite. As one Fenian reflected, it marked 'the beginning of that necessary double dealing which was to play such an important part in the events of the Easter Week'.[202] It also illustrated the extent to which the actions and fortunes of the UVF (and their powerful supporters within the British military and political establishment) shaped those of the Irish Volunteers. Noting the tremendous impact of Howth, one Volunteer recalled: 'Neither of the Volunteer movements impressed itself on the public mind as a force to be reckoned with, until the Larne Gun-running coup was carried out by the Ulster Volunteers'.[203] The effect of the Curragh mutiny and the gun-running in Larne was to render the Government's legislation for all-Ireland Home Rule unworkable.

By the summer of 1914, the possibility of revolution in Ireland was no longer a Fenian fantasy, as the alarmed tone of the inspector general's reports to Dublin Castle indicated. Two months before Howth, he reported:

> In Ireland the training and drilling in the use of arms of a great part of the male population is a new departure which is bound in the not distant future to profoundly alter all the existing conditions in life...If the people become armed and drilled effective police control will vanish...Events are moving. Each county will soon have a trained army far outnumbering the police, and those who control the Volunteers will be in a position to dictate to what extent the law of the land may be carried into effect.[204]

The condition of Ulster, he warned, 'could hardly be surpassed in gravity except by open insurrection'. By June, he was predicting imminent civil war. Just one week after the dramatic events in Howth, Irish politics was once more transformed but by violence on the streets of Sarajevo rather than Dublin or Belfast.

3

The Soul of the Nation

War

The outbreak of the Great War transformed the political atmosphere in Ireland, at a stroke postponing the implementation of Home Rule, defusing the impending crisis in Ulster, and forcing nationalists to take a stance on the war. In the longer term, the war would create the long-awaited opportunity for rebellion but its immediate impact on separatist fortunes was overwhelmingly negative.

The origins of the Easter Rising remain sketchy: the conspirators planned it with the utmost secrecy, few records of their plans survived, and all of the military council's members were executed within three weeks of the insurrection. Consequently, a surprising number of basic questions, most notably whether the leaders thought they had any reasonable prospect of military success, remain unresolved. It was only a small inner circle of the IRB, the military council, rather than the IRB leadership as a whole that planned the insurrection, but their objectives were dependent on the willingness of the wider Volunteer movement to fight. This chapter examines the role of ordinary Volunteers, as well as that of the leadership, using new evidence from the Bureau of Military History to assess the Rising from the perspective of both advocates and opponents of the insurrection. It begins by tracing how the war gradually radicalized Irish nationalism, undermining public confidence in the Irish Party and offering the separatists an opportunity to strike.

I

Young men throughout Europe greeted the news of war with excitement, as a wave of jingoism swept the Continent. Perhaps surprisingly, in light of the political crises that preceded it, the war also provoked considerable enthusiasm among Irish nationalists. For separatists, popular support for Britain provided a depressing reminder of their marginal status: 'The effect in Ireland was immediate', one Dublin Volunteer recalled, 'People who were what one would have thought rebels on Sunday were completely pro-British the following Sunday'.[1] 'Ireland', one northern nationalist complained, 'became pro-England and ardently pro-English virtually overnight'; 'war fever had gripped Ireland', a Limerick Volunteer observed, 'probably 90% of the population regarded anyone who was not "pro-Ally" as a traitor'.[2] Such sentiments appeared widespread throughout the country. 'When the war started in August 1914', an IRB man stated, 'the town of Galway went recruiting mad. It was not a question of "will you join up", but "what regiment are you joining?"'.[3]

Ireland's separatist minority failed to counter this wave of enthusiasm for a war which soon dominated every aspect of public life. The physical presence of the British army had never been so apparent: 'large numbers of troops were on the move to the boats at the North Wall for transport to England and France and large numbers of British recruits were brought over to Ireland for training. The streets of Dublin and the military centres all over Ireland were packed with the British army'. The mobilization of 58,000 military personnel and reservists on the outbreak of the war and the initial popularity of recruiting—210,000 Irishmen in total would serve in the armed forces—suggested a nation united behind the British war effort:

> Troops started to arrive from all parts of the country...They were carried away in the mail boats and in liners escorted by destroyers. There would be troops packed everywhere, in the lifeboats, on the bridge, from stern to stern. All the other ships in the harbour would blow their sirens, while everybody sang *Rule Britannia*...and *God Save the King*...There was hardly a family in Dublin that was not affected.[4]

Images of the war were omnipresent: 'No matter where you looked', a Citizen Army man complained, 'there was khaki. Every bit of wall space seemed papered with one kind of recruiting appeal'.[5] 'The streets were full of uniforms', one nationalist remembered, 'The hoardings and dead walls were papered over with posters calling on Irish youth to join up and do their bit for King and Country...Nearly every dead wall in the city had an enormous outsize picture of Kitchener's forbidding countenance'.[6] It was, one separatist observed, 'a sickening sight in those days for anyone who loved Ireland': 'the hoardings plastered with recruiting posters—"Your King and Country need you". "Join an Irish Regiment to-day". "Come, boy, and lend a hand"...With the exception of the faithful few—the Irish Volunteers—the country was reeking with imperialism'.[7]

The campaign for Home Rule and the clash between unionism and nationalism which had so energized the Volunteer movement were pitched into irrelevance when the Government placed the Home Rule Act on the statute books on 18 September, postponing its implementation for the duration of the war. In some areas, 'the Volunteer movement fell into a feeling of apathy and indifference'.[8] Even some nationalists who had previously been enthusiastic Volunteers felt themselves 'torn between conflicting ideals of duty, conflicting appeals and conflicting emotions. In my own case I hardly knew where I stood', Kevin O'Shiel recalled, 'I found every day more and more of my contemporaries...donning the khaki'.[9] On a more practical level, the organization lost most of its military instructors who were called up as reservists. In Castletownroche, this 'finished the company'.[10] In areas with a strong tradition of British army recruitment, the organization also lost many members. A Belfast organizer described the movement as 'virtually crippled' after it 'lost at least 700 men, either as reservists or through enlistment, during the first ten days' of the war.[11]

An unfamiliar and, for some, disconcerting sentiment percolated Irish public opinion: goodwill towards Britain. In Tyrone, normally a reliable hotbed of sectarian tensions, the RIC county inspector reported 'a revolution in the state of party feeling': 'the Ulster Volunteers and the Irish Volunteers turned out together on different occasions with their respective bands and torchlight processions to escort the soldiers to the trains'.[12] For the first time in many months, the inspector general could report some positive news to Dublin Castle:

All classes displayed a strong patriotic and anti-German feeling, and joined irrespective of creed and politics in giving a hearty send off to the Reservists...Popular feeling is undoubtedly in sympathy with Great Britain and hostile to Germany. Sinn Feiners, and other extremists, are here and there making efforts to stir up anti-English feeling…but it has not yet affected the public mind to any serious extent. There is a general dread of German invasion.[13]

Propaganda, particularly the sensational reports of German atrocities in 'Catholic Belgium', reinforced the war's grip on the public imagination. The emotive press coverage of the destruction of Louvain provoked mobs to burn down German-owned pork shops in Dublin, while separatist attempts to counter such propaganda fell on deaf ears: 'we tried to break up recruiting meetings but we generally got beaten up ourselves'.[14] The war brought economic rewards, further pacifying the country. 'Our fathers, uncles and other near relatives were, as reservists, called to the British colours', a Volunteer in one garrison town recalled, 'A large number of young men with no alternative careers of note also joined, and the town—Haulbowline—and district boomed with increased employment in the British war effort'.[15] In south Armagh, like other rural areas, 'Prices for all classes of farm produce were high and the farmers making money. Any person who worked had piles of money to spend and many were spending it freely'.[16]

The Volunteers initially remained popular throughout much of the country but not for the reasons envisaged by its founders: 'In the hectic excitement of that early war period, volunteering became suddenly fashionable', Peadar Doyle complained, 'The Volunteer movement was inundated by members who at the time had no real sympathy with the real ideas of the Volunteers. Rapidly the Volunteer movement was being converted into a recruiting instrument for the British Army'.[17] 'After the war started', an Enniscorthy IRB man related, 'things began to change in the Volunteers. The ex-British soldiers who used to drill us began looking for recruits. They told some of us that we would only be fighting to serve our own country and, when we came back, that we would get Home Rule'.[18] Popularity again proved a curse as the most unlikely supporters began to raise money for the movement. 'All the seóniní flocked into their ranks', one Volunteer complained, 'Lord this and that would call in to the office'.[19] The Earl of Meath, the Marquis of Conyngham, and Lord Powerscourt leant their support to the movement, the latter tactlessly presenting Bray's Volunteers with a Union Jack.[20]

The war posed different challenges for separatists and constitutional nationalists. Despite the Irish Party's instinctive ambivalence towards British imperialism, John Redmond would eventually come to adopt a policy of unambiguous support for the war effort, a stance he first signalled in the House of Commons on 3 August 1914 when he urged Britain to withdraw its troops from Ireland, leaving its defence to Irish and Ulster Volunteers. Calling for a British military withdrawal was hardly an unpopular suggestion for a nationalist to make but, in a speech at Wood-enbridge on 20 September, Redmond went much further, pledging the Government the support of Irish Volunteers 'wherever the firing lines extends, in defence of right, of freedom and religion in this war'.[21]

Redmond's decision to stake his political future—and that of his party—on the war is often regarded as both a disastrous miscalculation and a turning point in Irish history.[22] It was, nonetheless, consistent with his personal and political principles. Redmond had always argued that a Home Rule Ireland would prove 'one of the strongest bulwarks of the Empire'.[23] He personally identified with the war, regarding it as a just struggle for the right of small nations to freedom, and he believed that the experience of fighting a common enemy had the potential to reconcile Ireland's two political traditions. Moreover, despite his obvious sympathy for the war effort, he did not commit himself to active support for Irish enlistment in the British army until his speech at Woodenbridge, two days after he had finally succeeded in persuading an initially reluctant British Government to place the Home Rule Bill on the statute book.

Less idealistic (or naïve) nationalists could rationalize their support for Britain in more pragmatic ways. The status of Ulster had yet to be resolved—both the extent and duration of partition remained unclear—requiring the leaders of nationalism and unionism to compete for influence with the British Government. Reflecting his party's traditional distrust of British motives, Redmond's more nationalist-minded deputy, John Dillon, observed: 'that section of the Irish nation which has done best on the battlefields of France will be strongest in the struggle which may then be thrust upon us'.[24] But the most compelling reason for the Irish Party's support for the war was the lack of a viable alternative, even if some nationalists would later complain that a harder bargain should have been struck.

That separatists viewed the nationalist public's enthusiastic response to the war with despair demonstrates that Redmond's gamble had initially paid off: 'The country generally had lost its old national spirit. We were sinking very low nationally.'[25] This reaction reinforced the pessimistic belief of some republicans that Irish nationality was on the verge of extinction: 'Between the soldiers and their women it seemed as if we were getting more English than the English themselves and that there would soon be no room for anything but khaki in the city'.[26] Paradoxically, though, for the most committed separatists, rather than emphasizing the futility of their militant aspirations, it only reinforced the urgent necessity for a defiant protest. The IRB, moreover, had always regarded England's difficulty as Ireland's opportunity, a logical position in light of the impossibility of defeating Britain's superior military forces without a powerful international ally. The 'declaration of war between Britain and Germany', Joseph Lawless recalled, 'caused a flutter of tense excitement in Volunteer circles. Now, we thought, our chance had come; a war in Europe would so distract the forces of the army that surely this was a providential opportunity to strike for freedom'.[27] As early as September 1914, the IRB supreme council had resolved to support a rebellion before the end of the war.

II

First, however, it was necessary to respond to Redmond's bold decision to commit the Volunteers to the war. On 24 September MacNeill and twenty members of the executive announced the expulsion of the Redmondites from the leadership and called on the rank and file to back them. Throughout the country, companies assembled to choose between Redmond and the separatists, debating the issue at stormy and sometimes violent meetings. The IRB's influence over many Volunteer officers allowed it to frame the split in the most favourable light: the men of E Company, in Dublin's Third Battalion, were told to decide whether they wished to 'side with Ireland' or 'support the British Empire'.[28] Kilkenny's Volunteers were asked whether they 'stood for Ireland and the Green Flag' or 'England and the Union Jack'.[29] In Rathfarnham, County Dublin, the company adjutant 'explained that Redmond wanted us to fight for England and that Pearse wanted us to fight for Ireland'. In contrast, Captain Crosbie put forward the Irish Party's case to the Volunteers of Cork at a meeting in Millfield:

> 'We are actually at war with Germany and the boom of her guns may at any moment be heard on our shores'. At this point he was interrupted by a member of the committee who said, 'We are not at war with Germany; England is, but we are not'. Crosbie replied, 'That is all very well, but if we

are invaded and you tell that story to a German soldier his answer would be a crack of a rifle butt across your head, and what would our women and children do?' The interrupter answered, 'Our women and children could not fare worse than they recently did at the hands of the British at Bachelor's Walk'.[30]

The Irish Volunteers (as the minority separatist faction continued to be known) were overwhelmingly defeated. British intelligence sources estimated that the separatist leadership retained the loyalty of only 13,500 (7%) of the 188,000-strong force; the inspector general, probably more accurately, placed the strength of the militant faction at 9,700 (6%) out of a membership of 156,750.[31] In Belfast, 3,000 men joined the new Redmondite force (renamed the Irish National Volunteers or National Volunteers), leaving only fifty men remaining within the Irish Volunteers. This meant, as one member of the Belfast executive observed, that the original force 'had lost many good genuine men who had been good Volunteers before the Devlinite supporters came into the organisation'.[32] In Cork city, a former stronghold, less than a hundred Irish Volunteers remained active; in County Louth, around thirty out of one thousand Volunteers remained with the separatists. The split was less one-sided in some areas—including, importantly, Dublin—and in a handful of towns (including Castlegar and Athenry in County Galway, Ferns and Enniscorthy in County Wexford, and Tralee in County Kerry) support for the Irish Volunteers held firm. In most areas, however, the disheartening experiences of Michael Leahy in Cobh proved typical:

> The meeting seemed unanimous. I attempted to speak but was struck... The chairman, however, secured me a hearing and I was put upon a seat. I objected to recruiting the Volunteers for the British Empire, and said they had been established to fight for the freedom of Ireland. I asked any man who believed as I did to follow me out of the Hall. Fifteen of us walked out. We were jeered and hissed, and barely escaped being beaten up.[33]

Indeed, given the scale of the split it appeared 'as if it was the men who organised the Volunteers who got expelled from that body' rather than the other way round.[34] A similar if less devastating pattern occurred within Cumann na mBan, considerable numbers of members deserting the more radical leadership. Máire Fitzpatrick, who founded Cumann na mBan's Enniscorthy branch, was 'heartbroken' by the desertion of all but one of her hundred-strong company: 'I gave my speech and asked any member that was against Redmond to stand on my side of the hall, but Mrs Green and I were standing alone'.[35] Only the Fianna, which had always been a separatist force, was largely unaffected by the split.

But it was not all bad news for the separatists. The split clarified—to a certain extent—the ideological vagueness of the movement, separating 'the wheat from the chaff': 'At last we had a real body with a real purpose'.[36] 'If we were small in number', Gary Holohan observed, 'we had got rid of any ambiguous feeling which existed that we were only bluffing'.[37] Purged by the split, the new movement could be rebuilt on firm foundations: 'those who remained...meant business'.[38] The split also strengthened the IRB's grip over the organization: many of the remaining officers were Fenians and they regarded those Volunteers who stayed as 'men who would participate in an insurrection when the right moment was revealed'.[39] But these advantages were probably more evident in hindsight than at the time, particularly as the movement continued to decline after the split. Although E Company, in Dublin's Third Battalion, was reduced from 130 to 70 men on the night of the split, only 25 turned up for the next parade, while, several weeks later, its strength had dropped to 7: 'Even with that small number de Valera carried on as if he had a full company and solemnly issued orders to form fours with the seven men'.[40] F Company, in the Second Battalion, initially declared for the Irish Volunteers, but the 130-strong unit soon dwindled to 12 men. Some of these, like Liam Archer, had subsequently dropped out because they felt 'confused and disappointed' by the split.[41]

There were plenty of reasons for disillusionment. The organization had lost many of its weapons, which were owned by individuals rather than companies. The doors of meeting halls were again closed to Volunteers. The collapse in numbers was also attributed to the influence of the older generation: 'their fathers and mothers advised them to keep away from the Irish Volunteers because the old people at the time had been backing Redmond'.[42] The organization became the focus of renewed harassment by the authorities, prompting local government employees and public servants to leave the movement, although these tactics did not deter committed separatists as it remained difficult for public bodies to dismiss Volunteers without firm evidence of subversion.[43] Many who fell under suspicion merely stopped drilling, or joined companies that met secretly. It was possible to transfer recalcitrant public employees—wartime England was a particularly unpopular destination—but this could prove counterproductive. After Patrick O'Mahony, a postal officer in Tipperary, rejected the Chief Secretary's instruction that he leave the Volunteers ('I said it was known to me that officials of the Post Office in Belfast held office in the Ulster Volunteers'), he was transferred to potentially sensitive censorship duties in Valentia, where he soon made contact with the local IRB. He was then transferred to Dungarvan, in County Waterford, because there were no Volunteers there, a situation he remedied by forming a new company.[44] In contrast, such intimidation proved more effective when adopted by private employers. A company in Blarney, Co. Cork, was disbanded by its own officers 'due to pressure from their employers'; 'considerable pressure was put on many Volunteers by their employers', one Tralee Volunteer recalled, 'My own company was, in fact, practically wiped out in this way during 1915'.[45]

The greatest difficulty facing the Volunteers after the split was the resurgence of hostility against the movement, with the AOH again to the fore: 'We were actually afraid to appear in public, afraid of our own people', one Belfast Volunteer recalled.[46] The Irish Volunteer movement collapsed in Galway city after a night of violence that culminated in physical attacks on Volunteers and their homes and businesses.[47] In County Cork, which had been a relative stronghold, the movement was devastated: 'We were ostracised by our neighbours, by our bosses and by some of our priests. We were jeered at in public and spat upon', a Cork city Volunteer recalled, 'There were incidents when people spat into our collection boxes'.[48] The position was no better outside the city. In west Cork, opponents of the Volunteers 'availed of every opportunity to jeer at, insult and attack the Ballinadee men, even lying in ambush on the roads leading to the town for the purpose of attacking them with stones and other missiles'.[49] The Clonakilty Company collapsed, while Volunteers in nearby Lyre and Ahiohill were assaulted. In Dunmanway, the movement was reduced to eight men: 'The people generally took no interest, even men who turned out good afterwards. They said we were only leading the boys into trouble. Some were hostile and set the dogs on us when we were collecting'.[50]

In early 1915, it would have been difficult to see how England's difficulty was Ireland's opportunity. Redmond's decision to back the British government appeared successful: it had allowed the Irish Party to seize control of the Volunteer movement, isolating its separatist founders and their supporters within a marginal rump. In doing so, the Irish Party had

earned the gratitude of the British Government, and reasserted its dominance as the unchallenged representatives of Irish nationalism at home.
What could possibly go wrong?

III

Almost all the Irish Party's problems were rooted, one way or another, in
its support for the war. Had the war ended quickly, as most people had
assumed it would, Redmond would surely have been vindicated. As it was,
the length of the war, and its increasing unpopularity, strained the credibility of the party. Redmond's difficulties had begun almost immediately,
when Lord Kitchener's War Office appeared to treat the UVF more
favourably than the National Volunteers. While the loyalist militia was
incorporated into the 36th (Ulster) Division in a way that was perceived
to preserve its political identity and command structure, Redmond's
appeals for a similar nationalist ethos for the 16th (Irish) Division went
unheeded. 'Had Kitchener possessed even a tincture of sympathy with the
Irish national sentiment', the Chief Secretary, Augustine Birrell, later
complained, 'the Irish attitude towards the war would have been materi-
ally affected'. After a year of relative enthusiasm, which saw tens of thousands of National Volunteers enlist (nearly half of all Irish recruits came
from the National and Ulster Volunteers), recruitment dropped sharply in
mid-1915. Among those with no desire to serve in the British army, enthusiasm for the National Volunteers melted away. Aside from encouraging
enlistment, the movement lacked any purpose except, nationalists feared,
to potentially mark one out as recruitment fodder should conscription be
introduced. 'My battalion, though one of the first after the split to proclaim
its allegiance to John Redmond', Kevin O'Shiel (a young law graduate
living in Dublin) recalled, 'just withered away and vanished into thin
air'.[51]

Wider political developments contributed to Redmond's difficulties. In
May 1915, as a result of growing criticism of his conduct of the war, Asquith
was compelled to form a coalition government. The appointment of the
Tory leader, Bonar Law, and leading unionists, such as Edward Carson
(both of whom had openly defied the Government in 1914), to the Cabinet
heightened nationalist suspicions about the Government's long-term
commitment to Home Rule and raised fears about the possibility of

conscription. Redmond, in accordance with the Irish Party's traditional policy, refused the invitation to join the Cabinet which meant that he continued to be seen as partly responsible for wartime policy in Ireland while lacking much ability to influence it. The shift in power in London also increased unionist influence within Dublin Castle, undermining Birrell's alliance with the Irish Party, as was demonstrated by the appointment of Sir James Campbell, a diehard loyalist, to the position of Irish Attorney General in 1916.[52]

Against this background, nationalist public opinion began to shift. Kevin O'Shiel described it as 'changing from strong pro-allyism, through disillusionment, to neutralism'. But most nationalists, he believed, continued to steer clear of separatists: 'whatever abstract sympathy they might have had with their target—an Irish Republic—they counted its achievement an utter impossibility and regarded them as an ill-balanced lot of idealistic "rainbow-chasers" '.[53] However, O'Shiel felt that separatism did begin to appeal to his own age group: 'Subtly, clearly and constantly, they appealed to and drew out the latent and nationalist separatism inherent in nearly every young Irishman, thereby developing in us an extremely critical attitude towards the Party and the Liberal Government'. This reading of the prevailing mood chimes with that of the inspector general who reported that Sinn Féin 'by quietly representing that the government has no intention of giving Home Rule, and by urging young men to join the Irish Volunteers and to be trained to resist conscription and fight for national independence instead of joining the army, has already acquired an influence which its comparatively small membership would scarcely warrant'.[54]

In contrast to the purposelessness it bestowed on the National Volunteers, the war provided the Irish Volunteers with a clear and potentially highly popular cause: opposition to the war. Despite the prosperity it brought, the war—or, to be more precise, the idea of being compelled to fight in it—was very unpopular in rural areas. The county inspector reported that west Cork's Volunteer companies were 'almost entirely composed of farmers' sons of military age' who had turned against their local constitutional nationalist leaders because of the latter's support for the war.[55] The omnipresent wartime propaganda which had so depressed republicans during the summer of 1914 now presented endless opportunities for subversion. By altering one word ('his' to 'her') of the slogan on one of the most popular posters—'England expects every man to do his duty'—separatists made an effective and widely accepted point.[56] When an unfortunate Enniscorthy chemist lost his arm in the war, local separatists spotted an opportunity to counter the latest poster campaign: 'The wording on the poster was "Join the army and lend a hand". Some member of the IRB had slips printed and put under the poster: "Mike Kelly lent a hand but never got it back"'.[57]

As 1915 progressed, recruitment meetings were broken up as anti-war protesters grew bolder. In Killarney, armed Volunteers marched through a meeting addressed by Tom O'Donnell, one of the few Irish Party MPs not to have deserted the recruitment platforms: 'all present except military and police, followed the Volunteers, and this finished all active recruiting in this area'.[58] The inevitable coercive response to such protests served only to boost the popularity of the Volunteers. In Westport, a dozen Volunteers were arrested for disrupting a recruiting meeting addressed by Lord Sligo: 'I walked out of court without signing anything, and I believe the others did the same', one of the accused recalled, 'This incident sent our stock soaring amongst the people of Westport, and we felt proud of ourselves and obtained a status we had not got before our arrest. It swung a lot of people in our favour'.[59]

Opposition to the war offered separatists an opportunity to rebuild their shattered movement. The decline of the Irish Volunteers was halted and then reversed as new companies evolved from anti-war activist networks. In Millstreet, Co. Cork, a company was established after local separatists distributed leaflets calling on locals to 'Boycott England's Immoral Army'.[60] Although Máire Fitzpatrick (the Cumann na mBan leader who had been deserted by her followers in Enniscorthy) 'got a very rough handling from the crowd' while protesting at one British army recruitment meeting, she recalled that the 'Irish Volunteers got more members and we got back most of our women'.[61] Eamon Ahern's success in breaking up a recruitment rally revived the Volunteers in Dungourney:

> I got five or six of the local lads to go through the congregation to ask the men to assemble at the Tallow side of the village after Mass. About one hundred men, young and old assembled. We put them in fours and told them what we proposed to do...we then marched our body of men right through the meeting...When we got back in a few minutes the meeting had broken up and the people scattered...Captain Donnellan went to the Parish Priest...and decided to form a company of Volunteers.[62]

Inevitably, anti-recruitment activism overlapped with pro-German senti-ment. The sister of Cork Volunteer leader Terence MacSwiney recalled that 'we all were with the Germans in spirit in their fight against England'.[63] Despite the famous banner outside Liberty Hall declaring that the Citizen Army owed allegiance to 'Neither King nor Kaiser', the ICA marched to songs such as *The Germans are winning the war me boys*.[64] For many, this stance was merely an opportunistic one: 'we were pro-German, insofar as Germany was Britain's enemy, and we would have been pro-anything else that would oppose the ancient tyrant that held our country in bondage throughout the centuries'.[65]

The return of marching feet to the streets provided an early indication of the revival of the movement. On Whit Sunday, 23 May 1915, fifteen hundred Volunteers marched behind Austin Stack in Killarney: 'There was hardly a townland in Kerry that was not represented'.[66] On the same day a Volunteer parade in the city of Limerick, targeted as a recruitment stronghold of the Munster Fusiliers, proved more turbulent. As the Volun-teers paraded through the city's densely populated slums, they were assailed by stones, bottles, and cabbage stalks: 'They had been told that these men had cheered and gloated over every disaster that had befallen the Munsters', one Limerick man complained, 'and so their hearts were filled with bitter hatred of the pro-German Sinn Féiners, as they called the Irish Volunteers'.[67] The Volunteers were not attacked in more affluent parts of the city but, one recalled, 'the silent contempt of the citizens was almost as bad to look at'.[68] Women (almost invariably described by Volun-teers as 'separation women' in reference to the allowance paid to depend-ents of serving British army soldiers) played a prominent role in the violence. Alphonsus O'Halloran walked through 'a barrage of abuse from thousands of excited females'; another Volunteer claimed that 'it was the women on the street shouting all kinds of insulting epithets that finally whipped up the mob to frenzy'.[69]

In August a more successful demonstration occurred in Dublin, which had remained a relative Volunteer stronghold. The timely death of Jeremiah O'Donovan Rossa, one of the founding generation of Fenians, had provided an opportunity for an elaborate funeral to display the move-ment's growing organizational abilities, as armed men took over the city centre. One recalled with delight how Thomas MacDonagh, the Second Battalion commandant who organized the procession, ordered the 'arrest' of a DMP superintendent who had attempted to obstruct proceedings.

The involvement of the ICA, as well as representatives from Sinn Féin, the GAA, and the (unarmed) National Volunteers demonstrated an unprecedented display of unity for a separatist-controlled event. The funeral offered an opportunity to display the growing strength and confidence of the Volunteers, and to test public opinion (now judged by one participant as 'no longer severely hostile').[70]

It also provided the ideal setting for the most powerful speech of Patrick Pearse's oratorical career, a remarkably indiscreet and defiant statement of revolutionary intent in the guise of a traditional graveside tribute to the 'rather unattractive' figure of Rossa:

> Life springs from death; and from the graves of patriot men and women spring living nations. The Defenders of this Realm have worked well in secret and in the open. They think they have pacified half of us and intimidated the other half. They think that they have foreseen everything, think that they have provided against everything; but the fools, the fools, the fools!—they have left us our Fenian dead, and while Ireland holds these graves, Ireland unfree shall never be at peace.[71]

Many of those who participated in—or merely observed—O'Donovan Rossa's funeral were profoundly moved by the experience. 'The funeral was most impressive, skilfully organised and carried out', Father Curran (secretary to the Catholic Archbishop of Dublin) noted in his diary: 'It was a challenge to Dublin Castle and a deeply significant lesson to the Irish people'. He was struck, not so much by Patrick Pearse's famous graveside oration (which few people would have been able to hear), as the volley of shots fired by the Volunteers: 'It was more than a farewell to an old Fenian. It was a defiance to England by a new generation in Ireland'.[72] For many spectators, it was the sight of armed men that demanded attention. Leslie Price was one of many observers who instinctively grasped the significance of a very public ritual orchestrated by a secret society:

> When the armed Volunteers passed I then suddenly realised that the men I had seen—Tom Clarke, The O'Rahilly, Seán McGarry—looked as if they meant serious business. This aspect of the funeral and the reading of Pearse's oration the following day made such a deep impression on my mind that on the following Thursday night I joined the Árd Craobh of the Cumann na mBan. I joined from conviction and on my own volition.[73]

Many others, including former members of the National Volunteers, did the same, prompting an influx of recruits into the ICA and Irish Volunteers.

Similar public demonstrations followed. Armed rallies marked the anniversary of the Manchester Martyrs in November 1915 and a series of well-organized parades were held on St Patrick's Day in March 1916. In Cork, Volunteers who had previously refused to march in public with their rifles, regarding it as an unnecessary risk, enthusiastically turned out with their guns.[74] In Dublin, some fifteen hundred men participated in 'a monster parade' allowing the Volunteers to again seize control of the city centre: 'I remember seeing on that day British soldiers...being stopped and ordered to proceed on alternative routes and having no choice but to obey the directions of our men. A large force of armed policemen were simply powerless to intervene'.[75] Approving, or merely curious, onlookers were regaled by band music and displays of drill. One Volunteer, who attended a special Mass for the Volunteers, described its potent cocktail of patriotism, camaraderie, and piety:

the scene had a profound effect on me which will never leave my mind. A guard of honour in full uniform had been drawn up around the altar and the chapel packed to its utmost capacity with Volunteers. At the elevation the guard of honour drew their swords to the salute while the bugles rang out with a clarity that was astounding...Patrick Pearse, The O'Rahilly, Seán MacDermott and the executive who were in close attendance near the altar, appeared to look in their uniforms as if receiving a special blessing from God, and undoubtedly every man attending that Mass received such a blessing. Suddenly a rich baritone voice burst into the hymn to our Patron Saint *Hail Glorious St Patrick* and it was taken up by the whole congregation in such a fervent manner that a lump rose in my throat and I wanted to burst out crying or to do something to prove that I was worthy of being in their company.[76]

Of course, not everyone was as impressed by these displays. A Belfast-born Protestant who observed the same parade found the military posturing 'of young clerks and middle-aged labourers' a comical sight: 'Most of them had no uniform, and their cheap, ready-made clothes had an extraordinarily unwarlike look that was made almost ridiculous by the bandoleers and the long, obsolete bayonets and the heavy, out-of-date rifles they carried'.[77] It was a telling divergence of perceptions, as many of those in positions of authority shared such condescending and complacent attitudes.

These public demonstrations formed part of a broader trend towards open, and potentially violent, defiance of the authorities in the months before the Rising. In Craughwell, Co. Galway, Volunteers won the right to march openly with arms after facing down the local district inspector and a large force of his men: 'He went into consultation with our O/C who told him that Carson's Volunteers were carrying rifles in the north without any hindrance and that we would do so in the south, and he got away with it'.[78] Throughout the country, such small but symbolic acts of defiance emboldened local Volunteers, furthering the erosion of British authority set in motion by the Ulster Volunteers. Liam Tannam, captain of the Third Battalion's E Company, refused an RIC sergeant's order to disperse his men: 'I...asked him why he did not go up north and arrest Carson's Ulster Volunteers for parading. He threatened to arrest me and I drew a .38 revolver and invited him to go on with the arrest. He did not go on with it'.[79] Separatist leaders were well aware of the liberating effects of such defiance, intended to undo the deference ingrained by decades of British rule. Donal O'Hannigan, an IRB leader, refused to concede to his arrest by a force of twenty policemen at a meeting in Meath: 'I said "I have an automatic and a Colt revolver here and 13 rounds of ammunition, and 13 RIC will die before I am arrested and then perhaps not either." This bold statement gave the Volunteers great heart as it was the first time anyone had spoken to them in that manner'.[80]

Connolly's Citizen Army—which was even more committed than the Volunteers to revolutionary violence—was involved in similar stand-offs. Helena Molony and James Connolly dramatically broke up a police raid on Liberty Hall a month before the Rising. Molony was the first to arrive on the scene: 'I always carried a revolver', she recalled, 'I held up the revolver and said to the police, "You can't seize the paper"'.[81] Another comrade described what followed: 'Connolly came down quickly, walked quietly to the counter with drawn gun in his hand. A few feet away Miss Molony was already covering the police with her automatic. Connolly looked sternly at the police and gave his command to them: "Drop those papers or I will drop you"'.[82] The impact of such defiance on morale, both that of the ICA and of the police, was evident:

> to see the order backed by a wicked .45 was terrible and unthought of. The G man dropped the papers like hot coals and the other three stared without a word for fully a minute. During this time Jim Connolly told them never to come into the shop again for any papers no matter who sent them. If they did they would be carried out.[83]

The raid was followed by a dramatic mass mobilization to defend Liberty Hall from any reprisal: 'all jobs stopped, men running out of foundries, fitting shops, forges and building jobs. Carters left horses in the street and ran for their rifles and equipment'.[84] From that day on, Liberty Hall was defended by a permanent armed guard. 'It was just what the lads were aching for—action', one ICA veteran recalled, 'I have never met such a crowd of men from that on. Comradeship would be too empty a word to describe it. We were like a lot of brothers'.[85]

Public displays of strength and armed resistance to the police rendered the Volunteers and ICA a more credible threat, winning respect and recruits and making the option of an armed insurrection more practicable. But how strong were the Volunteers on the eve of the Rising? The appointment of full-time organizers, such as Liam Mellows in Galway and Terence MacSwiney in Cork, had resulted in more effective training, improved morale, better contact between companies, and the formation of battalion and brigade structures. After MacSwiney's appointment in July 1915, one Volunteer remembered, 'companies cropped up like mushrooms' and Cork soon (characteristically) considered itself 'the best organised county in Ireland'.[86] The autumn of 1915 saw the final disappearance of Redmond's National Volunteers; new Irish Volunteer companies were often established just as rival National Volunteer units disintegrated. Nonetheless, the strength of the movement should not to be exaggerated. The decline of the Volunteers had been reversed but, numbering around fifteen thousand men, it remained weak. The organization barely existed in some counties such as Kildare, Cavan, and Longford. The entire county of Wexford could muster only eighty-three Volunteers for the Manchester Martyrs' commemoration at Vinegar Hill in November 1915. With around 125 members, the Belfast Volunteers remained a negligible force while, with the exception of parts of Tyrone, the movement had little presence throughout the rest of Ulster. But the general trend was heartening for separatists, and it was obvious that Redmond's difficulties would only increase as the war continued, particularly if conscription (as was being increasingly rumoured) was imposed. Against this background, the idea of an insurrection was no longer a fantastic proposition.

IV

As it happened, the two men most responsible for the Rising, Tom Clarke and Seán MacDermott, were committed to this course regardless of the strength of the Volunteers. In September 1914 they had persuaded the IRB supreme council, despite opposition led by Bulmer Hobson, to authorize an insurrection before the end of the war. How had they managed this, given the unfavourable circumstances at that time? Their argument boiled down to the absolute necessity of staging a rebellion during the war. Clarke's greatest regret, one of his confidants explained, was the failure to rise during the Boer War:

> He never understood it and never gave up thinking of it...The old feeling of humiliation at the failure of his generation...was still with him and he wanted to do all that one man could do to assure that should another war come, it would be proved to the world that there were still in Ireland men who were willing to fight and die for Irish freedom.[87]

It was this argument that ultimately prevailed. When Pat McCartan questioned the wisdom of embarking on an insurrection without popular support (a position which contravened the IRB's 1873 constitution) at a meeting of the supreme council, Denis McCullough, the president of the IRB, pointed out that 'we had been organising and planning for years for the purpose of a protest in arms when an opportunity occurred and if ever such an opportunity was to arrive, I didn't think any better time would present itself in our day'.[88]

The issue of motivation is crucial: the most disputed aspect of 1916 remains whether the organizers believed that they were likely to be successful or whether they acted in the knowledge that there was little prospect of victory. For many, Patrick Pearse's commitment to a 'blood sacrifice'—the belief that only a Christ-like act of sacrifice could redeem the Irish nation—lies at the heart of this controversy. Although this was an appealing notion for many of Pearse's deeply Catholic generation, subsequent critics would identify it as central to what they saw as the irrational and unmandated violence at the heart of the Rising. Recent historical accounts which argue that the Rising was intended as a serious attempt to overthrow British rule are partly a response to these criticisms.[89] Arguably, the preoccupation with blood sacrifice has distracted from consideration of the organizers' motives: at the time the IRB leadership agreed to rise, Pearse was a relatively new recruit with limited influence.

The decision to rise during the war was—from the IRB's perspective—a rational one. At what other time could they secure the support of a major power? Separatists also argued, for a variety of reasons, that an insurrection during a time of war did not have to be successful to be effective: 'what results were to be hoped? The Republic? Hardly! It was expected that the Rising, if it coincided with a big German offensive in France, would divert large British forces, and later on compel the enemy to negotiate'.[90] In a more realistic appraisal of their prospects (if not the rules of international law), Tom MacDonagh told Volunteers that even defeat would lead to success (providing that Germany won the war): 'if we were able to stand up against the British for one week as a uniformed disciplined force we would be able to claim recognition at the peace conference that would be held at the end of the war'.[91]

Such arguments appear naïve but they provided vital ammunition in the all-important, unceasing debate as to whether there should even be a rising. In the spring of 1916 Thomas MacDonagh outlined a fanciful level of German support in an attempt to persuade a sceptical W. T. Cosgrave of the Rising's viability: 'MacDonagh enquired as to whether my opinion would be affected by such developments as a German naval victory—neutralisation of the British fleet of submarines, importation of arms on a large scale—the landing in Ireland of the 69th regiment. I agreed that developments such as these would completely alter the situation'.[92] Some leading separatists felt that the military council's members did not actually believe that Germany would lend support on this scale. Ernest Blythe recalled that when MacDermott told him, one month before the Rising, of Germany's plans to land not only arms but men from submarines, 'I did not believe a word'.[93] Days before the insurrection, when MacDermott was forced to admit to an alarmed Denis McCullough that the rebellion was going ahead, he attempted to mollify him by assuring him that an invading German force would lead the fighting. 'I put little faith in the latter statement and I don't think Seán did either', McCullough later reflected, 'I can't decide, in my own mind even yet, whether or not he was trying to deceive me or was deceiving himself'.[94]

The decision to rise during the war strengthened the hand of those who favoured a rebellion against those who wanted to await a more favourable opportunity (which the insurrectionaries, conscious of the risk of the movement's suppression, feared might never arrive). If, as the supreme council had reluctantly agreed, it was necessary to rise during the war, the fear that the war might end provided the insurrectionaries with a compelling reason to act regardless of the preparedness of the Volunteers. Connolly frequently told his supporters 'he knew we would fight but would we be in time?'[95] Ceannt, one Dublin officer recalled, 'was always saying that something would have to be done before the war between England and

Germany ended'.[96] MacDermott warned that 'before America was forced into the war we would have to fight'.[97] During the week before the Rising, rumours abounded of a secret parliamentary session at Westminster to consider peace proposals, leading rebels to despair that 'the country will be lost without a blow'.[98]

A wartime insurrection, even one likely to fail, was not only rational but a moral and historical imperative if Fenianism was to retain any credibility or future. The IRB's belief that Irish freedom could only be won by the use of physical force at a time of international conflict committed them to act before the war ended. Paradoxically, their awareness that most Irish people disagreed with them made it more rather than less important to fight: if the separatist claim to independence rested, at least in part, on a supposed historic tradition of unbroken resistance to British rule (rather than the support of the majority), a failure to rise would prove all the more devastating. Their willingness to act, John MacDonagh argued, was more important than the outcome: 'Every generation of Irishmen had risen to show they wanted freedom for their country and they—the Volunteers—were prepared to lay down their lives, if necessary, for the same ideal'.[99] The military council, despite their many ideological differences, were agreed on this. 'If this thing passed off without us making a fight I don't want to live', MacDermott confided to a leading Brother, 'And Tom [Clarke] feels the same'.[100] Shortly before the Rising, Eamon Ceannt, the Third Battalion commandant, justified his decision to his wife along much the same lines: 'We Volunteers, an armed body, could not let this opportunity pass without striking a blow while England is at war. We would be a disgrace to our generation'.[101] 'Consider how we would look', Pearse told one of his students, 'if we said, "Well, after all the British are too strong and we don't feel like fighting them." The people would just laugh at us and our movements would collapse in laughter'.[102]

Although the war provided the rationale for rebellion, Irish separatists were motivated by emotion as well as reason: the Rising was born out of frustration, shame, and pessimism. While Tom Clarke felt humiliated by the failure to rise during the Boer War, Pearse remained preoccupied with the events of 1803: 'Dublin has one great shame to wipe out and that is that no man risked his life to save Robert Emmet'.[103] Connolly, the military council member least in thrall to romantic nationalism, expressed similar views; during one of his lectures, a Belfast Volunteer recalled, Connolly 'spoke very strongly about periods in Irish history when the Irish people had opportunities of fighting for freedom and did not avail of them...He felt so strongly about this that he stated, in my hearing, "If the Irish people don't fight, then by God I'll go out and fight myself"'.[104] Connolly's frequently stated (and presumably genuine) intention to fight, regardless of whether the Volunteers joined in with his tiny force, suggests that he was 'less concerned that a rising should succeed than that it should take place'.[105]

For revolutionaries, even a rebellion partly motivated by pessimism about the deracinated state of the country could still be justified on the grounds of its potential impact. The Rising, it has recently been argued, 'fits into a powerful strand of separatist thinking, one of a series of moments that should cause a communal epiphany'; 'it was nearly impossible to see a difference between Ireland and England', one Dublin Volunteer more prosaically put it, 'something big should happen to reawaken the country'.[106] But for critics like Hobson, this desire to fight regardless of the chances of success amounted to an irrational blood sacrifice. The IRB, he complained, had fallen under the sway of Pearse's zealous extremism:

> He was a sentimental egoist, full of curious Old Testament theories about being the scapegoat for the people, and he became convinced of the necessity for a periodic blood sacrifice to keep the national spirit alive. There was a certain strain of abnormality in all this. He did not contribute greatly to the hard grinding work of building up the movement, but as soon as we had succeeded in getting a small organisation and a handful of men he seized the opportunity to bring about the blood sacrifice.[107]

Nor was Pearse the only conspirator committed to mystical notions of sacrifice and redemption; the other poets on the military council, Plunkett and MacDonagh, expressed similar ideas which partly reflected the romantic nationalist zeitgeist of the generation of 1914 who willingly sacrificed themselves on the battlefields of Europe.[108] Hobson questioned the motives and sanity of this faction: Plunkett 'was in a very advanced stage of T.B'., he observed, 'his condition was far from normal'.[109] Shortly before the rebellion, Eoin MacNeill expressed similar concerns, arguing that an insurrection could not be justified 'by a sense of feebleness or despondency or fatalism or by an instinct of satisfying their own emotion or escaping from a difficult and complex and trying situation'.[110]

Some of those who lived through the Rising also described it as a blood sacrifice. 'The men who signed the Proclamation knew that they were finished', one Dublin Fenian asserted, 'These men, I think, came to the conclusion that something must be done to save the soul of the nation'.[111] Conceding that Hobson's defensive strategy was more sensible than that of Pearse, Eamon Martin reflected:

> This is not to say its soundness or practicability would have diverted my own course. I believe that Pearse's doctrine, no matter how impracticable from the military aspect, had a greater appeal for those who had become tired of waiting for favourable opportunities. And I think it was generally felt that the European War which had been going on for eighteen months might end without any attempt being made to take advantage of England's difficulty, that this would be shameful and disastrous, and that even a glorious failure would be better than no attempt at all.[112]

Despite his reference to 'Pearse's doctrine', it is clear that what Martin meant by blood sacrifice was not a mystical embrace of martyrdom as an essential prerequisite of national regeneration but rather the much more widespread and perfectly rational belief that it was necessary for separatists to be prepared to fight even if they would probably be defeated. This belief, shared by all the organizers, is often conflated with Pearse's more specific (but considerably less rational) notion of blood sacrifice because the language in which both concepts were expressed was so similar. In an address to Tralee Volunteers in 1914, Seán MacDermott declared that 'the Irish patriotic spirit will die forever unless a blood sacrifice is made in the next few years'. But, as his speech made clear, such martyrdom was not willingly sought in the egotistical belief that a Christ-like sacrifice was necessary to spiritually redeem the nation but reluctantly accepted as an unavoidable means to a more modest end, the preservation of the separatist tradition: 'it will be necessary for some of us to offer ourselves as martyrs if nothing better can be done to preserve the Irish national spirit and hand it down to future generations'.[113] Speaking only a month before the Rising, MacDermott was still thinking about the credibility of the physical-force tradition rather than fetishizing an irrational death wish: 'Who will listen to the appeals of men who are not prepared to sacrifice their lives, if necessary, in defence of their country?'[114]

When it came to this fundamental rationale for the Rising, there was little difference within the military council between its romantic intellectuals, professional Fenians, and sole revolutionary socialist, who oscillated between predicting success and hedging his bets on a more long-term result: 'at the worst the laying down of their lives shall constitute the starting point of another glorious tradition', Connolly wrote of the ICA men he would lead into death, 'a tradition that will keep alive the soul of the nation'.[115] Connolly's pessimism was motivated more by the destruction of working-class solidarity on the fields of Europe than the decline of Irish nationality but his remedy was the same. As with the Fenians, his embrace of insurrection was a desperate response to frustration and disillusionment.[116]

If a single belief united the organizers it was not blood sacrifice but the conviction that action was preferable to inaction; that the potential advantages of defeat—the reassertion of separatist credibility, the long-term survival of the physical-force tradition, the possibility of inspiring popular support and of destroying Home Rule—outweighed the advantages of inaction. The Rising represented a last throw of the dice: in a phrase used at the time, 'the last fight' before the extinction of Irish nationality. As John MacDonagh argued, the strategy that united his brother and his comrades on the military council was pragmatic, rational, and ultimately successful:

> They were men exalted by their mission to strike once more with arms, as had been done in every generation against the British oppressor, and this purpose was so all-embracing that it completely dominated their lives, and no consideration, such as family or strict adherence to any formal procedure, could be allowed to interfere with their accepted destiny, to which they gladly dedicated their lives. It was not a question of military success or failure, though there is always a hope for brave men. Armed protest would revive the national spirit and demonstrate to the world that Ireland...still preserved her national spirit to resist the invader.[117]

Of course, the arguments against insurrection were even more pragmatic and rational. They were championed within the Volunteers and the IRB by Eoin MacNeill and Bulmer Hobson but many separatists sympathized with their views. Some opposed the timing of the rebellion: resigning from the supreme council in 1915, P. S. O'Hegarty told MacDermott that he felt the Volunteers should be preserved 'against the possibility of conscription'.[118] Hobson opposed not just the timing but the very notion of a 1916-style insurrection on the not unreasonable grounds that they had never succeeded in the past. He argued that the Volunteers should be built up as a military force: if they were to fight, it should only be if there was some compelling reason that would guarantee popular support, such as an attempt to disarm them or to introduce conscription. And, if they fought, they should adopt guerrilla war tactics rather than occupying buildings in the capital and awaiting the arrival of enemy artillery. On one level, as some leading Volunteers recognized, the cleavage between both factions was not so much about tactics and strategy as temperament, psychology, and morality.

Hobson later claimed that the 'great majority of the Irish Volunteers, and the great majority of the IRB would have been definitely hostile to a demonstration like the 1916 insurrection had it been possible to consult them'.[119] This is a difficult claim to evaluate, although the low numbers who turned out lend it some credence. After the Rising, not everyone would be as honest as veteran Fenian Augustine Ingoldsby who stated: 'I did not approve of a rising as I thought it had no chance of success against the forces that the British Empire could oppose to it'.[120] Hobson's doubts were certainly widely shared. W. T. Cosgrave, a Fourth Battalion officer (and future head of the Irish government), thought that the rebellion was 'little short of madness' due to their lack of men and weapons: 'I was not impressed with gaining a moral victory; that while there was a certain glamour in maintaining a succession of risings against British domination, our policy should be directed towards leaving things better than we found them'.[121] IRB and Volunteer leaders outside the capital, such as MacCurtain and MacSwiney in Cork, were generally even more sceptical than Dublin-based separatists: 'Tomás was a very practical man, and he would not undertake a thing that he believed had not a reasonable chance of success. In plain language, the two of them thought the Dublin crowd were daft'.[122]

V

Those opposed to the Rising were always unlikely to deflect a determined minority from their course. At the heart of the conspiracy were Tom Clarke and Seán MacDermott. Born in 1857, Clarke was the more experienced revolutionary, a veteran both of the Fenian dynamite campaign of the early 1880s and of a gruelling life sentence in English jails. Frail, reclusive, taciturn, and partially deaf, he was a determined if uncharismatic leader. He spent much of his time behind the counter of his Parnell Square tobacconist shop, his prison record ensuring that he remained in the background, but he was the guiding spirit behind the Rising: 'To him the Irish nation was very real', Seán McGarry admiringly recalled, 'To fight England was to him the most natural thing in the world for an Irishman'.[123] His closest confidant was the younger and more charming Seán MacDermott, a former tram conductor from Leitrim who, despite being almost crippled by polio, provided the organizational dynamism behind the conspiracy.

Although Clarke and MacDermott provided the inspiration, they subcontracted the actual planning of the Rising to a committee (or 'military council') consisting of Joseph Plunkett, Eamon Ceannt, and Patrick Pearse formed in May 1915. Its deliberations were characterized by extreme secrecy, unwavering dedication to its objective, and ruthless duplicity. It was an autonomous body: 'The only curb on the military committee was the executive', recalled one IRB leader, 'The Supreme Council did not count so much at all'.[124] The active members of the executive consisted of Clarke and MacDermott, as the IRB president, Denis McCullough, who lived in Belfast, was excluded from the military committee's deliberations. Over the next year, the military council expanded as Clarke and MacDermott (September), James Connolly (January), and Thomas MacDonagh (April) joined.

In terms of ideology and social background, the military council was remarkably diverse. Patrick Pearse, who in death would become the public face of the Easter Rising, had only recently joined the IRB, having been previously blackballed by Clarke due to his earlier enthusiasm for Home Rule. Intense, unworldly, 'undeniably odd', Pearse had devoted his career to the education of children and the Irish language, editing the Gaelic League's newspaper and running a Gaelic-speaking school which teetered permanently on the edge of bankruptcy.[125] Like many Irish-Irelanders who threw in their lot with the IRB, he had previously regarded it as an anachronism: 'a lot of old Fenians who had run to seed or were doting and used to talk in public houses'.[126] Pearse's rhetorical abilities and revolutionary zeal led Clarke to overlook his shortcomings (including his lack of a sense of humour), and place him at the heart of the conspiracy. Despite his painfully introverted personality, many ordinary Volunteers regarded Pearse as the most charismatic of the leaders: 'there was something about him I cannot explain. He seemed different to other men'.[127] Praising 'the clarity and strength of his purpose' and 'nobility of his soul', another Volunteer recalled how 'one got a feeling of addressing a being who paid short visits to the earth, but had his normal habitation elsewhere'.[128]

Pearse was not the only other-worldly presence on the military committee, a peculiar combination of old-school Fenian revolutionaries and middle-class cultural nationalist intellectuals. Thomas MacDonagh, dramatist, critic, and academic, struck one Fenian as 'a dreamer and possibly one of the least likely men who would have been a physical force man'.[129] Others thought MacDonagh—author of such poems as 'The Suicide'—insecure, melodramatic, and emotionally volatile.[130] Despite his eccentricities, it was another poet, Joseph Mary Plunkett, who was given ultimate responsibility for the military planning of the rebellion (possibly because he was the Volunteers' Director of Military Operations). A member of a wealthy Catholic family, Plunkett had fashioned a role in public life as a man of letters, mystic, and (despite being an invalid since childhood) Volunteer leader. A 'charming fantasist', whose emaciated features and penchant for sombreros, capes, and jewellery lent him a distinctly odd appearance, he was an unconventional choice for the role.[131] Grace Gifford, who married Plunkett on the eve of his execution, conveyed something of his bohemian character: 'he was completely reckless about his health. He would ramble about the house in his pyjamas, looking for books. He was terribly careless. He was all the time composing poetry'.[132] His brother Jack felt 'he had all the attributes of a man who, you would think, would never undertake anything practical. He took, however, a frightful lot of pains about his poetry'.[133] A Dublin surgeon who operated on Plunkett at his Mountjoy Square nursing home recalled a 'very thin and highly-strung' figure who made for an implausible military leader despite his entourage of aides:

> I remember once finding a group of them seated round his bed with note-books and pencils in their hands, while he was sitting up in bed, apparently giving them instructions. I, frankly, did not take this at all seriously and remarked: 'Napoleon dictating to his marshals'—a remark which was not well received. On another occasion I joked with him, saying: 'I suppose you sleep with a revolver under your pillow' and, to my surprise, he said, 'I do' and pulled one out.[134]

The conspirators, however, placed considerable faith in his abilities, as did Plunkett himself despite the fact that his military experience was limited to a stint in the cadet corps at Stonyhurst public school. MacDonagh described him as 'a wonderful man on a committee, thinking of everything, foreseeing everything down to the smallest detail'.[135] Another insider insisted: 'They all thought Joe Plunkett the cleverest from the point of view of military organisation'.[136]

James Connolly brought the most organizational experience to the military council. As acting general secretary of the largest trade union in the country and leader of the ICA, he was the pre-eminent figure of the Irish Left. In contrast to the rest of the military council, he had some actual military experience (having served in the British army in his youth). Short, stocky, fiercely determined, abrasive, and self-educated, Connolly was the most experienced agitator on the military council: heckled at one public meeting ('How do you know so much about revolution Mr Connolly?'), he had stylishly replied: 'My business is revolution, madam'.[137] As with Pearse, Clarke was willing to overlook Connolly's previous criticisms of the IRB for the greater good although his presence, according to one leading Fenian, did not add to the harmony of the military council:

> Connolly was a man of massive intellect, of great resource and of immense value to the committee but he was as temperamental as a Prima Donna. He was impatient, irritable and petulant. The slightest upset annoyed him...His method of revolution differed from that of Tom Clarke. He wanted to shout it from the housetops, did not care how soon it started or with how many men. He believed that once the standard of revolt was raised the people—his people—would rally to it and he was afraid of a sudden collapse of the war...Tom, who had infinite patience in a matter of this kind, had his hands full.[138]

The military committee had several functions. It was responsible for devising an overall strategic plan for the Rising, assigning Volunteer officers to implement it, and supervising all necessary preparations. Its most difficult and important task was to secure German military support. The military council's contacts with Germany were complicated—and ultimately compromised—by its reliance on the IRB's American wing, Clan na Gael, to communicate with the German authorities. The presence in Berlin of Sir Roger Casement, a Volunteer leader who regarded himself as a sort of revolutionary ambassador, further complicated matters. A dashing but volatile figure of questionable judgement, who had forged an unlikely career in the British Foreign Office as an anti-imperialist humanitarian, Casement had travelled to Berlin to win German support for an insurrection. Joined by Plunkett in the summer of 1915, they submitted the detailed 'Ireland Report' outlining how German support could facilitate a successful rebellion. It called for a naval invasion to land 12,000 soldiers and 40,000 rifles in Limerick which, they argued, would spark a nationwide revolt, effectively pitting Ireland on the side of the

Central Powers. The proposal was rejected by the German General Staff and Foreign Office, either because the rebels were not taken sufficiently seriously or because naval considerations made such an operation impractical. Plunkett did, however, secure a commitment of Germany's willingness to assist the rebels if they could prove that a rising was a credible prospect, an undertaking that ultimately resulted in the *Aud*'s ill-fated mission to Kerry.[139]

One obvious difficulty facing the military council was how to organize an insurrection involving the participation of up to 15,000 Volunteers without compromising its secrecy. The solution was ingeniously simple: the Volunteers would be mobilized without being told why. Although Bulmer Hobson subsequently condemned the military council for bringing out Volunteers 'unprepared and unaware of what they were being let in for', the reality was more complex.[140] In the months leading up to the Rising, Volunteer officers were lectured on various aspects of insurrection in a series of talks at GHQ. Compared with the earlier lectures on military history, the syllabus was pointedly practical. 'It was becoming apparent that things were coming to a head', one officer recalled, 'Connolly gave us lectures on street fighting and on tunnelling from house to house and on the erection and manning of barricades'.[141] Another officer, who attended lectures by MacDonagh, de Valera, and Ceannt, felt that each gave 'the impression that in a very short time the Volunteers would be going into action'.[142]

The purpose of these lectures, one senior IRB leader claimed, was not merely to instruct the Volunteers but 'to attune their minds to participation in an insurrection'. They were intended to ensure that the Rising would not come as a shock to those who would be expected to take part in it and to counter the suggestions by Hobson and MacNeill that the Volunteers may not have to fight. Eamon Ceannt assured his wife that the men of his battalion 'had been warned repeatedly that some day they would go out and not return'.[143] The First Battalion commandant, Ned Daly, told his men that Dublin 'would be their battle ground...before another twelve months'.[144] Con Colbert warned his Fourth Battalion company that he 'did not intend wasting his own time and theirs unless they made up their minds definitely as to their action "when the day came"'.[145] The closer the Rising, the more stark the warnings: three months before Easter, one officer recalled, Ceannt 'took a crowd of us out one Sunday beyond Blessington; he sat on a stone wall and got us all around him. He told us what to prepare for and said "Get guns and ammunition, honest if you can, but get them".[146]

The most indiscreet—and inspiring—of the Volunteer leaders was Patrick Pearse. Oscar Traynor, a future government minister, described one of his powerful performances:

> Patrick Pearse was wearing his greatcoat, a Volunteer green, and a slouch hat, when he entered the room. His brother, Willie, helped him to take these off...Pearse rose amidst dead silence, stared over the heads of the Volunteers assembled in the room, and paused for almost one minute before he spoke. The first words he uttered sent a thrill through the persons present...'I know that you have been preparing your bodies for the great struggle that lies before us, but have you also been preparing your souls?' These words made such a deep impression on all present that there was dead silence for a considerable period.[147]

A Cumann na mBan member recalled his lecture on Wolfe Tone in similar terms: 'I'd swear he did not see anybody in the room; he had his mind and eyes fixed on the vision he saw. We were nearly in tears. He talked about the sacrifices that had been made and would again have to be made for Ireland. He all but told us that a rising was to take place'.[148] Pearse's rhetorical power rested on his ability to convince his audience, jaded by years of patriotic cant, of his absolute sincerity: 'you felt impelled to believe that he did actually believe that there should be some attempt'.[149]

These lectures and speeches had the desired effect. After hearing Pearse insist that those who were not prepared to fight should leave the organization, Michael Walker recalled, 'I made up my mind I would face up to the obligations which I had not taken when I joined the movement'.[150] Others dropped out when they realized, as one put it, 'that these men were in earnest'.[151] Tom Byrne, like many Volunteers, insisted that 'it was generally understood that there would be a fight'.[152] It was even more widely understood within the ICA as James Connolly had personally asked each of its members whether they were prepared to fight: 'This was not hidden or spoken of with bated breath', Jim O'Shea insisted, 'We all knew and discussed openly our aims and objects and we told everyone what we were drilling for'.[153] Indeed, it was precisely this openness that resulted in Connolly's inclusion in the military council as the members of the latter grew increasingly worried that the ICA would precipitate a rebellion. The intensification of the Volunteers' training and the growing urgency of their efforts to arm the movement alerted many others to the imminence of a rising.

Volunteers and IRB men began returning from Britain, not just to avoid conscription but to play a role in the final preparations. Around eighty Volunteers (dubbed the 'flagboys' or the 'refugees' in a not entirely complimentary allusion to the threat of conscription that hung over them in Britain) ended up in the Plunkett family's derelict mill, at Larkfield, Kimmage. Like their Irish-based comrades, most 'had no idea of what the plans were' or 'the date it was to start' but were aware 'that a fight was bound to come'.[154] Remarkably, many of these men—including twenty-one-year-old William Daly—had been born in Britain:

> My mother was born in Kerry and had never seen Ireland since she was four years of age. My father (who died before I was fourteen years old) was born in London of Irish parents, and I was born in Dockhead, a rough and ready quarter of London. I knew nothing of Ireland except in a hazy kind of way until I joined the Gaelic League. So, in a sense, I adopted Ireland as my own country until it adopted me at Easter 1916.[155]

The largest contingent, numbering around fifty-six men, came from Scotland, products not only of expatriate branches of Na Fianna and the Irish Volunteers but the radicalizing impact of an eclectic range of Scottish nationalist and socialist revolutionary influences.[156]

Their British backgrounds—and accents—provoked surprise and mistrust from both separatists and the authorities. When Daly made his way to Tom Clarke's tobacco shop (to present him with a rifle that he had smuggled from London under his long overcoat) Clarke—taking him for a 'tout' due to his cockney accent—told him 'to take myself and my rifle away to h[ell] from him'. During the Rising, Daly and his London-Irish chum, 'Blimey' O'Connor, were taken prisoner by their comrades when they arrived at an outpost without anyone to vouch for them.[157] Glasgow-born John McGallogly, who had never been to Ireland before 1916, encountered similar difficulties; at one point during the rebellion he and a friend from Liverpool found themselves lost in the city centre, unable to find the GPO. Later, he was singled out for abuse as imprisoned rebels argued the merits of the Rising with their British army captors: 'I ventured a remark and one of the guards, a red-haired Irishman, said "You shut up, you Scotch bastard. You only came over here to make trouble." '[158] William Stapleton was instructed to keep an eye on another London-Irish Volunteer during the Rising due to his 'marked English accent' and to arrest him if necessary. The same rebel was later victimized in Knutsford Jail: 'He suffered badly at the hands of the military warders who, apparently, believed he was an Englishman because of his accent, and eventually he was sent to a lunatic asylum completely broken down in mind and body'.[159]

Although the refugees' presence at Larkfield allowed Tom MacDonagh to boast that 'we have a standing army at last', there could be no rising without arms or ammunition.[160] In 1907, following the lapse of legislation dating back to the Land War, gun ownership had become something of a legal grey area, enabling anyone with the permission of two magistrates to form a gun club. In December 1913, less than two weeks after the formation of the Irish Volunteers, new controls were brought in to ban the importation of arms and ammunition without a permit, but they were allowed to lapse after the outbreak of the Great War. The Irish Volunteers took advantage of this to begin importing arms, although the police also used their wartime emergency powers to seize any they could find.[161] Volunteers deployed an ingenious range of methods to arm themselves; rifles, when possible, were legally imported or purchased within Ireland. Volunteers from overseas returned with legally held pistols and rifles. Arms and ammunition were stolen from trains, railway goods' stores, hardware shops, and the National Volunteers. Small arms, ammunition, and explosives were illegally brought in by Irish workers in Britain, and consignments of rifles were smuggled into the country by various means, including the postal service.

The British army proved a particularly generous source of weapons: 'In some cases soldiers whom we knew gave us their rifles; in others, we bought them', one Volunteer recalled: 'where soldiers were not prepared to give them or sell a row was picked and in the melee which followed the rifle disappeared'.[162] Alcohol proved the undoing of many a soldier: 'At that time publicans were forbidden by the authorities to serve soldiers with drink if they were carrying rifles. Soldiers on leave lost many a rifle when they handed them to someone who obligingly offered to look after them while they had a drink in one of the pubs on the quays'.[163] 'These soldiers were always short of money and they would sell their shirts, socks, boots and brushes to get drink', another Volunteer recalled, 'After a time, there were so many guns missing, it was arranged to disarm the soldiers in England before they took the boat'.[164] Edward Handley, a sergeant in the Royal Dublin Fusiliers, often stole guns from Wellington barracks: 'there were huts where men used to go for lectures on wet days. They often left their rifles outside the huts and it was an easy matter to take a few'.[165]

Weapons and ammunition were also manufactured: 'when not drilling', one of the Larkfield refugees recalled, 'we were engaged in making ammunition. The ammunition consisted of shotgun cartridges filled with large slugs, larger than peas. We sometimes worked a 24-hour shift. We also made hand-grenades...On the night of a peak load our output would be 5,000 lead pellets. The output of hand-grenades, when we had the material, would be twenty an hour'.[166] At St Enda's, Pearse's boys manufactured ammunition under the supervision of their science master: 'Every evening we spent in the "University Room" making hand-grenades, filling cartridges with shot and fashioning batons'.[167] 'When raids for ammunition became more frequent', one student recalled, 'Pearse made us all carry around several hundred rounds of .303 concealed on our persons, on trams, in the streets, everywhere till the alarm died down'.[168] In Liberty Hall, the ICA set up a munitions factory on the first floor:

> Improvised hand grenades were being manufactured. Cartridges were being altered to fit rifles and guns for which they were not meant. Bayonets, of an old French type, were being heated over a blow-lamp and bent or reshaped, to fit an old German Mauser rifle. It was quite a common thing, on entering the armour room, to find a man sitting over the fire, brewing a can of tea on one side of it, while melting a pot of lead on the other side; two or three men at a bench, making some repairs to a rifle, while, at the same time, two or three others were stretched on the bare floor, snoring, fast asleep.[169]

The women of Cumann na mBan played a more genteel role, making field dressings 'for the men'. 'Our rooms', Min Ryan recalled, 'were entirely given over to bandage making'.[170]

Despite such resourcefulness, the Irish Volunteers—particularly outside Dublin—failed to arm more than a tiny proportion of its 15,000-strong force. By 1916, it probably had less than 2,000 rifles; the UVF, in comparison, was thought to have 55,000.[171] While shotguns did prove useful in the close-quarters street-fighting in Dublin, the bombs churned out in such vast numbers would pose more of a danger to the Volunteers than British soldiers. The arming of the rebels as a credible national force remained dependent on the arms promised by Germany.

VI

How did the military council manage to keep its preparations from discovery by both the authorities and the many Volunteers opposed to an insurrection? The secrecy and discipline of the IRB helped; as far as was practicable, the organizers relied on Volunteers who were Fenians. Volunteers in strategic positions who were not Fenians were pressured to join what was described to them as 'the inner organisation which was behind the Volunteers'.[172] The ceremony, as described by Liam Tannam, was often perfunctory: 'Eamon Ceannt swore me in looking over the wall of the Liffey'.[173] Ceannt swore another Volunteer into the Brotherhood on a busy Dublin street: 'He said: "You needn't raise your right hand. Just remove it from the handlebars of your bicycle." '[174] John MacDonagh recalled that when he joined Ceannt was unable to remember the oath.[175] The extent to which such recruits (including Ceannt, a devoutly Catholic Irish-Irelander who had only joined the IRB in late 1912) could be considered Fenians in any meaningful ideological sense is questionable: it seems evident that the movement had become little more than a convenient means of secretly coordinating the insurrection.[176]

From early 1916, IRB men in key Volunteer positions were informed that a rising was imminent or simply told not to leave Dublin without permission: 'This we took to be a hint that something was brewing'.[177] Officers who had previously appeared to leave the movement in order to avoid police attention reappeared, while important figures just as mysteriously disappeared to avoid the risk of arrest. From early March, an ever-widening circle of IRB men and Volunteers received vague but unmistakable warnings which, at least in Dublin, began to permeate down the ranks: 'whilst there was a certain amount of indefiniteness about it', one Dublin Volunteer recalled, 'most of us expected something would happen at Easter'.[178] Shortly before the Rising, Harry Colley noted, 'Everybody seemed to expect to go into the fight at any moment'.[179] According to Helena Molony, 'the atmosphere was like a simmering pot'.[180]

Crucially, though, few Volunteers knew precisely what was to happen or exactly when or where it was to occur. The Volunteers' realistic training exercises, such as the seizure of the city's canals and mock attacks on Dublin Castle, lulled some within the authorities into a degree of complacency at the sight of armed men moving around the capital. Outside Liberty Hall, a large blackboard advertised detailed notices for each weekend's military manoeuvres: 'You know the story of Wolf', explained James Connolly when asked the reason for such indiscretion.[181] A fortnight before the Rising, senior officers were informed of their roles and asked to carry out reconnaissance of their positions and submit field plans. Finding nothing useful on street-fighting in his British army manual, Thomas O'Donoghue enterprisingly 'went to the National Library and looked up the records of the fighting in Moscow'.[182]

The military council alerted Volunteer officers throughout the country by courier and telegram. Pearse favoured farming-related coded messages such as 'Send on the Cattle', 'The butter will arrive', 'The grass-seeds on order will be delivered', and cryptic references to 'Mrs Hawkins' timber'. With few exceptions—Countess Markievicz, who declared to another member of the ICA that 'the scrap was definitely fixed for Easter', was one—those in the know remained close-lipped.[183] But by Holy Thursday, word inevitably began to seep out. One young member of Cumann na mBan was angered when a comrade told her that Sunday's manoeuvres were a pretext for the Rising: 'Don't you think you are terribly indiscreet to say that to me? And to think that so many men's lives could be jeopardised by telling me, a real raw recruit!'[184] Miko O'Dea, a Fifth Battalion Volunteer, learned about the Rising from an IRB man on Easter Saturday: 'he was in McCormack's bar having a bottle of stout'.[185] By the weekend, as last-minute arrangements to secure weapons, arms, and food supplies were put in place, and Liberty Hall began to fill with armed men, the mood was electric: 'Something marvellous and extraordinary was about to break. You felt it in the air everywhere'.[186]

How confident were the rebels on the eve of the Rising? The leaders were elated by the imminence and likely impact of the insurrection but fatalistic about their own prospects of survival. Sent up from Cork on Spy Wednesday to find out what was going on, Annie MacSwiney was disturbed by Tom Clarke's 'joyous elation': 'He was exhilarated. His whole spirit seemed to burn in his glowing eyes. He spoke with enthusiasm of help from Germany, and said that John Devoy had a document, signed by the Kaiser, recognising the Republic of Ireland'. When she expressed doubts about his confidence, Clarke told her that victory was assured 'though, we in the front rank, of course, go down. We know that, but the Republic is safe, nothing can prevent that'.[187] 'The whole atmosphere', she remarked, 'was electric'.[188] Ned Daly, the First Battalion commandant, was in a similarly ecstatic frame of mind. Shortly before the Rising, Daly startled Jerry Golden by telling him how 'he was sure I would do my duty as a soldier of the Republic':

> This was the first mention I had heard from anyone about a Republic, and when I asked him what he meant by it . . . he replied that . . . the Irish Republic would be proclaimed by the provisional government of the Republic. Every Volunteer in arms would be expected to defend the Republic with his life if necessary and some of the leaders would fall in the fight, but the others would carry on even in face of overwhelming odds. While he was speaking to me I noticed his eyes. They appeared to shine, and I saw that he was in earnest in every word he spoke.[189]

MacDermott, MacDonagh, and Connolly also made it clear that they expected to die.[190] The normally reserved Eamon de Valera, according to one of his officers who met him on Camden Row on Holy Saturday, was equally fatalistic: 'We stopped to talk and tell each other how near we were to it and he said a remarkable thing. "We'll be alright, it's the women who will suffer. The worst they can do to us is to kill us, but the women will have to remain behind to rear the children." It was one of the few times that he ever really revealed himself to me'.[191] Those leaders who doubted the wisdom of an unprovoked insurrection shared this sense of fatalism but without the compensating elation. On Holy Thursday, J. J. ('Ginger') O'Connell, who had been given command of the Volunteers in Kilkenny and Carlow, bleakly confided to another executive member that 'he could see no hope of success' given the forces at their disposal: 'he could see no other course than to dig in at Scalloge Gap and hold out there until wiped out'.[192]

Ordinary Volunteers, who knew there was to be a rebellion but had no idea of what was planned or of the extraordinary difficulties that had beset the organizers over the final days, were generally more optimistic: 'there was a considerable confidence that victory was within our grasp', Joseph Lawless believed, 'The younger ones of us never doubted, of course, that arms would be made available at the right moment. We had a supreme confidence in the leaders of our organisation'.[193] With 'outside help I thought it could be successful', Joseph O'Connor recalled, 'I thought that every man would rush in to help'.[194] Others were more realistic: 'there were some of our lads who believed they were going to drive the British into the sea', a Dublin Fenian related, 'It was not on my mind, I can assure you'.[195] Incarcerated in Wakefield prison after the Rising, Michael Knightly was asked by a unionist warder how things went in Dublin: 'I said they went as we expected. "Did you not expect to succeed?" he asked. I said that surely he did not think that we were such simpletons as to expect a handful of men with a few antiquated rifles and shotguns to beat a modern equipped army'.[196] His realism was shared by Leslie Price, a member of Cumann na mBan, who learned about the insurrection on Holy Thursday:

> it made a shocking impression on me. Immediately I went kind of cold. I thought of all the men I knew, and I could not visualise success when I realised the strength of the British Empire. It terrified me . . . I did not sleep that night. I intensified my prayers.[197]

Why, despite all the preparations and rumours, did the authorities fail to realize the imminence of the Rising? 'Of all the division in the Volunteer Executive, of all the moves and countermanoeuvres, the Government knew absolutely nothing and this is all the more extraordinary because so many people, including some on the fringe of things, knew that a revolt was to take place', the historian Leon O'Broin concluded, 'The British intelligence system in Ireland had failed hopelessly'.[198] The failure was partly bureaucratic. At least five organizations within the United Kingdom received intelligence about Irish separatism, but most failed to share their most important secrets with Dublin Castle, let alone each other.[199] Despite this, as is often the case, the intelligence failure stemmed more from the authorities' inability to act on the evidence in its possession than a lack of knowledge. British naval intelligence, which had broken Germany's wartime codes, was aware of the plans to land guns in Kerry in advance of a nationwide rising. Although the Admiralty was understandably unwilling to jeopardize the secrecy of its remarkable intelligence breakthrough, it did provide Dublin Castle with clear warnings that went unheeded. A secret despatch in March, for example, stated that an 'absolutely reliable source' had established that a rising would occur by Easter Saturday.[200]

Considerable responsibility for this arguably lay with the Irish police forces, which failed to penetrate the Volunteers and the IRB in the same way as they had previous Irish revolutionary movements. The only accurate human intelligence came from a source named 'Chalk' who reported on Saturday 22 April that Thomas MacDonagh had told a group of

Volunteers (on the previous Wednesday) that 'we are going out on Sunday. Boys, some of us may never come back'.[201] His report was still filtering through the system when the Rising broke out. Although it was considered an all-powerful adversary by many separatists, the DMP's infamous 'G Division' had less than a dozen detectives assigned to political work in 1916. These men were sufficiently intimate with the Volunteers to have earned nicknames (Johnny Barton, one of the most notorious, was 'Calf's Head' and another colleague was 'Sheep's Eyes') but their methods were distinctly old-fashioned.[202] Prominent separatists were followed from place to place and their public speeches were recorded but little effort was made to penetrate the movement from within. Policing, however, functioned within a wider political context: the infiltration of separatism had not been a government priority since the election of the Liberals in 1906, and funding for secret service work had been severely curtailed during this period.

Indeed, the greening of Dublin Castle (the policy of recruiting more Catholic nationalists to work within the administration) meant that the rebels' penetration of Dublin Castle was more thorough than the authorities' infiltration of separatism: 'for some reason which I am unable to fathom, a large proportion of the people treasonable to England', Matthew Nathan, the Under-Secretary, remarked, 'are to be found in the lower ranks of the government service'.[203] Although lacking the ruthless level of professionalism developed during the War of Independence, the military council received intelligence from policemen, sympathizers in government departments, and telegraph operators (some of whom had the ability to decode police communications).[204]

Ultimate responsibility for the intelligence failure lay with the political leadership at the Castle. Since his appointment as Chief Secretary, Augustine Birrell had made little effort to reform the RIC or DMP despite his awareness of their deficiencies; he was, by 1916, 'a worn out, dispirited minister whose only ambition was to quit'.[205] In addition, he had failed to act on the DMP's recommendation of 'drastic action' against the separatists in early April. Judging Birrell 'primarily responsible' for the failure to prevent the Rising, a subsequent royal commission of inquiry concluded that 'the main cause of the rebellion appears to be [the] lawlessness that was allowed to grow up unchecked, and that Ireland for several years has been administered on the principle that it was safer and more expedient to leave law in abeyance if collision with any faction of the Irish people could thereby be avoided'.[206]

This was a reasonable conclusion but Birrell's policy of avoiding confrontation was a rational one which was supported by the Irish Party leadership (treated by Birrell as the Home Rule government in waiting). Any attempt to coerce the Volunteers would have provoked a response potentially more violent than the one that did occur. Inaction was an effective response to the strategy of MacNeill and Hobson who believed that government coercion was not only inevitable, but were relying on it to rally nationalist opinion against the repression of the Volunteer movement. Prior to the Rising, one historian has judged, Birrell's policy of refusing to 'make martyrs of the militants' in order 'to deflate their popular appeal and maintain the predominance of constitutional nationalism' appeared 'remarkably successful'.[207] Possibly Birrell's greatest failure was one of imagination rather than intelligence or logic: 'in my wildest dreams', nationalist Ireland's most sympathetic Chief Secretary conceded, 'I never contemplated the possibility of what actually happened'.[208]

Given the complacency of Dublin Castle, it was those separatists opposed to insurrection who represented the greatest threat to the rebels' ambitions. In contrast to the authorities, they were under increasingly few illusions as to what was being planned. The weeks before the Rising saw the intensification of a remarkably public debate between both factions. On 16 April, speaking at a Cumann na mBan concert in Parnell Square, Bulmer Hobson warned of the danger of precipitate action which would result in the suppression of the Volunteer movement: 'I said that no man had a right to risk the fortunes of the country in order to create for himself a niche in history'.[209] Hobson's speech, one of the audience noted, provoked 'a certain breathlessness in the hall. One could see glances passing between those who were probably aware of what decisions had already been taken. When it was all over there were groups talking earnestly, some denouncing him and others praising his speech...those who knew most about the plans regarded it as disastrous'.[210] Down from Belfast, the IRB president Denis McCullough felt 'very distressed' to witness such open divisions: 'I left the Hall and on my way out met Seán MacDermott limping in. I told him what Hobson was saying inside and with a good, round oath Seán said that we would "damned soon deal with that fellow"'.[211]

The military council acted skilfully and brazenly to frustrate their opponents: their methods included secrecy, lies, and (in Hobson's case) kidnapping. They shrewdly exploited the fact that neither the IRB nor the Irish Volunteers were, in principle, opposed to an insurrection. On Spy

Wednesday, the 'Castle Document'—an ostensibly leaked document exposing a government decision to arrest the Volunteer leadership—was circulated by the insurrectionists in an attempt to win the waverers over. Eoin MacNeill, a more gullible and less consistent opponent of the insurrection than is often assumed, initially believed it was genuine, issuing a general order urging the Volunteers to prepare to resist their suppression. 'Whoever forged that?', a more cynical separatist remarked to Willie Pearse.[212] According to Eugene Smith, the government official who smuggled the original document on which it was based out of the Castle, the document that was publicized was an edited version of an authentic despatch outlining the army's plans in the event of the imposition of conscription.[213]

When MacNeill finally discovered the insurrectionaries' plans on Holy Thursday (after one of his students casually mentioned his orders to blow up a bridge), he initially sought to prevent the Volunteer mobilization on Sunday, before backing down when he was persuaded that there was nothing he could do to prevent it.[214] However, the dramatic news of the arrest of Sir Roger Casement in Kerry in the small hours of Good Friday and the British interception of the *Aud* early on Saturday convinced him that the rebellion had no possibility of success. At an emotional meeting on Saturday night, attended by members of the military council and their opponents, MacNeill announced that 'he had come to the conclusion that the enterprise was madness, would mean a slaughter of unarmed men and that he felt it to be his bounden duty to try and stop it'.[215] A carefully worded 'countermanding order', which was distributed overnight by messengers and reported in the national press on Sunday morning, was sufficient to prevent the mobilization of Volunteers throughout much of the country.

Devastated by the failure of the two most essential components of their plans—the arms shipment and the general mobilization—the military council met in Liberty Hall early on Sunday. Normally careful to project an air of confidence, the leaders were visibly crushed. 'It was the first and only time', one Volunteer remarked, 'that I saw Seán [MacDermott] really angry and upset'.[216] Nora Connolly recalled her father's reaction when she told him how the mobilisation in Ulster had collapsed the preceding evening: 'The tears ran down his face...I remember saying: "Are we not going to fight now", he said, "the only thing we can do is to pray for an earthquake to come and swallow us up, and our shame." '[217] After spending several hours debating how to respond, they decided the Rising should be deferred until noon on Monday, to allow for a partial remobilization of willing Volunteers. Although there was no longer any chance of a successful mobilization, there was little to be lost by proceeding as the movement would now be suppressed whether they rose or not. In contrast, a failure to rise would expose it to ridicule. Given that the military council had long resolved to fight regardless of the odds (as demonstrated by its willingness to proceed despite the failure of the *Aud*'s mission the previous day), its decision was not surprising.

According to his daughter, Connolly had recovered his composure by Sunday afternoon: 'he was going around the room, singing a song which he usually sang when things were going well with him—"We have got another saviour now. That saviour is the sword." '[218] In contrast, the rest of the military council remained stunned into speechlessness by the near unimaginable train of disasters that had occurred. MacDermott complained that he was 'so annoyed and upset that his mind refused to act'.[219] Tom Clarke was 'crushed'.[220] 'I never saw Pearse so silent and disturbed', Desmond Ryan recalled, 'He simply could not speak to anyone'.[221] Marie Perolz who brought a message to the organizers on Sunday evening was shocked by their demeanour: 'They struck me like men going out into a losing cause'.[222]

The news of events in Kerry and the countermand also led to confusion and demoralization among rank-and-file Volunteers. Many Volunteers learned of the countermand from the *Sunday Independent* after attending early morning Mass. Some assumed that the mobilization would go ahead, others remained at home. Those who mobilized were either sent away or hung around awaiting orders in an atmosphere of confusion, anxiety, and disappointment. The outraged Larkfield refugees spent the day plotting revenge against MacNeill. At Liberty Hall, where Countess Markievicz dramatically brandished a pistol and vowed to shoot MacNeill and Hobson, the mood was bleak. 'We will be all dead in a short time', Jim O'Shea was told by Michael Mallin, who was eager to fight on regardless of what the Volunteers decided: 'I told him I was willing to go down as long as I could bring a good crowd with me'.[223] Others assumed they would be arrested before they had a chance to fire a shot. 'I didn't want to live any longer', Marie Perolz remembered, 'We were all in a state. Tom [Hunter] cried like a baby'.[224] Some of those Volunteers who knew what had been planned were openly defeatist; others, demoralized by the confusion and what they saw as bungling by the Volunteer leadership, declared that they would not obey any further orders. However, one advantage of the secrecy of the plans was that relatively few people knew just how fundamentally they had been compromised: there was probably as much confusion and uncertainty as pessimism among the Volunteers. Wherever they gathered in numbers on Sunday night, an air of anxiety and excitement prevailed. At the Fr Matthew Hall, where a concert was held, 'the atmosphere seemed charged'.[225] 'Everybody seemed to be on edge' at the militant Keating branch of the Gaelic League that night, 'the atmosphere was quite abnormal'.[226] At Liberty Hall, the regular Sunday night concert went ahead in front of a packed audience: 'We had...a sing-song', O'Shea remembered, 'for what we believed was our last night on earth'.[227]

4
Walking on Air
The Rising in Dublin

The extraordinary battle which raged throughout the centre of Dublin from Monday 24 April until the following Saturday has formed the subject of intense political and historical controversy. There is little disagreement about what happened—around 1,600 rebels occupied a ring of prominent buildings, fortified them, and awaited the arrival of British army soldiers whose superior numbers and firepower soon crushed their resistance—but more about its significance. Much controversy has centred on the military strategy of the rebels. Why were buildings of obvious strategic or symbolic value—such as Trinity College and Dublin Castle—not occupied? Why were positions of negligible military value, such as St Stephen's Green, seized? Underlying these questions is a debate not so much about the tactics of the rebels as their fundamental motives. Was the Rising an attempted *coup d'état* or an irrational blood sacrifice?

Recent studies of the IRB have emphasized the symbolic nature of the event: 'the 1916 rising was not a national insurrection, but a citizens' revolt or the last 1848-style rebellion in European history, when would-be "free citizens" simply "manned the barricades" in defence of a cause of "national" liberty against an unaccountable monarchical government and virtually waited to be shot to pieces'.[1] Describing the rebellion as a 'unique example of insurrectionary abstract art', Peter Hart has gone further than this, arguing that it lacked even the rudimentary *coup d'état* ambitions that characterized the 1848 model of insurrection:

The surprise, the proclamation, the tricolour, the seized buildings and barricades were all there, but the targets seem almost purely symbolic or even arbitrary: instead of the arsenal, city hall or barracks, they occupied a post office, a bakery, a public park. There was probably some military rationale involved—it's hard to tell since no record of the plan has survived—but there was certainly no intention of seizing power.[2]

Regardless of its rationale or strategic limitations, a powerful nationalist narrative emerged within months of its suppression: the Rising was seen as a heroic fight by selfless patriots who had recklessly taken on the might of the British Empire, the nobility of their cause and vindictiveness of the British response resurrecting a quiescent Irish nation. From the Rising followed the rise of Sinn Féin, the war against Britain, and ultimately Irish independence.

Long commemorated by republicans as the Irish equivalent of the storming of the Bastille, historians have naturally adopted a more complex and critical perspective since the Rising first became a subject of scholarly inquiry in the 1960s. Writing in a context in which a simplistic, heroic narrative still held sway, many historians (pilloried as 'revisionists' by their nationalist critics) drew attention to 'the conspiratorial, undemo-cratic, and destructive nature of the rebellion'.[3] Particular criticism was directed at two aspects of the insurrection: the absence of a democratic mandate for the actions of the rebels and their military futility. 'The plan-ning and conduct of the Rising', one leading historian has recently argued, 'provided chilling confirmation that military victory was not its primary objective':

> By raising their tricolour in the centre of the main shopping area and close to Dublin's northside slums, the rebels ensured massive human and material losses once their position was attacked. It is difficult to avoid the inference that the republican strategists were intent upon provoking maximum blood-shed, destruction, and coercion, in the hope of resuscitating Irish Anglo-phobia and clawing back popular support for their discredited militant programme.[4]

In this reversal of the traditional heroic narrative, it was the ordinary people of Dublin who were sacrificed for the nation, and the achievement of the rebels was not to strike a blow for freedom but to kill the Irish Party's efforts to fashion a peaceful path to independence. Underlying much of the controversy surrounding the Rising is the difficulty of disen-tangling its violence from that which followed, not only during the War of Independence but also the Civil War and the more recent Northern Irish Troubles which can all be seen as consequences of the military coun-cil's successful revival of the physical-force tradition. Interestingly, the

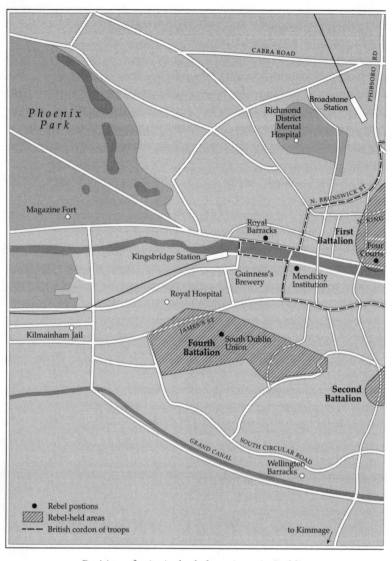

Position of principal rebel garrisons in Dublin

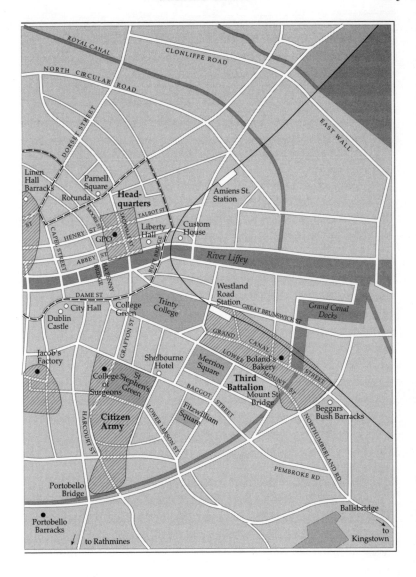

notion that the rebellion had inflicted unjustified violence on the civil population was widely expressed both at the time and over the next decade by a broad section of opinion including unionists, Home Rulers, and, perhaps most controversially, the iconoclastic dramas of the socialist playwright Seán O'Casey. By the 1930s, however, such criticisms were voiced much less frequently as a more pious attitude to the rebellion came to prevail in southern Ireland.

The next three chapters of this book examine the Rising from the perspective of the rebels and other contemporary participants and observers as it unfolded at the time. Rather than focusing on military aspects and high politics, which have been authoritatively reconstructed in two recent studies, it seeks to convey how the rebellion was experienced, particularly by ordinary Volunteers and civilians whose involvement has attracted much less attention than the actions of leaders such as Pearse and Connolly.[5] The Rising was planned by a secret cabal but it relied on the cooperation of a large body of supporters without whom its organizers would have been powerless to act. Telling the story from below, despite its many discordant voices, also illuminates broader debates about the motivations and expectations of the rebels.

I

The insurrection could not have begun in a more chaotic manner. Mobilizers received less than an hour's notice to alert their companies, a process that normally took at least four hours. At 10 a.m. Liam Archer received an order to mobilize his section of the company—for 10 a.m.: 'My first two calls at Jones Road and Clonliffe Road drew blanks, both members had gone out for the day. At this point the motor cycle combination broke down...I set off on foot for Blackhall Place, giving up the idea of mobilising my Section'.[6] Seán Kennedy 'only contacted those within reasonable walking distance'.[7] John Kenny ignored the mobilization order he received, joining his friends on an outing as 'we were still sore about the fiasco of the previous day'.[8] The Third Battalion's quartermaster told his mobilizer that he (like many other Volunteers and British army soldiers) was going to the Grand National horse race at Fairyhouse: 'I said to him: "What will the battalion do, they are depending on you?" He said they would have to get a horse and car'.[9] In contrast, more zealous Volunteers were delighted that the day had finally come. Annie Cooney recalled the excitement of Christy Byrne and Con Colbert, a former Chief Scout of the Fianna, who had devoted years of activism to bringing about an insurrection:

> During the time I was buckling him up Con—who has not a note in his head—was singing 'For Tone is coming back again' he was so excited and charmed that at last the fight was coming off. He thought of nothing else. The pair went off, wheeling their bicycles which were loaded up with pikes, their rifles and small arms.[10]

For many, the Rising was a family affair: fathers, brothers, sisters (and the occasional mother) fighting together. Michael O'Flanagan was mobilized with his father and two brothers, one of whom was killed. Molly Reynolds was joined by her father and three brothers. Some parents were prepared to sacrifice their children for the cause. Pat Fox thrust his young son—who was killed the following day—towards Frank Robbins as the rebels marched from Liberty Hall: 'Here is my lad; take him with you for the Irish Citizen Army. I am too old for the job'.[11] Some parents were willing to sacrifice themselves, leaving their children behind. After the Rising, John MacDonagh 'was struck by the sight of a wife keeping step with her husband, Séamus Murphy, both prisoners. I knew both of them, and knew they had left their young children at home'.[12] Some were motivated to fight because of their children, as one elderly rebel explained to MacDonagh: 'I was never able to do much for them but isn't this the grandest thing I ever could do for them'.

Many Volunteers mentioned their parents' support for their decision; few, perhaps understandably, recalled their opposition. 'My father showed emotion, but my mother was calm and controlled', one Dublin Volunteer who left to fight alongside his brother recalled: 'She gave us her blessing, told us to fight well, and added: "Remember that your deaths are ordained by God and not by the English." '[13] In contrast, Charlie D'Arcy's father told his eighteen-year-old son to choose between Liberty Hall and his family: 'He immediately, and without hesitation, chose the Hall. I was present and I admired him with all my heart', Jim O'Shea recalled, 'He was killed on Henry & James' roof, a bullet between the eyes'. Frank Robbins' father, a veteran Fenian, called to Liberty Hall with the same purpose in mind: 'I guessed immediately the nature of his visit and for the first time in my life purposely tried not to see him'.[14] O'Shea parted with his own family on bad terms: 'My people thought we were mad to try anything and were not as sympathetic as I would wish', he recalled: 'I was sorry I parted with my people as I did but I considered I had done my best and I felt a savage exultation thinking of what we were about to do'.[15]

Other parents positively encouraged their children to fight. Joseph Lawless was handed his mobilization order by his father: 'his eyes were alight with the excitement of joyful news'.[16] Patrick Kelly described the enthusiasm of his father, an elderly Fenian, as his mother made his sandwiches: 'He worked the bolt of the rifle, sighted it and fired imaginary shots. As he handed me the rifle he remarked, "if I was a few years younger I would go with you" '.[17] The Plunkett brothers actually did have to turn their elderly father away from the GPO. Some parents demonstrated a remarkably defiant spirit to the authorities. When James Kavanagh's family home was raided, the sympathetic officer in charge told his mother (who, he knew, had five sons in the Rising) that he was sorry for her: ' "I'm sorry too", she said to him, "sorry I haven't five more out with them" '.[18] Family loyalties, at least in some cases, outweighed professional ones. On Monday morning, the DMP knocked on the door of Joseph Byrne, who was home on leave from the Royal Irish Rifles, to tell him to report to his barracks as there was trouble in the city. He reported instead to his family home to join up with his two Volunteer brothers. 'My mother put her arms around me', he recalled, "God bless you, I knew you would do it", and she burned my British uniform'.[19]

Given the dramatic events of the weekend, most Volunteers knew, or quickly realized, that they had not been called out for routine manoeuvres. Fifteen-year-old Vinny Byrne—who would become an experienced killer in Michael Collins' 'Squad' during the Tan War—was ordered home by his lieutenant to keep him out of danger. Seeing him crying, his section commander took pity: 'Come along out of that, and don't mind him'.[20] Throughout the city, Volunteers made hurried arrangements for the worst. Announcing to his children, 'I am going off to war', James Foran told his brother-in-law: ' "Goodbye, and if anything happens to me will you look after the wife and kids?". "Right", said he'.[21] Their leaders were more certain that they would not be returning home. Tom MacDonagh parted from his children on Sunday night: 'the boy did not wake up but the little girl did and put her arms around his neck'.[22] Áine Ceannt described her husband's poignant farewell to her and their young son on Monday morning: 'Turning to Ronan, who was watching us, he kissed him and said, "Beannach leat a Ronain [Goodbye, Ronan]", and the child replied, "*Beannacht leat a Dhaide* [Goodbye, Dad]." "*Nach dtiubhraidh tu aire mhaith dod mhaithrin?* [Won't you take good care of your mother?]", he asked. "*Tiubhrad, a Dhaide* [I will]", said Ronan, and so they parted forever'.[23]

Inevitably, the mobilization resulted in a disappointing turnout. Arriving at Blackhall Place, where two of his battalion's company captains had failed to arrive, Liam Tobin 'was struck by the small number who turned up...I had often seen our company, C Company of the 1st Battalion, muster a bigger number than the whole battalion did on that morning'.[24] Most First Battalion companies reported a turnout of one-third, amounting to less than 300 men rather than the battalion's full strength of 750. The Second Battalion fared worse, assembling just over 50 men after two attempts at mobilization. Some Third Battalion companies mustered only 30 Volunteers (rather than their full strength of 120), amounting to a meagre mobilization of less than 150 men: in addition, the vice-commandant, adjutant, quartermaster, and two company captains also failed to appear. The Fourth Battalion's turnout was just as disappointing: 'I would say there were only a hundred men at Emerald Square'.[25] It was also late. Having 'bade what at the time I thought was a last farewell to my wife and family', an embarrassed Peadar Doyle found himself 'parading for about half an hour attired in a semi-military uniform, fully armed [with] 500 rounds of ammunition', his 'only companion a policeman'.[26] The total number of Volunteers who mobilized on Monday morning was considerably less than 1,000, rising to around 1,300 later in the week, less than half the number Joseph Plunkett had identified as a minimum requirement to implement his plans. More impressively, 219 men and women turned out for the ICA, representing almost two-thirds of those who had previously assured Connolly that they were prepared to fight.[27] The proportionally higher ICA turnout reflected its greater militancy and undivided leadership.

The poor turnout was not simply due to the confusion and disappointment of the previous day. Although many leading officers had been careful to emphasize the organization's ultimate revolutionary intent, it had always been something of a gamble as to whether the great majority of Volunteers would follow them into an insurrection launched without any obvious provocation. There were numerous reasons why Volunteers were unwilling to fight, not least self-preservation. 'Some men used to say that it was only nonsense to be talking about peace', Thomas Doyle observed, 'but I happened to mobilise some of these same men in 1916 and they did not turn out'.[28] When Patrick Kelly reached Blackhall Place, he was dismayed to see his company captain rushing past him: 'I learned afterwards that Alright had lost his nerve and ran away when he discovered what was to take place'.[29] But what some attributed to cowardice, others regarded as a pragmatic—or even principled—decision; another Volunteer recalled a more disconcerting reason for Captain Alright's departure: 'This officer said that the whole thing was lunacy'.[30] Many refused to fight because they were opposed to an unprovoked insurrection or because they felt compelled to obey the orders of Eoin MacNeill, the commanding officer of the Volunteers, rather than a self-appointed military council. Some chose not to fight because they believed that the demoralizing impact of the countermand had destroyed any possibility of success. Joseph O'Connor (who did fight) was shocked when de Valera told him they were to go into action at midday: 'I asked him were they mad? His reply was: "I am a soldier and I know you are a soldier also"'.[31]

Some opponents of the military council's strategy took part in the Rising despite acknowledging its futility. Liam Ó Briain and Michael ('The') O'Rahilly, who had spent the previous day carrying MacNeill's countermand across the country, felt they had no choice but to join in once it began. Michael Hayes, a lecturer in French at University College Dublin, recalled that although his 'immediate inclination was to side with MacNeill' he presented himself for service (along with a similarly ambivalent Gerry Boland): 'I entered Jacob's very early in the morning having made up my mind that this was the only course but that the venture was a hopeless one. There must have been a number of people in the Rising who, if they had been given an opportunity of coming to a conclusion would not have taken part at all'.[32] Louise Gavan Duffy, secretary of Cumann na mBan, sought out Pearse in the GPO on Monday afternoon:

> I now think it was very insolent of me because I said to him that I wanted to be in the field but that I felt that the rebellion was a frightful mistake, that it could not possibly succeed and it was, therefore, wrong...I suppose what I meant was that I would not like to be sent with dispatches or anything like that, because I felt that could not be justified. He asked me would I like to go to the kitchen.[33]

Even Eoin MacNeill, by midweek, reportedly felt compelled to participate in the Rising. He was dissuaded by Bulmer Hobson, who pointed out that it 'would place all the men who had obeyed his orders in an impossible and false position'.[34] Perhaps the most famous—certainly the most dapper—last-minute recruit was the former Boer War veteran Major John MacBride, who, 'well-dressed in a blue suit, carrying a cane and smoking a cigar', joined MacDonagh's Second Battalion, declaring that 'he would like to give these amateurs a hand'.[35] Several hundred Volunteers—who either didn't receive or had ignored their mobilization order—joined in after the fighting had begun, although the overall turnout remained disappointing. Many of these latecomers joined the GPO garrison which increased in size from around 150 to about 400.

Had the mobilization occurred as originally planned, the military council would certainly have brought a much larger number of Volunteers on to the streets. Camaraderie and peer pressure may have kept many of them there once the fighting began. Desmond Ryan, who spent Easter week in the GPO, felt the countermand 'broke the nerve of the Rising... We had Easter Week instead of a revolution'.[36] Given the other disasters which preceded Easter Monday this seems unlikely, but the botched mobilization deterred many who would otherwise have fought. When Blackrock's company captain refused to turn out on the grounds 'that the mobilisation order had not been issued by the duly authorised officer', his small unit melted away: 'The long wait, the absence of their captain and then the sound of fighting had unnerved them'.[37] For some, this would become a source of shame. One of the Blackrock men, Tim Finn, spent weeks brooding over his failure to play an active part in the Rising before suddenly disappearing: 'Not many months afterwards we learnt of his death on the Western Front'.[38]

The poor turnout had serious consequences. Most obviously, there were insufficient numbers of men to implement Plunkett's plans. Many Volunteers would later attribute their poor tactical deployment to lack of numbers:

> the occupation of the city was incomplete from the start. Trinity College and the Provost's House should not have been neglected. Shortage of men forbade the occupation of the commanding Shelbourne Hotel in the Stephen's Green area. With more men, de Valera could have occupied the stretch of the canal on either side of the Mount Street Bridge instead of only a house or two, and so on.[39]

The failure to occupy strategic locations, such as Broadstone Station and Kingstown station and harbour (which became transport hubs for British reinforcements), was also attributed to lack of manpower. De Valera found

himself with one—rather than five—hundred men to occupy his extensive positions around Boland's bakery.[40] This problem was compounded
by the size of some of the locations chosen as garrisons, such as the South
Dublin Union's sprawling fifty-acre site. In some cases, however, the low
turnout provided a convenient excuse rather than the reason for poor
tactics: the decision to deploy the men in St Stephen's Green in trenches
rather than the buildings that overlooked it made no sense regardless of
numbers. The military council has also been criticized for not sufficiently
adapting its plans.[41] Forced to deploy much smaller amounts of men than
expected, the responsibility instead fell to individual commandants to
make spur of the moment adjustments to their orders with little coordina-
tion between the various garrisons.

As Volunteers gathered at their various mobilization points throughout
the city, the mood varied considerably. Some officers, like Joseph
O'Connor, told their men what to expect: 'I told them we were going
into action...for the glory of God and the honour of Ireland. I told the
men that any man who felt he was unable to take the final step was at
liberty to leave'.[42] Daly's announcement at Blackhall Place—'Now, boys,
the time has come...you have the chance of striking a blow for Irish
freedom'—was greeted 'with a great cheer'.[43] 'The men', one Volunteer
insisted, 'were all in good spirits and joked about who would fire the first
shot'.[44] At Larkfield, where the refugees had been verging on mutiny since
Sunday morning, George Plunkett's announcement met with similar
enthusiasm: 'The company broke ranks cheering and ran for kits and arms
without being formally dismissed'.[45] Other Volunteers, however, were
kept in the dark: 'our company O/C did not enlighten us very much as to
what was about to take place...He simply told us that the battalion was
going to occupy various buildings'.[46] At Emerald Square, where Ceannt's
Fourth Battalion assembled, there 'was a lot of confusion and no one
seemed to know what was going to happen'.[47] 'While a number of us felt
that we were marching out that day to take part in a rising', one man
recalled, 'quite a number of Volunteers who paraded had no idea where
they were going and what was to take place'.[48]

As midday approached, around a thousand members of the Volunteers,
Citizen Army, Fianna, and Cumann na mBan, trailed by the occasional
G man or DMP constable, were making their way, in 'gloriously fine'
sunshine, towards their positions. Led by a sword-wielding George Plunkett, sixty of the Kimmage refugees—armed with rifles, shotguns, pikes,

crowbars, pickaxes, and assorted small arms—boarded a tram for the city centre: 'Plunkett insisted on paying the conductor for tickets'.[49] The Rathfarnham Volunteers, accompanied by boys from St. Enda's 'with shopping baskets filled with .303 ammunition', commandeered an open-top tram: 'the driver got orders "full steam ahead to O'Connell [Sackville] Street"'.[50] Shortly before noon the largest contingent, led by Connolly and Pearse, left Liberty Hall on foot, the elderly Clarke and disabled MacDermott travelling ahead by car. Joseph Plunkett (like his brother brandishing a sword) was 'beautifully dressed, having high tan leather boots, spurs, pince-nez...like any British brass hat staff officer. Connolly looked drab beside him in a bottle-green thin serge uniform'.[51] Others were less impressed by the appearance of Plunkett, who had absconded from his sickbed in a nearby nursing home, and wore a large brightly coloured handkerchief, 'cowboy-fashion', to mask his gaping neck wound: 'He was looking very bad, very thin and ghastly, as if he were going to pass out', Catherine Byrne recalled, 'I thought it very funny seeing a man wearing a bangle'.[52] Countess Markievicz also attracted attention, not only as a woman in uniform (albeit a rather odd one consisting of 'an Irish Citizen Army tunic, a pair of riding breeches and puttees and a lady's hat with an ostrich feather') but one with a fur coat and dog (Poppet) in tow.[53] Although the propaganda images of the Rising almost invariably depict the rebels in uniform, many were dressed in ordinary clothes, something which would have fatal consequences for the city's civilian population once the British counter-attack began.

How did the rebels feel in these final moments, knowing what they were about to do? Desmond Ryan felt sick, exhilarated, and awed: a 'dream-like sensation' that would last much of the week.[54] Conscious of being untested in battle, Seán Prendergast remembered his 'restrained excitement', but also his anxiety over whether he would be able to retain his composure under fire and his difficulty in controlling his physical 'tremors of dread and fear'.[55] Marching along the quays, Séamus Robinson felt as if he 'were walking on air'.[56] Others similarly experienced 'a vast elation'.[57] Jim O'Shea, like many men, described a curious feeling of detachment:

> little things that never mattered before came up in our minds. Home, people, friends and the chances of the fight, what it would be like to be killed, what of the next world. Those remote things that never gave you a thought before seemed important at the moment. It did not fill you with sorrow or foreboding, only a kind of abstract removal from realties.[58]

'I could not help thinking of the thousands making for trains for the races, seaside and country', he added, 'I smiled to think that at 12 noon, a matter of minutes, we would be fighting for our lives and for our country. I wondered how they would take it'.[59]

Other Volunteers already had a fair idea of how they would take it. Marching towards Jacob's factory, the Second Battalion were rounded on by 'separation women...hysterical in their abuse of us. The mildest of their remarks was, "Go out and fight the Germans"'.[60] Gestures of support were rarer. Marching towards the GPO, Ryan heard children cheering from doorways and the shouts of an elderly man: 'Hurrah for the Volunteers! Hammer the [shit] out of them!' O'Shea was approached by 'an old man, tall and stout, black soft hat and flowing beard', whom he took for a Fenian: 'He wished us luck and God's help in our terrible task...tears fell down his face as he walked away...I suppose he had been through it before I was born'.[61]

But most people who encountered the Volunteers that morning took them no more seriously than usual, despite their weapons. One former Volunteer who passed the Larkfield refugees observed that many of them were armed with twelve-foot pikes: 'that, to my mind, was very ridiculous'.[62] On Grafton Street, O'Shea recalled, a policeman 'passed a remark about playing soldiers'.[63] The manager of the Abbey Theatre found the sight of passing Volunteer wagons, piled high with cauliflowers, 'irresistibly comic'.[64] John Regan, a soldier in the Royal Irish Rifles, passed a group of rebels near Portobello Barracks: 'as they waved to us we waved to them'.[65] Entering the GPO just before noon, Lieutenant Chalmers of the Royal Fusiliers (who would spend the rest of the day trussed in wire in a telephone box) spotted the main body of rebels marching towards him: 'Just look at that awful crowd: they must be on a route march'.[66] Some Volunteers continued to experience a feeling of unreality, even as they stormed the GPO:

> When in front of the GPO, Seóirse [George Plunkett] gave his company the order to left turn, charge, and, as some of the men could not believe their ears, he had to say, 'Take the GPO'. One of them gave such a whoop of delight that something was actually going to happen that it threatened to disorganise the whole plan.[67]

'This ain't no half-arsed revolution', one excited Volunteer exclaimed to bewildered Post Office officials as they piled into the vast building, 'This is the business'.[68]

The GPO was taken without difficulty. The sole constable on duty at the main entrance was persuaded to surrender, while its small guard of five soldiers, lacking ammunition for their rifles, could do no more than barricade themselves into the instrument room, capitulating after their sergeant was shot in the face. Startled workers and customers were cleared from the building at bayonet point, while policemen and soldiers were ejected or taken prisoner. Similar scenes were unfolding throughout the city. South of the Liffey, de Valera's Third Battalion occupied Boland's bakery and Westland Row train station, the Citizen Army filed into St Stephen's Green, the Second Battalion seized Jacob's biscuit factory, and the Fourth Battalion took over the South Dublin Union. The First Battalion captured the Four Courts, the only northside garrison other than the GPO, after a short conversation with its sole guard, a policeman manning the gate at Chancery Place:

> We asked him to open the gate and he refused. We asked him to hand out the keys and he also refused. I threatened him with a revolver and he then handed out the key. We searched the place to see if anyone was in it and we collected any police that were there and put them into the central hall.[69]

The capital fell into rebel hands with a minimum of fuss. 'The Irish Republican Army had taken Dublin', one Volunteer reflected, 'with little more noise and excitement than many a public meeting creates'.[70]

The GPO's defences were secured as the provisional government prepared to proclaim an Irish republic. Two flags were raised over the GPO—a green flag (inscribed with 'Irish Republic' and featuring a golden harp) and a much less familiar green, white, and orange tricolour. The Citizen Army's 'starry plough' standard was flown from the roof of the Imperial Hotel (owned by Connolly's nemesis, William Martin Murphy, who had led the employers during the bitter 1913 Lockout). At around 12.45, with a minimum of fuss, Patrick Pearse formally proclaimed the Irish Republic beneath the shadow of the GPO's porch. Connolly grasped his hand when he finished: 'Thank God, Pearse, we have lived to see this day!'[71]

Primarily a poetic call to arms—'Ireland, through us, summons her children to her flag and strikes for her freedom'—the Proclamation was a progressive document, eschewing a narrow Catholic nationalism (that many Volunteers, as the subsequent history of the Irish State demonstrated, would not have objected to) in favour of a more generous social and political vision. Addressed to the nation's women as well as its men, it asserted 'the right of the people to the ownership of Ireland' and guaranteed 'religious and civil liberty, equal rights and equal opportunities to all'. Alluding to the Protestant minority, it rejected 'the differences carefully fostered by an alien government, which have divided a minority from the majority in the past'. More controversially, it asserted that the provisional government's mandate for violence derived from 'the dead generations':

> In every generation the Irish people have asserted their right to national freedom and sovereignty. Six times during the past three hundred years they have asserted it in arms. Standing on that fundamental right and again asserting it in arms in the face of the world, we hereby proclaim the Irish Republic as a Sovereign Independent State, and we pledge our lives and the lives of our comrades-in-arms to the cause of its freedom, of its welfare, and of its exaltation among the nations.

Like the stream of orders, declarations, and manifestos that followed over the next five days, the Proclamation presented an intentionally misleading appraisal of events. The Rising was not, as it claimed, endorsed by either the IRB or the Irish Volunteers. The rebels had hardly 'waited for the right moment' to reveal themselves, nor struck 'in full confidence of victory'. In contrast to the democratic programme of the First Dáil, there was no attempt to outline a political programme; with a striking economy of detail it simply stated that the provisional government would 'administer the civil and military affairs of the Republic in trust for the people' pending the election of 'a permanent National Government'.

Few Volunteers or civilians appear to have witnessed this momentous occasion but hundreds of copies of the Proclamation, which had been hurriedly printed in Liberty Hall over the preceding weekend, were quickly distributed. Volunteers handed them out to the curious crowd milling around the GPO, and pasted them on the walls of the surrounding buildings. Newsboys distributed (or, more enterprisingly, sold) copies throughout the city, cynics remarking that their value would increase after the signatories were hanged. Of the leaders, Pearse (who had drafted much of the Proclamation) seems to have been most aware that the Rising's importance would lie in its symbolic rather than military impact; when told of the attention the posters were attracting, his 'eyes lit up with intense joy'.[72] The rebellion, the Proclamation made clear, was a stunningly ambitious act of imagination calculated to inspire the nation's 'children to sacrifice themselves' for the 'august destiny' of a Republic willed into existence. Possibly this was why it was Pearse—rather than the chief signatory and more senior IRB figure Tom Clarke—who was named president of the provisional government and commander-in-chief. It was ultimately the romantic spirit of Pearsean nationalism rather than traditional Fenianism that would capture the public imagination and shape the powerful legacy of 1916.

Despite the 'distinctly muted response' (even among Volunteers) to this modest ceremony outside the GPO, it is difficult to overstate its importance.[73] The Proclamation—with its dramatic revelation that the Rising had been coordinated by a single revolutionary body—succeeded in uniting, at least for posterity, the fragmented coalition of secular republicans, Catholic intellectuals, Irish-Ireland activists, and revolutionary socialists that had brought about the rebellion.[74] Its ritualistic re-enactment over the years would create a powerful illusion of ideological coherency that the Rising did not embody at the time. Revealingly, many rebels were surprised to learn that a republic had been declared: the Irish Volunteers was not a republican organization, and the IRB's shadowy influence over it was not widely known. It was a testament to the enormous success of the Rising as an act of propaganda that the republican flag which commanded so little recognition at the time, even among rebels, would soon be taken for granted as the unquestioned symbol of the independence movement, and the republic its natural objective.

The republic proclaimed, Pearse and Connolly returned to the GPO to organize its defence. Hours of feverish activity followed as Volunteers finally got the chance to apply their street-fighting lessons. Windows and doors were cleared of glass and barricaded with mail bags, furniture, and ledgers; loopholes were cut into external walls, while internal walls were broken through to facilitate movement and communication. Defensive points were established, and men and ammunition distributed throughout the garrisons and the surrounding outposts. Food and other essential supplies were secured. Every available container was filled with water, and first aid stations were established. Barricades were erected throughout the city, to disrupt movement rather than to fight behind. Dick Humphreys described the headquarters of the new republic:

> Inside the central postal hall, round the three sides of which run the newly-built counters, all is bustle. Every inch of space between the counters and

windows is occupied with uniformed men, boxes of ammunition, pikes, blankets, mess-tins, bandoliers, knapsacks, and all the paraphernalia…Ammunition of every description overflows counters, tables and chairs, while revolvers and automatic pistols of all shapes and sizes are scattered among them.[75]

Located at the centre of the widest and busiest street in the capital, the rebellion was a remarkably public event: ultimate street-theatre, orchestrated by a military council dominated by dramatists.[76] One local priest, appalled by 'the frivolity and recklessness of the crowd', estimated that there were over a thousand spectators in the vicinity of the GPO.[77] 'O'Connell Street was thronged with sightseers', one Volunteer noted, 'some dumbfounded at the sight while others raised a cheer'.[78] Charles Saurin watched excited youths tear British army recruiting posters from the pillars of the GPO's portico: 'the citizens greeted us like a victorious army, numerous young men jumping with joy and cheering us, but resisting our invitation to fall in'.[79] Desmond Ryan spent the afternoon observing events from the roof of the GPO:

Below the crowd watches curiously and waves its greetings…Talbot Street is blocked up by a tram-car and a barricade. Children dance and ring the bell inside the car…We hear the kids singing below in the distance: 'We are the Volunteers…we'll whack the British army'.[80]

Businessman Ernest Jordison observed incongruous scenes as delighted children, inquisitive sightseers, opportunistic looters, and earnest young revolutionaries converged on Sackville Street: 'I actually saw boys with cricket bats and balls, playing in the middle of the road, before reaching Nelson's Pillar where I saw two dead horses lying in the road, on the left hand side of the Pillar, and an immense lot of blood all over that part of the road'.[81] Others witnessed confusion and disbelief rather than festivity, with many onlookers refusing to take the performance seriously:

Crowds of people were wandering up and down or standing about in an expectant manner. All around me I could hear men and women asking the question which was general that day in Dublin, 'What's it for?'…Some of the rebels were distributing bills, in which the heads of the provisional government announced the establishment of an Irish republic. Someone began to deliver an oration at the base of the Nelson pillar, but the crowd had no taste for oratory, and it did not last long…when one saw how young they were, there came again into the mind that sense of the ridiculousness of it all, and one thought, 'This is all very well, this playing with rebellion and establishing a republic; but wait—just wait until the police catch you at it'... 'It'll be over when dinner time comes', someone said to me... 'Silly young asses!' people were saying, 'they'll only get into trouble'.[82]

II

By early afternoon, the rebels had fortified six garrisons throughout the city with relatively little bloodshed. Few policemen offered more than token resistance. A typical confrontation occurred near O'Connell Bridge, when a DMP man approached Volunteers as they broke into a shop: 'He was held up at the bayonet point', Arthur Agnew recalled, 'He exclaimed "Don't do that. I will go back to barracks. Those are my instructions if anything happens" '.[83] Some DMP men showed considerable bravery during the week: the same policeman repeatedly attempted to walk away despite being threatened with death if he did so: 'I had to break into something bordering on blasphemy before I could get that good-natured, and only mildly-scared bobby to stand until we could get inside the building', Séamus Robinson recalled: 'I did not want to shoot the man, but also I didn't want him to go away too soon to tell his precious military that we were out—until I was in'.[84] John MacDonagh recalled how a 'very officious' constable refused to move away from the entrance to Jacob's despite his brother's threat to kill him: 'I whispered to Tom, advising patience, but he answered that it might be necessary to shoot some of these policemen and detectives to show our own men that we were at war'.[85] Seán Prendergast was among a group of Volunteers who shot and overpowered a burly constable who insisted on passing through their lines: 'In the midst of the melee he could be heard to say, "I'm as good an Irishman as any of ye". We admired his pluck but not his indiscretion'.[86]

By early afternoon, six policemen had been shot, two fatally. At St Stephen's Green, St John Greer Ervine, manager of the Abbey Theatre, stumbled upon 'a pool of congealed blood. I almost sickened at the sight of it'. It was the blood of Michael Lahiff, a twenty-eight-year-old constable, who was shot three times in the head as he confronted rebels (allegedly by Countess Markievicz, who was reported to have shrieked in delight, 'I shot him! I shot him').[87] Following several such incidents, the authorities withdrew the unarmed force from the streets. 'We had to report to our barracks in the normal way as if reporting for duty during that week', a DMP sergeant related, 'No one interfered with us'.[88] Some policemen were sent back on to the streets in plain clothes to monitor rebel movements but their withdrawal from active duty gave the rebels an edge in the fighting that followed; as the royal commission of inquiry subsequently noted, if Dublin, 'like Cork and Belfast, had been policed by the Royal Irish Constabulary, a thousand armed and disciplined policemen, knowing every nook and cranny of the city, would have been a formidable addition to the thousand soldiers who were available when the rebellion first broke out'.[89]

Civilians, as well as policemen, were subject to sporadic acts of violence in the first hours of the Rising. A raid on the army's Magazine Fort in Phoenix Park by young Volunteers and Fianna boys disguised as footballers, timed to coincide with the storming of the GPO, resulted not in the destruction of the city's armoury but the pointless murder of the fourteen-year-old son of the fort's commandant. Gary Holohan, a member of the Fianna, spotted the boy running from his home:

> He stopped and spoke to the policeman who was in the middle of the road...when he got to the corner of Islandbridge Road he ran towards one of the big houses, evidently with the intention of giving the alarm. I jumped off my bicycle, and just as the door opened I shot him from the gate.[90]

Many of these confrontations resulted from civilian opposition to the rebels' attempts to barricade the streets and commandeer vehicles. One eyewitness described how people gathered at the Green to mock the rebels despite their guns:

> A man was standing inside the gates, holding a rifle and looking intently down Grafton Street. Some girls were chaffing him, and asking him if he was not scared to death, and what would his mother say if she could see him, and was he not afraid that she would give him a beating. But he paid no heed to their chaff, though now and then, when someone obscured his vision of the street, he gruffly ordered them away and, if they did not move speedily, threatened to shoot them, 'G' long with you!' they would say, still chaffing, but a little uncertain.[91]

A surprising number of people refused to relinquish their cars or possessions until they were threatened or even shot. The writer James Stephens' description of the 'surprise and fear and rage' of a wealthy businessmen ordered to hand over his vehicle by working-class youths at St Stephen's

Green suggests that class tensions may have been a factor. As much as 55% of those arrested in Dublin after the Rising were labourers, shop assistants, salesmen, and clerks, while another 30% were tradesmen: the young age and working-class composition of the insurgents would have sharpened the resentment of wealthy Dubliners in what remained a very status-conscious society.[92] Stephens also witnessed the brutal killing of Michael Cavanagh as he attempted to retrieve his cart from a barricade:

> The man was picked up and carried to a hospital beside the Arts Club. There was a hole in the top of his head, and one does not know how ugly blood can look until it has been seen clotted in hair. As the poor man was being carried in, a woman plumped to her knees in the road and began not to scream but to screech. At that moment the Volunteers were hated.[93]

Such violence must have accounted for much of the resentment of the rebels expressed by Dubliners that week. St John Ervine, who, like Stephens, spent much of the week walking through the city, heard 'the strongest expressions of hatred' for the rebels. He described the furious response of women from the tenements who had gathered at the edge of St Stephen's Green when a man suggested that they bury a dead rebel lying inside the park: 'one of them, when she heard what he said, rushed at him and beat him with her fists and swore at him horribly. "No, you'll not get him out", she yelled. "Let him lie there and rot, like the poor soldiers!"'[94] Observing the same scene, Maurice Headlam, an English civil servant, noted with satisfaction that 'the "people" were sound'.[95] Most rebels accepted that public opinion was strongly against them. One Volunteer, returning from the races at Fairyhouse as news of the Rising began to spread, observed:

> In the railway carriage on the way back there was a good deal of violent criticism of the Volunteers for provoking a hopeless conflict and endangering the lives and property of citizens. The criticism...could, I think, be taken as a fair cross-section of feeling among the big majority of the populace.[96]

In the absence of the expected retaliation from the authorities, most of the Volunteers' casualties on Monday were self-inflicted. At the GPO, there were numerous accidents as the inexperienced Volunteers clambered into the building through broken side windows. Peadar Slattery and Jack Kiely shot themselves (the latter fatally), while another Volunteer who fell on jagged glass was carried from the GPO 'with his leg literally hanging off'.[97] At Westland Row, Tom Scully was shot by a comrade as they entered the railway station, while another rebel shot himself crossing a wall between the railway and bakery. At Jacob's, John MacBride responded coolly to an uncomfortably close blast, picking 'a few pellets out of his moustache, saying "that shotguns should be treated carefully"'.[98] The rebels' home-made bombs (tin cans packed with nuts, bolts, and gelignite) provided another hazard. One exploded in the GPO as it was being passed through a window to Liam Clarke: 'When I saw him he was bleeding freely from the face and knee. He never recovered fully from these wounds'.[99]

The fighting that occurred that afternoon, as surprised military columns stumbled across rebel positions, proved less lethal, at least for the Volunteers. Several British army soldiers were shot when a military convoy, escorted by lancers, passed Chancery Place while Ned Daly's men were seizing the Four Courts.[100] Another section of Daly's First Battalion, garrisoned in the nearby Mendicity Institute, attacked a large party of soldiers passing along the quays: 'Two shots were fired rapidly and the Commanding Officer dropped', Dick Balfe recalled, 'The column halted right opposite to us after the two shots and it was a case of fire and one could not miss'. Another convoy was attacked in the same area several hours later: 'It was just a matter of firing as rapidly as possible into a solid body. This column also broke up and ran in all directions. No man got past Queen Street Bridge'.[101] The GPO garrison scattered a column of lancers—killing four—as they trotted down Sackville Street towards the GPO: 'We all crowded to the windows and thrust our weapons through the barricade and just as the first two lancers came into view of my window, someone let off a shot and with that I immediately gave the order to fire. Some lancers and several horses were shot and the remainder of them galloped away'.[102]

These exchanges demonstrated the ability of the well-fortified rebels to inflict casualties on even large military contingents in relative safety. At this point, however, the advantage of surprise lay with the Volunteers: these army units were trying to bypass rather than confront the rebels. Indeed, the rebels were later criticized for lacking ambition and initiative on this crucial first day of the Rising. Important targets—such as the telephone exchange on Crown Alley—were not taken despite their light defences; as the wife of the Post Office secretary noted: 'Had they taken it we should have been absolutely powerless, unable to send messages or telegrams for troops'.[103] The greatest missed opportunity, as noted in the

Introduction, was Dublin Castle, the centre of British power in Ireland. Not only would its seizure have represented a tremendous propaganda coup, it would have netted leading members of the Irish administration and provided the rebels with a strategically important stronghold. Given Pearse's obsession with Robert Emmet's 1803 rebellion, the military council must have considered the possibility at some length. It may have been rejected, as a confidant of Connolly insisted, because 'it was a big straggling building requiring a large number of men to hold it and commanded in some places by higher buildings which overlooked it', but this seems unconvincing given the decision to locate garrisons in equally sprawling but more peripheral locations lacking both strategic and symbolic value.[104] The Castle, which dominated the centre of the city, could not have been ignored in the same way as a biscuit factory or a bakery, nor would it have been so casually flattened by artillery as a post office.

The Castle's remarkable vulnerability, moreover, was exposed by the ease with which the small Citizen Army raiding party—with orders to occupy the adjacent City Hall building—penetrated its defences. Helena Molony was among this patrol which fired the first shots of the Rising: 'We went right up to the Castle Gate, up the narrow street. Just then, a police sergeant came out... When [Seán] Connolly went to go past him, the sergeant put out his arm; and Connolly shot him dead'.[105] The shooting of Constable O'Brien was witnessed by another policeman, Peter Folan, from a ground floor window beside the gate: 'The second shot of the Rising was fired at me'. His account indicated that the Castle was even more vulnerable than Molony suspected: 'The military fired no shots, because they carried nothing but the rifles and pouches of blank ammunition'.[106] Despite this, by the time Major Price, the army's chief intelligence officer, had rushed out of his meeting with the Under-Secretary, Sir Matthew Nathan, the raiding party had begun to withdraw from the Castle yard.

For Arthur Norway, the Secretary of the Post Office who had urged the Irish executive to take the separatist threat more seriously, there must have been a grim irony at finding himself besieged in Dublin Castle. He had escaped the occupation of the GPO by minutes when he was summoned to the Castle by Nathan whose plight he now felt little sympathy for:

[Nathan] had formed the habit, possibly on instructions from Mr Birrell, of consulting John Dillon upon every step he took, and viewing everything through the eyes of that old and inveterate rebel. Under this influence, and on the accepted policy of avoiding all measures which might be provocative, he had omitted all precautions, making no arrests and leaving the city during that critical weekend denuded so far of troops that when the Castle gates were shut on himself...there was no force nearer than the Curragh which could be used to restore us to freedom.[107]

Nathan, Norway harshly observed, 'was shaken and bewildered at the moment of the outbreak, it is little wonder. His reputation was gone'.

Dublin Castle—the traditional stronghold of the Ascendancy class which had enjoyed centuries of domination over the Catholic majority—did not fall to the rebels but, like its Under-Secretary, it was badly shaken. In the separatist imagination, the Castle represented an undivided bastion of British oppression. The reality was rather different: the administration in Ireland was divided between diehard unionists, moderate supporters of Home Rule (including an increasing proportion of Catholic civil servants), and pragmatic politicians and officials such as Birrell. The mood in the Castle, which remained vulnerable until it was relieved by a battalion of South Staffords at dusk, was one of tension and paranoia. 'I had no communication with the outside world, I might as well be in prison', Constable Folan recalled, 'During the week there was an atmosphere of mistrust. One did not know what people's thoughts or feelings were, and one did not like conversing with anybody'.[108] John Regan, a soldier in the Royal Irish Regiment, experienced a similar sense of unease, harshly criticizing some of the police and soldiers—'damned cowards'—for their reluctance to venture out.[109]

While the military council must have been pleased by the ease with which they occupied their garrisons, they could not have predicted that they would initially face most resistance from ordinary members of the public. At Church Street Bridge, near the Four Courts, local women attempted to pull down a rebel barricade: 'one of the women, using her finger nails, scratched me badly down the face. We eventually drove them away'.[110] Liam Archer's company was forced to fix bayonets to repel a mob close by: 'immediately a very fat dame in spotless white apron and voluminous shawl leapt in front of us and beating her ample bosom with clenched fists called on me to "put it through me now for me son who's out in France"'.[111] Outside Jacob's, on the other side of the Liffey, Volunteers were also attacked by the 'ladies of the separation allowance'.[112] Matt Walton was shaken when one of his comrades shot a woman as she went to strike him: 'I just remember seeing her face and head disappear as she went down like a sack. That was my baptism of fire and I remember my knees going out from under me. I would have sold my mother and father and the Pope just to get out of that bloody place'.[113] In nearby Malpas Street and Blackpitts, a frenzied crowd danced to jingoistic songs, pelting the rebels with stones: 'One man in the crowd was very aggressive. He tried to take the rifle off one of our party', Vinny Byrne remembered, 'I heard a shot ring out and saw him falling at the wall'.[114] An outpost in nearby Fumbally Lane was withdrawn due to the intensity of attacks by civilians. Unable to follow the retreating Volunteers into Jacob's, a mob stood outside, pushing paraffin-soaked rags under the door until dispersed by shotgun fire.[115]

Further to the west, similar scenes occurred outside the South Dublin Union. C Company's attempts to enter Roe's Distillery were blocked by an irate mob: 'we were practically attacked by the rabble in Bow Lane, and I will never forget it as long as live. "Leave down your [fucking] rifles," they shouted, "and we'll beat the [shit] out of you". They were most menacing to our lads'.[116] Patrick Egan's unit came under attack from a large crowd outside the distillery—'The women spat at us and shouted jingo slogans, while the men started to pull down the barricade'—until they clubbed several of them into unconsciousness.[117] Outside Marrowbone Lane Distillery, Tom Young encountered a group of unarmed Irish soldiers accompanied by their families: 'It was only the soldiers' wives that attacked us. We were on bicycles. The ladies pulled us off the bicycles and we had to use the butts of our rifles to defend ourselves'.[118]

Not all rebels were so restrained. The patience of the St Stephen's Green garrison was stretched to breaking point, and possibly beyond, by the inhabitants of the York Street slums. As they retreated under British fire from the Green to the nearby College of Surgeons on Tuesday, they came under repeated attack: 'one of the soldiers' women, who had been screaming most of the morning, rushed at [Michael] Mallin with the intention of tearing at him', Jim O'Shea recalled, 'I had my bayonet fixed and nearly got her, but Mallin knocked it up'.[119] Frank Robbins reacted similarly when he encountered a tirade of abuse as he ran towards the college:

My patience was exhausted from the previous day's experience when watching her continual interference with our outposts.... With my mind firmly made up I ran into the centre of the roadway, dropped on one knee with the feeling that this woman would be a good riddance...Lieut. Kelly, who was now almost at the door, guessed my intention...ran out into the roadway and grasped my arm. I felt sore over it and wondered would the same consideration have been shown by the opposing forces if they were to be obstructed in the same way.[120]

The most striking aspect of these accounts is the prominence of women. While escorting prisoners to Jacob's, Thomas Pugh was attacked by women from the Coombe 'in a terrible state, they were like French revolution furies and were throwing their arms round the police, hugging and kissing them, much to the disgust of the police. I got a few kicks...but somebody fired a shot to clear them off and they went away'.[121] In contrast, attacks by men were rare. This may simply have been because the rebels were far more likely to shoot them, but the abuse and violence appears to have been largely driven by women. The rebels attributed their anger to the fact that they were married or related to serving soldiers and, less charitably, to their fear of losing their army allowances, but some women were clearly enraged by the danger the rebels had placed them and their families in. There was an obvious class dimension to the violence: the most hostile citizens were described as 'the lower classes', 'loafers', 'rabble', and 'the female dregs of Dublin life'. Many of the female assailants wore shawls, the uniform of Dublin's working-class poor, and most of the violence occurred in inner city slums. The residents of the more prosperous south Dublin suburbs may have been just as pro-British or aggrieved at their neighbourhoods being turned into a war zone but, perhaps sensibly, did little about it.

In contrast to some of the more isolated outposts, the rebels around Sackville Street faced less violence from civilians. They did, however, have to contend with an equally alarming and depressing phenomenon when looting broke out on Monday afternoon. Curiously, the first targets on a street lined with expensive businesses were sweet shops and toy stores, a phenomenon which James Stephens considered 'almost innocent and child-like'.[122] But more valuable targets were soon identified: 'I saw a young fellow standing on the ledge of McDowell's Jeweller's at the Pillar, breaking the window, taking out fistfuls of watches and chains and throwing them to the crowd'.[123] An appalled Volunteer described the chaos that ensued:

> The plate-glass of Noblett's is shivered. The crowd breaks in. A gay shower of sweet-stuffs, chocolate boxes, huge slabs of toffee tosses over amongst the crazy mass. Tyler's suffers in its turn. The old women from the slums

literally walk through the plate-glass panes. Heavy fragments of glass crash into their midst inflicting deep gashes and bloody hurts, but their greedy frenzy is unchecked. Purcell's tobacco shop and the Capel Shoe Co's store are also attacked. Lawrence's next falls a victim. Volunteers emerge and remonstrate, baton and revolver in hand. They deal sturdy blows with rifles butts and threaten with the bayonet's point when all else fails. Rifles are levelled threateningly and once or twice discharged over the looters' heads... [Seán] MacDermott limps across the street and protests vehemently.[124]

James Connolly may have been less concerned than some of his comrades about this assault on private property; warned earlier about the possibility, he had replied that it would 'be one more problem for the British'.[125] Although it has been suggested that the looting may have been partly motivated by revenge for the injustices of the Lockout, most of the rebels were disgusted by the scenes they witnessed. The military council had anticipated the disorder, manufacturing wooden batons to arm Volunteer police, but the shortage of men left them unable to maintain order. Jeremiah O'Leary was one of those given the hopeless task of dispersing hundreds of looters: 'there was such a dense, milling crowd', he recalled, 'that we became broken up and submerged by the crowd immediately'.[126] 'I fired my first shot for Ireland', another Volunteer remembered, 'to disperse daring looters up the street... the effort earning me a scared reproachful look from someone in front and rebuke from an officer behind'.[127] Both rebels and British soldiers fired on looters, killing some, but with little effect. As one priest observed in his diary, the 'foolhardiness of the looters—mostly women and children—is amazing'.[128]

Bizarre scenes ensued as the looting spread throughout surrounding streets, the crowd now targeting residences as well as shops:

> The gamins take charge of a hat-shop, and come out dressed in 'toppers', hunting caps and bowlers, which give them the most grotesque appearance imaginable—seeing that the rest of their garments are nothing but rags of the filthiest description. They loot a sports emporium, and rush out into the road to play mock cricket and golf. They seize a cheap book-shop, and immediately offer to sell armfuls of the paper volumes to the now rapidly-growing crowd. The more adult hooligans, intent on more profitable spoils, smash a huge plate-glass window of a boot-shop and emerge with stacks of expensive footwear and hurry away to their hovels.[129]

One Volunteer encountered five people struggling home under the weight of a large piano: 'We fired a few shots over their heads as a warning and they dropped the piano and made off'.[130] 'Ragged women and children were seen calmly sitting in the window trying on boots and shoes', another eyewitness reported, but they remained too frightened to smash the windows of the most opulent store on the street: 'old women passed up and down gazing longingly at fur coats and silken raiment and saying sorrowfully... "Isn't it a great shame that Clery's is not broke!"'.[131] Even some of the rebels found it impossible to resist the opportunity of seeing how the rich lived: sent to Clery's to secure materials for bandages, Bridget Foley recalled how she and her comrades 'started trying on fur coats'.[132]

In general, though, the looters were regarded not merely as a nuisance whose actions besmirched the dignity of the Rising but a real threat after they set fires which quickly encroached on Volunteer outposts. Eamon Bulfin watched from the roof of the GPO as Lawrence's toy emporium went up in flames despite the efforts of the fire brigade:

> all the kids brought out a lot of fireworks, made a huge pile of them in the middle of O'Connell Street, and set fire to them. That is one thing that will stick in my mind forever. We had our bombs on top of the Post Office, and these fireworks were shooting up in the sky. We were very nervous. There were Catherine wheels going up O'Connell Street.[133]

The situation deteriorated further when pubs and bonded stores were ransacked. After the waxworks were broken into, costumed and sword-wielding drunks returned to Sackville Street, beating each other with empty alcohol bottles to the point of hospitalization.[134] Some rebels considered the drunken gangs rampaging through the city a greater menace than the soldiers. 'Men, women and even children seemed to have gone mad', Denis Daly recalled, 'In the cellars of one house in Henry Street I saw them wading in wine more than a foot deep'.[135] Emerging from the GPO on Tuesday evening, Áine Heron 'felt scared for the first time' when she was confronted by 'a crowd of drunken women who had been looting public-houses... they were too drunk to attack us'.[136]

As with the violence against Volunteers, the part played by women was widely remarked on: 'all the ringleaders were women', one priest claimed, 'then the boys came along'.[137] Class and ethnic prejudice may have added to the disgust of some. 'The Dublin hooligans have come out of their holes like rats out of a sewer', an English clergyman wrote home, 'The slums of the north and south banks of the river have vomited their horrible brood'.[138] A hint of titillation can be discerned in his vivid descriptions of an unconscious young looter—'The upper part of the body is quite naked...A costly silken gown, now torn to shreds, partially conceals the lower limbs, and the fair head is split open like a cocoanut'—and a foul-mouthed drunk 'with the proportions of a plump goddess only barely hidden by the tattered garments which hang about her'.[139]

A similar lack of empathy seems evident in the description, by the English wife of a senior civil servant, of a raid on a 'high-class fruiterer' during the latter part of the week when food was in short supply:

> I never saw anything so brazen. The mob were chiefly women and children with a sprinkling of men. They swarmed in and out of the side door bearing huge consignments of bananas, the great bunches on the stalk, to which the children attached a cord and ran away dragging it along. Other boys had big orange boxes which they filled with tinned and bottled fruits. Women with their skirts held up received showers of apples and oranges and all kinds of fruit which were thrown from the upper windows by their pals; and ankle-deep on the ground lay all the pink and white and silver paper shaving used for packing choice fruits. It was an amazing sight, and nothing daunted these people. Higher up at another shop we were told a woman was hanging out of a window dropping loot to a friend, when she was shot through the head by a sniper, probably our man; the body dropped into the street and the mob cleared. In a few minutes a hand-cart appeared and gathered up the body, and instantly all the mob swarmed back to continue the joyful proceedings![140]

Other observers expressed more nuanced attitudes. Eileen Drury, a Gaelic League activist stranded in Dublin, was disgusted by the looting but added: 'I saw people in the Gresham Hotel with jewellery they had bought from the looters'.[141] 'Men and women and children surged up from the foulest slums in Europe and rifled the shops', St John Greer Ervine observed, 'but I doubt whether in similar circumstances in any city in the world there would have been so little looting as there was in Dublin on those days'.[142]

Did the abuse directed at the rebels by Dublin's poorest citizens, and the rioting that followed, have a political dimension? Those who abused the rebels may have been motivated by their loyalty to serving family members or understandable concerns about their livelihood and homes rather than any particular attachment to Britain, but they were clearly opposed to the Rising. Not all looters were opposed to the rebellion—and they evidently weren't very keen on law and order—but many were openly derisive of the rebels. Moreover, although hundreds of Dublin's poor were willing to risk their lives looting, binge-drinking, or destroying property, relatively few of them were willing to join the rebels. As one sympathetic Volunteer, who felt that 'economic conditions and low wages for their labour made them more determined to grab all they could', reflected: 'It was a pity to see them, especially able-bodied men doing this kind of thing, instead of being in the firing line with us'.[143] As he stood beside a dismayed Pearse ('tragedy written on his face'), watching these scenes from the GPO, Desmond FitzGerald felt profoundly depressed that their willingness to sacrifice their own lives 'weighed as nothing in the scales against the opportunity it afforded to go home with a sackful of boots'.[144] Among the poorest, those whom the Citizen Army saw itself as representing, there was little revolutionary—or anti-British—sentiment evident. The irony was not lost on Bulmer Hobson, who had tried so hard to convince Connolly that Ireland was not ready for revolution:

> His conversation was full of clichés derived from the earlier days of the socialist movement in Europe. He told me that the working class was always revolutionary, that Ireland was a powder magazine and that what was necessary was for someone to apply the match. I replied that if he must talk in metaphors, Ireland was a wet bog and that the match would fall into a puddle. I thought of this later as I watched the Dublin mob, not joining Connolly in the Post Office, but looting the shops in O'Connell Street, and I thought of this again when I read in the press how the British soldiers after the surrender had to protect their prisoners from the violence of the Dublin mob.[145]

III

Despite expectations of a swift and savage response, few garrisons encountered serious opposition before British reinforcements entered the city in strength on Wednesday. There were exceptions: machine-gun fire from the Shelbourne Hotel, which overlooked St Stephen's Green, forced the Citizen Army to pull back to the College of Surgeons; the South Dublin Union came under sporadic attack from the outset; and small but lethal battles erupted throughout the city without warning. But, during the first part of the week, many eyewitnesses were struck by both the lack of fighting and the absence of a British armed presence throughout much of the city: the 'Government seemed to have thrown up the sponge', one

St Stephen's Green resident complained, 'There was not a policeman to be seen, or a soldier or any person in authority'.[146] 'Some machine guns were firing and a few explosions were heard', Father Curran noted in his diary on Tuesday morning, 'On the whole, everything is much quieter than one would expect. No military or police are to be seen'.[147] As late as Tuesday evening, Lord Donoughmore could drive from Thurles, Co. Tipperary, into the city centre without observing anything more unusual than empty roads: 'Having seen no sign of military or police we had no apprehensions. People seemed to be walking about in the streets without fear, but we noticed that no trams were running'. It only dawned on him that the city remained in rebel hands when he was fired on near St Stephen's Green.[148]

Normality coexisted alongside surreal and violent scenes. Public houses were allowed, by order of the Lord Lieutenant, to remain open during the afternoons throughout the week. Thirty Volunteers heading across the Ha'penny Bridge towards a gun battle at the Exchange Hotel were surprised to be approached by the toll collector: they flashed their guns at him.[149] The *Irish Times* was published and sold on the streets of the capital until Wednesday. A disappointed reader complained that the Tuesday edition included 'a long account of Gilbert and Sullivan's operas which were to have been performed' but little about the rebellion.[150] The Royal Dublin Society's spring show continued, apparently oblivious to the carnage inflicted by the Third Battalion's outposts only hundreds of yards away.[151] It remained relatively easy to move about the city, despite sniping between Volunteer outposts and scattered groups of soldiers and armed unionists (such as the Trinity College OTC) who found themselves stranded in the city when the fighting broke out. As late as Wednesday, large numbers of sightseers continued to assemble in the city centre: 'An ever inquisitive crowd is standing in D'Olier Street and O'Connell Bridge, right between the two firing parties. They appear quite unconcerned. Indeed, one would think from their appearance that the whole thing was merely a sham battle got up for their amusement'.[152] 'There was no use in warning these people about the danger', one Volunteer complained, 'Bullets were whining but they did not seem to mind'.[153] A senior civil servant encountered a group of old women sitting on chairs on the street near St Stephen's Green: 'they had come out to see the battle'.[154]

The lack of British soldiers in the city centre allowed the rebel garrisons to remain in contact with each other, and enabled Volunteers to belatedly report for duty during the first half of the week. Min Ryan walked from the suburbs to the GPO on Tuesday afternoon: 'when I was passing by Trinity College I had a feeling that there was something going on there. You could see an odd man peeping out from behind sandbags or you would see the muzzle of a gun. There was odd shooting, and people would go off the street and come back again'.[155] Volunteers from as far as Maynooth, Co. Kildare, reached the GPO on Tuesday night without encountering opposition: 'Many of the residents were on the streets or in their windows. Some of them advised us to go home or we would be slaughtered, others cheered us on'.[156]

A few, genuine, volunteers joined the rebels during the week. After Judge Law Smith's car was commandeered to form part of a barricade near the GPO, his chauffeur remained on to fight.[157] When the Volunteers occupied a dispensary near Boland's bakery, a doctor initially tried 'to throw us all out but when he saw the situation he offered to serve with us'.[158] James Connolly dealt with one of several offers of assistance from passing drunks with uncharacteristic tact: 'will you go home now, have a good sleep, and when you are sober come back and tell me that you still want to fight for Ireland and I'll give you a rifle'.[159] But there were not that many volunteers, and their lack of military training limited their usefulness. Charles Donnelly described how 'a big burly man of the dock-labourer type came to the window and said he wanted to fight with Mister Connolly'. After failing to master a rifle, he was given a pike and told to guard the main entrance of the GPO. Donnelly watched him die later that week: 'He seemed to have lost his head, as he was unarmed and was moving along in a pugilistic attitude. He was riddled with bullets'.[160] Two foreign sailors, motivated by the geopolitical intricacies of wartime Europe, poked their heads through a window of the GPO to offer their services (but only until Thursday when their ship was due to disembark):

> The smaller of the two spoke. He said, 'I am from Sweden, my friend from Finland. We want to fight. May we come in?' I asked him why a Swede and a Finn would want to fight against the British. He said: 'Finland, a small country, Russia eat her up'. Then he said: 'Sweden, another small country, Russia eat her up too. Russia with the British, therefore, we against'.

More enthusiastic than competent, they were transferred to bomb-making duties in a questionable attempt to keep them out of trouble after one of them accidentally shot a Volunteer.[161]

What did the rebels do during the first days of the Republic, other than preparing for the onslaught? What did it feel like to be inside the GPO? The garrison, according to Dick Humphreys, had been transformed into a model of efficiency by Tuesday morning:

> Upstairs on the top storey of the building the P.O. restaurant has been turned into the Volunteer mess-quarters. Desmond FitzGerald, at the head of a busy ration party, is preparing breakfast for the few hundred defenders of the GPO. Five or six 'Tommies' have also been requisitioned. By this time everyone has been allotted to his different station, and the building no longer presents the appearance of an overturned anthill, as was the case the evening before. All street-facing windows have been barricaded and manned by single, double or treble guards of Volunteers, as the case may demand. An ambulance department and hospital have been prepared. Armourers have collected all the loose and spare ammunition, rifles, revolvers, pikes, etc., into one central depot. Another room has been set apart for hand and fuse grenades. Chemical fire extinguishers are distributed at the different danger points, while in the yard outside other parties are busy filling sandbags.[162]

Others remembered it a little differently: 'there appeared to be a superabundance of officers hanging around with nothing particular to do', one visitor noted, 'There seemed to be one officer to every three men'. Desmond FitzGerald complained that 'many of the men for a large part of the day and the night would have no particular duty assigned to them, and for want of anything better to do would stroll along to the restaurant to pass the time eating and talking'.[163]

Pearse may have been commander–in–chief but it was James Connolly, who had been appointed 'Commandant-General' of the 'Dublin Division', who led the forces in and around the GPO. This was an interesting decision, in light of both the earlier tensions between the Volunteers and the Citizen Army and the prevalent clerical and nationalist disapproval of Connolly's socialism. But it was not that surprising given the alternatives: Clarke was old, MacDermott lame, and Plunkett ill. Pearse was a charismatic and inspirational figure but hardly a commanding presence except when orating. Opinion remains divided as to Connolly's strategic abilities but his demeanour and leadership impressed most in the GPO. His 'physical energy and strength were amazing. He was always on the move', James Kavanagh recalled, 'He seemed to take no notice of rank. He would call out a number of men and then say to one of them "Tom" or "Pat" or whoever it might be, "take these men and go to such a place and do so and so and report back to me"'.[164] He toured the surrounding outposts ceaselessly, returning to the GPO to dictate detailed orders to his secretary, Winnie Carney. Countless Volunteers described how Connolly personally led them to their outposts, inspected their positions, and resolved any crises which arose. His principal weakness as a leader, Oscar Traynor suggested, was his indifference to his own safety:

> We reached Eason's in Abbey St and, although at this time, heavy firing was taking place, Connolly insisted on walking out into Abbey St and giving me instructions as to where I should place a barricade. While he was giving these instructions, he was standing at the edge of the path and the bullets were actually striking the pavements around us. I pointed this out to him and said that I thought it was a grave risk to be taking and that these instructions could be given inside.

This apparent recklessness was presumably a deliberate attempt to project an air of calm rather than bravado, and many Volunteers were duly impressed by Connolly's 'remarkable coolness'. William Whelan was among a group of Volunteers, shaken by the looting crowds, who had started firing wildly: 'The panic was spreading and Connolly came out of the Post Office and marched up and down the road in front of it. He said, "Steady, we are going to have a good fight". He quelled the panic'.[165] However, Connolly's willingness to expose himself to unnecessary danger saw him shot twice during the week, the second—more serious— wound effectively ending his command during the final days of the rebellion.

The military contribution of the other members of the provisional government was more modest: 'The headquarters people were not doing any fighting in the GPO', Min Ryan observed, 'They were watching things'.[166] Clarke and MacDermott were not Volunteers, and did not wear a uniform. Like Connolly, they sought to project a sense of composure and purpose: 'They calmed and steadied us, they encouraged us and laughed with us, so that our nerves were soothed and our hearts inflamed with determination not to show the white feather'.[167] Charles MacAuley, a surgeon who was called to the GPO on Monday night, was greatly impressed by the sight of the elderly Tom Clarke 'with a bandolier across his shoulders and a rifle between his knees'. 'He was silent and had a look of grim determination on his face', he remembered, 'It was as if he thought his day had come. He never spoke'. Leading Fenian Seán McGarry thought Clarke was never cooler: 'His normal air of business seemed to have been accentuated and he gave his orders decisively and as calmly as if he were in his own shop'.[168]

Although Patrick Pearse was criticized by Michael Collins for penning 'memoranda couched in poetic phases', compounding what he memorably described as the 'air of a Greek tragedy' about the Rising, many Volunteers found Pearse ('moving about slowly, as if in deep thought') an inspiring, if undeniably otherworldly, presence. His military abilities were admittedly less reassuring. After delivering an urgent despatch, a Cumann na mBan messenger 'asked him whether he remembered my message. He said "yes" in a vague tone, as if he were up in the clouds, so I went to O'Rahilly and repeated the message to him, so as to be sure the grenades would be sent'.[169] Numerous observers admired his charismatic presence: 'such soldierly bearing that the word "Napoleonic" shot at once through my brain'.[170] This persona may have been somewhat cultivated—another visitor to the GPO described him as standing 'very solemn in a Napoleonic attitude with his right hand on his breast'—and probably owed more to Emmet than Napoleon but it inspired confidence nonetheless.[171] Pearse's manifestos leant gravitas to the rebels' actions, just as his impromptu speeches inspired a heroic sense of purpose. Many who arrived in the GPO during the week received a personal address, something which Oscar Traynor recalled as a 'terribly thrilling moment': 'Pearse assured them that they had done a great and noble work for their country, and said that if they did not do anything else they at least had redeemed the fair name of Dublin city, which was dishonoured when Emmet was allowed to die before a large crowd'.[172] The men from Maynooth received the same treatment: 'He told us how glad he was to have us with them in the fight; that our action in marching in from Kildare, even if we did no more in the rebellion, would gain us a place in history'. 'With my knowledge that my name would live in history', Patrick Colgan recalled, 'I felt elated'.[173]

Morale in the GPO remained high during the first half of the week: Bridget Foley described 'an atmosphere of great elation and excitement'.[174] The leaders were generally careful to maintain a positive outlook, reassuring their followers that 'they expected the whole country to be out under arms shortly'.[175] They even published a newspaper, *Irish War News*, which outlined Pearse's optimistic reading of the military situation:

The Republican forces everywhere are fighting with splendid gallantry. The populace of Dublin are plainly with the Republic, and the officers and men

are everywhere cheered as they march through the streets. The centre of the
city is in the hands of the Republic, whose flag flies from the GPO . . . reports
to hand show that the country is rising.[176]

In reality, the provisional government had a pretty realistic view of its
position. The elation of the leaders was based not on any complacency
about what lay ahead but rather satisfaction at the scale of what had finally
been achieved. Min Ryan's account of her long conversation with Tom
Clarke in the kitchen of the GPO on Tuesday night indicates how the gap
between Pearsean blood sacrifice and Fenian pragmatism had continued
to narrow:

> The gist of it was—that people naturally now would be against them for
> rising and coming out like this; that one of the reasons for being against
> them would be because of the countermanding order, but that they had
> come to this conclusion that it was absolutely necessary that they should
> have the Rising now, because if they did not have it now, they might never
> have it; that when the men had been brought to a certain point they had to
> go forward; that, in any case, a rebellion was necessary to make Ireland's
> position felt at the Peace Conference so that its relation to the British Empire
> would strike the world. I asked him: 'Why a republic?' He replied: 'You
> must have something striking in order to appeal to the imagination of the
> world'. He also said that at all periods in the history of Ireland the shedding
> of blood had always succeeded in raising the spirit and morale of the people.
> He said that our only chance was to make ourselves felt by an armed rebel-
> lion. 'Of course', he added, 'we shall be all wiped out'. He said this almost
> with gaiety. He had got into the one thing he had wanted to do during his
> whole lifetime.[177]

Rank-and-file Volunteers, however, continued to differ widely in their
expectations. Some clearly had a realistic grasp of their position. At
midnight on Tuesday, Jimmy Grace and Mick Malone sent home the
other two members—'mere boys'—of their Northumberland Road outpost:
'the Lieutenant called me aside and told me we could not hope to win
owing to the confusion caused by the GHQ countermanding order, and
also the overwhelming odds against us, and the failure of the expected
German aid to arrive'.[178] At Jacob's, many Volunteers were equally fatalistic: 'That the Rising was a gallant but hopeless venture which could not
end but in early defeat seemed the general feeling'.[179] Their pessimism may
also have been accentuated by the ineffectiveness of that particular
garrison. John MacBride, MacDonagh's deputy, told one Volunteer 'that

the fighting should have taken place in the country. He did not seem to have any knowledge as to why Jacob's had been occupied'.[180]

In the GPO, when asked by J. J. McElligott how things would turn out, Michael Knightly pessimistically replied: 'Of course we shall all be wiped out'. 'What matter', McElligott had agreed, 'it will keep up the old spirit'.[181] But Knightly felt that their fatalism was not shared by other Volunteers: 'I had concealed my pessimism from those with whom I had been on duty for they were burning with enthusiasm and convinced that we were going to win'. Many Volunteers, having no reliable information about events outside their own garrisons, had an unrealistic view of their position. Joe Good worried that his comrades in the GPO garrison were 'unduly optimistic'.[182] Desmond FitzGerald felt 'depressed and distressed' when he heard ordinary Volunteers 'talking of victory', expressing a guilty sense of responsibility that some other leaders did not appear to share: 'If they of their own choice had come out to certain defeat and death it would have been a very different thing from coming out because they thought that their leaders had chosen to act with a view to victory or probably victory'.[183] When the Kildare Volunteers reached the GPO, they were taken aback by Connolly's candid appraisal of their chances: 'Connolly paraded us and said, "it didn't matter a damn if we were wiped out now as we had justified ourselves". I thought this was a bit rugged'.[184] Sensibly, the leaders generally shielded their followers from the reality of their military position for as long as possible, particularly as the disciplined manner in which the rebels subsequently faced defeat would prove an important aspect of the Rising's later impact. Volunteers who arrived in the GPO from the provinces were warned 'not to tell anyone of the conditions in the country' while, only hours before the evacuation of the burning GPO, Connolly had continued to declare: 'Courage, boys, we are winning'.[185]

The only information most Volunteers received came from wild rumours. Some, such as the reports of gas attacks, were alarming.[186] Others were more bizarre: it was rumoured that bishops were being shot down on the streets, that the Archbishop's Palace was under attack, that Irish-American forces were landing, and that the Dublin Fusiliers had mutinied. Most of the rumours were heartening in one way or another: 'the Germans had landed here, there and everywhere—a German submarine was coming up the Liffey—the Volunteers were marching in from the country—the whole of the country was up in arms...The German fleet was in the Bay!'[187] Such rumours spread like wildfire. Learning, in the

GPO, 'that thousands of Germans had landed at Kerry and were marching on to Dublin', Ignatius Callender passed the good news on to the Four Courts men who 'were delighted that help was so near'.[188] Some officers deliberately spread misinformation to sustain morale: 'despite the rumours which we helped in circulating among the men that the remainder of the country had risen', Joseph O'Connor recalled, 'I was fairly satisfied myself that we were alone in this fight'.[189] In the Four Courts, 'an official statement was circulated that help was at hand as two German warships had arrived in Dublin Bay'.[190] Some Volunteers doubted whether these rumours 'served any useful purpose'; others felt they 'gave us hope that we could at least make a stand for some time'.[191]

During the first half of the week an unexpected threat to morale was posed by the tension and boredom arising from long periods of inactivity: 'the suspense in waiting for the fight to begin was far worse than the actual battle'.[192] The fires spreading through Sackville Street added to a growing sense of unease by midweek: 'We sat behind our loopholes. Time dragged. We even wrote letters. We watched the bleak and deserted street tumble into ashes. We watched the smouldering ruins rise. We watched for the soldiers who never came'.[193] Diarmuid Lynch passed some of his time reading the RIC's mail: 'We chuckled at the fact that all their spying was now in vain, and that neither they nor their superiors realised the imminence of the climax'.[194] More ambitiously, some rebels occupied the Atlantic School of Wireless in Reiss's Chambers, where they reassembled a transmitter, broadcasting news of the insurrection which was reportedly transmitted on to America.[195] Less successfully, an attempt was made to blow up Nelson's Pillar outside the GPO.

In Jacob's biscuit factory, a dimly lit building where men 'covered with flour from head to toe' moved around like ghostly apparitions, the mood was lightened by music and practical jokes. Volunteers discovered a gramophone recording of *God Save the King*, which was played whenever MacDonagh inspected his men, and 'a miniature ceilidh' was organized.[196] 'A piano was strummed occasionally in an upper portion of the building in contrast with the rifle fire', Seosamh de Brún recalled, 'The book-case in the library was broken open and pillaged'. Volunteers smoked, chatted, and read books, while self-improvers began diaries or formed study circles: 'I can distinctly remember the interest evoked by quotations from *Julius Caesar*'.[197] James Kavanagh recalled 'a good deal of fun' in the GPO; Volunteers raided the nearby waxworks for costumes and musical instruments, and effigies of Wolfe Tone and King Edward were placed in the windows of the GPO where they attracted heavy fire.[198]

But there was a lot more praying than joking or dancing. Volunteers were armed not only with guns but rosary beads, scapulars, and holy water. Confessions were heard, conditional absolution was granted, and the rosary was endlessly recited. 'Each night we said the Rosary and indeed at frequent intervals during the day', one GPO Volunteer recalled, ' 'Twas not an unusual sight to see a Volunteer with his rifle grasped firmly in his hands and his Rosary beads hanging from his fingers'.[199] Every evening in the South Dublin Union, the 'rosary was recited and prayers said, and all retired for the night'.[200] 'Every man in the place went to confession', recalled one of the Jacob's garrison.[201] There were many incongruous scenes. In the GPO, a priest set up a confessional beside the ammunition dump: 'The men queued up for confession'.[202] In Boland's bakery, Father McMahon 'made a confessional in a four-wheel bread van. We said our penance in a nook in a huge stack of flour bags'.[203] A large white car was designated the 'general Communion building' in Jacob's.[204]

The rebels' devotion to Catholicism was not fully reciprocated by the clergy, at least at the time. But although he considered the rebellion foolish and futile, the Archbishop of Dublin confined his public statements to issues of public welfare, urging Catholics to remain at home during the crisis. Significantly, he rejected a plea from Dublin Castle, whose incompetence he blamed for the Rising, to call on the rebels to end the insurrection.[205] Some clergy did demonstrate support for the rebels. The 'wonderful' nuns of St John's Convent, where the First Battalion was headquartered, 'did everything possible to help'.[206] There was little doubt where the sympathies of several members of the Capuchin Franciscan Friary on Church Street lay. After making his confession, Patrick Kelly recalled being told by Father Albert: ' "Go forth now my child and if necessary die for Ireland as Christ died for mankind." I felt exalted and could have faced the entire British Army single-handed'.[207] Éilis Ryan described Father Augustine's spiritual support: 'Rosary after rosary was recited during the last twenty-four hours as the British military were closing in on the area. The firing was intense on Saturday...Father Augustine was still on his knees; he consoled the wounded and staff alike and prayed for the success of the men in action'.[208]

Some priests offered more practical support. At Jacob's factory, 'when the mob were loudest in their abuse of us, an old priest came along and,

before them all, made the sign of the Cross at all parts of the building',
Joseph Furlong recalled, 'This acted like magic on the mob, and they
melted away'.[209] However, most priests were strongly opposed to the
Rising, which clearly failed to meet the Church's criteria for just war.
Several priests had to be ejected from Boland's bakery when they urged
Volunteers to 'go home and stop our madness', while others only desisted
from doing so after being threatened with expulsion.[210] Pauline Keating
and her comrades were denounced by a Franciscan friar in the Four
Courts: '"Girls, girls, you don't know what you have done; you have
blown up the whole of Dublin"...We thought we were heroines, but
when he had finished with us, we thought we were all criminals'.[211]

Some priests, such as Fr John Flanagan from the Pro-Cathedral, were
more opposed to the rebels than they would later publicly recall. Flanagan's
account of his experiences (one of many such articles subsequently published
by the *Catholic Bulletin* that tended to glorify the Rising) revelled in his role
as unofficial chaplain to the GPO. Leslie Price, who arrived at his presby-
tery after a perilous journey to Marlborough Street on Thursday, described
a different attitude:

> I said to him 'I have been sent over by Tom Clarke for the priest'. He said,
> 'You are not going to the Post Office. You are staying here. No one here
> will go into the Post Office. Let those people be burned to death! They are
> murderers'...I knew then, by some other remark Fr O'Flanagan made that
> it was the linking up with the Citizen Army he did not like. It took a certain
> amount of courage to fight a priest. I said...'I feel sure that every man in
> the Post Office is prepared to die, to meet his God, but it is a great consola-
> tion to a dying man to have a priest near him'. Whatever effect I had on
> him, he said, 'Very well! I will go'.[212]

Price was further outraged when Flanagan passed by a dying man, with
'drink taken', on Moore Street, but stopped to give absolution to another
'who was respectable'. At the GPO, Price recalled, Tom Clarke quietly
ordered that 'on no account was the priest to be let out'. Regardless of the
basis for Price's criticisms, many priests, including Flanagan, placed their
spiritual duties ahead of personal or political misgivings, demonstrating
bravery in ministering to rebels, soldiers, and civilians throughout the
week. Jim O'Shea recalled how an elderly canon, who shook with fear as
he was ejected from St Stephen's Green at gunpoint, turned back when a
young Volunteer asked for confession: 'I thought it was a very brave action
for an old man in such a nervous state'.[213]

The remarkable piety of the Volunteers reflected the nature of Irish society at this time, but probably also the zealous and moralistic outlook of the rebels, many of whom clearly viewed their cause as a sacred one. One Volunteer described how he surprised Eamon Ceannt, commandant of the Third Battalion, during a lull in the fighting: 'I knocked, opened the door and saw him kneeling in the room, his rosary beads in his hand, and the tears running down his cheeks'.[214] Even bad language was frowned on by many. Michael Collins proved a strikingly irreverent exception on both counts, angrily rounding on one comrade for seeking solace in prayer rather than fighting on when the rebels' resolve began to collapse at the end of the week: 'Are you [fucking] praying too?'[215] The piety of the rebels also reflected the consolations of religion (and the importance of receiving absolution) in the face of death. 'During the week some of the fellows began to cry when they heard shots, because they were a long time from confession', one of the Marrowbone Lane Volunteers recalled, 'Father Ciaran and another priest came down from Mount Argus, and they gave us all Agnus Deis'.[216] The first thing Cumann na mBan members were asked by the paternalistic Desmond FitzGerald when they entered his commissariat was: ' "Now listen, girls. Have you been to confession?" '[217]

What was the ideological significance of all this? Accounts of the piety of the rebels, particularly the executed leaders, formed an important aspect of the transformation of public opinion after the Rising. As a result, the non-sectarian (if deeply religious) ethos of the Proclamation was overshadowed by the popular perception of the Rising as an event steeped in Catholicism—which, in many respects, it was. For most Volunteers, their preparation for the Rising began with religious devotions at the weekend: 'The scenes in almost every chapel on Saturday night were amazing—the chapels were crowded with men and boys for confession. Similar scenes were witnessed on the Sunday morning, thousands of men and boys receiving Holy Communion'.[218] The men of the Second Battalion's F Company were blessed by a young curate before they left Fr Matthew Hall on the morning of Easter Monday:

> It was while he was speaking to us as we all knelt each on one knee before him clasping our rifles in both hands that Peter Traynor came round the corner and halted suddenly at the scene before him...I caught the look in his eyes and could see that he was struck by the drama and by something deeper than just drama in the young priest holding up the Crucifix and

exhorting the kneeling armed men before him to think on what it represented and of our brief mortal life.[219]

Moments before the Rising began, Count Plunkett called on the Archbishop of Dublin to inform him that he had visited the Vatican on behalf of the rebels to seek the Pope's blessing, and to assure him that the rebels 'wished to act as Catholics'.[220] Many of the leaders, such as Ceannt, emphasized the significance of Count Plunkett's visit to the Pope, telling their men 'that we had the Pope's Blessing'.[221] Even Thomas MacDonagh, who was not particularly religious, declared: 'Do you know that the Pope has blessed this thing?'[222] The Catholic spirit which infused the Rising influenced even the few non-Catholics involved, including the foreign sailors who volunteered their services in the GPO: 'The Finn was not a Catholic. He had no English but before he left he was saying the Rosary, in Irish'.[223] Others, like John MacBride, were sufficiently moved by the experience to return to the sacraments after a long absence. Pearse, it is clear, was far from alone in viewing the Rising in explicitly religious terms: when one Volunteer was asked by an anxious comrade if he had received confession, he replied: 'No, I do not think it matters as I believe I would go straight to heaven if killed here'.[224] Others observed miraculous occurrences, such as the rebel saved from a sniper's bullet when he kneeled for the Angelus, or the picture of the Crucifixion 'left untouched although the wall all round was torn with bullet marks'.[225]

The Catholicism of the rebels remains a contentious issue. Before 1916, Irish republicanism distinguished itself from constitutional nationalism not just through its commitment to physical-force separatism but also its rejection of faith and fatherland politics. While there was, arguably, no necessary contradiction between the Catholic (and Gaelic) outlook of the rebels and the non-sectarian aspirations of Irish republicanism, there were obvious tensions given their desire for a united Ireland that would include a large minority that was neither Catholic (nor Gaelic). The form of republicanism which triumphed after 1916 did not reflect the more secular ethos of nineteenth-century Fenianism with its call for 'no priest in politics'. Like many of the rank-and-file rebels, Eamon de Valera—the only commandant to escape execution who would go on to dominate Irish politics for the next half-century—conceived of his country as a Catholic and Gaelic nation.[226]

Few Protestants fought with the rebels and those that did (literally) stood out: when a Volunteer in the Hibernian Bank outpost was killed,

Leslie Price recalled, 'we all knelt down to say a prayer and Arthur Shields stood in a corner because he was not a Catholic'.[227] Revealingly, there were even fewer left by the end of the week. Cathal McDowell, one of a tiny number of Protestant rebels, converted to Catholicism during an emotional ceremony in Boland's bakery: 'He laid down his Howth rifle beside him and the priest baptised him'.[228] Claiming to have experienced an epiphany during the Rising, Countess Markievicz (the only Protestant among the leaders) also converted to Catholicism. Tom Clarke's wife, Kathleen (who also experienced an epiphany after the Rising), was not alone in describing the Easter Rising in the religious language of apparition, divine mission, and sacrifice.[229] Much as it would later discomfort secular republicans, it was hardly surprising that many Irish people would come to see 1916 and Catholicism as intertwined.

Similar tensions between the progressive rhetoric of the Proclamation and the underlying realities of Irish society at that time are highlighted by the role of women in the rebellion. Around two hundred women—mostly members of Cumann na mBan and the ICA—took part in the Rising in Dublin.[230] Inevitably, discussion of their experiences has centred on their gender. Although some male rebels later testified to their 'courage and devotion', the women they praised had to overcome the obstacles imposed by their male comrades in order to make this contribution. Ned Daly had assured Phyllis Morkan that 'if there was going to be fighting, they would need all the women they could get' but her company waited in vain for his orders to join them in the Four Courts. When Daly finally ordered the women under his authority to demobilize on Monday evening, many ignored him. 'You know the Volunteers, the kind of men they were; they thought that we should be away from all that danger', Leslie Price recalled, 'Bríd Dixon and I decided that we were not going home. Here was something that would never happen in our lives again. We decided to go down to the centre of the city, to see what was going on, and get into any building that was available'.[231] Min Ryan had the same idea, disconsolately loitering outside the GPO until she found someone willing to invite her in.[232] When Catherine Byrne asked a Volunteer to allow her in to the GPO: 'he said, "No, I was to go home". He added: "I'll tell Paddy on you" (that was my brother)'. She refused to take no for an answer, literally smashing her way in to the GPO:

> I hung around...I asked Frank Murtagh to lift me up to the side window at the corner...and I kicked in the glass of the window. I jumped in and

landed on Joe Gahan, who was stooping down inside performing some task. He started swearing at me, asking: 'What the bloody hell are you doing here?' I cut my leg and arm with the glass as I jumped and he drew my attention to the bleeding which I had not noticed.[233]

It was not until Monday evening, after their leaders had gone to the GPO to protest their exclusion, that a formal mobilization order was drafted for Cumann na mBan members. Despite this, female rebels were still not permitted into Boland's bakery, and they had to argue with Volunteers before they were allowed into Jacob's biscuit factory, its commandant Thomas MacDonagh protesting: 'We haven't made any provision for girls here'.[234] Some of the military council, notwithstanding their egalitarian instincts, were also unwilling to expose female family members to danger. Kathleen Clarke begged her husband in vain to allow her to fight beside him in the GPO.[235] James Connolly refused to allow his daughters to serve with him, sending them to Tyrone where he must have known there was little likelihood of much fighting.[236]

Those determined women who succeeded in forcing their way into the garrisons found their roles there rigidly demarcated by gender: 'We busied ourselves mainly with the washing up and the cooking'.[237] Pearse's manifesto to the citizens of Dublin espoused a similar gendered division of labour: 'There is work for everyone: for men in the firing line, and for the women in the provision of food and first aid'. At Marrowbone Lane, Lily Cooney recalled, 'Our main activity was preparing food and generally looking after the welfare of the men'.[238] Like Father Ted's housekeeper, another victim of Irish patriarchy, the women of the Four Courts 'spent a lot of time making tea and sandwiches'.[239] Even within these areas, their autonomy was further subordinated to men: the GPO's commissariat was run by Desmond FitzGerald, while the 'men of the first aid detachment' took charge of the casualty station.[240] Nor were these women always treated with respect. Bridget Lyons's 'most vivid recollection' of the Rising was a rather tactless summons to a small outpost: 'Somebody said "call that fat girl that came up from the country". I resented the slight, but my patriotism asserted itself... It was a hazardous expedition over broken glass and with bullets flying'.[241] Most persevered, although Mairead O'Kelly (who, like many women, spent Easter week in the kitchen) left the Four Courts because she felt she was not 'doing work of great value'.[242]

The ICA proved a partial exception. Its female members were allowed something approaching a combatant role at St Stephen's Green. However, most of these women were not armed and at least one ICA man insisted that the services of 'the women's section of the Citizen Army' were only called on due to the shortage of men. Although Marie Perolz initially 'felt very proud' when she was asked to be a messenger—'Said Mallin with his heavenly smile "Is it dangerous enough for you?"'—she subsequently experienced 'a bitter feeling of frustration, as I did not take part in the fighting'.[243] In contrast, Margaret Skinnider, a maths teacher from Glasgow, cited the Proclamation to insist on her right to throw a grenade through the window of the Shelbourne Hotel. Although shot three times while attempting to burn down the Russell Hotel, Skinnider survived to write a memoir of her experiences.[244]

Preoccupation with the subordination of women and the roles they were denied should not detract from the important contribution that they did make. Their duties were not always glamorous—Éilis Ui Chonnaill recalled bathing Ned Daly's 'feet and giving him fresh socks with plenty of boric powder'—but they were not insignificant or lacking in danger. Their logistical role freed up Volunteers for combatant duties. Women repeatedly risked their lives as despatch carriers, braving military cordons and sniper fire to maintain rebel communications. They carried weapons, ammunition, and other supplies, and scouted the streets to facilitate the movement of Volunteers. Mary McLoughlin brought money, ammunition, and food to the College of Surgeons and conveyed messages between the GPO and Jacob's; when her distraught mother finally locked her into a room for her own safety, she escaped through the window, returning to the GPO. Máire Smart forced herself to walk past dead civilians to bring food and ammunition to Boland's Mill: 'I was terrified but I went'.[245] Ignatius Callender turned to his mother to get his supply of .303 ammunition to the Four Courts:

> I did not like to do this, but the question was, how was I to get it through, as there were hundreds of soldiers between our house and Church St. I gave it to her. She put it inside her blouse and taking 2/6 and a milk jug went off on the pretence that she was going to Stoneybatter to get milk, eggs and rashers for breakfast for Lieutenant Anderson and Captain Connolly of the Pals RDF...One of Mrs Murnane's daughters got it safely over the barricades in King St.[246]

Women were far less likely to be shot on the streets and much more likely to talk their way through the cordons that began tightening around the rebel positions by midweek. Some were not above exploiting their gender. One woman dressed in widows' black, placing a British emblem on her coat to ease her passage through checkpoints; others told 'pitiful stories about sick relatives'.[247] Marie Perolz borrowed her 'little niece who was dressed in a blue velvet coat and bonnet' to accompany her as she set off to deliver a basket of revolvers. She did, at least, tell her niece the purpose of their mission: ' "O Mamma, can I come too to drive out the English?" said she to her mother'.[248] Women's work became increasingly dangerous during the week: Leslie Price was terrified when Tom Clarke ordered her to convey a message across Sackville Street which was under heavy machine-gun fire: 'I had seen Connolly brought in when he had gone out under the arches in front of the Post Office and had been wounded. I remember saying to myself, "Here's good-bye to you"...I could have cried but, when I looked at his courageous old face, I said, "Alright" '.[249]

Women, as one Cumann na mBan activist related, were also assigned emotionally demanding tasks: 'One fellow—Hurley from Cork—who had come over from London to be in the fight, was brought in dying from a bullet in the head. I had to sit by him till he died'.[250] Bridget Foley, who set up a first-aid post near the GPO, assisted in an operation on a civilian with a gaping stomach wound: 'I stuck it out as long as the doctor was doing his part, but when I took away the bowl of water I got good and truly sick. I think he died soon after'.[251] Min Ryan was sent to the homes of mobilized Volunteers to let their families know where they were; later in the week she delivered messages to the wives of captured British army soldiers: 'I always remember the look on the women's faces when they read the messages. They looked at us as if we were awful women'.[252]

The involvement of female combatants was inevitably seen as exotic or sinister. In one of his many colourful revelations to the press, Lieutenant Chalmers, who was held hostage throughout the week, claimed that 'the girls' in the GPO were dressed 'in the finest clothes', accessorised with 'white, green and orange sashes' and 'knives and pistols in their belts'. The male hostages, he claimed, were appalled to find themselves 'under the charge of a woman in male attire, who flourished a big loaded revolver'.[253] Countess Markievicz, the only woman to occupy a position of command (albeit a possibly self-appointed one), attracted particular contempt. Arthur Norway referred to her as 'that virago', while another observer was surprised (given her role in feeding the poor during the Lockout) by the 'remarkable fury' directed towards her by working-class Dubliners.[254] Recalling the 'shrieks of hatred' of the 'savage women' they encountered,

Bridget Lyons felt that a 'lot of it seemed to be directed against the Countess' breeches and puttees'.[255]

Ultimately many of the Volunteers, despite their separatist radicalism, regarded the role of women in much the same light as did their imperialist enemies. Those who believed that women should be allowed to play a part in the Rising felt that they should do so in the kitchen or the hospital rather than the firing line and, in most garrisons, the women came under pressure to leave before the British assault began. Many refused to do so or, like Min Ryan, insisted on returning to the fight: 'we were determined to get back. It would be absolutely idiotic not to; if the men were to die, we would too; that is the way we felt'.[256] But it would be simplistic to suggest that such gendered concerns exclusively divided men from women. Many women, including members of Cumann na mBan, shared the prevailing values of their times. Nell Humphreys initially felt ashamed of her 'unwomanly' sister, Sighle, when she learned 'that at times it was difficult to keep her from taking a shot herself, [and] that the way she gloried when the enemy fell was inhuman'.[257]

Feminist historians argue that 1916—because of both the egalitarian nature of the Proclamation and the active role which women actually played—advanced the status of women within the revolutionary movement and the Irish State that it created. Others view the issue of gender, like the Catholicism of the rebels, as another example of the tensions between the progressive rhetoric of the Proclamation and the underlying social conservatism of the separatist movement. As with so much else, the leaders disagreed on this important issue: James Connolly, Helena Molony recalled, 'gave out revolvers to our girls'; de Valera notoriously refused to allow them into Boland's bakery.[258] The Rising can be seen as an inspiring example of the revolutionary nature of the struggle for independence: 'Even before the Russian Army had women soldiers', Molony proudly declared, 'the Citizen Army had them'.[259] But a more accurate portent of the place of women in the Irish Republic that ultimately emerged was the experience of the many women who spent Easter week out of sight in the GPO, confined to the kitchen at the back of the building: 'we were very busy and we did not get invitations to come down'.[260]

5

Glorious Forever

The Fall of the Republic

The extent to which the insurrection took the civil and military authorities by surprise was demonstrated by the remarkable vulnerability of the capital on Easter Monday. Only 400 of the 2,400 soldiers on active service scattered throughout Dublin's military barracks were available for immediate deployment. The Chief Secretary, Augustine Birrell, and Maj.-Gen. Sir Lovick Friend, the Irish commander-in-chief, were in London, and many of the army's officers were enjoying a day at the races at Fairyhouse. Oddly, no plan had been put in place to deal with the well-publicized Volunteer manoeuvres expected on Sunday. The rebels were also fortunate that a long-planned crackdown on the Volunteer leadership had been delayed. Despite the concerns of the Lord Lieutenant, Lord Wimborne, his discussions with Nathan and the heads of the police and military over the weekend had ended in a decision to postpone the arrests. This was partly due to Birrell's absence—as well as Nathan's reasonable assumption (in light of the *Aud*'s discovery and Casement's arrest) that the moment of danger had passed—but it also reflected the Castle's long-standing reluctance to move against the separatist faction for fear of creating greater disturbances.

The military response to the insurrection was prompt and effective. Because of the rebels' failure to seize control of communications, contact between London and the civil and military authorities in Ireland had been restored by late on Monday afternoon.[1] The army command's first impulse was to secure the Castle. All available troops were sent there, many encountering resistance en route. By Monday evening, a sufficiently large force had gathered there to begin assaulting the surrounding rebel-held buildings such as City Hall. The rebel garrisons were largely ignored while strategic locations such as Dublin harbour and Amiens Street railway station (where reinforcements from Belfast began arriving that night) were secured. By Tuesday morning, the balance of military forces in the city had radically shifted. Brig.-Gen. William Lowe—who commanded operations throughout most of the week—and the 1,600-strong Curragh mobile column arrived in the early hours of the morning, closely followed by General Friend from London. It was Lowe who devised the strategic response which would shape the fighting over the next week: 'the establishment of a central axis of communication running from Kingsbridge to the North Wall and Trinity College, followed by the cordoning off of the main rebel positions'.[2]

The response of the civil authorities was less impressive, although other than sending urgent requests to the War Office for reinforcements there was not a whole lot that could be done once the fighting had broken out. In Birrell's absence, Sir Matthew Nathan was the effective head of the administration in Ireland (although the brandy-fuelled Lord Lieutenant issued a stream of orders from 'splendid viceregal isolation in Phoenix Park').[3] The Secretary of the Irish Post Office, Arthur Norway, who worked closely with Nathan that week, has left a devastating portrait of the Under-Secretary's performance—'His manner and actions were those of a man who was not cool and steady, but rather bewildered'—which he attributed to Nathan's awareness of his culpability for the outbreak of the insurrection.[4] On Tuesday Wimborne declared martial law in Dublin, extending it to the rest of the country the following day. His decision (apparently made without consulting the Attorney General) reflected the gravity of the crisis and the collapse of law and order in the capital, but it was probably unnecessary given the extensive wartime powers provided by the Defence of the Realm Act which the administration had been using to coerce republicans without recourse to civil law since the summer of 1914.

The disadvantage of martial law, aside from its powers being notoriously difficult to define, was that it ceded a propaganda success to the rebels at a time when the Government was striving to portray the insurrection abroad as a local riot, and it had the potential to alienate moderate nationalist opinion without providing meaningful additional powers. Birrell, while en route to Dublin, wrote to Asquith urging the Government not to extend martial law to peaceful parts of the country. The Cabinet's rejection of his advice, perhaps understandable given the discrediting of his conciliatory policy, set an important precedent for the next months: the wartime political and military interests of English politicians and the British army would prevail over local political concerns about the impact of government policy. Like so much else about the Rising, the alacrity with which the Government set aside the rule of law reflected its wartime context: 'When the Cabinet declared martial law across the whole of Ireland for an indefinite period, and placed Ireland under a military governor, it was sending a deliberate signal. The suppression of the rebellion, by whatever means, was the overriding priority'.[5]

Although General Friend had four thousand troops available for combat by Tuesday evening—twice as much as his overgenerous estimate of the rebels' strength—he waited until the arrival of further reinforcements from England before moving decisively. On the morning of Wednesday 26 April, the main body of these reinforcements began marching from Kingstown harbour towards the city centre. Significantly, their orders made it clear that any resistance encountered en route should be methodically crushed before proceeding: 'the head of the columns will in no case advance beyond any house from which fire has been opened, until the inhabitants of such house have been destroyed or captured', Brigadier-General Lowe decreed, 'every man in any such house whether bearing arms or not may be considered as a rebel'.[6]

I

For many of these soldiers, the Irish rebellion would prove a perplexing experience. In Kingstown, where most embarked, they were bemused to find that crowds had 'turned out to cheer them, giving them food, cigarettes, chocolate, and everything the hospitable inhabitants could provide'.[7] Like the Volunteers, many soldiers had received little information about their destination or mission from their officers. When Fr Michael Doyle, an Irish chaplain in the British army, entrained for Liverpool, he was told that they were taking a precautionary route to France due to the threat of submarine attacks: 'On boarding the boat he lay down to rest and after some time was called and, to his utter amazement, found that he was at Dun Laoghaire [Kingstown] Pier'.[8] Some soldiers—including one Cockney sergeant who 'wondered how everyone he met spoke such good English'— initially assumed that they were in France.[9] In many areas, they were welcomed as liberators. One Volunteer—recalling the 'very hostile' reception his men had received since Monday—wryly noted the local response when a British machine-gun corps paused for a rest: 'within a few minutes every man had a cup of tea. Upper Leeson Street was loyal to the Empire'.[10] However, any complacency that the army's progress through Dublin's affluent southern suburbs may have instilled was to be shattered by the reception that awaited it on Northumberland Road.

On Wednesday morning, the 178th Infantry Brigade—one of two infantry brigades which had been rushed to Ireland to put down the rebellion—began its march on Dublin. The two Nottinghamshire battalions took the coast road, approaching the city through Ballsbridge, while the Derbyshire battalions followed an alternative route that lay slightly inland, marching through Donnybrook towards the city centre. The latter reached the capital without mishap; the two thousand men of the 2/7th and 2/8th battalions walked into the most devastating fighting of Easter week. Anticipating the likelihood that the army would approach from Northumberland Road, Eamon de Valera, the commandant of the 3rd Battalion, had placed two outposts along a short stretch of the road approaching Mount Street Bridge: No. 25 Northumberland Road contained just two men, while another four Volunteers waited in St Stephen's parochial hall a little further to the north. In addition, just north of Mount Street Bridge, two outposts overlooked Northumberland Road: Clanwilliam House (held by seven men) and Robert's builders' yard (held by four Volunteers). This short stretch of Northumberland Road also lay within range of Volunteers positioned on the Grand Canal Street Bridge, a railway embankment at the docks, and several large water tanks on the roof of the railway workshops.[11] Collectively, these outposts would form the most lethal killing zone in the city.

Forewarned both by the Irish Command and many of the residents they met en route, Brigadier Maconchy expected resistance as he led his Nottinghamshire troops towards the city.[12] Having received a despatch reporting that five hundred troops were heading their way, the Volunteers were no less prepared. William Christian was visited by his father just before the battle began: 'he begged me to come home with him, but having taken up my post nothing but death would make me desert it'.[13] Shortly after midday, the main column of soldiers—preceded by an advance guard moving along both sides of the road in single file—reached Northumberland Road. Demonstrating a degree of tactical nous and

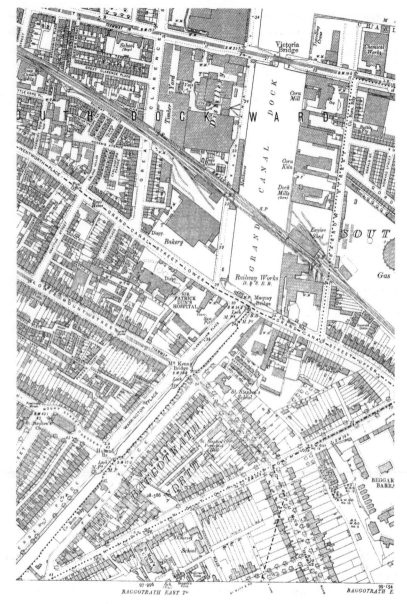

Clanwilliam House and Mount Street Bridge area

composure absent among many other Volunteers, Mick Malone, a twenty-eight-year-old carpenter, waited until the advance guard had passed his outpost before opening fire from No. 25; Clanwilliam House and the other outposts then added to the withering fire. From the parochial hall, William Christian witnessed the devastation that ensued:

> As the British troops drew nearer, the bullets fell on the roof of the school opposite like a shower of hail. Excitement gripped us and we braced ourselves for the encounter. Because of our position we had to wait until the British troops actually passed us before we could fire on them; and then they came—hundreds and hundreds of them—stretching right across the road—and so intent were they in gaining their objective—the capture of Clanwilliam House—they completely overlooked our post. We opened fire and men fell like ninepins. Those who got past us had scarcely reached the bridge before they had to face a battery of fire from Clanwilliam House. We emptied our guns on those who thought to turn back on the line.[14]

During the next hours, wave after wave of infantry charged relentlessly towards Mount Street Bridge, an appalling spectacle which was observed by a large crowd of Dubliners from the city side of the bridge. James Walsh, one of two brothers in Clanwilliam House, described the decimation of the soldiers who succeeded in reaching the bridge:

> Those who managed to get by '25' ran towards the bridge and took cover anywhere they could find it, on house steps, behind trees, and even in the channels of the roadway. We kept on blazing away at those in the channels, and after a time as they were killed, the next fellow moved up and passed the man killed in front of him. This gave one the impression of a giant human khaki-coloured caterpillar.[15]

When, several hours later, the Sherwood Foresters finally crossed the bridge, their position remained lethal until they were able to identify the precise location of the outposts: 'they did not seem to know what their objective was or where they were going', a Volunteer from Robert's yard stated, 'Those who came in our direction were completely wiped out. The bridge and Northumberland Road was strewn with dead and wounded'.[16] The carnage would have been more horrific but for the doctors, nurses, and civilians who bravely ran onto the street between the lulls in fighting to retrieve the dead and wounded on white sheets.[17] The tiny number of Volunteers at the centre of the storm experienced extremes of fear and exhilaration. The onslaught was so intense, Jimmy Grace recalled, 'that I trembled from hand to foot in a panic of fear and it was only when I was able to reply to the fire that I overcame the fear'.[18] They were thrilled by their success. Moments before he was shot dead, a euphoric Paddy Doyle exclaimed: 'Boys, isn't this a great day for Ireland?'[19] Looking down on the carnage, James Walsh thought 'we had accounted for the whole British army in Ireland. What a thought! What joy! What a day!'[20]

Several hours into the battle, Brigadier Maconchy, horrified by the mounting cost of the assault, ordered one of his companies to attempt a flanking movement. He was overruled by General Lowe, who insisted that the frontal assault should continue. Some time later, Maconchy recalled, 'I returned to Ballsbridge (not a very nice walk) to the telephone and asked Irish Command if the situation was sufficiently serious to demand the taking of the position "at all costs" saying that I could take it with another battalion but that we should lose heavily. The reply was to "come through at all costs"'.[21] He returned to inform his officers, many of whom were wounded: as one Volunteer noted, 'It was easy to see the officers with revolvers leading them on'.[22]

The battle eventually turned due to sheer weight of numbers—the 2/8th Battalion relieving the shattered 2/7th—and superior British fire-power (bolstered by the belated arrival of grenades and machine guns). The outpost at No. 25 fell at around 5 p.m., although the battle was sufficiently intense two hours later for the brigade to call for 'at least' another battalion to finish the job.[23] As increasing numbers of troops secured positions on the northern side of the canal, Clanwilliam House came under an unsustainable hail of fire. James Doyle (who had been knocked unconscious) awoke to find that his outpost, shredded by bullets, had become an inferno:

> I heard a terrible explosion and almost the whole ceiling in the room fell down and I could see very little with dust and smoke...We had to rely on our revolvers now as all the rifle ammunition was used...We went down the stairs...I saw Paddy Doyle and Dick Murphy lying dead. Murphy was still holding his rifle. Poor Reynolds was on the floor, in a pool of blood. Tom Walsh was lying beside him...I got a cup of water out of a basin, but it was dirty from falling plaster. I held it to his lips. He said 'God' and then said 'Mick, Mick'. I could never recall what happened after this, nor do I know how I got out of the house...I had an idea that the landing collapsed, or that a large wooden beam came down.[24]

As the battle ground to its grim conclusion, the Sherwood Foresters began to cheer and sing. They were joined by local residents, 'all of a good class', who had gathered to watch the battle. Another, more disturbing, sound emanated from the hundreds of wounded men lying around the bridge: 'a horrible sound—something between a "wail" and a "shout" '.[25] The smell of the burning corpses of dead Volunteers in Clanwilliam House added to the horrors of the scene. Over two hundred wounded or dead soldiers lay scattered 'along the Northumberland Road, on the house steps, in the channels, along the canal banks, and in Warrington Place'.[26] A youth who witnessed the scene recalled: 'The place was literally swimming with blood'.[27] Remarkably, seventeen men had held an army brigade for nine hours, at the cost of only five of the Third Battalion's Volunteers. Four British officers had been killed and another fourteen wounded, while 216 other ranks had been killed or wounded.[28] At least four residents— including the caretaker (and his wife) of a school mistaken for an outpost—had also been killed.

How can the carnage at Mount Street Bridge—which accounted for almost half the British army's total casualties in the Rising—be explained? The necessity for a frontal assault on such well-fortified positions seems inexplicable considering that two alternative routes into the city were known to be undefended. The shortage of grenades, ammunition, and Lewis guns (which had been left at Liverpool docks) gave the Volunteers an edge for much of the battle.[29] Although the Rising is sometimes characterized as a clash between spirited amateurs and trained professionals, the reality was rather different. As Capt. Arthur Lee observed: 'most of our "men" were merely boys, Derby Recruits, who had not been in uniform about 6 or 8 weeks. They had not passed their musketry course and many had never fired a rifle'.[30] 'The young Sherwoods that I had with me had never fired a service rifle before', complained Captain Gerrard, 'They were not even able to load them'.[31] This opinion was shared by some Volunteers who saw them in action: 'They were mostly lads...poorly trained'.[32] Another remarked of the soldiers generally: 'Most of them were young fellows who did not know one end of a rifle from the other as far as I could see'.[33] In contrast, despite the obvious limitations of their weaponry, the Northumberland Road Volunteers were reasonably well-trained, disciplined, and highly committed, while some, such as Malone and Grace, were excellent shots. The British army had little experience of street-fighting, whereas the Volunteers had at least studied and trained for it.

The tactics which led to the debacle at Mount Street Bridge have also been attributed to the influence of the Great War: the sight of waves of soldiers repeatedly charging towards well-fortified positions at the sound of an officer's whistle was undeniably reminiscent of the Western Front, as was the refusal of the army command to authorize anything other than a full frontal assault.[34] This stubbornness may have been influenced by professional pride (or frustration) at their failure to overcome a motley band of amateurs, but it also accorded with Lowe's previous instruction that all resistance be crushed before proceeding.

Although the battle for Mount Street Bridge appeared to justify the military council's optimism about the advantages enjoyed by a defensive force in an urban environment, it also exposed serious tactical shortcomings among the Third Battalion's leadership. Most notably, the seventeen Volunteers in the most effective outposts were not reinforced by de Valera despite ample requests and opportunity to do so.[35] As occurred elsewhere throughout the week, the vast bulk of Volunteers (garrisoned only hundreds of yards away in Boland's bakery) played no part in the fighting: indeed, men in one valuable outpost were ordered to withdraw while the battle was still raging.[36] With the exception of North King Street and Church Street (which formed part of the Four Courts garrison), the strategy of reinforcing numerous well-positioned small outposts which proved so effective at Mount Street was not successfully replicated elsewhere. Instead, most Volunteers remained inside their garrisons, unable to challenge the advance of British forces. The Mount Street rebels had also been fortunate because the Sherwood Foresters had lacked the heavy weapons necessary to overwhelm their fortified positions. The use of heavy machine guns, artillery, and improvised armoured trucks ensured that there would be no repetition of this in the fighting that followed. Indeed, given the difficulties facing the British army—the inexperience of its young soldiers, its ignorance of the strength and location of the rebels, and the novelty of street-fighting—its prompt suppression of the Rising has been judged an impressive achievement.[37]

It may have proven the most significant and deadly confrontation of the week but the battle of Mount Street did not set the pattern for the fighting that followed. None of the rebel garrisons would face a full-frontal assault; instead, they were individually isolated by military cordons, allowing the main body of soldiers to advance towards the GPO which was subjected to intense machine-gun and artillery fire. Consequently, relatively few rebels were engaged in direct combat. The most obvious example of this was provided by Jacob's factory which—virtually ignored by the British army—witnessed almost no fighting, but even the more effective garrisons did little to shape the battle for Dublin. 'During the whole of my time in the Four Courts', George O'Flanagan recalled, 'I never saw a single man of ours killed or wounded'.[38] (In contrast, the small outposts beyond the Four Courts were in the thick of the fighting.) Even in the GPO, there was little direct engagement with British forces. Like many Volunteers, Kevin McCabe spent much of the week in an outpost of the GPO 'waiting for something to happen. We did practically no shooting as there was no target'.[39] Only nine of the Post Office's garrison were killed in action, and most of these casualties resulted from the chaotic retreat on Friday.

Although there were dramatic close-quarter battles in some areas, particularly the South Dublin Union and the streets north of the Four Courts garrison, much of the fighting consisted of long-range sniping duels. As the military council had assumed, the rebels' defensive positions helped to even the odds against their better-armed and more numerous opponents. Soldiers had to advance through streets where they could be fired on from almost any angle. John Regan, a Royal Irish Regiment officer, noted the problems posed by snipers: 'Some we got on the roofs of houses, but those who fired from inside a room, over a blanket stretched across it and through a window from which the glass had been removed were nearly impossible to spot'.[40] Frequently, British soldiers opened up on each other in the ensuing confusion.

These difficulties partly compensated for the inadequacies of the rebels' weapons and ammunition. Many Volunteers were armed with 'Howth rifles', antiquated Mausers which, although reliable and accurate, 'had a kick like a mule and only fired one bullet before having to be reloaded'.[41] Robert Holland recalled, with some understatement, that 'it was a bad weapon for street fighting': 'Flame about three feet long came out through the barrel when it was fired and a shower of soot and smoke came back in one's face. After three shots were fired from it, it would have to be thrown away to let it cool and the concussion of it was so severe that it drove me back along the floor several feet'.[42] The Volunteers' medley of weapons—which included shotguns, revolvers, rook rifles, antique rifles, and modern rifles—required different types of ammunition and expertise. Joseph O'Connor, who fought in Boland's bakery, outlined the resulting problems:

In the whole garrison of, we'll say one hundred men, to the best of my belief there were not more than fifty rifles. A number of the rifles were

Martini-Henry, Mark 6 and Mark 7. They, with the ordinary Lee-Enfield, used .303 ammunition, but in the case of the Mark 6 and Mark 7 Martini they fired a different .303 type of cartridge. This caused us great confusion and we frequently had to stop to change the ammunition supplied to the men even in the hottest of corners. In addition, we had the Howth rifles which fire an altogether different ammunition, and then we had the shot-guns, the cartridge of which had been loaded with heavier shot... With this extra loaded shotgun ammunition used in these inferior shotguns they were positively dangerous.[43]

II

Historians have accused the rebels of seeking to provoke maximum blood-shed, and both sides accused the other of atrocities. How much evidence is there for these claims? In order to understand the rebels' attitudes to violence, it is important to understand how they perceived themselves as a military force. For the military council, the Rising was—above all else—an act of propaganda, intended to inspire the Irish people and win international support for their cause: consequently, a 'clean fight' was imperative. The Proclamation urged the rebels not to dishonour their cause 'by cowardice, inhumanity or rapine'. For Pearse, the behaviour of the rebels was as important as their achievements. 'The valour, self-sacrifice, and discipline of Irish men and women', he predicted, will 'win for our country a glorious place among the nations'.[44] The belief that they constituted a conventional army engaged in a legitimate form of warfare was crucial to the rebels. This was one reason for their enthusiasm for the trappings of militarism; the GPO's officers assigned themselves orderlies, aides-de-camp, and adjutants, ate in a commissariat, and reportedly even socialized in an officers' mess. The importance of conventional military behaviour was impressed on Volunteers. 'Wilful damage was as severely eschewed as indiscriminate shooting', Desmond Ryan stated, 'Orders were given that prisoners were to be treated courteously. No firing was to take place except under orders or to repel attack'.[45]

In general, the rebels attempted to live up to these standards. Policemen and unarmed soldiers were not systematically targeted, and Volunteers avoided unnecessary bloodshed. Father Curran noticed with surprise how a large group of DMP men stood at Nelson's Pillar throughout Monday afternoon, while the GPO garrison fired on British soldiers. He was struck also by the rebels' restraint in not shooting easy targets, such as a drunken unarmed soldier who stood 'eating something, in an act of bravado, right under where the Volunteers were firing'.[46] Father Flanagan observed how soldiers on leave stood around watching the fighting with their friends and family: 'Though in khaki, and well within the danger zone, they did not seem to fear being shot at by Volunteers'.[47] Some policemen also seemed remarkably complacent about their non-combatant status. One Volunteer recalled how a detective casually leaned over his barricade to ask him 'how long we thought we could hold out. I told Pearse about this and asked if we could shoot him. He said: "No, let him go" '.[48]

There were acts of chivalry on both sides. When a drunk or deranged soldier staggered into the lethal crossfire on Sackville Street—'I'm a bloody Dublin Fusilier. I don't give a damn about anyone'—a Volunteer 'with a white flag, went over to where he lay, knelt down, said a prayer over his body, and dragged him in to the side'.[49] Seán Nunan observed a similar act of kindness: 'Despite the fact that the street was swept by machine gun fire from the Parnell Street end, George Plunkett took a water-bottle from the man alongside me, crossed Moore Street, gave the soldier a drink, and then carried him back to our headquarters'.[50] Such chivalry was often reciprocated: some British officers allowed Volunteers to rescue their wounded and bring them to hospital. Harry Colley believed that his life was saved by the treatment he received from the Royal Army Medical Corps: 'We were well treated'.[51] The most unusual example of cooperation between both sides was the twice-daily ceasefire at St Stephen's Green that allowed the park-keeper to venture out to feed the ducks.[52]

But there were also less palatable occurrences: civilians, policemen, and unarmed soldiers were killed by rebels. Outside Jacob's, Volunteers killed an unarmed man (who they assumed was a policeman) because he refused to leave the area: 'one of our best shots was at the barricade and he opened fire and shot the man dead'.[53] Connolly's Citizen Army—many of whom regarded themselves as revolutionary socialists rather than romantic nationalists—were more ruthless than Volunteers when it came to shooting policemen. The acrimonious legacy of the Lockout may have played some role in this. Advising his men how to deal with policemen, Connolly—one ICA officer recalled—'left that question to our discretion with the words: "Remember how they treated you in 1913" '.[54] The same thought occurred to Patrick Kelly, a Volunteer behind the barricades at the Four Courts, when he found a policeman within his sights:

> I took steady aim at him and was about to press the trigger when Captain Laffan knocked up my rifle and asked what I was doing. I pointed to the policeman and said I was going to shoot him. He said, 'you can't do a thing like that, the man is unarmed'. I remarked that I was unarmed in 1913.[55]

Citizen Army members were involved in several dubious killings, particularly around St Stephen's Green. By his own admission, Frank Robbins was prevented from shooting hostile civilians, policemen, and unarmed soldiers by his officer (who also favoured shooting policemen but had been ordered by Thomas MacDonagh to avoid unnecessary bloodshed).[56] His comrade Jim O'Shea was even more trigger-happy: 'I was constantly using my rifle, firing down Dawson Street at any movement of cars'. O'Shea fired on a policeman (in retaliation for a sarcastic remark about playing soldiers), attempted to bayonet an abusive woman, and shot an unarmed British soldier who harangued him from the gates of the Green:

> He stopped directly in front of us and started to curse and swear about tin soldiers and told us if we were any good we would go and fight for our king and country...I then realised he was not drunk and was convinced he was spying...He called me a b[astard] and a lot of other names...He passed a remark about prostitutes fighting with us...He became worse so I picked up a shotgun and shot him at close quarters.[57]

Much of the criticism of the Rising, then and subsequently, was based on the perceived immorality of its violence. It was an issue that also troubled some of the leaders. Pearse and Plunkett debated whether their actions were ethical during the Rising, while the publication of MacNeill's moral objections to the insurrection in the early 1960s would come to form one of the first articles in the 'revisionist' controversy that dominated Irish historiography for several decades.[58] The debate over the ethics of the rebellion's violence was also influenced by the actions of anti-Treaty republicans during the Civil War who cited 1916 as a justification for their defiance of the majority, and consciously emulated the defensive military tactics of the rebels in the initial fighting in Dublin in June 1922 (with much the same results).

There is little evidence to suggest that ordinary Volunteers (who appear to have generally viewed themselves as soldiers following orders) were preoccupied by these issues although some did agonize about having to take a life. Thomas O'Donoghue, a founder of the Fianna who would later

1. Irish Volunteers return from Howth after landing a shipment of German rifles in July 1914. This propaganda coup resulted in a surge in Volunteer numbers.

2. 'We serve neither King nor Kaiser'. The Irish Citizen Army parade outside Liberty Hall, the labour movement headquarters subsequently destroyed by the shells of the *Helga*.

3. (*opposite*)Fianna boys practice first-aid. The formation of Na Fianna Éireann, a response to Baden Powell's scouting movement, anticipated the pre-war militarization of separatism.

4. (*above*) Cumann na mBan member Rose McNamara—one of around two hundred women who took part in the Rising despite the reservations of many male rebels—served in Marrowbone Lane Distillery.

5. Despite her ascendancy background, the flamboyant Countess Markievicz (1868-1927) was a leading separatist. Many prominent rebels made clear their revolutionary intentions in poems and plays in the years before 1916.

6. Tom Clarke (1858-1916). A veteran of the Fenians' 1883 dynamiting campaign, Clarke was central to the revival of the IRB and planning of the Rising after his return from imprisonment and exile in 1907.

7. Seán MacDermott (1883-1916). A former barman and tram conductor, the popular and charming revolutionary was the most active Fenian organizer in the years before the Rising.

8. Poet, cultural nationalist, educationalist and president of the Republic proclaimed on Easter Monday, Pearse would come to personify the idea of the Rising as an act of blood sacrifice.

POBLACHT NA H EIREANN.

THE PROVISIONAL GOVERNMENT

OF THE

IRISH REPUBLIC

TO THE PEOPLE OF IRELAND.

IRISHMEN AND IRISHWOMEN : In the name of God and of the dead generations from which she receives her old tradition of nationhood, Ireland, through us, summons her children to her flag and strikes for her freedom.

Having organised and trained her manhood through her secret revolutionary organisation, the Irish Republican Brotherhood, and through her open military organisations, the Irish Volunteers and the Irish Citizen Army, having patiently perfected her discipline, having resolutely waited for the right moment to reveal itself, she now seizes that moment, and, supported by her exiled children in America and by gallant allies in Europe, but relying in the first on her own strength, she strikes in full confidence of victory.

We declare the right of the people of Ireland to the ownership of Ireland, and to the unfettered control of Irish destinies, to be sovereign and indefeasible.   The long usurpation of that right by a foreign people and government has not extinguished the right, nor can it ever be extinguished except by the destruction of the Irish people.   In every generation the Irish people have asserted their right to national freedom and sovereignty ; six times during the past three hundred years they have asserted it in arms.   Standing on that fundamental right and again asserting it in arms in the face of the world, we hereby proclaim the Irish Republic as a Sovereign Independent State, and we pledge our lives and the lives of our comrades-in-arms to the cause of its freedom, of its welfare, and of its exaltation among the nations.

The Irish Republic is entitled to and hereby claims, the allegiance of every Irishman and Irishwoman.   The Republic guarantees religious and civil liberty, equal rights and equal opportunities to all its citizens, and declares its resolve to pursue the happiness and prosperity of the whole nation and of all its parts, cherishing all the children of the nation equally, and oblivious of the differences carefully fostered by an alien government, which have divided a minority from the majority in the past.

Until our arms have brought the opportune moment for the establishment of a permanent National Government, representative of the whole people of Ireland and elected by the suffrages of all her men and women, the Provisional Government, hereby constituted, will administer the civil and military affairs of the Republic in trust for the people.

We place the cause of the Irish Republic under the protection of the Most High God, Whose blessing we invoke upon our arms, and we pray that no one who serves that cause will dishonour it by cowardice, inhumanity, or rapine.   In this supreme hour the Irish nation must, by its valour and discipline and by the readiness of its children to sacrifice themselves for the common good, prove itself worthy of the august destiny to which it is called.

Signed on Behalf of the Provisional Government,

THOMAS J. CLARKE.
SEAN Mac DIARMADA,   THOMAS MacDONAGH.
P. H. PEARSE,   EAMONN CEANNT.
JAMES CONNOLLY.   JOSEPH PLUNKETT.

9. An inspirational call to arms, the Proclamation became the foundational text for the independent Irish state.

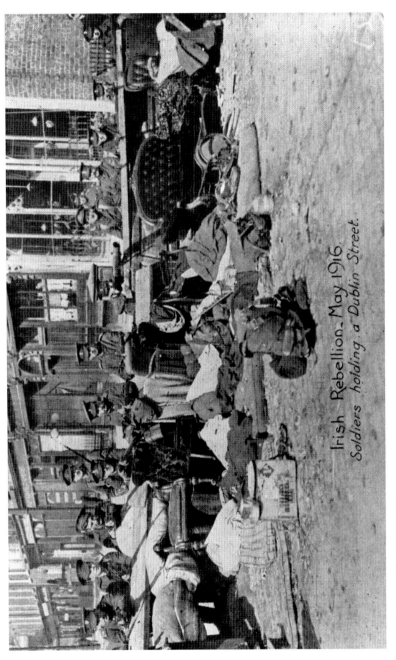

10. British army soldiers hold a Dublin street.

11. The occupation of the Shelbourne Hotel (which overlooked the rebel garrison in St Stephen's Green) by British soldiers forced the Volunteers to withdraw to the Royal College of Surgeons.

12. The British army's use of improvised armoured cars (manufactured from old boilers by workers at Guinness's) proved an effective street-fighting tactic.

13. The disruption to civilian life accounted for much of the public anger directed at rebels during Easter week.

14. The arrest of over three thousand suspected rebels in the wake of the Rising, including many innocent people, created immense logistical and political problems for the authorities.

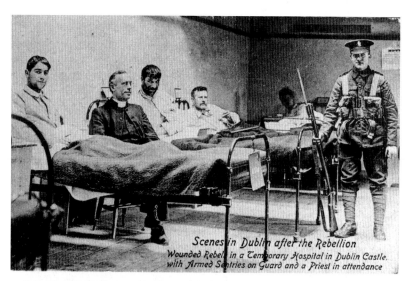

Scenes in Dublin after the Rebellion
Wounded Rebel in a Temporary Hospital in Dublin Castle.
with Armed Sentries on Guard and a Priest in attendance

15. Wounded rebels in a temporary hospital in Dublin Castle. Harry Colley attributed his survival to the treatment he received from the Royal Army Medical Corps.

16. Sackville Street between Abbey Street and North Earl Street. Many contemporaries compared the destruction to Ypres, images of which had dominated the press before the rebellion.

17. Abbey Street and Sackville Street. Nelson's Pillar survived the rebellion, despite British shelling and a rebel attempt to destroy it. It was blown up by the IRA to mark the fiftieth anniversary of the Rising.

18. Children search for firewood amidst the rubble. Children (and women) were prominent among the looters from the inner-city slums who contributed to the chaos of Easter week.

19. (*opposite*) Many individuals—including nurses, doctors, firemen, ambulance-drivers, priests, and civilian volunteers—risked their lives during the Rising.

20. Spectators view the destruction. During Easter week, rebels and soldiers had been unable to prevent sightseers from coming to watch the fighting unfold.

21. A new Ireland: despite being abused by many Dubliners when they surrendered, the rebels were greeted as heroes on their release from internment in 1917.

become a priest, 'felt bewildered at the prospect, because I had never taken part in any kind of a fight and always shuddered at hurting anybody'.[59] Some of their opponents felt much the same. Lieutenant Jameson, an officer in the Leinster Regiment, 'felt horrid' after killing his first rebel. But many found that after the initial shock of firing a rifle, or even shooting a man, it became routine, and even exhilarating. Jameson (who had to suppress an instinctive urge to 'apologise and help' his first victim) noted: 'I very soon got over that and was very annoyed when I missed anybody'.[60] Con O'Donovan experienced an ambivalent satisfaction on killing his enemy:

> We were really suffering from the strain of looking for a soldier to fire at, and I remember well the callous and, shall I say, brutal pleasure I felt when I 'picked off' one who was crossing Grattan Bridge, although he dodged from side to side, and kept his head low most of the time. Another who fell to one of our group was too easy a mark. He walked out of Chancery Street in full kit...Here was a soldier, armed and probably looking for a chance to fire on us. One bullet did it, and then the marksman raised his hat, and said, 'He's dead, or dying now, anyhow. May the Lord have mercy on him'.[61]

Although the rebels considered themselves chivalrous combatants, they were widely accused of atrocities by unionists and the British press. The most controversial incident was the shooting of seven members of the Volunteer Training Corps (a force of reservists popularly dubbed the 'Gorgeous Wrecks' due to their *Georgius Rex* armbands and mature profile) as they returned to Beggar's Bush barracks on Monday afternoon after a sham fight in the Dublin mountains. 'From our house in Northumberland Road', Áine O'Rahilly recalled, 'we saw everything...The poor old things were carrying their rifles, but we did not know they had no ammunition for them'.[62] Four of the men were killed. Jimmy Grace, like other Volunteers who participated in this attack, refused to accept that he had done anything wrong: 'the plea has been made that these Yeos were not armed and had no ammunition, but that is false'.[63] Some of the reservists appear to have been armed but none had apparently been issued with ammunition (although there is no reason why the Volunteers should have known this). But atrocity and murder are strong terms to describe the shooting of uniformed soldiers who were aware that an insurrection had occurred and were returning to their barracks under orders to assist in its defence.[64]

Another criticism levelled at the rebels concerned their use of dumdum (or expanding) bullets, which had been banned by international law. Lord Donoughmore, who was fired on when he drove too close to a barricade near St Stephen's Green, was convinced that his passengers were shot with dumdums, as were some of the doctors who treated the wounded.[65] After the surrender, some British soldiers were disgusted by the ammunition they discovered on rebels: 'An old sergeant roars out as he waves a Howth bullet in our faces that the British Army wasn't a herd of elephants'.[66] But the use of soft-nosed bullets was motivated by necessity rather than malice: some Volunteers had spent the weeks before the Rising paring down soft-nosed bullets into the conventional pencil shape. Another rebel, much to the amusement of his comrades, retorted to his arresting soldier: 'Well, you wouldn't let us get the right stuff'.[67]

The rebels were accused of abusing prisoners, as well as exploiting them—and civilians—as human shields. Large numbers of prisoners were taken; there were around thirty-five in the GPO, and another thirty in the Four Courts.[68] They were mainly policemen or soldiers who had been captured during the initial occupation of the garrisons or who later stumbled into them; it is less clear why other prisoners were taken. Laurence Kettle, a senior Dublin Corporation official, was held as an 'important prisoner' in the College of Surgeons on the dubious grounds that he was known to visit a military barracks (presumably to visit his brother Tom, a former Irish Party MP who had enlisted). Like many of the prisoners, he voluntarily helped the rebels, making barricades out of books from the well-stocked college library.[69] The GPO garrison was fortunate enough to seize an Indian army medical officer who cheerfully offered his expertise to his captors. More controversially, Tom MacDonagh sent armed men to force a doctor from the Adelaide hospital to come to Jacob's, while some Volunteers forced civilians to carry out dangerous tasks such as moving supplies or building barricades under fire.

The experiences of these prisoners varied widely. At one extreme, a Dublin Fusilier offered his services to the rebels in the GPO; he was assigned potato-peeling duties instead.[70] Some clearly enjoyed the experience but others were terrified: the first, disturbing, sight one Volunteer encountered in the GPO was a traumatized 'DMP man lying face downwards on the floor, resting on his arms and moving his head from side to side'.[71] The captured soldiers were generally stoical, even good-humoured, as a soldier on leave from the horrors of the Western Front might well be. In the GPO's kitchen, Michael Knightly observed, 'The soldiers were preparing tea and were as cheerful as if nothing out of the ordinary had taken place. I asked one of them if he thought the place would be stormed. "No", he said,

"I think it will be shelled"'.[72] This was the prevailing wisdom among the soldiers. Asked what the army would do, another captured officer replied: '"Oh", he said, "shell them out". He was good-natured and good-humoured about it and admitted that Britain was in an embarrassed position'.[73]

Prisoners endured minor indignities. The soldiers in the GPO were put to work with the women in the kitchen. Fifteen-year-old Vinny Byrne recalled how two policemen were placed under his authority at Boland's bakery: 'It must have been a strange sight indeed to see the two men, six-feet high, looking down on the young lad of about four feet who was guarding them'.[74] At Jacob's, two equally sturdy constables were escorted to the kitchen for potato-peeling duties by a diminutive Fianna boy armed with a double-barrelled shotgun: 'This daily parade as it passed brought smiles to the faces of many if not the prisoners'.[75] Some of the prisoners, however, were mistreated. One Volunteer filled a policeman's hat with bullets, 'saying he would like to put one of them through his head'.[76] Prisoners in the GPO, James Kavanagh recalled, were forced to carry bombs through the building while fires raged about them:

> The look of the RIC man was terrible at this time. His eyes were staring from his head, he was pale and terror-stricken. He was afraid of the bombs he was carrying. He was afraid to cross the courtyard with its rain of fire, but he was more afraid of the young Citizen Army man who was urging him on with a forty-five stuck in his back.[77]

In general, most prisoners were treated well. Considering he was shot without warning and almost bayoneted, Lord Dunsany, an officer in the Third Battalion of the Inniskilling Fusiliers, was unreserved in praise of his assailants.

> The man that took me prisoner, looking at the hole in my face made by one of the bullets, a ricochet, made a remark that people often consider funny, but it was quite simply said and sincerely meant: he said, 'I am sorry'. He led me back to the rest, and one of them came for me with his bayonet, now cleared of its scabbard; but the bullet having made my wits rather alert than otherwise I saw from his heroic attitude that there was no malice about him, but he merely thought that to bayonet me might be a fine thing to do. When the other man suggested, with little more than a shake of his head, that it was not, he gave up the idea altogether. 'Where's a doctor? Where's a doctor?' they shouted. 'Here's a man bleeding to death'....my chauffeur was allowed to go freely to a hospital, and I was sent, with a generosity for which I shall always be grateful, to the hospital in Jervis Street.[78]

The GPO's prisoners were placed under the protection of Michael O'Rahilly, who, Min Ryan testified, took his duties seriously: '"If it's the last bit of food in the place, it must be shared with the prisoners, and if any man does not follow my instructions he will get this"—and he pulled out a gun'.[79]

Two of the most controversial allegations—that prisoners were left 'to die like rats' in a cellar full of bombs and that they were used as a human shield during the evacuation—originate from the same dubious source: Lieutenant Chalmers.[80] In reality, the prisoners, as Joe Good insisted, appear to have been treated as reasonably as could be expected during the chaos of the evacuation:

> Our military prisoners whom we had captured during the week appeared terrified, as was only natural in the confusion. I suggested to O'Rahilly that they be let go and take their chance of escaping. It looked to me as if we were trapped. O'Rahilly misunderstood me at first, thinking I wanted to exploit the prisoners in some way and he almost struck me. Then he saw my point and apologised.[81]

One soldier was killed and another wounded as they ran into a hail of bullets, their army uniforms offering little protection in the smoke, confusion, and darkness of the retreat. The refusal of many prisoners to identify their captors after the surrender suggests that they were satisfied with their treatment, even if fear rather than gratitude may have influenced some. When Ned Daly released a large contingent of DMP men from the Four Courts 'his last words to them were "Forget all you have seen" and this met with a chorus of "Yes, sir, we will"', one Volunteer officer recalled. 'Apparently, they thought at first he was going to shoot them and were surprised to get away so easily'.[82] Some captives—including Lord Dunsany—even helped rebels to escape after the surrender.

The most serious charge was that the rebels deliberately targeted civilians. One Dublin surgeon claimed that 'the Sinn Feiners have been sniping at all and sundry, regardless of persons or sex', an allegation endorsed by numerous (usually unionist) eyewitnesses.[83] 'There was absolutely no safety anywhere from the snipers', Louisa Norway wrote in a letter to her family, 'man, woman or child, nothing came amiss to them. It was dastardly fighting, if it could be called fighting at all'.[84] 'In Merion Square', another woman claimed, 'the Sinn Feiners were in most of the houses potting from the roofs and from the windows, with crowds looking on. A boy of twelve was brought in to the hospital, shot through the stomach while he was giving a wounded soldier a drink—the doctor says he will recover'.[85] The rebels were also criticized for firing from hidden positions. Two feisty 'ladies of the Vigilance Committee' who came upon a wounded soldier while on night patrol 'walked up to the railings of St Stephen's Green and gave the Sinn Féiners a regular dressing down, telling them they were skunks and cowards to shoot people down from behind bushes and asking them why they did not come out and fight in the open like men'.[86] Conversely, the rebels confidently attributed the shooting of civilians to the British army. The reality, as an incident witnessed by James Kavanagh suggests, must often have been less clear-cut: 'On one of my journeys when returning to the Post Office I was halfway across the metal bridge when I saw two people, a man and woman, fall shot dead at the corner of Liffey Street and Bachelor's Walk. I don't know where the shots came from'.[87]

It is not possible to be certain why some people were shot, or by whom, but the rebels had no reason to shoot civilians unless they appeared to be hostile, even if there can be no doubt that frightened or curious civilians were killed by the rebels for acting suspiciously. In contrast, as some unionists acknowledged, the British army had a pretty good reason to shoot civilians: 'it was impossible to tell friend from foe, and, as the Sinn Feiners wore no uniform, many innocent and loyal people suffered…it was safer to shoot at sight, as any loafing idler might pull a revolver from his pocket and shoot'.[88] Louisa Norway had assumed that her hotel was under attack from a 'very active' sniper until discovering that it was routinely being fired on by passing military patrols: 'People were constantly pulling up their blinds for a moment with the lights on to look at the city on fire, and the military have orders to fire on anything that resembles signalling without asking questions'.[89]

Both sides shot people who did not obey their orders, particularly drivers who failed to halt at barricades. Even uniformed officers found driving through their own lines a hair-raising experience due to the British army's 'excessive vigilance'.[90] Sir Horace Plunkett's car was riddled with bullets by soldiers 'having so lost their heads after a night of sniping that they expected me to hear them say "Halt" at 100 yards and opened fire on me at about ninety yards, firing at myself and another old gentleman sitting beside me with our hands up'. Plunkett was unharmed, but the driver behind him was seriously wounded.[91] Lord Dunsany encountered much the same response at a rebel barricade:

> They stood up from behind the barrels with their rifles already at their shoulders, with the bayonets fixed and the scabbards still on the bayonets, and as soon as they were standing they began to fire. We had stopped the car and were forty yards away, and they were standing shoulder to shoulder all the way across the broad street. Though Dublin must have been echoing to those volleys, to us they were firing in complete silence, for the crash of bullets going through the air drowns all other sounds when they are close enough. We saw the men's shoulders jerked back by the recoil of their rifles, but heard no sound from them except the tinkling of their empty cartridges as they fell in the road. I got out and lay down in the road, and many bullets went by me before I was hit. My chauffeur, Frederick Cudlipp, was shot at the wheel, but not fatally.[92]

The claim that the rebels deliberately targeted civilians is unconvincing. It seems more likely that most civilian casualties were caused by the British army, not only due to its inability to discern rebels from civilians but also as a result of the difficulties of street-fighting and its use of artillery, incendiary shells, and heavy machine guns. John Regan, a Royal Irish Regiment officer, reported that the English troops 'had a gruelling time coming into Dublin and did not know friend from foe. They regarded, not unreasonably, everyone they saw as an enemy, and fired at anything that moved'.[93] Captain Gerrard described one such appalling incident: 'One of my sentries in Beggars Bush Barracks, about Tuesday evening, said to me, "I beg your pardon sir, I have just shot two girls." I said, "What on earth did you do that for?" He said, "I thought they were rebels. I was told they were dressed in all classes of attire"'.[94] Many civilians were killed simply for being in the wrong place. Ernest Cavanagh, a political cartoonist, was 'riddled with bullets fired by soldiers in the Customs House' as he entered an empty Liberty Hall.[95] Curiosity or carelessness killed others. Thirteen-year-old Margaret Veale was killed because she used binoculars to look out of the window of her Haddington Road house.[96] Teenager Dominic O'Donoghue was shot by a sniper because he climbed a clock tower in the North Dublin Union to observe the fires in the city centre. Looters and drunks were also shot.

The rebels, for their part, accused the British army of atrocities. Pearse condemned British troops for 'firing on our women and on our Red Cross'.[97] Volunteers cited numerous examples of their opponents breaking 'the rules of war': snipers dressed in women's clothing; soldiers who fired from hospitals and church towers; ambulances that ferried soldiers, weapons, and despatches through the city; and officers who ignored Red Cross flags over buildings. Some British army officers believed that the rebels were not entitled to the same treatment as a conventional military force. When Father Augustine asked an officer not to shell a hall on Church Street which was being used as a makeshift hospital he was told: 'we were all rebels and outlaws and that we would get none of the ameni-ties of war'. The officer reconsidered when he was informed that there were also wounded soldiers inside.[98] Albert Mitchell, a Protestant busi-nessman who drove a Red Cross ambulance during Easter week, claimed that he was prevented from taking Michael O'Rahilly (who he found lying wounded in a gutter in Moore Lane) to hospital: 'When back in the lorry, I asked the sergeant what was the idea? His answer was—"he must be someone of importance and the bastards are leaving him there to die of his wounds—it is the easiest way to get rid of him"'.[99]

Allegations of drunkenness, looting, and brutality by soldiers were widespread. Robert Barton (who claimed that his fellow soldiers routinely robbed their prisoners) was told that the War Office was greatly concerned by the extensive looting, 'an offence for which they would have been shot if they were in France'.[100] Albert Mitchell kept the personal possessions of the corpses he collected for safekeeping on the assumption that they 'would be seized by the first soldier who got an opportunity'.[101] In Dublin Castle, John Regan was shocked by the heavy drinking of some officers and privates during the week: 'I do not think I ever saw a larger collection of empty bottles than that stacked in their common room. The senior officer was very drunk indeed'.[102] Patrick Bermingham, a DMP constable, arrested a soldier 'who was very much intoxicated firing indiscriminately in the air and at windows and doors'.[103] George Duggan, the manager of the Provin-cial Bank at College Green, was fortunate to escape with his life during an encounter with a drunken sergeant as his son related:

> On Wednesday afternoon, there was a ring at the Bank House door in College Street. My father opened it, and a very young subaltern, a sergeant (the worse for drink) and a number of British soldiers entered and began to search the house, insisting that sniping was going on from the building...The sergeant became truculent, threatened that he would shoot my father out of hand as being in league with the rebels, and ordered him down to the base-ment...where he proposed that the shooting would take place. On the way down, my father appealed to the subaltern to exercise his authority and not allow an innocent person to be shot...When they reached the second floor, my father took him into the drawing-room and showed him the photographs

of my two brothers in uniform, one a Captain in the Royal Irish Fusiliers, the other a Lieutenant in the Royal Irish Regiment, who were killed in August, 1915, at Suvla Bay... This convinced the subaltern of the truth of my father's assertions and he ordered the party to leave the Bank.[104]

Given that Duggan's wealthy, Protestant, and loyal background failed to protect him from such a terrifying ordeal, it is not surprising that the corpses of innocent Catholic civilians were found in basements in at least one working-class district of Dublin. Volunteers Jimmy Grace and Dan McCarthy claimed that they were saved from summary execution by the intervention of army officers.[105] Patrick Colgan escaped a similar fate when he was captured near the GPO:

> I was taken by a little brat of a 2nd Lieutenant of the Royal Irish Regiment who kept prodding me with his revolver and telling me what a pleasure he would have in killing me...We were put up against the front of a house beside the barricade...He ordered the soldiers to kneel on one knee; the soldiers had levelled their rifles at us. Then a voice above and behind us spoke and enquired what was happening. The brat said he was going to shoot us swine. The voice said he was an Irishman, he was against us, we had fought a clean fight and if the officer gave the order to fire he would fire on him... The voice reminded the brat that only for the rebellion they would be in France and he wouldn't like it if taken prisoner to be shot out of hand.[106]

The two most notorious atrocities of Easter week were committed by the British army. Three men were murdered in Portobello Barracks on Wednesday morning by a firing squad acting under orders from Capt. J. C. Bowen-Colthurst, an Anglo-Irish officer in the Royal Irish Regiment, who was judged to have lost his mind by a subsequent military inquiry. Of the three victims, only Francis Sheehy Skeffington is now remembered, partly because he was a well-known and eccentric pacifist from a prominent family (who had spent the first days of the Rising trying to raise a civil force to prevent looting), and partly because the other two victims—Thomas Dickson and Patrick MacIntyre (editors, respectively of *The Eye Opener* and *The Searchlight*)—were considered 'very unsavoury' characters due to their involvement in scurrilous, strike-breaking journalism.[107] As so often occurs, the subsequent scandal was a consequence not only of the murders, appalling though they were, but the way in which the deranged behaviour of Bowen-Colthurst (who had murdered a teenage boy in front of forty soldiers during a rampage through Portobello the previous evening) was initially ignored and then covered up.[108]

The killing of fifteen people in a short stretch of North King Street raised similar concerns. A military court of inquiry, which judged 'the South Staffords a quiet and respectable set of men', and concluded that responsibility could not be attached to individual soldiers (due to a lack of witnesses), was widely if somewhat unfairly considered a whitewash. A confidential assessment of its findings, commissioned for the Prime Minister, attributed many of the deaths to the fact that the soldiers 'had orders not to take any prisoners, which they took to mean that they were to shoot anyone whom they believed to be an active rebel'.[109] Much of the public outrage, however, concerned the fact that the killings were believed to have occurred not in the heat of battle but in a systematic follow-up operation supervised by officers.[110] Embarrassingly, the city coroner's inquest into two of the victims, who had been hastily buried in a shallow grave in the cellar of 177 North King Street, found that they were 'unarmed and unoffending' residents who had been killed by soldiers.[111]

Why, contrary to the impression created by contemporary press reports, were British troops involved in more atrocities than the rebels? Although many soldiers behaved professionally, there were vastly more of them— some twenty thousand—and they were both more mobile and spread over a much greater area than the rebels. Many were Derby recruits with less than two months' training. They lacked the rebels' idealism, and were understandably bewildered by the task of having to suppress a rebellion in a major city of the United Kingdom. The confusion and frustration of street-fighting was also to blame for lapses in discipline. Rebels might surrender in one outpost, only for their comrades to fire on soldiers from another house further up the street.[112] As General Maxwell, in a surprisingly candid press interview, explained:

> These rebels wore no uniform, and the man who was shooting at a soldier one minute might, for all he knew, be walking quietly beside him in the street at another...Nearly everything had to be left to the troops on the spot. Possibly unfortunate incidents, which we should regret, may have occurred...but how were the soldiers to discriminate? They saw their comrades killed beside them by hidden and treacherous assailants, and it is even possible that under the horrors of this peculiar attack some of them 'saw red'. That is the inevitable consequence of a rebellion of this kind.[113]

It was perhaps no coincidence that the regiment responsible for the North King Street massacre had witnessed the carnage at Mount Street Bridge.[114]

The fact that many of the civilians, who had failed to evacuate North King Street before the fighting began, appear to have been sympathetic to the rebels may also have been a factor. Moreover, in those areas where British soldiers encountered stiff resistance (fourteen soldiers were killed and another thirty-three wounded in a twenty-eight-hour battle for 150 yards of North King Street), the troops appear to have regarded anyone in the area as legitimate targets.[115]

Whatever the circumstances, much of the moral responsibility for the civilian deaths must be attributed to the military council's decision to base the insurrection in the densely populated inner city, a decision which conflicted with their perception of themselves as a conventional military force fighting by conventional means. Some 2,600 people were wounded during the Rising, and another 450 were killed. Civilians constituted over half the total number of these fatalities; British combatants accounted for less than one-third, and rebels (including those subsequently executed) less than one-fifth.[116] It remains difficult to understand why it was considered acceptable to locate a garrison in the South Dublin Union, the largest poorhouse in the country which housed over three thousand sick and destitute inmates, when other locations would have served equally well. Volunteers also occupied convents, hospitals, and houses. That they were often polite about it was of little consolation to those whose families, homes, or livelihoods were destroyed. The Volunteers who occupied Clanwilliam House were forbidden to break through the walls or smash the windows as their officer had rashly 'promised to hand back the house the way we had got it'. They left behind a smouldering shell. Patrick Colgan awoke in his outpost to find 'a middle-aged woman was whacking me with an umbrella...Her premises, which she valued at £5,000 had been destroyed'.[117] Some Volunteers were reckless with lives as well as property. Seán Cody recounted how he entered a large inhabited house overlooking Broadstone station to fire on British soldiers: 'There was no replying fire until I was back on the street below again when the whole house was peppered with rifle fire. I got back safely to my unit and on my way back could see British soldiers from the Broadstone taking up positions on the bridge in front of the building'.[118] Against this, the decision to fight in the city made undeniable military sense, and the reaction of the leaders to the plight of civilians when they finally witnessed it at first hand after their evacuation from the GPO suggests a shocking lack of foresight rather than a cynical intention to wreak havoc on Dublin's civilian population.

III

By the latter part of the week, the pressure on the rebels had mounted to barely tolerable levels: exhaustion, the constant fear of attack, lack of information, the fearsome noise and impact of artillery creeping closer, and the inferno raging through the centre of the city took an increasing toll on morale. Food supplies became a pressing issue. Volunteers who, several decades later, could recall little else about the Rising remembered what they ate, or went without, that week. Some, such as Mary McLoughlin who 'saw a whole salmon cooked laid on a dish' for the first time, remembered the culinary highlights.[119] Captain Lindsay, an officer of the Inniskilling Fusiliers imprisoned in the Four Courts, claimed 'the curious hardship of subsisting for the best part of the week on sherry, champagne, port, claret, and Benedictine; for food was very scarce and the cellars were well stocked'.[120] Others fared less well. Liam Tannam's final meal of the rebellion was 'a raw egg and a square of Chivers Jelly'.[121] By the end of the Rising, the rebels in the College of Surgeons were debating whether to eat the horses in a nearby stable. The occupation of Jacob's—a biscuit factory—initially proved something of a treat for younger Volunteers. Teenager Vinny Byrne had 'a great time eating plenty of cocoa chocolate and biscuits galore'; 'we gorged ourselves', another youth cheerfully recalled.[122] However, after several days of a diet of biscuit ingredients—including unlimited supplies of figs for the company's celebrated fig rolls—most 'would have given a lot for an ordinary piece of bread'.[123] One of the few victims of the Rising in Jacob's was the young Fianna boy who downed a large cake with such 'remarkable speed' that he was incapacitated by the 'dire results': he bravely refused to go home.[124]

Food was plentiful in the GPO early in the week—'I can still see the vision of the big sides of beef going into the ovens for their lunches'—although some of the men received little from the outset.[125] The garrison at Boland's bakery had, unsurprisingly, ample supplies of bread, supplemented by margarine, Oxo cubes, tinned coffee, and tea. However, because much of the garrison was exposed to sniper fire 'the real trouble was in getting the food distributed to the posts'.[126] The Four Courts garrison was well supplied with tinned food, fresh meat, and the ubiquitous Oxo cube (a recent invention of the food industry) and supplied with bread from Monks' bakery. The master of the North Dublin Union and the nuns of St John's Convent also supplied the Four Courts with ten-gallon cans of hot soup nightly. Most garrisons were situated close to grocery shops from which supplies could be requisitioned. Volunteers were also supplied with food parcels by friends and family. At Clanwilliam House, James Walsh's brother arrived with a parcel which was tied to a rope and hauled into the building: 'The parcel contained steak (hot), bread, butter, etc., also a note telling us how proud they, at home, were of the news from all parts of Dublin, and not to be worrying about them'.[127]

The outposts in the vicinity of the South Dublin Union were the worst supplied: 'dying of hunger', Con Colbert's men were forced to withdraw from the Ardee Street distillery.[128] At Marrowbone Lane Distillery, hunger proved such a problem that Volunteers had to be prevented from eating roasted malt. The enterprising rebels resolved the crisis by posting Tom Young as a lookout on the first floor of the building to signal whenever supplies were passing:

> I signalled that there were three cattle being driven along Marrowbone Lane towards Cork Street. Ned Neill opened the gates and drove the cattle through them. He closed the gates. In a few moments the owner of the cattle came along and stood in consternation. I asked him what his trouble was, and he replied by asking me had I seen three heifers. I, of course, assured him that no cattle had passed that way.

They also intercepted a bicycle messenger with a basket of trussed chickens destined for the Viceregal Lodge: 'Ned Neill took the basket of chickens off the bicycle and told the boy to give the Lord Lieutenant Ned Neill's compliments. The boy's reply was: "For [fuck's] sake, Mister, take the [fucking] bicycle as well." '[129] Rose McNamara's diary indicates that the Volunteers of Marrowbone Lane Distillery became proficient highway robbers, commandeering one bread van, two vats of milk, twenty-eight chickens, three cows ('God forgive us'), and 'a load of cabbage'.[130]

But even in the well-stocked GPO, many were experiencing real hunger by the end of the week. 'The only thing I remember getting the whole week was a ration of two thin slices of dry bread and a quarter of a mess tin of vegetable soup made from powder', one Volunteer complained: 'One small packet of this powder was put into a mess tin of hot water and was divided between four men'.[131] By Thursday, Desmond FitzGerald was refusing food to men who had not eaten for two days: 'He gave me a bucket filled with tea and two or three old empty salmon tins to drink from', Patrick Colgan recalled, 'the nice strong tea had been given us in a bucket which contained Jeyes Fluid'.[132] On Thursday evening Séamus Robinson, who hadn't eaten since Tuesday, 'was told that it was past tea time and that was that'.[133] Many Volunteers blamed FitzGerald, a future government minister, who was probably the most unpopular man in the garrison: 'we thought him very niggardly in dishing out the grub. He was evidently expecting a long sojourn in the GPO'.[134] Even the members of the provisional government had to wait until he was out of sight before helping themselves to a last meal of mutton chops, tinned peas, and pears. Cumann na mBan members, who had to make dangerous journeys from their outposts, were outraged by his insistence that they return to the GPO with written orders before they could receive rations.[135] FitzGerald, Liam Tannam recalled, 'was heartily cursed in every jail in England where men were confined when, starving with hunger, they thought of the food they had left behind them in the GPO. I myself even dreamt of it'.[136]

Lack of sleep, combined with hunger, led to debilitating exhaustion. Many Volunteers claimed to have slept only once or twice during the week and some not at all: 'I never slept one single hour of that week. Once the first two days passed I never thought of sleep, just lived without sleep and never thought of it'.[137] Deprived of sleep, the week seemed 'like one long day' to Tom Harris.[138] Séamus Robinson did not sleep between Monday and Thursday: 'I felt overpowered...I had to keep knocking my knuckles against a granite stone window-sill to keep awake...my head was swimming'.[139] In the smaller outposts 'you just slept at your post when you got a chance' and, on occasion, the entire staff of outposts fell 'asleep on their feet' despite the obvious dangers.[140] By the final days of the Rising, considerable numbers of Volunteers were unable to remain awake, let alone fight.

The response of the Volunteers' untested leaders to these extreme conditions varied widely. Some—such as Eamon Ceannt, Cathal Brugha, and Con Colbert, all of the South Dublin Union garrison—demonstrated remarkable resilience and courage. Others were less impressive. Two battalion commandants—de Valera and MacDonagh—appeared unable to cope with the pressure. At one point de Valera—who issued contradictory and bizarre orders during the final four days of the insurrection—appears to have been temporarily relieved of his command (although the precise circumstances remain disputed).[141] Exhausted, disoriented, or traumatized Volunteers fell victim to paranoia and hysteria, and desertions occurred on both sides. At Boland's, where one deranged Volunteer was shot by his own men after killing one of his officers, George Lyons glumly recalled the paranoid atmosphere: 'Everyone seemed to be thinking in terms of sanity and insanity'.[142] British soldiers, just as young and inexperienced, endured similar trials. One of the worst incidents occurred in Guinness's Brewery where Sgt. Robert Flood of the Royal Dublin Fusiliers succumbed to paranoia, killing two nightwatchmen and two of his lieutenants.[143]

The pressure on the rebels was intensified by the artillery bombardment which began on Wednesday. At 8 a.m., on 'a lovely sunning morning', Volunteers woke to the sound of a British vessel, the *Helga*, shelling Liberty Hall (possibly for symbolic reasons as the trade union headquarters was empty). Four eighteen-pounder field guns joined in from Trinity College, reducing the building to a shell. After two days of relative inactivity, the GPO now took on a siege atmosphere as Sackville Street and the surrounding area emptied, save for the soldiers massing at either end of the street. Messengers were still able to move between garrisons but only at much greater risk. The centre of Sackville Street was effectively turned into a no-man's land by machine-gun fire, rendering the GPO's contact with the outposts opposite increasingly hazardous. Sniping between Volunteers on the roof of the GPO and encroaching British soldiers intensified. Connolly, who continued to believe that the British authorities would baulk at flattening 'the second city of the empire', continued to deploy men in the buildings around the GPO in expectation of an infantry assault. Elsewhere, Jacob's and the South Dublin Union remained relatively quiet: 'Wednesday was the day of calm before the storm'.[144] The Four Courts came under attack from Wednesday, but remained in a strong enough position to occupy the nearby Linenhall Barracks (capturing forty unarmed members of the Army Pay Corps) and burn it to the ground. But Wednesday also brought the surrender of the first substantial outpost, the Mendicity Institute: 'the place was just plastered with machine gun and rifle fire and we seemed to be surrounded as we were being fired on from all sides'.[145]

On Thursday, under 'a burning sun glowing in a cloudless blue sky', the bombardment grew more intense. 'I don't know what others felt', Bridget Foley stated, 'but I was terrified'.[146] Pearse responded with another optimistic address, claiming that the rebel garrisons remained intact, the country was rising, and that the men of Wexford were marching on Dublin.

Privately, the leaders were aware that the end was approaching, as Connolly's refusal of an offer of help from a volunteer who presented himself at the GPO indicated: 'Too late now, man; it's a hopeless case'.[147] As the shelling of the southern end of Sackville Street intensified, the surrounding rebel outposts were gradually withdrawn. The GPO's first serious casualties occurred, most notably Connolly himself who was put out of action by a serious leg wound. Late on Thursday afternoon, the GPO came under direct artillery fire. 'They were shrapnel shells', Oscar Traynor recalled, 'and the amazing thing was that instead of bullets coming in it was molten lead, actually molten, which streamed about on the ground when it fell'.[148] By Thursday night the GPO and the other rebel garrisons, surrounded by constricting military cordons, could do little more than prepare for the end, but only the South Dublin Union had yet seen significant combat. On Thursday, 'this most terrible night', the bombardment intensified; it was, for Molly Reynolds, 'beyond description'.[149]

Throughout all this period, the rebels expected the final assault to occur at any moment: 'The ever-lasting wait for the unexpected is terribly nerve-wracking'. Sensing the growing despondency in the GPO, Michael O'Rahilly urged the Volunteers to sing *The Soldier's Song*. Morale appears to have remained reasonably firm, with many Volunteers fatalistic about what lay ahead; 'The future was often discussed by us and what would be the outcome of it all; there were no regrets or complaints for what we had started'.[150] Louise Gavan Duffy assumed 'we were going to stay in the building until we died'.[151] Desmond Ryan anticipated a glorious last stand of the sort his former headmaster at St Enda's would have approved:

> Fire and death and the beginning of the end but we have lost all fears and cares. The noble side of war appeared. The great strength and goodness of Ireland shone vividly before me. And a deep respect and admiration surged up in me for these men and women in this doomed building...I felt we were in for a jolly death.[152]

Ryan's desire for a glorious demise was dashed by the inferno which would consume the GPO—and much of Sackville Street—within a day. Aside from unnerving the Volunteers, and forcing the evacuation of the roof, the shelling on Thursday afternoon had inflicted little real damage on the GPO. The incendiary shells which rained down on Sackville Street that night would prove more devastating. Volunteers watched from the GPO as an awesome firestorm swept the opposite side of the street:

> The interior of our room is as bright as day with the lurid glow of the flames. Reis's jewellery shop is a mass of leaping scarlet tongues of light. Behind it huge mountains of billowing jet black smoke are rolling up into the heavens. A roaring as of a gigantic waterfall re-echoes from the walls...Suddenly some oil works near Abbey Street is singed by the conflagration, and immediately a solid sheet of blinding, death-white flame rushes hundreds of feet into the air with a thunderous explosion that shakes the walls. It is followed by a heavy bombardment as hundreds of drums of oil explode. The intense light compels one to close the eyes...The whole thing seems too terrible to be real.[153]

The overnight destruction of the finest street in Ireland produced 'a sublime and appalling spectacle' which riveted people throughout the city and beyond. 'It was the most awe-inspiring sight I have ever seen', Louisa Norway wrote to her sister:

> It seemed as if the whole city was on fire, the glow extending right across the heavens, and the red glare hundreds of feet high, while above the roar of the fires the whole air seemed vibrating with the noise of the great guns and machine-guns. It was an inferno! We remained spell-bound, and I can't tell you how I longed for you to see it.[154]

Many people grasped that something more than shops and offices had gone up in flames. 'It is the most impressive sight I have ever witnessed', an English clergyman wrote, 'because I know that it means so much more than the burning of a city—it means the ruin of a cause, the grave of a hope, the dissipation, perhaps for many years, of a great political dream'.[155]

The Volunteers witnessed beautiful and terrifying sights. Oscar Traynor watched the 'huge plate-glass windows of Clery's stores run molten'.[156] Patrick Colgan remembered 'globular fire balls rising into the skies and dying out' above Hoyte's (a pharmaceutical and oil warehouse), and the 'flames licking up the glass tower' over the DBC restaurant, 'the tower twisting and bending and finally collapsing'.[157] Horses ran wild through the streets as the opposite block became 'one huge leaping flame'.[158] Volunteers were forced to run through machine-gun fire as they fled their burning outposts: 'they wrapped themselves round with big mattresses and ran across the street'.[159] Inside the GPO, the heat 'was so intense that in spite of playing hoses on the barricades of mail bags they were continually

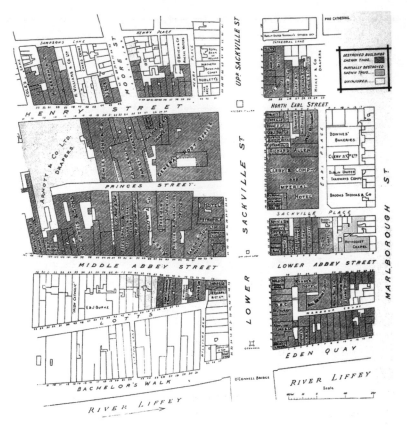

Destroyed buildings in GPO area (issued by Hibernian Fire and General Insurance Company)

bursting into flames'.[160] Volunteers responded to the inferno in different ways. Kevin McCabe called the fire brigade: 'I was answered, rather to my surprise...and was then told they intended to let us burn out'.[161]

The awesome scale of the destruction brought home to the rebels the gravity of what they had done: 'This will have a terrible effect upon the country'.[162] The sight 'unnerved a great number of the men' in Boland's bakery: 'One officer particularly, his nerves completely shattered, lost his head and fired at a Volunteer who was standing near me'.[163] In contrast John MacDonagh recalled that, in Jacob's, the fires 'heartened us, for it showed the magnitude of the Rising, which we knew would change the whole position of Ireland'.[164] Even Pearse, Desmond Ryan related, seemed overwhelmed by the spectacle:

> I stood beside him as he sat on a barrel looking intently at the flames, his slightly flushed face crowned with his turned-up hat. He suddenly turned to me with the question: 'It was the right thing to do, wasn't it?' 'Yes', I replied in astonishment...'When we are all wiped out, people will blame us for everything. But for this, the war would have ended and nothing would have been done. After a few years they will see the meaning of what we tried to do...Dublin's name will be glorious forever', he said with deep passion and enthusiasm. 'Men will speak of her as one of the splendid cities, as they speak now of Paris!'[165]

Pearse, who had long anticipated a glorious death in battle, was perhaps more sanguine than most of his comrades. Desmond FitzGerald observed 'a marked collapse in the general optimism' of the garrison after the fires caught hold: 'They felt, as we did, that these fires were the beginning of the end'.[166] Ryan also felt that the mood in the GPO had darkened: 'Connolly wounded, P.H.P.'s address to us, the news we heard from a visitor of the despondence in the city as well as the news that the country has not risen. We are in the middle of a circle of fire'.

IV

The rebels were not the only ones within the circle of fire. Most accounts of the rebellion focus on the combatants: how did ordinary Dubliners experience Easter week? Boredom, rather than fear, was a surprisingly common complaint from many people, including St John Greer Ervine:

> If this was war, we thought to ourselves, then war is an uncommonly dull business. We became bored by bullets. When the surprise of the rebellion was over, most of us became irritable. We could not get about our ordinary affairs, we could not take our customary pleasures, and the rebellion itself had become flat.[167]

Louise Norway similarly observed that 'the noise of battle after the first two days seemed to produce nothing but boredom'.[168]

Despite the danger, many people continued to ignore the official procla- mations instructing them to remain indoors. Describing the 'terrible sights',

Elsie Mahaffy (the daughter of the Provost of Trinity College) felt herself 'drawn towards' the violence.[169] 'The overmastering desire to see what was happening will draw the most craven to the scene of disaster', Ervine observed, 'people went every day to "see the fighting" in Dublin'.[170] He was surprised that several days into the rebellion some people continued to walk into the city centre to get to work despite the potential consequences:

> I heard the sound of heavy boots on the pavement below, echoing oddly in that silence; and then I heard shots, followed by a low moan...I stood there counting the dying man's moans. He said, 'Oh!' four times, and then he died...Just off the pavement, in front of the door of my home, lay the body of an old man, a labourer, evidently, who had been stumping to his work.[171]

The staff of essential services, such as fire brigades and ambulances, remained at work despite being fired on by both sides. They were assisted by civilian volunteers who carried stretchers, drove ambulances, collected the wounded, and buried the dead. Some, such as Louisa Norway's son Nevil (a popular novelist in later life), enjoyed the drama: 'This week has been a wonderful week for N. Never before has a boy of seventeen had such an experience'.[172] But much of the work was grisly. Albert Mitchell, who collected the dead from hospital and morgues, estimated that he 'buried over 200 bodies of civilians and Irish soldiers, also some English soldiers in Deans Grange'.[173] Despite his efforts, corpses lay scattered throughout the city, covered over with sacks, decomposing in the unseasonable warmth. Volunteers and civilians alike burned in the buildings where they were killed; all that was found of those who fell in Clanwilliam House was a single charred leg.[174] The dead were buried in gardens (even in Dublin Castle), yards, or wherever a hole could be dug, and many corpses were never afterwards recovered despite the efforts of family members. The streets were littered with the bodies of animals, including curiously large numbers of cats and dogs. The sight and smell of a dead horse decomposing on a pavement opposite St Stephen's Green brought home the strange transformation of the city and the absence of law and order to many of those who passed by: 'People came to one and said, "Have you seen the dead horse?" In whatever way conversation began, always it seemed to end with that question, "Have you seen the dead horse?"'.[175]

The doctors and surgeons of the hospitals located near the fighting worked through the most difficult conditions, treating civilians and combatants alike. Surgeon Alexander Blayney did not leave the Mater

Hospital all week: 'He was operating day and night. There was neither gas nor electricity and he had to operate by the light of candles brought from the sacristy. There was no sterilisation of instruments or dressings as there was no boiling water at hand'.[176] The wounded, one nun recounted, started to arrive at the Mater on Tuesday:

> One of the badly wounded, Margaret Nolan who was a fore-woman in Jacob's factory died that day, as did also James Kelly—a schoolboy who was shot through the skull. Another schoolboy John Healy aged 14, a member of the Fianna whose brain was hanging all over his forehead when he was brought in, died after two days.

By the end of the week, close to half of the seventy-three people admitted to the Mater had died. Jervis Street Hospital—which like other hospitals came under direct fire—treated over six hundred people, principally for bullet wounds. At Richmond Hospital, where over three hundred patients were treated, the 'deadhouses' overflowed: 'It was a gruesome sight to see the dead piled on top of each other in the morgues where there were not enough marble slabs on which to place the bodies'.[177]

Priests played an important role, ministering to the frightened, wounded, and dying, helping to organize medical care, and mediating between soldiers and rebels to minimize the violence. Many performed small acts of heroism, such as the priest who braved the heavy gunfire to paint a red cross on a building: 'We marvelled at him, for the bullets were falling all around the place he was painting the sign'.[178] 'In the middle of the fighting when the bullets were flying and the road strewn with the dead or dying, Fr Wall of Haddington Road came along on his bicycle', recalled Áine O'Rahilly, whose house overlooked Mount Street Bridge, 'He was visibly frightened, but he left his bicycle against a railing and went from one body to another administering the Last Sacraments'.[179] Priests tended to soldiers—even reluctant ones—as well as rebels. With the authority natural to an Irish priest, Fr James Doyle proved more than able for the aggressive English soldiers he encountered:

> I said to them: 'are there any Catholics among you? If there are I am going to give general absolution now'. One of the soldiers spat on the ground and said, 'naw-a-o, Church of England'. I said, 'how dare you, I will report you to your superior officer'. They all stood to attention. I again told them I was going to give absolution. I then gave the Field Absolution. I saw one man at the back bless himself. Some of these fellows were killed ten minutes afterwards.[180]

Priests, like doctors and anyone else who was prepared to travel through the city by day and night, faced considerable risks. In Father Doyle's own parish one priest, Father McKee, was killed, another was shot, while Doyle was fired on by an unknown assailant. Several doctors and priests, including the Archbishop's secretary, claimed that they were deliberately targeted by soldiers despite being clearly identifiable by their clothes.[181]

Many ordinary citizens demonstrated a quiet bravery. The vital central telephone and telegraph exchange was kept going by twenty women who were unable to leave the building throughout the week. It was to be expected that the 'male staff would stick to the posts', one of their (male) colleagues later wrote,

> but one would not have wondered if the nerves of the ladies had proven unequal to the strain. Such, however, was not the case even when the operators were at intervals told to lie on the floor during the rattle of rifles and machine guns. They wept but carried on the work notwithstanding the fact that the switchboard and ceiling were scarred with bullets.[182]

Such workers were not necessarily politically motivated. Some—such as the porter of the Provincial Bank who was killed by a stray bullet on his daily journey home from work to care for his invalid wife—were motivated by loyalty to their employer or the economic necessity of protecting their workplace.[183] The staff of Monks's bakery returned to work during lulls in the fighting so that their neighbours would not starve: at least one of them was killed. Throughout the city, many bakeries remained open, some giving out free bread, others rationing it at the usual price.

Louisa Norway was struck by the bravery of ordinary people—'there has been no trace of fear or panic among the people in the hotel, either among the guests or staff'—as well as their fatalism which she attributed to the shadow cast by the Great War: 'Life as it has been lived for the last two years in the midst of death seems to have blunted one's desire for it, and completely changed one's feeling towards the Hereafter'.[184] James Stephens also attributed the surprisingly buoyant atmosphere in Dublin to the same cause: 'In the last two years of world war our ideas on death have undergone a change . . . So Dublin laughed at the noise of its own bombardment, and made no moan about its dead—in the sunlight'.[185]

Despite such stoicism, boredom was increasingly replaced by fear for those who remained within the military cordon as the week progressed: 'the rattle of machine guns made us all sit up', Ervine noted, 'One sat there, frankly afraid, and imagined a perpetual flow of bullets pouring across the green, killing and wounding and terrifying'. The roar of artillery made sleep impossible for long periods, while some found 'the awful silence' between bombardments more nerve-wracking: 'When the roar of the guns ceases you can *feel* the silence'.[186] Lord Dunsany, recovering in Jervis Street Hospital, described the sound of approaching artillery:

> one heard it coming methodically nearer, as house after house was bombed; one crash, and then a tinkling rain from every window in the house. And so on from house to house. I can hear the sound yet; bong, tinkle–tinkle–tinkle; and this going on and on like a symphony, with only one bar of music in it, repeated again and again...For the rest of that night I heard men dying, and when the cries seemed to have reached an apex beyond which one had not thought that horror could go, one voice was lifted up more horrible than anything else in that night, and this came from a wounded dog.[187]

People were evicted without warning from homes, hospitals, and hotels, while others fled as shells, bullets, or flames came ever closer. The elderly, infirm, and poor suffered most. On Friday, Fr John Flanagan 'prepared for death a poor bedridden man whose house soon became his funeral pyre'.[188] On Thursday night, Nancy Wyse-Power 'saw a procession of women bearing a white flag crossing Sackville Street at the Parnell monument. These were inhabitants of the Moore Street–Parnell Street area leaving their homes for safety'.[189] In some areas, only the women were allowed to leave: 'I heard this order shouted by the enemy: "Females advance and males stand"—before the fighting commenced'.[190]

Of the many basic hardships—including the absence of public transport and gas for cooking, heating, and lighting—the most urgent problem was the shortage of food. Some Dubliners were initially amused by the sight of well-to-do suburban residents (whose groceries would normally be delivered by messenger-boys) foraging for food. 'The moment the trouble started all differences in social standing disappeared', Father Doyle asserted, 'I saw one man, a K.C., walking along the road with a salmon or a cod in his hand. I saw another prominent man wheeling a perambulator full of groceries; all the artificialities of life suddenly disappeared'.[191] In reality, the poor, who had least resources and were most dependent on bread as a staple food, suffered most. Much of the fighting took place in the poorest and densely populated inner city, the affluent middle classes having long migrated to the leafier suburbs beyond the canals. Scarcity of food was exacerbated by the non-payment of wages, the suspension of separation and other welfare payments, and the closure of banks and post offices (which undoubtedly accounted for some of the hostility against the rebels). Profiteering added to these difficulties: 'nothing could be got in Dublin except at exorbitant prices'.[192]

As early as Tuesday, Volunteers in Monks's bakery had to brandish their guns to repel 'a mob of some hundreds' clamouring for bread. They put some of the hungry to work building barricades in exchange for food. By Thursday, the *Weekly Irish Times* reported, 'something approaching a food famine was imminent' in the north Dublin suburbs, resulting in food riots and the looting of shops and flour mills.[193] By Friday, Father Curran noted in his diary, 'Whole districts are without provisions—milk, butter, bread or meat'. He received reports of 'great distress through scarcity of food' and heard that some hospitals had closed their doors due to a lack of food.[194] Joseph Byrne looked on as a woman he knew, who was returning home with a loaf of bread, was shot in the head outside his Boland's bakery garrison.[195] Mairead O'Kelly saw numerous civilians killed as they tried to reach the Four Courts in search of food.[196] After the garrison surrendered, Bridget Lyons was approached by two elderly men whose families had not eaten for days: 'I gave them ham, bread and butter. I remember I took back a loaf, a piece of butter and a large piece of ham from one of them. I shall never understand why I did that'.[197] The threat of starvation was alleviated by the military authorities who commandeered food stores and warehouses on Thursday, distributing food to those in distress.[198]

Strangely, despite these conditions, 'the streets outside and around the areas of fire were animated and even gay', James Stephens claimed: 'Almost everyone was smiling and attentive and a democratic feeling was abroad...Every person spoke to every other person, and men and women mixed and talked without constraint'.[199] People naturally interpreted the extraordinary events of the week according to their own political outlook. Many northern unionists, like those Eileen Drury found herself confined within the Gresham Hotel, felt 'the rebels should all be shot'.[200] Supporters of Home Rule felt almost as betrayed. St John Ervine, for example, expressed 'anger, because I saw in it the wreck of the slowly maturing plans of the better ordering of Irish life'.[201] However, many moderate southern unionists and British observers were also highly critical of northern unionists—blaming them for provoking the Home Rule crisis—and the Liberal government for failing to tackle the resulting paramilitary threat. While many moderate nationalists assumed that the insurrection had destroyed any possibility of Home Rule, some English observers—such as the senior civil servant Maurice Headlam—cynically, but more astutely, disagreed: 'with the present Government you will probably have Home Rule all the sooner'.[202]

Unionists—who (as a result of their social background) wrote a disproportionate number of the published civilian accounts of the Rising—almost certainly exaggerated the public hostility to the rebels. Although he acknowledged that popular feeling was strongly against the rebellion, James Stephens observed that almost all the men he met were careful not to reveal their personal sympathies. In contrast, he noted that most women, particularly the richest and poorest, denounced the rebels, often in 'viciously hostile' terms.[203] Some observers, although opposed to the futility of the rebellion, were impressed by its audacity. Francis Sheehy Skeffington denounced the Rising as 'a hopeless enterprise' but added that it was 'noble folly'.[204] Charles Wyse-Power, a barrister with republican sympathies, recalled his conversation with Sir Simon Maddock, a prominent Freemason and unionist: '"What do you think of this, Sam?" He said: "Charlie, you have caught us on the wrong hip this time". I said: "What do you think is going to be end of it?" He said: "It is a brave thing to have done and brave men always win"'.[205]

Individual recollections suggest that public opinion was more fluid than was first reported. Ernie O'Malley, one of many young men who 'laughed and scoffed' at the Volunteers before the Rising, initially considered offering his services to the Trinity College OTC, until a friend's observation that this would mean shooting 'fellow Irishmen' caused him to question his own lack of patriotism. The bravery of the rebels, he claimed, produced the first 'faint stirrings of sympathy' that would lead him to pick up a rifle in support of their cause.[206] John McCoy's description of how he and his friend (both of whom had recently applied for British army commissions) responded illustrates a similar remarkable volatility:

> He asked me did I hear the news and then what I thought of it all. I told him I didn't know what to think of it, that I thought the people who started in Dublin were foolish as they had little hope of success. He then said that they were worse than foolish that they were doing a disservice to the country and betraying the Irish men who volunteered for the British Army and that the Rising was a fatal stab in the back to the cause of Home Rule. I replied that I didn't look on it at all in that way...I had admiration for their courage; that I believed the cause was facing certain defeat. I told him that, 'blood being thicker than water', if I was in Dublin I would go to them and offer

them my services; that the men in Dublin were engaging in the same old fight that so many previous generations of Irishmen had engaged in with as little prospects of success. My chum seemed sorry for his outburst and told me that he did not consider the matter in that light...he finally asked me was I sincere in my intention to help the Volunteers if I was in Dublin. I told him undoubtedly I was. He then suggested that we should get ready and go to Dublin and that he would offer his services with mine.[207]

There is evidence of a shift in public opinion during the week. Although many Volunteers were dismayed by the hostility they encountered throughout the entire week, a Volunteer at the Four Courts claimed that 'We gradually got the sympathy or, if not, the respect of the great majority of the people when they saw for themselves that we were conducting the Rising in a fair and clean manner and with such small numbers against the might of England'.[208] Around Jacob's factory, another rebel recalled, the 'people who had been very hostile at the beginning of the week turned completely round and were giving us any information they could get'.[209] By midweek, James Stephens also detected a growing respect for the rebels' resilience: 'had they been beaten the first or second day the City would have been humiliated to the soul'.[210]

V

At 2 a.m. on Friday, Maj.-Gen. Sir John Maxwell arrived in Dublin, replacing Friend (possibly undermined by his absence from Ireland at the outbreak of the rebellion) as commander-in-chief. A Scottish career officer in his mid-fifties, he had spent the first two years of the war as GOC in Egypt. Although caricatured as the blimpish general who lost Ireland, Maxwell merely shared the conservative, imperialistic values characteristic of the British officer class.[211] Like many British observers, he blamed the Irish administration's failure to confront both unionist and nationalist Volunteers for the insurrection. Contrary to nationalist myth, he was not chosen in order to suppress the rebellion with unprecedented ruthlessness: the Prime Minister, Asquith, had advised the Secretary of State for War 'to send a competent man who so far as Ireland is concerned has no past record'.[212] But Maxwell was granted sweeping powers which made him military governor of Ireland, and his appointment sidelined the discredited Castle administration which would have adopted a more subtle response.

His arrival made little difference to the military suppression of the Rising, which was entering its final phase. Echoing the tone of Lowe's earlier pronouncement, Maxwell declared that he would 'not hesitate to destroy all buildings within any area occupied by the rebels', and he made it clear that nothing short of unconditional surrender would be acceptable.[213] The cordon continued to tighten around the garrisons and the bombardment of the GPO was intensified. There were now twenty thousand troops in the capital and the army's effective, if highly destructive, deployment of artillery rendered the fate of the GPO inevitable. Both the army command and Cabinet seem to have been at one that this crude strategy was the most appropriate one. The destruction of much of the centre of the capital was seen as an acceptable price to pay for the rapid suppression of the Rising. While an infantry assault on the GPO would surely have resulted in the scale of casualties inflicted at Mount Street, the option of simply waiting until the rebels were forced to surrender doesn't seem to have been considered (although this would also have entailed starving some of the civilian population). The ferocity of the assault may be another example of how the wartime context shaped decision-making during the Rising, but the authorities were also uncertain about the scale of the threat posed by the rebels, the risk of risings elsewhere in the country, and the possibility of German intervention, in Ireland or on the Western Front, if the Rising was prolonged. However, it may also have reflected Ireland's ambiguous semi-colonial status in the official British mind: it is difficult to envisage the same tactics being so readily deployed in a British city.

In the GPO on Friday afternoon Tom Harris watched, fascinated, as Volunteers armed with hosepipes struggled to extinguish a tiny fire on the roof of the GPO which had apparently been caused by an incendiary shell: 'I saw a little hole, just a circle, which came in the plaster, about the circumference of a teacup, and I could see this growing larger'.[214] Patrick Pearse characteristically assured his sceptical subordinates that the building was fire-proof and that there was no danger of the roof collapsing. By the evening, the upper storeys of the GPO had become an inferno. Burning debris and water poured down on the rebels who desperately sought to move explosive materials out of the path of the fire which spread inexorably downwards, floor by floor, filling the building with fumes. Their position gradually became untenable: 'The floors began to give way. Debris crashed in. Thick columns of smoke and flame rose steadily',

Desmond Ryan wrote, 'The fire roars through the building. Walls of flame seem to surround the yard. Sheets of flame seem to cover the top of the ground floor and the floor above. Cracks begin to show in the outer walls'.[215]

Lamenting how the imminent collapse of the GPO had 'deprived us of a glorious fight', the leaders debated how to respond. 'You can all go and leave me here', Tom Clarke valiantly declared, 'I'll go down with the building'.[216] The others, more pragmatically, decided that they should all evacuate the GPO. Pearse stood on the table to make a final address, paying tribute to 'the gallantry of the soldiers of Irish freedom who have during the past four days been writing with fire the most glorious chapter in the later history of Ireland'.[217] Retreat would prove infinitely more dangerous than defence. As soon as the Volunteers readied themselves to move off, men began to fall as they accidentally discharged their shotguns in each other's backs. Michael O'Rahilly agreed to lead a party of forty men out of the GPO to secure a line of retreat. It was an unenviable mission. The Volunteer in charge of the Henry Street entrance recalled that when he asked one of the men where they were going: 'In a most cynical voice he said "We are going to clear the British out of Moore St, fight our way to Williams & Woods jam factory in Parnell St, and then try to connect up with Ned Daly in the Four Courts"'.[218] Denis Daly was among the party: 'We were in two files, each file to take a side of Moore Street...No sooner had we entered Moore Street than we came under heavy fire. The O'Rahilly was shot and everyone in front of me was shot down...It was impossible to get forward'.[219] John Kenny was one of the first of these men to fall: 'The O'Rahilly drew his heavy automatic pistol and, pointing towards Moore Street, gave the order to "charge for the glory of God and the honour of Ireland"...I only got about 30 yards when I was hit and fell'.[220]

There was reportedly little panic among those still waiting in the GPO, despite the increasing likelihood of the ceiling collapsing. Lighting a cigar, which he had requisitioned from the Metropole Hotel, Liam Tannam 'walked up and down trying to appear as nonchalant as possible', before launching into the *Soldier's Song* to steady nerves.[221] The Volunteers assembled at the Henry Street entrance, the only one not yet in flames: 'There was something of a crush, but no panic'.[222] At around 8 p.m. the order to evacuate was given. One Volunteer recalled that it proceeded 'in a very orderly manner'; another described how they poured onto Henry Street 'with no semblance of order'.[223] All recalled the intensity of the gunfire they immediately faced from Mary Street. 'I could see the bullets like hailstones hopping on the street', Fergus Burke stated, 'With head down as if running against heavy rain, I ran as I never ran before or since and got into Henry Place without a scratch'.[224]

The Volunteers crossed the street into Henry Place, a dark and narrow lane (which led towards Moore Street) where they encountered 'a state bordering on chaos. Men were trying to get shelter in doorways and against the walls from the fire, which no one seemed to know whence it was coming'.[225] Further up the lane, Volunteers who had taken shelter in a white-washed house were unintentionally firing on their comrades: 'There were shouts of "You are firing on your own men" from our part, but the firing persisted. I saw one or two men fall while trying to pass the house', Joe Good recalled, 'Some Volunteers tried to break down a large door with their rifle butts, but in doing so shot three or four men who were behind them'.[226] A woman who came to the door of her house to see what was happening was shot dead by a Volunteer who was immediately disarmed by his comrades.[227] Discipline began to collapse: 'There was no cohesion. Nobody seemed to be in charge once we left the Post Office; it was every man for himself'.[228] Into this vacuum stepped Seán McLoughlin, a determined twenty-year-old Volunteer familiar with the area, whom a stretcher-bound James Connolly had promoted to 'commandant-general' in order to lead the retreat.[229] The final obstacle on the short route to Moore Street was a concentrated hail of machine-gun fire which commanded Henry Place from a barricade some distance back from its junction with Moore Lane. A motor-van was pushed across the junction to provide some cover but the gap remained treacherous:

> as each man darted past it there was a spurt of gun fire which spattered itself on the opposite wall. As each man rushed across and received his burst of fire, the next man would pause before making his dash. As there were some hundreds of us to get through it became a very tedious job, as well as nerve-wracking, wondering who would be the first to be hit.[230]

Several hundred Volunteers made it to the shelter of Moore Street's tenement houses that night where they began the slow and laborious process of knocking through connecting walls, house by house, burrowing north towards Sackville Lane. The boring was carried out as silently as possible, in darkness, to avoid giving away their position: 'We were using a very large crowbar, and each man would take his turn at the bar for a few minutes and then stop to rest, a fresh man taking his place'.[231] Most of the rebels were now in terrible shape: 'we were practically exhausted by this time from lack of food and sleep. 'Twas impossible to keep awake. As soon as one sat down, one's head began to nod over one's rifle'.[232] Some were so exhausted that they had to be carried, unconscious, from house to house.

For the first time, many of the rebels were exposed to the horrors which they had inflicted on Dublin's civilian population. 'I felt very sorry for the people who lived in these houses', James Kavanagh reflected, 'By going into them we were bringing death and destruction...mostly we would find we had burst from a hall or landing into a living or bedroom where frightened people were huddled together'.[233] An attempt to shoot through the lock of one door killed a young girl and wounded her father in the chest.[234] A Liverpool Volunteer groped around in the dark trying to find another girl who had been shot in similar circumstances: 'He thought he put his fingers into her mouth as he thought he felt her teeth, but when he struck a match he found that it was through a hole in her skull he had put his fingers'.[235] Remarkably, the rebels received encouragement from some of those whose walls they knocked through: 'many blessed us and said prayers for our safety before they left their homes'.[236] When Kavanagh burst into one house, an elderly woman began to abuse her son: ' "It's out helping these men you should be" she said, "instead of sitting here as you are" '.[237]

Despite his admission of regret, Kavanagh placed much of the blame for the civilian casualties around Moore Street on the British army which fired 'at everything that moved in the street, and at such short range their shooting was deadly. I saw three men attempting to cross the street killed by three shots, 1, 2, 3, like that'. He heard an old man, crying for water, slowly die as he lay on the street: 'Later, when daylight came, a little girl, about four or five years, came out of the shop and started bawling "Mammy, mammy, my granddad is dead". She kept repeating this over and over again. Her mother was inside the door calling her in and afraid to go out herself'.[238] Some Volunteers sought to persuade fleeing residents to remain where they were, but neither option was safe given that the area was under artillery as well as machine-gun fire. Eamon Bulfin witnessed one house take a direct hit: 'It went down like a house of cards'.[239] Civilians were shot as they advanced towards the British barricades, despite waving white flags or their arms in the air.[240] Oscar Traynor came across the corpse of a man who had insisted on leaving his home to find a safe place for his daughter and grandchildren: 'I saw the old man's body lying on the side of the street almost wrapped in a white sheet, which he was apparently using as a flag of truce'.[241]

By break of day on Saturday the situation was bleak: 'We were completely surrounded. The military were entrenched behind a high barricade at the end of Moore Street. We could see from our windows dead bodies of civilians lying out on the path opposite'.[242] Rebels lay where they had fallen the previous night: one Volunteer recalled the disturbing sight of a Volunteer (whom he identified, probably mistakenly, as Michael O'Rahilly) 'lying on his back, his arms outstretched, blood oozing from his body in a pool under him and flies buzzing about his head. Two or three others lay dead near him'.[243] The mood of the rebels was grim: 'Most of the men by this time were utterly tired, exhausted and apparently despondent. A large number in the more or less darkened rooms were saying their rosaries'.[244] Holed up in Hanlon's Fish Shop, the members of the provisional government discussed their options. Seán McLoughlin gamely advocated a 'Death or Glory Squad' charge on the barricade.[245] When George Plunkett called for twenty men with bayonets to come forward, Diarmuid Lynch was impressed by the enthusiastic response, which recalled for him the Irish Brigade at Fontenoy. Fergus Burke was less gung-ho: 'I had the awful temptation of getting rid of my bayonet as no-one was looking, but thank God I overcame such a cowardly action and proceeded to join the men out in the yard'.[246] The men were rewarded with a final meal—two raw eggs—and advised to say their prayers. Just as they were about to depart, Burke learned that the charge had been postponed: 'The relief to me anyhow was like an answer to a prayer'. It turned out to be a prudent decision, another Volunteer realized when he later saw what lay behind the barricade:

> The barricade at the Parnell Street end of Moore Street was simply crammed with British soldiers bending over it and more standing behind them again and on it were two machine-guns. Facing up Cole's Lane . . . was a piece of artillery . . . Every house in Parnell Street was crammed with British soldiers and an overflow of the troops were lying down on the paths.[247]

As the firing died down, rumours of negotiations circulated: 'The hours passed slowly enough', Fintan Murphy recalled, 'some of us managed to collect some food of sorts from the shops, others were unconcernedly shaving themselves and smartening up their appearances; some lay around asleep, exhausted'.[248] The provisional government's decision to surrender provoked mixed reactions. Fergus Burke was one of few Volunteers to record any relief: 'To say that I was glad and thankful to God would be putting it mildly'. 'All I really felt at the time', Charles Saurin recalled, 'was that I was hungry'.[249] Many Volunteers were too exhausted to care and a considerable number, like John McGallogly, were actually asleep: 'When I awoke the Rising was over and I hadn't fired a shot'.[250] Others who awoke to the news were depressed or angry, and many wanted to fight on. Some continued to cling to the fantasy that they could fight their way to the Four Courts and on to the Dublin mountains, others simply preferred to die fighting rather than accept the humiliation of surrender.

Despite their exhaustion, the option of fighting on was not as rash as it might seem given the Volunteers' strong defensive position which would have presented real challenges for the army (as the ferocious battle for North King Street demonstrated).[251] Joe Good recalled that 'something close to mutiny erupted' (particularly among the Kimmage refugees who feared being shot as deserters) until Seán MacDermott's powerful appeal restored order:

> He suggested that we take a long look at the dead civilians lying in the street outside our windows. He asked us to imagine how many more of them would be lying there if we fought on. He also stressed that the civilians nearest us were all very poor and would be butchered with us. He said that the rest of 'this beautiful city' would be razed...He told us that the worst that would happen to the Irish Volunteers from England would be a 'few years' in jail. He said we'd 'fought a gallant fight' and we'd only lose now by fighting further. He told us that our only remaining duty now was to survive...He ended by insisting quietly, and still smiling, that, 'We, who will be shot, will die happy—knowing that there are still plenty of you around who will finish the job'.[252]

At around 12.45 p.m. on Saturday, Elizabeth O'Farrell approached the British military cordon carrying an improvised white flag, and informed the army command that Patrick Pearse wished to discuss surrender terms. She returned almost two hours later to report that General Lowe had demanded an unconditional surrender. At 3.30 p.m., after subsequent attempts to improve on these terms were rejected, General Lowe met Pearse at the top of Moore Street to accept his surrender. Six days after its proclamation, the Irish Republic had fallen.

6

Charlie Weston, Are You Gone Mad?

The Rising in Provincial Ireland

The focus on Dublin has overshadowed the significance of events outside the capital. Large numbers of Volunteers mobilized in the south, west, and north of Ireland on Easter Sunday, while bands of Volunteers roamed through the countryside during the week that followed. Despite this, more attention has been devoted to what did not happen outside Dublin than what did. The failure of a nationwide rising to occur is generally attributed to the discovery of the *Aud*'s mission, the secrecy of the military council's plans, and the impact of Eoin MacNeill's countermanding order. The evidence from local Volunteers, however, presents a more complex picture of events beyond the capital. Although the confusion and failures of Easter weekend did play a large role in what followed, inadequate planning, poor communications, and more deep-rooted differences between provincial leaders and the organizers over the viability of an insurrection also played an important part in the collapse of the Rising in rural Ireland.

Like many important aspects of the rebellion, the military role ascribed to the Volunteers outside Dublin remains disputed. Some Volunteers insisted that a nationwide insurrection was an integral part of the military council's plans, while others maintained that the leaders had reconciled themselves to the fact that the fighting would be generally confined to Dublin.[1] In the absence of surviving records, the military council's intentions have been surmised from numerous, often conflicting, sources. P. S. O'Hegarty, then an IRB supreme council member, claimed that the original plan (in May 1915) called only for a rising in the capital ('as a forlorn hope to awaken the people'), and that the proposal for a nation-wide insurrection came as an afterthought.[2] In contrast, the Ireland Report which Plunkett submitted to the German authorities at around the same time suggests that the military council did envisage an ambitious role for the provincial Volunteers. But it is clear that the organizers primarily focused their efforts on Dublin: partly because the Volunteers were better organized and armed there than elsewhere, and partly because it was the capital. In contrast, there was little possibility of serious resistance in the many parts of the country where the Volunteers and IRB were poorly organized. In addition, German reluctance to commit anything more than a shipment of captured rifles to the venture must have necessitated some modification of Plunkett's original proposal.

By April 1916, the proposed site for the landing of arms had shifted south to Fenit, Co. Kerry, but the military council's strategy continued to hinge on both the seizure of Dublin and a popular nationwide uprising to be triggered by the arrival of the arms shipment. On close scrutiny, however, the actual plans for this insurrection appear more aspirational than strategic. Once armed, the Volunteers of Cork, Kerry, Limerick, and Clare had been urged by Pearse to 'hold the line of the Shannon'. The role of the Cork Volunteers, who were to mobilize in the west of the county to facilitate the distribution of arms from Kerry, was particularly impor-tant.[3] Volunteers in the midlands, parts of Leinster, and Ulster were expected to move towards the fighting in the west. Volunteer units closer to the capital, in Louth and Meath, were ordered to fight alongside the Volunteers of north County Dublin and Kildare, the latter linking up with rebel forces in Wicklow and south County Dublin. As Donal O'Hannigan, the commander of the Volunteers in Louth and Meath, explained: 'we would form a ring around the city. The ring would extend from Swords via Blanchardstown—Lucan—Tallaght and from thence across the hills to the sea'. Its purpose, he believed, was to prevent British reinforcements reaching the city, and to hold a line of retreat open towards the west.[4]

Whether all this amounted to a coherent strategy remains a matter of opinion. While some aspects of the plan, such as the possibility of a popular uprising in the west, seem plausible, others—such as the expectation of German troop landings or the notion that Volunteers could march from Tyrone to Galway—were not. Some details of the plan clearly owed more to their symbolic than military value. When Donal O'Hannigan complained that Tara was an unsuitable location for mobilization, Pearse told him 'that for historical reasons Tara was important and he wanted the Proclamation of the Republic read there'.[5] Crucially, even if all this could be considered a coherent strategy, it was not clearly conveyed to the provincial Volunteers by the secretive military council. Only two weeks before the Rising, the Cork leadership was still under the impression that the purpose of the Easter manoeuvres was to secure the arrival of an arms shipment rather than the pretext for a full-blown insurrection; the military council's arrangements to receive and distribute these arms, moreover, were clearly inadequate.[6] Remarkably, many of the provincial commandants only learned the real purpose of the mobilization a week before the Rising, leaving them effectively unable to plan, train, or prepare for the insurrection.[7]

The vague nature of those aspects of the plan that are known, and the lack of realism demonstrated by some of the military council, has left its intentions subject to widely divergent interpretations. Historians who regard the Rising as 'reckless, bloody, sacrificial and unsuccessful' base this opinion partly on the lack of serious effort to provide support to the rebels in Dublin.[8] In contrast, some well-informed participants, such as Liam Ó Briain, insisted that 'it was never the plan to allow the Dublin brigade to be cooped up in the city, surrounded and forced to surrender':

> the seizure of Dublin city and Dublin Castle by the Dublin Brigade was meant to electrify the country; cause it to rally to the support of the Volunteers who would be rising everywhere, in some places receiving the German arms which would be in process of distribution. After a few days the Dublin Brigade, if forced to do so, were to leave the city and beat a fighting retreat westwards.[9]

The Ireland Report submitted to the German government also stated that 'the plan for dealing with Dublin depends on relief coming, or a diversion of the British opposition being brought about by the end of a week'.[10] More optimistically, others have discerned a plan to trap British forces between the five thousand-strong rebel force in Dublin and the Volunteers who would converge on the capital from the country, an interpretation endorsed by some recent accounts.[11] That this strategy, hinging on the notion that the combined efforts of German U-boats and Irish Volunteers could prevent reinforcements arriving from Britain, was unrealistic does not mean that it was not advocated by the military council.

This chapter focuses on what actually happened rather than what may have been intended, drawing on the testimony of hundreds of provincial rebels to shed new light on some key questions. To what extent did rural separatists support the idea of an insurrection? What did they think it would achieve? Why did so many Volunteers fail to act that week despite their knowledge of what was happening in Dublin? It begins by examining the reasons for the failure of the national mobilization by focusing on the key areas of Cork and Belfast; it then examines those areas where the Volunteers did rise including Galway, where the rebels achieved little, and north County Dublin where Crown forces were more successfully engaged. It concludes by considering the Rising in Enniscorthy, the only substantial town outside Dublin seized by the Volunteers, which provides some insight into what a more successful provincial insurrection may have achieved.

I

The most striking feature of the lead-up to the Rising in Cork was the utter confusion that had enveloped the local Volunteer leadership. Patrick Higgins, a member of the brigade council, described how the Cork commandant, Tomás MacCurtain, and his deputy, Terence MacSwiney, had become increasingly alarmed by the impetuousness of 'the people in Dublin': 'Tomás and Terry believed the Dublin men were going to fight whether anybody else did or not. They did not approve of that'.[12] As Higgins noted: 'both of them were greatly influenced by MacNeill, but had lost almost all faith in some of the Dublin men'. These misgivings were not only due to the likely lack of popular support for an unprovoked insurrection, but also their concerns about Germany's role: 'they believed the Germans were just using the Irish Volunteers in their own interests'. They were also troubled by the split within the leadership of the movement: 'Tomás and Terry feared that the dual control of the Volunteer organisation, which they knew existed in Dublin, would result in uncertainty and, possibly, in conflicting or even contradictory orders'.[13]

Their fears were confirmed by the arrival of no less than eight conflicting despatches from Dublin between Spy Wednesday and Easter Monday. On Good Friday evening, the Volunteers' Chief of Inspection, J. J. O'Connell, arrived in Cork with an order from MacNeill rescinding MacDermott's previous orders, and placing himself in control of the Munster Volunteers. MacSwiney's sister, Annie, described the 'gloom and depression' among the local leadership occasioned by his arrival: 'they were suffering from abnormal strain'.[14] Worse was to follow. In the early hours of Saturday, the shocking news of Casement's arrest and the capture of the *Aud* reached Cork. This was followed by the arrival of Jim Ryan with yet another despatch from MacDermott which reported that both factions had agreed to support the insurrection which would now go ahead as originally planned.[15] Despite the disastrous turn of events in Kerry, MacCurtain, cheered by the news of unity in Dublin, sent Ryan back to the capital with the resolute message: 'Tell Seán we will blaze away as long as the stuff lasts'.[16]

Rising at dawn on Sunday, Volunteers throughout County Cork began to make their way to eight designated assembly points. A force of 163 men from the city's battalion left Cork by train for Crookstown. It included over forty Volunteers from Cobh and Dungourney who had arrived the previous night, and twenty-five of the Fianna's 'bigger boys'.[17] The low level of mobilization in both the city and county (in total just over a thousand men, about 60% of the total force, turned out) in what was widely considered the best organized county outside Dublin, raises questions about the provincial Volunteers' commitment to an insurrection.[18] Although MacNeill's countermanding order had not yet reached Cork, less than one-third of the city's 120-strong D Company mobilized: 'The instructions that had been received were for an ordinary two-day exercise, but rumours were going about towards the end of the week that it was "Der Tag"', Liam Murphy recalled: 'When most of the men were advised to go to confession on Saturday, colour was given to the rumours and many did not parade because of the possible consequences'.[19]

The position was similar in the countryside. Questioned by MacSwiney about the likely turnout 'in a serious emergency', Carriganima's company captain had been cautious: 'I expressed the opinion that 70% of the company would turn out. He asked me what support we would be likely to get outside the company, that is from the people generally, and I said I thought not very much as we were not then taken very seriously'.[20] Less than half of the hundred-strong Ballinadee Company—regarded by the Hales brothers as 'the best armed, trained and equipped company in the county'—turned out.[21] Several Volunteers from Ballinhassig, who were informed of the real purpose of the mobilization, revealed that they were ordered 'not to tell anyone else in the company of this. We were afraid they would not turn out if they knew'.[22] Only four of Jeremiah O'Carroll's thirty-strong Farnanes Company mobilized: 'maybe they were lackadaisical, or maybe it was some other reason that nobody would care to

remember now'.[23] Only seven of Kanturk's thirty-five Volunteers mobilized, and only one of them was armed.[24] In the village of Ballinspittle,
only one Volunteer obeyed the order to mobilize: he set off on foot to join
the rest of his battalion in Macroom.[25] Such accounts call into question the
belief that a serious rising was ever a possibility in the provinces.

How many of those who turned out knew what was planned? Many
leading Volunteers and IRB men had either been told or had received clear
hints from MacCurtain or other senior officers that some form of action was
imminent. However, until the week before the Rising, the leaders themselves
assumed that any such mobilization would be for the purpose of providing
security for an arms shipment, or defending themselves against a decision by
Dublin Castle to suppress the movement, rather than an offensive insurrection. As in Dublin, the possibility that some form of conflict might occur
was allowed to filter discreetly down the ranks. When the officers of Lyre
Company were briefed by MacSwiney in early April, 'one question was
asked but not answered; would we come back from this march?'[26] Some
officers, in turn, made it clear to the men under their command 'that we
were out for more than a route march'.[27] A small minority of the rank-
and-file were aware that violence was likely but a greater number had no
inkling of this. A majority of Volunteers fell somewhere between these two
extremes: 'We sensed that something was going to happen, but what that was
we did not know'.[28] None of his company had 'any definite information that
action was contemplated', one Ballingeary Volunteer stated, 'but all understood that it was a possibility'.[29] As in Dublin, they were tipped off by the
unusual preparations, such as the distribution of first-aid kits, the urgent
efforts to secure weapons and ammunition, and the tense atmosphere. The
recollections of Patrick Harris from Cork City were characteristic:

> We had no definite information as to what was intended, but there was a
> general feeling that it was something serious. Rumours were plentiful, and
> when the officers advised everyone to go to confession, and when we saw
> the preparations being made in assembling ammunition and so on, it was
> clear to everybody that it was gong to be more than an ordinary exercise.
> At the Hall in Sheares Street on Sunday morning, scapulars and medals,
> which had been sent by some convent, were distributed, and it was evident
> that there was going to be a fight, but we did not know where we were
> going or what plans had been made.[30]

The indiscreet instruction, given in Cork and elsewhere, that Volunteers
should receive confession on Saturday night would have aroused more

suspicion had it not coincided with the Easter services. Like many officers, Brian Molloy 'advised all members of my company to go to confession and to offer up Communion on Sunday morning for the freedom of Ireland'.[31] 'All the Cork Volunteers went to confession', Bob Langford recalled, 'There was tension and everyone felt the day had come'.[32] The presence of armed men at Mass on Sunday morning attracted unwelcome attention from the police, as did the fact that 'practically all Volunteers received Holy Communion'.[33] In this period, most Catholics received Communion, which required spiritual preparation, infrequently; in Dungourney, it 'was only when they saw so many of the Cork Volunteers going to Holy Communion on Sunday morning that they began to suspect something unusual was on'.[34] Some priests, whether due to political or religious scruples, were unimpressed by these displays of armed piety: 'the job was to get the Canon to let them into the church in full kit', one enterprising officer recalled, 'I told him that I used this in order to entice the men to go to their Easter duties'.[35] The clergy in Upton proved less gullible: 'Our appearance aroused the interest of the priests there and they commented on our foolishness in going out, poorly armed as we were, against immense and powerful forces'.[36]

A considerable number of those who turned out on Easter Sunday did so in the knowledge that they might not come back. As his company marched towards Macroom, Patrick O'Sullivan recalled, 'my uncle, Dan Harrington, asked me: "Do you expect to come back to-day?"'.[37] Cornelius Murphy and his three brothers 'had no doubt but that we were going into something from which none of us may return. We made our arrangements accordingly'.[38] For those, like the Murphys, who had joined the movement as a family, difficult choices had to be faced: 'We held a discussion as to whether we would take Tadgh or not. He was very young. We decided finally . . . that he had a better chance armed with us than unarmed at home'.[39] In Tuirmdubh, the Ó Tuama brothers asked their father for permission to turn out, letting him know 'that serious business was intended and that they might not return': 'I can recall how he closed his lips tightly and then said "Well if it be God's will. Let ye go. Ye have my blessing"'.[40] Other parents were less willing to see their children in danger. When a company (in Wexford) failed to turn out, a Volunteer was sent with a second mobilization order for its commanding officer: 'Kennedy's father met the man who carried the orders and told him that if he did not leave the town he would shoot him'.[41]

The rebels ranged in age from the teenage boys of the Fianna to elderly IRB veterans well past their fighting prime: 'An old Fenian—Bill Connors from Crookstown—came along and joined us near Coolcower. He marched to Macroom, and was the oldest man in the whole parade. I said to him, "You have no gun" and he answered, "Well, I'll stop a bullet anyhow." '[42] In Belfast, Seamus Dobbyn recalled a similar determination by his father, an IRB veteran of the Land War, who had intentionally not been informed about the mobilization: 'he told Denis McCullough that he had lived all his life for that day and that he was going to be in it whether McCullough liked it or not'.[43] Some companies, such as Balli-nadee, chose not to mobilize the Fianna, while officers in other areas ordered them to return home: 'Many of them cried, but I succeeded in getting them back'.[44]

Aside from such determination, the Volunteers possessed few advan-tages. With the exception of the city companies—whose members were almost all armed with rifles, shotguns, or revolvers (many commandeered from comrades who had refused to mobilize)—few units in the county were well armed. Most possessed some shotguns, often borrowed from local farmers, but few had rifles. Ballinadee Company, despite having only twelve Mausers and eight Lee Enfield rifles for the forty-eight men who turned out, was one of the best armed rural companies; numerous compa-nies did not possess a single modern rifle.[45] Ballinhassig's fifty-strong company possessed three rifles, several shotguns, and twelve pikes. Donoughmore's forty Volunteers possessed seventeen shotguns, thirteen pikes, and two revolvers.[46] Some of the rifles, relics from earlier Fenian campaigns, posed more of a threat to the Volunteers than the Crown forces; other men were armed only with air guns. In terms of rifle ammu-nition, only the Volunteers from the city possessed 'a fair amount'. Every Volunteer may not have turned out in Cork city but efforts were made to ensure that every weapon and 'every round of ammunition in the company was out'. Those armed with shotguns relied on the home-made cartridges and slugs which had been manufactured during the previous months, the latter providing shotguns with a greater range and impact than buckshot. More enterprising Volunteers cut their cartridges: 'a wild-fowler's trick which makes a shotgun cartridge as dangerous as a bullet for about two hundred yards'.[47] Other home-made weapons included pikes, bayonets (made from garden shears and hedge clippers), and three-pronged spikes ('for use against cavalry').[48]

By mid-afternoon, over a thousand Cork Volunteers were marching west, oblivious to the postponement of the Rising in Dublin. The atmosphere was tense, as the realization that this was 'something more than an ordinary parade' dawned.[49] Some men were nervous, others confident: 'The morale of the Volunteers that morning was very high. They knew it was no normal parade', P. J. Murphy declared, 'They seemed to have sensed the time had come to strike a blow'.[50] The Dunmanway Volunteers marched behind Michael McCarthy, who 'played national airs on the bagpipes'.[51] The rebels travelled by whatever means were available: train, car, bicycle, and horseback; sixty Volunteers who arrived at Sheares Street on bicycles were armed with revolvers and placed into a hastily formed 'Cyclist Company'. Most Volunteers walked, despite having to carry arms, ammunition, kit, and two days' rations over long distances. The Volunteers of Lyre Company, like many others, sent their weapons ahead by horse and cart: 'Some of the men cycled to Dunmanway and some went on horseback'.[52] Tracton Company, Michael Lynch recalled, availed of more modern means of transport: 'the side car of my motor cycle was loaded up with ammunition, gelignite, powder, a few hand grenades, coils of fuse and detonators. I had a full load'.[53]

Unsurprisingly, this mass exodus attracted the attention of the authorities. Many companies were trailed through the countryside by a policeman, as was also often the case during routine mobilizations. The main contingent from the city was shadowed by a sole policeman as they marched towards Macroom: 'He followed for a few miles and halted when we halted…one of my section commanders wanted to use his bayonet'.[54] But relations with local policemen were often good. Dungourney Company was challenged by two RIC men as they waited at the station: 'Lee was a bit aggressive and wanted to know where the Volunteers were going. The Sergeant pulled Lee away. Gilroy was always friendly'.[55] The Dunmanway Volunteers took pity on the constable shadowing them when he proved unequal to the long march: 'one of the policeman got played out and Liam Duggan gave him a drop of whiskey'.[56] There was little likelihood of conflict as the police were not authorized to prevent Volunteers, even armed ones, from parading, and the Volunteers had received unambiguous instructions from MacCurtain: 'we were to get to the place where we were to meet him at all costs and not to fight unless attacked'.[57]

By late afternoon, as the Volunteers began to reach their assembly points, it became apparent that something had gone wrong. MacCurtain and MacSwiney had actually learned that the nationwide mobilization had unravelled shortly after the Volunteers left the city. If the thought of sending their men on a potentially dangerous operation which (given the seizure of the *Aud*) could not possibly succeed was not depressing enough, Jim Ryan had returned to Cork with Eoin MacNeill's countermanding order just after the main contingent had left the city. MacCurtain had decided that it would prove less demoralizing and less suspicious to allow the mobilization to continue as planned. Although it did occur to the Cork leadership 'that a few of the hotheads in Dublin may make trouble' regardless of the countermand, no serious consideration appears to have been given to the option of disobeying MacNeill's order.[58]

By Sunday evening, most Volunteers had received orders to demobilize as news of the debacle filtered down the line: 'Tomás spoke to me and said: "All is over, Casement is arrested and the guns are probably lost" '.[59] Some of the Volunteers returned home in good spirits—'many national songs were sung'—but those who knew that something more than a route march had been intended were dismayed. They faced a long march home through torrential rain: 'All the men were saturated to the skin'.[60] The sight of bedraggled and exhausted Volunteers, their faces dyed green from their hats, won the sympathy of at least one elderly Fenian who could remember the cold and stormy weather on the night of the 1867 rebellion: 'He was inclined to be critical of the rising generation—he thought they were only "playacting" with guns, but when he looked at our saturated clothes, he said that "the weather was always on the side of England" '.[61] One Cork-based British army officer cheerfully noted the demoralizing effects of 'wind and rain for 48 hours that you could hardly beat in the tropics'.[62] Volunteers may have been 'wet, sore and sorry' as they straggled home but their mood would turn to confusion, frustration, and anger over the next days as the news of events in Dublin filtered through.[63] Just why the best armed county failed to rise in support of their comrades in the capital during Easter Week will be considered shortly.

II

There were many similarities between the fiasco in Cork and events in Ulster, not least the misunderstandings and tensions between the local Volunteer leadership and the military council. In contrast to Cork, where

the Volunteers had an achievable objective (at least until the *Aud*'s interception), the debacle in Ulster was largely a result of the military council's
unrealistic plans. Determined to avoid sectarian conflict, the organizers
had decided that Ulster's rebels should march west towards Galway to join
the Volunteers of Connaught in holding the line of the Shannon. The
problem—as Denis McCullough, IRB president and leader of the Volunteers in Belfast, immediately pointed out to Connolly and Pearse when
they revealed their plan to him a week before the Rising—was that this
would necessitate a long march through unionist-dominated territory:
'the whole affair would have developed into a sectarian riot...we could
not have avoided a fight, somewhere on the way'.[64] The Volunteer leadership in Ulster was largely united in the belief that the plan, unveiled at a
'council of war' held in Beragh four days before the Rising, was
'impossible'.[65] Father Eugene Coyle, who attended the meeting, insisted:
'All the leaders there were strongly in opposition as it was considered not
practicable or possible to carry out those plans'.[66]

As in Cork, many leading officers also doubted whether an unprovoked
insurrection was a sensible idea; some of those who attended the meeting
in Beragh argued that 'the Rising should be postponed until the country
was better organised, as in many counties there did not exist any organisation whatever'.[67] The commandant of the Volunteers in County Tyrone,
Pat McCartan, one of the few representatives on the IRB supreme council
to have openly questioned the strategy of an insurrection without popular
support, complained 'that the leaders in Dublin seemed to imagine that
Dublin was Ireland...the position in the north then was that in all areas
except east and south Tyrone and Belfast city there was no organisation'.[68]
McCullough's failure to conceal his own 'perplexity at the orders he had
received and his feeling of inability to carry out those orders' cannot have
inspired much confidence among his subordinates: he later conceded that
he 'believed that MacNeill's orders were proper for Belfast, at least, under
the circumstances then existing'.[69]

These problems were compounded by weak leadership and an uncertain chain of command. Frank Burke, a Volunteer from Carrickmacross
who Clarke and MacDermott had rashly promoted to the grandiose military office of 'O.C, Ulster Forces of the Irish Republic', was described by
McCullough as 'a fool', an opinion endorsed by other leading officers.[70] In
Belfast, some Volunteers opted to travel south to fight in Dublin, such was
their lack of faith in the local leadership.[71] As in Cork, the issue of dual

control was at the heart of much of the trouble: the military council assumed it could call the shots despite having no formal authority over the Volunteer leadership. On Good Friday, the Tyrone Volunteers' 'priest commandants' (Father O' Daly and Father Coyle) summoned McCullough to a meeting with Pat McCartan near Carrickmore where they 'ridiculed the idea of a march to Connaught', claiming 'that the whole thing was engineered and inspired by Connolly; that it was not a Volunteer but a Socialist Rising; that it had no sanction from MacNeill'.[72] Notwithstanding his personal reservations about the plan, McCullough responded firmly:

> I stated specifically that my allegiance was to the IRB first and last; that I was satisfied that the proposed Rising was inspired and would be directed by the IRB through its leaders in the Volunteers, with Connolly and the Irish Citizen Army an integral part of any fighting force that would turn out; that I was taking my orders from the IRB through its military committee... I urged them to mobilise the men in the various districts where we had Volunteers units, and get them prepared to march on Sunday morning.[73]

The meeting ended indecisively. Although further contacts with the military council over the course of the following day confirmed MacCullough's claims, it failed to settle the underlying row about chain of command which rumbled through Saturday. By now, as groups of Belfast Volunteers began arriving in Coalisland, the pressure on McCullough was beginning to tell. At one point, he passed out at the side of a ditch after accidentally shooting himself: 'I was worn out and getting into despair'.[74] The news of events in Kerry cannot have helped; the county inspector subsequently attributed the failure to rise in Tyrone to the reports of 'the arrest of Casement and the sinking of the German vessel'.[75] Nor was Tom Clarke's message to McCartan, which arrived on Holy Saturday, particularly reassuring: 'it is hopeless but we must go on'.[76]

By Saturday evening, over a hundred Belfast Volunteers had arrived by train in Coalisland, from where they were supposed to march to Cookstown the following morning. This was not exactly an impressive turnout, particularly as they were armed with only forty rifles 'of mixed age and vintage'.[77] As in Cork, many of the Volunteers had sensed 'that it was the real thing' and were consequently 'disappointed at the absence of the local people expecting our arrival'.[78] In the early hours of Sunday morning, McCullough issued an ultimatum to the insubordinate Tyrone leaders: 'I stated that I had made up my mind that if they would not undertake to get their men moving and ready to start with mine for Connaught in the morning, I would order my men back to Belfast and disband them there'.[79] He then 'went to bed, worn out in mind and body': 'the responsibility for the lives of those I had with me weighed heavily on me. A number of them were married men with families and the greater number were young men and boys for whose lives and liberty I would be held responsible'.[80]

The following morning McCullough ordered his men to return to Belfast. Cathal McDowell, captain of Belfast's A Company, was one of the few officers to object, on the grounds that Pearse had personally instructed him to carry out his orders regardless of any attempt to cancel the mobilization. Opposed by McCullough, he was unable to convince his fellow officers that they should continue on.[81] Ordinary Volunteers had little say in the matter: 'None of us knew where we were bound for, nor what was happening...we were handed our railway tickets and found they were for Belfast...We had no choice in the matter, as we were not asked either to fight or go home'.[82] McCartan meanwhile had demobilized the Volunteers under his command in Tyrone, informing them that 'the contemplated rising in the north would only lead to slaughter'.[83] The mobilization had failed before it had begun. Its collapse, moreover, was primarily due to disagreement among the Ulster leadership of the Volunteers, and their lack of faith in the military council's strategy, rather than the impact of MacNeill's countermanding order which had merely compounded the disaster.

III

Given the paralysing confusion that preceded Easter Monday, the failure of much of provincial Ireland to rise was hardly surprising. It is more difficult to explain the Volunteers' inaction during the week that followed, particularly after it became clear that a major insurrection was taking place in Dublin. In Ulster, the Volunteer leadership appeared unable or unwilling to regroup after the debacle of the weekend. Weak leadership was partly to blame. 'McCullough was not moving about at the time, and his absence seemed to leave the Volunteers in a confused position', a member of the Volunteer executive in Belfast complained, 'There was no possibility of doing anything'.[84] In Tyrone, McCartan remained racked by indecision, holding a series of inconclusive meetings to consider a military response until his arrest later in the week.

For the minority who were inclined to fight, it was not clear how they should go about it. Did the original orders to march west still stand, despite the seizure of the *Aud*? On Monday, Ina and Nora Connolly (James Connolly's daughters) returned to Tyrone from Dublin claiming to have new orders from the military council—'an instruction from Pearse to mobilise all men in the county, seize all police barracks and hold up all trains with military supplies going south'—which contradicted the previous instructions to avoid conflict within Ulster at all costs.[85] Despite this, the Volunteer leadership in Tyrone appeared to have believed that its original orders remained valid, although by the end of the week some consideration was being given to the more realistic options of attacking local police barracks or moving towards Dublin. Small groups of Volunteers in towns such as Carrickmore, Coalisland, Dungannon, and Dunoughmore mobilized—or discussed the possibility of mobilizing—during the week but there was little obvious enthusiasm for action, particularly among the leadership. On Monday night, McCartan continued to insist to subordinates like Jimmy Tomney, IRB centre for Tyrone, that military action 'would be madness, and that I was to take my men home'.[86] When Belfast separatist Robert Haskin met him during the middle of the week to urge the mobilization of local Volunteers, McCartan told him 'that the Tyrone men were so disappointed with the mix-up in the plans that they would not be willing to take the field'.[87] Frank Burke claimed that his own attempts to mobilize his Volunteers in nearby Monaghan forced him 'to go "on the run" from my own men who resented my efforts to get them to do something'.[88]

Events in Cork unfolded in much the same desultory manner during Easter Week. On the morning of Easter Monday, the first of two messages from the military council arrived: 'We start here at noon today'. The slim possibility of a decisive response to this startling news was undermined by the absence of MacCurtain and MacSwiney, who had not yet returned from their tour of assembly points on the previous evening. Moreover, this first, unsigned, message was regarded with scepticism by the Cork officers: 'In view of the fact that nine separate dispatches arrived in Cork during those fateful days, some contradicting or countermanding, others affirming previous orders, it can be well understood how bewildering the confusion was'.[89] By now, the Cork leadership was not only suspicious but deeply critical of the Dublin leadership. Marie Perolz, an ICA activist, who arrived on Monday morning with a despatch for MacCurtain recalled that 'while Mrs MacCurtain was nice to me, I knew she did not want me...My impression was they did not want to find him. They said Cork will do its duty'.[90] Perolz, as one Cork Volunteer later confirmed, was correct in detecting a degree of personal hostility:

> Mary MacSwiney was in the hall and she took part in the discussion about what action was to be taken. She said in effect: 'Was a fine body of men like the Irish Volunteers to be dragged at the tail of a rabble like the Citizen Army?' There was comment that the messenger was not a Volunteer but a Citizen Army messenger.[91]

Bridget Foley, who arrived around the same time with the second of the military council's despatches, a message from MacDermott, encountered a more hostile response from MacCurtain's brother:

> His language was lurid, although he did not open the dispatch. 'Why the bloody hell don't they make up their minds in Dublin. We don't know what to do with all the commands and counter-commands'...I got the impression that neither MacCurtain's brother nor his wife was anxious that I should get in touch with Tomás...I could not describe the agony of mind I went through on the outward journey and I have the same feeling every time I think of it since.[92]

Any doubts about the authenticity of these messages were resolved later that day when the rumours of an insurrection in Dublin were confirmed by military telegrams (decoded by Volunteers) and press reports to the *Cork Examiner*'s offices. MacCurtain and MacSwiney returned to a fraught situation at the Sheares Street headquarters on Monday night: 'The atmosphere was very tense and strained. The younger officers particularly wanted to fight, and were resentful of the waiting policy adopted by the leaders'.[93] Both leaders appeared reluctant to commit their men to action regardless of what was happening in Dublin:

> I felt they had made up their minds not to call out the men again, and that they were justifying that decision by a recapitulation of all the arguments against such a course. They felt that the men would not turn out again if called upon. They seemed to have sensed the position in Cork, and to be to some extent influenced by consideration for the men, and the weakness of the arms position...The whole thing looked odd and mad at that moment...There had never been any plan for Cork except the concentration on the previous day, and they did not know what to do. Terry said something to the effect that he could not stand for the city being bombarded and being shot down.[94]

The Cork leadership resolved to defend their headquarters from attack but to take no action which might provoke the local military or RIC into violence.[95] Most Volunteers supported this decision, which was consistent with the local leadership's pragmatic belief that any resort to force must have a chance of success. Seán O'Sullivan, who had led the Cork men in the field on Sunday, believed that any violence that would follow would be futile: 'the most we could do was to create a moral effect'.[96] The brigade officers insisted that they lacked the means to take on the Crown forces: 'The Dublin Brigade, as they showed, had sufficient arms and ammunition to maintain a fight for a week, whereas the Cork Volunteers had scarcely enough to last five minutes'.[97] In contrast, some (generally younger) Volunteers questioned their leaders' decision to do nothing: 'A lead from them would have taken the majority of the Cork men into the fight in some way. Action in the city may have been inadvisable, but there was nothing to prevent the Volunteers mobilising outside the city on Monday or Tuesday'.[98]

Over the course of the next days, MacCurtain and MacSwiney resisted repeated attempts, fuelled by the wild rumours that circulated through the county, to change their minds: 'The Volunteers had captured Dublin Castle, the Custom House, the GPO! They were winning everywhere! Thousands of soldiers had been killed! Thousands of Volunteers had been killed! There was fighting all over the country!' A train driver, who had been ordered to take an armoured train to Dublin, called to Sheares Street to offer his services: 'He was willing to derail the train…but they would not take the responsibility of giving him an order'.[99] Macroom Volunteer Michael O Cuill went to Sheares Street demanding to know whether 'they intended to do anything': 'I said I was going to Dublin if there was to be no fight in Cork. They said everyone had the right to do what he thought best'.[100] Unable to find any transport, he would win local fame as the man who walked to Dublin: by the time he arrived, however, the Rising had ended. Frustrated Volunteers in outlying areas like Blarney urged the brigade command to smuggle rifles out of the city to enable a stand in rural Cork: 'a week of agony passed…here were we standing idle while our comrades were being surrounded in Dublin'.[101] An Annascaul Volunteer expressed a sense of frustration shared by many of the rural units: 'We heard that the boys in Dublin were out and we were all anxious to do something but no orders came'.[102] The Hales brothers' militant Ballinadee Company came closest to violence, ordering the local RIC sergeant out of the district and declaring an independent republic in their own corner of west Cork, but they were restrained from attacking the barracks in Macroom by their IRB and Volunteer superiors in the city.[103]

The most difficult appeal to ignore must have been the one that left the GPO shortly after midnight on Tuesday, when two of Edward Daly's sisters were sent from the capital with the military council's 'final messages'. 'The message to Cork was, "Tell Terry MacSwiney we are in action and we know he will follow us"', Eamon Dore recalled, 'To Limerick the message was less friendly'.[104] At midday on Wednesday, Nora Daly arrived at Sheares Street with her message: 'They both seemed to think Dublin was wrong and they were right. They said they had documents to prove they were right. In the course of discussion I told them I did not know why Dublin decided to go out on Monday but whatever Tom Clarke and Seán MacDermott did was right in my eyes'.[105] The local leadership insisted that 'Cork was ringed with steel and action was out of the question'.[106] Like many of the other, predominantly female, messengers who risked their lives to bring these unwanted messages to the provinces, Nora Daly reproached both herself—she referred to her mission as 'my failure'—and the provincial leadership: 'the only decision I could get out of Terry MacSwiney and Tomás MacCurtain was that they would not give up their arms. Before I left Cork on Thursday I heard they had actually handed them over to Bishop Cohalan'.[107] After a tense week holed up in Sheares Street, the Cork leadership faced the humiliation of surrendering themselves and their arms—in a deal which the Lord Mayor and bishop brokered with the authorities—without firing a shot: 'Their inaction haunted them for the rest of their lives'.[108]

IV

Aside from the dramatic role played by messengers like Nora Daly, women are noticeably absent from accounts of the Rising outside Dublin. The rural units generally did not allow women to take to the field with the men; where women were permitted a role, it was often because they volunteered for it rather than because they had been mobilized: 'Some girls came into our camp to help', one of the Meath rebels recalled, 'Those girls cooked, sewed and cycled 4 to 5 miles to other farm houses to procure bread and other necessities for us. They also carried important messages'.[109]

At many Volunteer headquarters, the role of women was similarly demarcated: 'We got in the dinners and made the teas ourselves in the Rink. The girls worked willingly and enthusiastically, and we were prepared to do our part in whatever happened that week'.[110] Some women, such as Máire Fitzpatrick who was appointed a despatch carrier in Enniscorthy, clearly sought a more active role: 'I knew what I would do when the real fighting started. I had a first aid certificate, but it's the rifle I would have preferred'.[111] The subordinate status accorded to women also meant that they were more likely to be unaware of the significance of the messages they conveyed. Annie MacSwiney was one of many who criss-crossed the country with despatches during the days before the Rising: 'My sister and I always... co-operated with the Volunteer leaders without asking for any explanations. Terry did not discuss Volunteer matters with us in such a way as to give any intimate knowledge or policy or intentions'.[112] As a result, some women who supported the insurrection unwittingly carried MacNeill's countermand across the country.

As in Dublin, those women who were active during Easter week had to demand the limited roles they were permitted. In Belfast, Nora Connolly insisted to McCullough that Cumann na mBan members had the right to travel to Tyrone with the male Volunteers: 'I had quite a lot of arguing. Finally, he agreed to six. I said he could not send the men out without anyone to give first aid'.[113] Connolly was soon given an opportunity to prove herself when a young Volunteer shot himself in Coalisland:

> I had the job of fixing him up; and they all gathered round, watching the process. Evidently, it was quite satisfactory. There was one big fellow there; he gave me a big whack on the shoulder, and said: 'You are coming with us'. I said: 'What do you mean by that?' He said: 'We want someone with us who knows the job'. I said: 'I have got a rifle and ammunition on one of the lorries. How do you know I don't want to use them?' He said: 'Come with us, and you can do both'.[114]

Although denied a combatant role, these women played an important logistical role as despatch carriers, cooks, nurses, and movers of weapons, arms, and supplies. There are some striking examples of women who refused to conform to the subordinate role that they had been assigned. In Tyrone, for example, Nora Connolly spent the week urging local IRB men and Volunteer leaders to fight.[115] Similarly, Maeve Cavanagh arrived in Kilkenny on the Wednesday of Easter week with a message from the military council ordering J. J. O'Connell, the Volunteers' demoralized Chief of Inspection, to lead the men of Kilkenny and Waterford into action:

> 'They should have awaited till there was conscription', O'Connell said, 'Look at that, it is all over already', showing me an English paper. I said: 'Sure an old woman could take Kilkenny today. If you are afraid to give the message, let me see the men and I'll give them the message and take the responsibility'. He replied, 'You shall certainly not see any man under my command'. To my consternation, he broke down and cried, and said, 'I deserve that, I'll be called a traitor'. I was very sorry for him as I saw he was under a terrible strain, but not of indecision... Afterwards... someone who was in gaol with O'Connell told me that he—O'Connell—wondered why they kept sending these hysterical women after him. I was amazed because if anyone was hysterical it certainly was not I. I had formed the conviction that day that he was not a revolutionary.[116]

V

The determination of such women counted for little given the state of confusion and disunity that existed not only in Cork but throughout much of the country. In Limerick city, as throughout much of the west, the Volunteers' mobilization was predicated on success in Kerry and, as in other places, it had been cancelled before MacNeill's countermand arrived.[117] On Monday afternoon, following the usual string of contradictory despatches and the news of the *Aud*'s failure, Commandant Michael Colivet's brigade council—believing that 'only the Citizen Army and a small section of the Volunteers had gone into insurrection'—decided that their 'orders could not be carried out'.[118] As in Cork, the leadership rejected pressure from some of their own men to reverse this decision during the week that followed. Alphonsus O'Halloran, a lieutenant in Limerick city's D Company, challenged his commandant about this shortly after the Rising:

> When I argued that we should have gone into action, Colivet said: 'What could we have done?' My reply was: 'Well, we could have gone down in a blaze of glory like the men of Dublin'. He then told me that from all he had heard at the time, he had assumed that it would be a case of 1803 all over again; that there would be something like a street riot, and that it would end at that, but that, had he realised that such a fight would be made, he would have ordered us into action... I believe he was quite sincere.

Having struggled to build a Volunteer force capable of serious military action, Colivet—like his comrades in Cork—was unwilling to commit the eight battalions under his authority (which extended north into Clare) to an apparently futile protest engineered by a militant faction of the movement. Significantly, O'Halloran (who at the time 'felt very bitter against Colivet and Clancy for not leading us into action') later reflected that 'after all those years I am inclined to think that...they really could not be blamed'.[119] His reflections highlighted the consequences of the military council's failure to convey the rationale behind the Rising. It seems probable that some provincial leaders would have proven no less willing to sacrifice themselves than their comrades in Dublin had they understood more clearly its purpose.

Throughout most of the country, the same reasons—or, in some cases, excuses—for inaction were cited: lack of organization, men, arms, or ammunition; contradictory, confusing, or unrealistic orders; the secrecy of the military council's plans; the logistical difficulties and demoralization caused by the countermand; incompetent, absent, or irresolute leadership; the unwillingness of Volunteers to mobilize; the apparent futility of military action; and the refusal of officers or units in neighbouring areas to act. There were countless examples of an unwillingness to cooperate between companies, rooted in local distrust or hostility between rival areas, and much passing of the buck for the inaction that resulted. Collectively, the response indicates that the military council's preparations and the state of the organization of the movement—as numerous Volunteer and IRB leaders insisted at the time—fell far short of what was required to mount a coherent nationwide insurrection.

These problems were compounded by the disunity within the national leadership. The rift between MacNeill and the military council led many to question the legitimacy of the latter's orders, with the involvement of the Dublin-based Irish Citizen Army subject to particular criticism. Sent by James Connolly to Waterford on Easter Monday, Maeve Cavanagh was met with suspicion by the local commander who refused to commit his men to the fight:'He talked about the Citizen Army pulling this thing off, mentioned this foreigner, Madame Markievicz'.[120] During the week that followed, it was rumoured 'that the Citizen Army had broken away from the Volunteers'.[121] There may have been little explicit discussion of ideology within the Volunteer movement but these reactions indicate a significant degree of conservative rural hostility towards Connolly's working-class socialist organization.

In addition, inadequate preparation, poor judgement, and plain bad luck paralysed large areas. In Kerry, Austin Stack was arrested when, against the advice of fellow officers, he presented himself at Tralee barracks on Good Friday after receiving a message from the head constable that an arrested Volunteer wanted to see him. Stack, who—as the county inspector accurately noted—'was in charge of everything', had to be replaced by an officer who had no knowledge of the plans for the county and lacked the confidence of his men.[122] In those areas where the Volunteers were weak the failure to rise may have been fortuitous but in towns like Tralee, where over three hundred Volunteers (ten times the number of police stationed in the town) had mobilized, it represented a missed opportunity to cause the sort of chaos that the military council had counted on. A retired British army officer who led a force of one hundred soldiers from Cork to reinforce the Royal Munster Fusiliers' depot was certain that Tralee had a lucky escape:

> When trouble began they had there a few NCOs, some 40-odd men, mostly wounded and recovering or decrepit old Home Service men, and a pack of raw recruits with less than a week's service. They had 26 rifles and 2,000 rounds of ammunition, and no support nearer than Cork. The barracks were old, the wall badly planned, and in many places without flank defence . . . twenty six men . . . all for whom there were rifles, could have done nothing against a resolute attack and the town was well armed and very ugly.[123]

Public hostility to the rebels also contributed to the failure to rise. In Cork, the Volunteer headquarters in Sheares Street came under attack from an aggressive mob during the week.[124] In Tralee, Roger Casement was subject to 'spitting and jeering' from dozens of women and children as the police led him through the slum district known as 'the lanes', while local Volunteers were also 'met by a barrage of dirt and abuse from the relatives of the British soldiers serving in France'.[125] In many large towns and cities—including Galway, Castlebar, Dundalk, New Ross, Wexford, and Drogheda—Redmondite Volunteers and unionists formed themselves into defence corps to defend strategic targets from separatist attack.

VI

Over a thousand Volunteers did rise in isolated parts of rural Ireland including Louth and Meath, north Dublin, Wexford, and Galway. The latter county produced the largest but arguably most militarily pointless mobilization in the country. As elsewhere, the Volunteers in Galway were mired in confusion during the days before the Rising. Even the arrival of a despatch from Eamon Ceannt (the only member of the military council from Galway) on Good Friday containing the agreed code for mobilization was met with suspicion due to the rumours of a split in Dublin.[126] Although messengers were sent to Dublin to get more information, it is clear that opinion in the county was sharply divided on the merits of a rebellion. Even prominent militants like Tom Kenny, IRB centre for County Galway and leader of a notorious Craughwell-based secret society, argued that 'the country was utterly unprepared and that it would be madness to go into action'.[127] A distraught Larry Lardner, who had replaced Liam Mellows as Galway Brigade leader after the latter's deportation in March, was equally unenthusiastic, being described by some of his own officers as 'funking it' on Easter Saturday.[128]

Following the arrival of the countermand on Sunday the Volunteers dispersed, many leaving the city. A subsequent despatch confirming that the Rising was off, which reached the city at 6 a.m. on Easter Monday, was contradicted by a message from Pearse which arrived later that afternoon: 'We have begun at noon today, carry out your orders'.[129] Confusingly, however, the orders in question called for the occupation of barracks in the city, while other Volunteer companies were to move south towards Clare to collect the arms that were supposed to be making their way by rail from Tralee before returning to Galway to begin a popular insurrection west of the Shannon. These orders made no sense in light of the failure of the *Aud*'s mission. As in Cork, the botched mobilization paralysed the Volunteers in the city throughout the week that followed: 'There was great confusion. We did not know what to do and as far as Galway city was concerned it was too late to do anything as the RIC and military were already alerted'.[130] One IRB man claimed that 'the Volunteers in Galway city were in such a weak position that it was almost impossible for them to act as a unit [or to]...link up with county units'.[131]

Outside the city, however, many rural units did rise: up to one thousand men mobilized throughout the county, five hundred of them taking to the field under the command of Liam Mellows, who had returned in disguise from England on Easter Monday. Why were so many men in Galway, compared to other counties, prepared to fight? It may have been due to the capable leadership provided by Mellows, who, in contrast to the many regional organizers appointed by the military council just weeks or even days before the Rising, had been chief organizer in Galway since early 1915. Mellows, who according to the RIC county inspector had 'succeeded in enrolling practically all the young men of the countryside', clearly had the confidence of local Volunteers.[132] Sensibly concluding that the original plans had been overtaken by events, he devised an alternative strategy based on a limited insurrection in the east of the county where his forces were strongest. They did not intend 'to do anything big', one officer explained, they merely hoped to 'bottle up the British garrison and divert the British from concentrating on Dublin'.[133] It was more than most other counties attempted.

Another factor accounting for the relative success of the mobilization in Galway may have been the unusual degree of agrarian radicalism in parts of the county; many of the rural Volunteers owed their primary allegiance to Tom Kenny's IRB-affiliated secret society which had enjoyed a well-organized and intermittently menacing existence since 1907.[134] Bridget Walsh witnessed a striking if extreme example of how this radical tradition may have added an edge to local proceedings when Clarenbridge was briefly occupied by Volunteers who arrested several policemen:

> A couple of Connemara men who were working with Mattie Niland were among the Volunteers. Mattie asked the Connemara men were they coming. They said: 'Where are you going?' He replied, 'To fight for Ireland'. 'If you are going sticking peelers we are with you', said the Connemara lads.[135]

This militant minority appear to have enjoyed more support in rural Galway than separatists elsewhere. Police reports indicate that the Rising won substantial popular support in parts of Galway, and it was one of the few counties where the rebels were joined by men who did not belong to the Volunteers and enthusiastically supplied with food by local people.[136]

Although the Catholic Church, the principal arbiter of nationalist public opinion, was assumed to be fervently opposed to the insurrection the evidence from Galway presents a more nuanced picture. In one of many examples of individual clerical support for the rebels, one Volunteer described the dismissive reaction of a priest when he brought him MacNeill's countermanding order: 'I shall always remember his remarks in reply—"that he personally did not give a hang who issued the orders if it (the Rising) only came off"'.[137] As in Tyrone, some priests behaved more like commanding officers than chaplains. 'Fr Feeney told us that the Rising was to take place', one Castlegar Volunteer stated, 'He advised us all to go to confession and receive Holy Communion on Easter Sunday'.[138] Before they went into action, another Galway rebel recalled:

> Father O'Meehan addressed the company, saying that the Rising was on in Dublin and that our company would very soon be engaged in the fight and that it was very likely that some of us would be going to our deaths...Fr O'Meehan then gave us General Absolution and told us to collect all the arms and ammunition we could in the town of Kinvara and neighbourhood.[139]

Feeney also accompanied the Volunteers into battle, dispensing confessions with—it was claimed—the approval of Bishop O'Dea of Galway; he was accompanied by two other priests, one a professor at the national seminary.[140]

These priests may have been influenced by the long-standing Sinn Féin presence in east Galway but most clergy opposed the insurrection, some deploying their considerable moral authority against the rebels: 'Father Tully, the parish priest, prevented them from taking the barracks at Clarenbridge. He spoke to them and told them the curse of God would be on them if they used any violence'.[141] Further north, Darrell Figgis attributed the failed mobilization in Castlebar to a local priest who 'had refused to allow the men there to make any move'.[142] Importantly, however, the rebels enjoyed the support of a significant minority of clergy. In his evidence to the royal commission, the county inspector for West Galway noted that 'some of the younger clergy were disaffected, but a good many of them were very loyal'. The county inspector for the more militant east riding went further, testifying that the rebels were aided by 'a considerable number' of priests, particularly 'the younger ones'.[143] Although those priests who supported the rebels probably represented a small proportion of the clergy, their stance was important in terms of the rebels' morale and legitimacy. It also challenges naïve depictions of the Volunteers as secular-minded republicans: many were simply Catholic nationalists with guns. The evidence on the ground in provincial Ireland, as in Dublin, attests to both the piety and religious homogeneity of the rebels. In Galway, the rebel force was entirely Catholic.[144]

Although the turnout in Galway was impressive, the Volunteers' strategy was not. A series of unsuccessful attacks on police barracks took place in Clarenbridge, Oranmore, and Gort on Tuesday. Another band of rebels encountered a patrol from Galway city at Carnmore crossroads at dawn the following day.[145] As would occur elsewhere, the large force of constabulary (accompanied by soldiers) did not distinguish itself in the skirmish which followed:

> The enemy advanced up to the cross roads and Constable Whelan was pushed by District Inspector Heard up to the wall which was about four feet high, the District Inspector standing beside Whelan and holding him by the collar of his tunic. Constable Whelan shouted, 'surrender boys, I know ye all'. Whelan was shot dead and the District Inspector fell also and lay motionless on the ground.[146]

Whelan's death illustrated the potency of shotguns in close-quarter combat. Shot by a man 'carrying a gun of antique pattern', a press report noted, 'the constable got a full charge of No. 3 shot in the head, blowing off the side of his face and killing him instantly'.[147] Volunteer John Hosty took no pleasure in Whelan's death, describing him as 'the most harmless man in the whole barracks'.[148]

By Wednesday, over five hundred rebels had converged under Mellows' command near Athenry but their objectives remained unclear. They did not seek to engage Crown forces in battle or to occupy the surroundings towns. Instead, they set up camp at a farm outside Athenry, subsequently retreating to further defensive positions at Moyode Castle and Lime Park. Their explanation for this strategy which, one Volunteer feared, may have appeared 'rather cowardly' was their lack of arms: 'we had about fifty full service rifles and about thirty rounds for each rifle...The argument in favour of Moyode was that we could defend it at least until our ammunition would be spent'.[149] The increasingly nervous contingent waited at a deserted 'big house' at Lime Park as rumours of the approach of vast military forces grew, diminishing in size as hundreds of Volunteers deserted the camp to avoid what must have seemed a pointless last stand. Mellows' fatalism ('it was better to die fighting') was not shared by the rest of his officers and men who finally disbanded on Saturday.[150]

VII

In striking contrast to events in Galway, a much smaller force of Volunteers from Dublin's Fifth Battalion was responsible for the most lethal military engagement outside the capital. Despite the impact of the countermand (an almost full strength mobilization of two hundred men fell to sixty when they regrouped on Monday) and an unwelcome order to send a further twenty Volunteers to the GPO, Commandant Thomas Ashe was determined to lead his men into combat. Joseph Lawless remembered Ashe shaking him by the hand 'saying something to the effect that "this would be a day to be remembered in Ireland for evermore", while his eyes shone with excitement'.[151] Surviving on commandeered sheep (butchered by one of the Volunteers) and locally purchased provisions, they travelled by bicycle, frequently moving camp and sleeping in stables, barns, or under the stars. On Tuesday, they were joined by another small contingent of Volunteers including the very capable future IRA chief of staff Richard Mulcahy, who 'without actually assuming command' soon came to be recognized as 'more or less in charge'.[152] Over the course of the next days, the Volunteers embarked on a remarkably successful rampage through north Dublin and Meath, attempting to blow up viaducts and railway lines, capturing barracks and post offices in Swords, Donabate, and Garristown, accumulating arms and ammunition, and dismantling telephone and telegram lines.

However, their objectives remained unclear. Like most Volunteers, they showed little desire to kill members of the Crown forces: captured RIC men, who generally surrendered with alacrity, were turned loose once they promised to take no further part in the fighting. Charlie Weston described one of these rather civil encounters at Donabate barracks: 'Ashe took the day book and looked up the entries... and the names of the Volunteers on parade on different dates. We had a chat with the police who had now got over their nervousness'.[153] In the absence of enemies to shoot or important buildings to occupy, they engaged in a series of symbolic acts. In Garristown, they exchanged the post office's stamps, money order books, and cash (Mulcahy informing the postmaster that 'This money is of no longer any value') for a receipt 'in the name of the Irish Republic'. The building's 'Imperial Coat of Arms' was replaced by 'the Tricolour on a brush handle [tied] to one of the high chimney pots'.[154] Despite these minor triumphs, the realization that the rest of the country had failed to rise had led to open protest by Thursday: 'some of the men started grousing that the thing was not right and that the Rising had not the sanction of the Irish Volunteer executive council. Dick Mulcahy gave all a lecture on our duty to the country and when he had finished he asked all those who were prepared to continue the fight to take a pace forward'.[155] All but a handful did.

The remarkable events of the following day would transform the despondent mood of the Fifth Battalion. On Friday morning, the Volunteers attacked a barracks defended by ten RIC men in the village of Ashbourne. Just as the outnumbered police were preparing to surrender, the sudden appearance of a seventeen-strong column of cars, containing at least fifty-four policemen (including a county inspector and district inspector), appeared to turn the tables. Impressively, Mulcahy prevented a panicked rout, persuading his startled and outnumbered men to hold their ground. Over the course of the next hours, Volunteers positioned in the fields along both sides of the road gradually closed in on the large police column, while a small party of Volunteers kept it helplessly pinned down, unable to advance or retreat:

> They were, apparently, hugging mother earth for dear life. Some of them had realised their mistake in getting under the cars and tried to get out of that position but were promptly dealt with by us, while those that remained were either dead or so badly wounded as to be incapable of any move-ment...All this time they were presenting beautiful targets to us and were crowding in on their comrades who were nearest to us.[156]

Completely surrounded, and exposed to relentless fire from all angles, the RIC men were gradually picked off: 'our fellows were making bets as to who would shoot the most', Bernard McAllister recalled, 'The police were acting like rabbits being driven from a ditch before a shooting party. We had a clear view and decimated them with our fire. Some took cover under the cars but were visible to us there'.[157]

By late afternoon, Mulcahy pressed home their superiority, fiercely urging his men forward: 'He was shouting "Will you surrender? By [God] if you don't we will give you a dog's death"'.[158] The proximity of both forces resulted in savage close-quarter fighting:

> John Crinigan of Swords looked through a gap in the ditch to locate any police, he was seen by D. I. Smith [Smyth] who fired at and shot him through the head with a revolver. Vice-Commandant Frank Lawless who was immediately behind joined fire on the D. I. with a Howth Mauser rifle at a distance of about 6 yards and shot him through the head.

At that point, Mulcahy forced a surrender by leading a bayonet charge 'while our men on both sides opened a rapid fire into the body of the policeman...When the policemen saw this party charge down on them with fixed bayonets they threw their rifles out on the road'.[159]

The aftermath of the battle produced some pitiful scenes: two Volun-teers had been killed but seven RIC men were dead and another sixteen lay wounded, including county inspector Alexander 'Baby' Gray who would die from his injuries: 'They looked a very sorry looking lot, covered with blood. At the time, I thought most of them must die, as there was so much blood about'.[160] 'Some of the wounded police were crying out for help', Jerry Golden recalled, 'They were a sorry looking lot, not the customary R.I.C. man's complex'.[161] A post office messenger who stumbled upon the scene—'a terrible sight with blood and bandages strewn on it'—agreed to clear away the corpses: 'I had eight dead men in the cart when I was finished'.[162] As he stood watching the bleeding policemen, lying on 'a road margined with death and pain and anguish', Richard Mulcahy was moved by the appeal made by one: 'an RIC man stretched out his arms impulsively to cry—"Oh, we are all Irishmen, Sir, we are all Irishmen. You know me, Sir, you know me Sir, I am Glennon the boxer"'.[163] As elsewhere, civilians had been caught up in the fighting. An unarmed chauffeur who drove one of the cars in the police convoy died after the amputation of his leg (wounded by an explosive bullet), while two commercial travellers who drove into the ambush were shot when they were apparently mistaken for Volunteers.[164]

The battle of Ashbourne was important for a number of reasons, not least because it was the only engagement of the Rising outside Dublin that could be considered a success in conventional military terms. Why did the Volunteers prevail over a much larger force? One recent account has convincingly disputed the myth of Ashbourne as a model ambush—an influential precursor to the flying column raids of the Tan War—in which careful planning, superior tactics, and steely leadership triumphed over greater numbers. In reality, the Volunteers were fortunate to find themselves in a superior position when the (unobserved) police convoy blundered into their midst, and Ashe had to be persuaded by Mulcahy to rescind his original order to retreat.[165]

But the rebels' victory was not only due to luck. In some respects, it did anticipate the War of Independence, showing what could be achieved by small, determined units willing to take the initiative. The mobility and firepower of the column—'most of the cyclists had three rifles or carbines slung across their shoulders or strapped to their bikes'—and its willingness to adapt to changing circumstances on the ground were important factors later emulated in the Tan War.[166] The police's tactics were also important. Ironically, had they not attacked the Volunteers in such large numbers, Ashe's men would have struggled to achieve any useful military objective.

A similar-sized band of equally determined Volunteers, who spent Easter week roaming around nearby Meath and Louth, and also succeeded in capturing barracks, policemen, and army officers, has largely been forgotten. The reason for this was that aside from the killing of one policeman in Castlebellingham (in an unauthorized shooting regretted by the Volunteers), the reluctance of Crown forces to attack them denied them an opportunity for glory.

Perhaps most importantly, the Volunteers at Ashbourne had more stomach for the battle than the RIC. They were, by their own account, committed and well trained: 'Most of the men were good natural shots, which is usual with young men from the country, while some of them were exceptionally good and could be said to be marksmen with a rifle'.[167] While showing no desire to kill policemen in cold blood, they relished the opportunity of a set-piece battle that accorded with their chivalrous notions of conventional warfare. A civilian described the euphoric mood after the battle: 'They were very excited and were cheering, as men would after a football match'.[168] One Volunteer recalled that 'The boys were in great form'.[169] Success in battle engendered such confidence that the news of the surrender in Dublin led to a near mutiny on Saturday. Joseph Lawless's account of the arrival of a column of Lancers leaves little doubt as to the Volunteers' resolve to fight on:

> They were a rather truculent swaggering lot...We were not intimidated either by their voluble oaths or their pennanted lances, but examined their horses and horsemanship with the critical eyes of countrymen to who such things were familiar. I think the feeling was general amongst us that these fellows would have been sitting ducks to us had they ventured to attack our camp.[170]

While Ashe's men were willing to die for their cause, the RIC—many of them Catholic nationalists—were less keen to sacrifice themselves for theirs. Remarkably, the column under fire had received no support from the large force of policemen in the barracks. Constable Eugene Bratton's account also indicated a lack of enthusiasm from some of those among the RIC column under attack:

> We knew what we were about and did not consider it was going to be an easy task. The Marchioness of Conyngham, who lived in Slane Castle...forced the County Inspector to go towards Dublin to meet them...Sergeant Shanaher was the first man to fall; he was shot though the heart...There was a feeling afterwards that this sergeant was shot by one of his own men.

Bratton succeeded in escaping to raise the alarm; admittedly he did return to Ashbourne but, as he put it, 'not in too much of a hurry'.[171] Another policeman who fled the ambush was found hiding under a bed in a nearby house, having stripped off his uniform.[172]

After the Rising, considerable numbers of rural policemen, whether due to their sympathies or fears, proved unwilling to side with the Crown against the rebels: in Galway, for example, all six policemen taken hostage by the rebels refused to identify their captors whom they knew well.[173] Policemen like J. J. McConnell who had joined the RIC when Ireland was at peace—'It never occurred to anyone that I was doing anything unpatriotic—not even the old Fenians and Land Leaguers who still survived, amongst them my father'—resented having to take the side of the British government against their own compatriots. The authority of the British State in Ireland was also challenged by other potent forms of local authority. Although an anonymous letter was sent to the RIC in Ballindaggin, informing it of the involvement of Pat Doyle and several of his comrades in the rebellion in Enniscorthy, the influence of the local priest, a separatist sympathizer, ensured that they were not arrested: 'Sergeant McGlynn showed the letter to Canon Meehan, P. P., Ballindaggin, who advised him not to take any action in the matter'.[174] The IRA was not slow to exploit the ambivalence and fear of Irish policemen in the guerrilla war that would follow.

It is difficult to gauge the civilian response to the rebels' success in Ashbourne. As elsewhere, clerical opinion was divided on the insurrection. Volunteers had left the camp between raids throughout the week to confess their sins to sympathetic priests and Ashe's men were blessed by a priest ('the son of a Fenian') before battle: 'We all knelt down and he gave us conditional absolution and his blessing'.[175] Shortly after the ambush, they met with a rather different response from two priests: 'They were very hostile to us and called us "murderers"'.[176] Local inhabitants were initially amazed by the sight of armed Volunteers cutting telephone wires and attacking post offices: 'The local people who knew me well were shouting "Charlie Weston, are you gone mad?"'.[177] Unsurprisingly, some viewed the rebels and police in a different light after the battle. John Austin, who worked in the local post office, was one of several frightened locals who refused to bring the corpses of the RIC men to Slane despite the promise of a police escort. 'When things had quietened down', he noted, 'the surviving police came down to the village ... They were very shaken and were shivering. One of them remarked to me that the rebels were great men, and I replied, "If you had won, I know what you would do"'.[178] After the rebels finally surrendered, Joseph Lawless described the reaction of one policeman who may have realized how the Rising would change his world and that of every member of the once-respected force:

> I saw Sergeant O'Reilly sitting by himself on the bank while his guard stood dejectedly by. What did he think about it? He did not look much like a victorious enemy as he gazed sadly about him...O'Reilly was one of those, I think, who, finding himself at middle age in the service of the enemy now at war with his countrymen, was seriously disturbed by his latent sympathy for their efforts, but yet felt bound by his contract of service as well as his dependence on it for the welfare of his family.[179]

Just as the rebels hoped, the violence of the Rising would polarize Ireland as never before: after 1916 policemen like O'Reilly would come under increasing pressure to make it clear where they stood, behind the Irish Republic or British rule.

VIII

These ambiguous responses raise the question of how ordinary people would have responded to a more successful rising in the provinces. The experience of Enniscorthy, the only rural town occupied by the rebels for a sustained period, offers some answers. Aside from the relative strength of the separatist movement there, the Enniscorthy battalion seems to have risen because it was one of the few units to receive clear and realistic instructions from the military council—to cut the railway line to prevent military reinforcements landing at Wexford from reaching Dublin—after the Rising had begun:

> On Tuesday and Wednesday rumours of all kind were circulating. Some said the Volunteers were sweeping the country; others that it was only the Citizen Army that had risen and that the Rising had been suppressed. Meetings of the officers were held, but in the absence of any definite or authentic information it was very difficult to decide what to do. However, Vice-Commandant Paul Galligan, who had gone to Dublin on Good Friday, arrived back in Enniscorthy late on Wednesday night. He had cycled all the way from Dublin...It was then decided to rise.[180]

In the early hours of Thursday morning one hundred Volunteers, armed with pikes, shotguns, and no more than two dozen rifles, seized the town.[181] The six policemen in the barracks put up little resistance—only one was wounded—before barricading themselves into their station. The Enniscorthy Volunteers appear to have had a realistic sense of what was achievable; Galligan told a local priest 'that we were only carrying out our orders and I believed that there was no hope of success'.[182] As in north Dublin, the Volunteers engaged in a variety of symbolic gestures. A club known as the Athenaeum was designated as their official headquarters and they paraded from it through the town: 'The republican flag was hoisted... and saluted with bugler and firing party'.[183] For Michael Kirwin, this was 'a thrilling moment', as were 'the first shots fired against the old enemy in Enniscorthy since the battle of Vinegar Hill on June 21st 1798'.[184] Unsurprisingly, Vinegar Hill was also reoccupied, if only to fire off a few ineffectual but symbolic rounds in the direction of the police barracks. As in Dublin, formal proclamations, instructions, and orders were issued. Some practical measures, such as the establishment of a republican police force, were also taken: 'We held the town and set up an administration'.[185] The banks were guarded, shops were ordered to close, and the pubs were locked up: 'during the four days of Republican rule', Fr Patrick Murphy noted with satisfaction, 'not a single person was under the influence of drink'.[186] Vehicles and bicycles were commandeered, and food, bedding, and clothing was requisitioned from local shops: 'Nobody was allowed to leave the town without an official permit and vouchers for provisions were given to deserving people'.[187] As elsewhere, Cumann na mBan 'attended to all the men's wants'.[188]

How did events in Enniscorthy, which the rebels occupied for four days, differ from the rest of the country? The Volunteers' success in capturing the town emboldened others to join them—'Recruits came in so fast that they constituted a problem to arm, equip and feed as well as billet'—suggesting that the military council's dream of a popular insurrection was not entirely fanciful in the right circumstances.[189] Attitudes to the rebels throughout the country were clearly shaped, in part, by the local context: for a brief period in Enniscorthy, a town that had a long-standing Sinn Féin presence, rebellion seemed more viable than futile. The behaviour of one soldier home on leave illustrated the pragmatic response of some nationalists to these changing circumstances: 'He threw off his uniform and joined the Volunteers. He rejoined his regiment when the Rising was over'.[190] Throughout the week, rebel reinforcements arrived from nearby towns such as Wexford, New Ross, and Ferns; non-Volunteers, like Michael O'Brien and Dan Carton, spontaneously 'decided to join up and be with the boys'.[191] As elsewhere, there were priests (including, as in 1798, a patriotic Father Murphy) on hand to provide their blessing, although the police would later claim that most of the clergy remained 'thoroughly loyal'.[192] However, the minority that did not proved influential. Sent to nearby Ballindaggin 'to cut all telephone wires, to close all public houses, to take over the parish hall, and to call on the young men of the district to join the Volunteers', Pat Doyle recalled how the 'parish priest, Canon Meehan, advised the young men to join, and about 100 did so'.[193]

Enniscorthy's 'four glorious days as a Republic' merit only a few lines in most accounts of the Rising but for local republicans its political and psychological impact was profound. The diary of Seán Etchingham, a future Dáil government minister, conveys the excitement and pride of the Volunteers on the liberation of their town: 'We had had at least one day of blissful freedom. We have had Enniscorthy under the laws of the Irish Republic for at least one day and it pleases me to learn that the citizens are appreciably surprised...a more orderly town could not be imagined'. 'The people of the town are great', he enthused, 'The manhood of Enniscorthy is worthy of its manhood'.[194] Máire Fitzpatrick, whose family had devoted long fruitless years to separatist struggle, experienced a euphoric sense of vindication:

> Mother and my sisters were making pots of tea. I went out on the street to see what was on. As long as I live, that morning sight will never leave my mind. A glorious day, Mike Moran...was standing at White's corner with a rifle covering the police barracks. Andy McKeever was at the other side of the street with a rifle. Dad with a can of tea and he feeding the sentries. He was an old man then with snow white hair. Nobody else about but an old man with a bucket of tea, two young men with rifles, and I knew then all our work was not in vain. We were on the road to freedom.[195]

Notwithstanding such individual experiences, the limits to what was achieved in Enniscorthy were also apparent. The Volunteers may have seized the town, but they failed to capture even the local police barracks. They were unable to inspire similar uprisings in the south of the county where support for Redmond was much stronger. In nearby Wexford and New Ross, the rebels were opposed by 'a lot of armed police and Redmond's

Volunteers', and the people remained 'very hostile'.[196] By Saturday, Galligan had run out of ideas, leading a fifty-strong column on a march to Dublin that made it no further than the next village.

Although the rebels were keen to emphasize the popular support they enjoyed—'there was no undue commandeering and no one was victimised on account of his political leaning'—the sectarian realities of Irish society inevitably conflicted with the idealism of the rebels.[197] The Rising did not represent liberation for the local Protestant (or, as Volunteers described it, 'British loyalist') population: the 'houses of nearly all the loyalists were visited by parties of Volunteers and motor cars and arms seized'.[198] Immediately after the rebellion, 'an exodus of church people began', a local Anglican minister claimed: 'Many were frightened by what had taken place, and were anxious to get to England or Northern Ireland'.[199] The police would also deny that there had been significant local support for the Rising: 'they terrorised the whole of the inhabitants into joining them'.[200] This seems unlikely but 'the people' were clearly more divided than separatists like Etchingham were willing to concede. After the surrender, when the RIC entered Enniscorthy, the county inspector was able to arm over two hundred locals to hold the town until the army's arrival: 'the National Volunteers, Hibernians, Unionists, and, in fact, everyone was most keen in helping the police'.[201] 'Things moved pretty fast', Máire Fitzpatrick remarked bitterly after the fall of Enniscorthy, 'The rats all came out of their holes to welcome the British soldiers'.[202]

IX

The mobilizations that occurred in Galway, north Dublin, Meath, and Wexford proved the exception: the debacles in Cork and Ulster reflected the experiences of most provincial Volunteers. Throughout much of the country, there was no attempt to mobilize. It did not necessarily follow from this that the Rising had little impact in these areas. Daniel O'Shaughnessy, one of many boys at the time who would go on to fight in the War of Independence, described the dramatic effect of the news of the rebellion in his remote village in southeast County Limerick:

At Easter, 1916, I was 14 years of age...Edmond Hayes was my teacher. His room was composed of three sons of District Inspector Reid and many other Protestants and policeman's sons, including two sons of Head Constable

Creedon. Then, one day early in the week, he evidently could not contain himself any longer. He burst forth into a speech and a tirade of abuse against the British government and all it stood for until he had us almost frightened out of our wits. At the end of his short but virile speech, he said—Irishmen's blood was flowing out there—pointing to the field outside—and the whole class involuntarily looked out the window to see the battle that was raging... We were really disappointed when we couldn't see the invisible battle.[203]

Opinion remains sharply divided as to the significance of the Rising in the provinces. A recent account of the rebellion in Galway, drawing on the new evidence provided by the Bureau of Military History, rejects the assumption of 'most historians that the aim of the insurrection was not a successful military victory', arguing that it 'was intended as a serious attempt to defeat the British military forces in Ireland'.[204] Were it not for the interception of the *Aud* and MacNeill's countermand, Fergus Campbell (and many others) argues, the Volunteers would have mounted a nationwide rebellion: 'the fact that 500 rebels in Galway, armed with less than 50 rifles, were able to take control of a substantial proportion of the county for almost a week suggests that if similar risings had taken place in other counties, a serious provincial insurrection was a possibility'.[205] Similar views were expressed by well-informed contemporaries including the RIC inspector general and General Maxwell who, in a secret report, warned: 'we have narrowly missed a most serious rebellion. Had any initial success been achieved it would have spread all over Ireland (except Ulster)'.[206]

This account of how the Rising was experienced beyond Dublin challenges these assessments. The notion that several thousand Volunteers could have taken on the British army in any conventional sense, given the disparity of military resources, seems absurd. For a multitude of practical reasons, conspiratorial rebellions were as unlikely to succeed in Ireland as elsewhere in modern Europe: 'Without access to real military resources, or without some catastrophic collapse of the opposing state and army, it was just a matter of the greater force prevailing'.[207] In contrast, the idea that a guerrilla war campaign, underpinned by strong public support, could have presented real difficulties for a British army under enormous pressure on the Western Front, forcing the Government to consider some form of compromise settlement, was not unrealistic, as the 1919–21 conflict would demonstrate. However, the advocates of this more viable strategy, including Bulmer Hobson and J. J. O'Connell, were to be found among the anti-insurrectionary Volunteer leadership rather than the military council.

The rebels' prospects must be evaluated in terms of their own objectives: the overthrow of British rule by an uprising of the sort that they planned for. Even in Galway, where the mobilization was unusually effective, the argument that the Volunteers could have met with any meaningful degree of success seems unconvincing. Only a quarter of the movement there ultimately took to the field in arms and, rather than controlling 'a substantial proportion of the county', they failed to capture a single police station, before retreating into a series of strategically pointless positions. Moreover, it was soon forgotten that large numbers of nationalists mobilized throughout the county to fight against them: indeed, one recent local study has argued that the humiliating failure of the Volunteers in Galway in 1916 contributed to their subsequent ineffectiveness during the War of Independence.[208] Much of the evidence from the provinces challenges the tendency to view the Rising as a potentially serious military venture.[209] Other recent local studies suggest that the obstacles facing the rebels—due to the secrecy of the military council's deliberations, the inadequacy of its strategy, its failure to convey clear or achievable objectives to the provincial leadership, the low level of mobilization, and the opposition of militant provincial leaders to the strategy of an unprovoked insurrection—were significantly greater than the capture of the *Aud* and the countermand, devastating though both of these incidents were.[210]

Moreover, in light of what we now know about British intelligence's knowledge of the plan to import arms, the shortcomings of the military council's arrangements to land and distribute those arms, and the depth of opposition within the Volunteer and IRB leadership to the Rising, it is difficult to envisage any circumstances in which it could have been successful. Given the circumstances, the argument that were it not for the *Aud* and the countermand the country would have risen seems rather like saying that had the Rising occurred in a different context to that which existed at the time the result would have been different. This preoccupation with the implausible counterfactual of a viable military uprising (a reaction to the opposing tendency to dismiss the Rising as an irrational blood sacrifice) overlooks another possibility. A more widespread insurrection—entailing a more ruthless and systematic coercion of separatist organizations—may have proved more harmful to the republican cause than the actual repression that followed which provoked 'maximum resentment, minimum fear'.[211] While the military council obviously hoped for a serious nationwide insurrection, the real question is whether they—and the provincial leadership—believed that one was possible at the time. Having worked towards building a force capable of serious military action, it is striking how many Volunteer leaders outside Dublin refused to commit it to a rebellion that appeared to them little more than a futile gesture.

7

A Good End

Punishment

The Rising ended in as chaotic a fashion as it had begun. Although Pearse signed a general order of surrender at the Irish Command's Parkgate Street headquarters on Saturday afternoon, the only other garrison to surrender that day was the Four Courts. Over the course of the following day, Boland's bakery, the Royal College of Surgeons, Jacob's biscuit factory, and the South Dublin Union followed suit. The dangerous and confusing position in Dublin accounted for some of the delay; communication and movement remained difficult, even for the British officers who escorted Elizabeth O'Farrell to the other rebel garrisons with Pearse's surrender order. The drawn out process also reflected the fact that many Volunteers—both officers and rank-and-file—were reluctant to surrender so long as it remained possible to fight on.

I

The rebel commandants were assisted in their efforts to persuade their men to obey the surrender order by the many priests present who urged them to consider the lives of Dublin's civilians. Despite the inferno on Sackville Street, many Volunteers in other garrisons were shocked when they learned that Pearse had agreed to surrender. When Elizabeth O'Farrell was brought to Jacob's on Sunday morning, Thomas MacDonagh (who had resolved 'that he would never surrender') refused to obey Pearse's order on the grounds that it was invalidated by his imprisonment.[1] Insisting that he would only negotiate with the General Officer Commanding the British Forces, and that his garrison could hold out until the course of the

Great War changed in Ireland's direction, he appeared to be unable to face reality.[2] When General Lowe personally made clear the consequences of a refusal to surrender, for both the rebels and the inhabitants of the area, MacDonagh finally relented. Some of his men felt just as strongly. The news that their commandant had agreed to surrender provoked 'incredible pandemonium and confusion' as Volunteers 'became hysterical, weeping openly, breaking their rifles against the walls'.[3] A near mutiny followed as rebels confronted a distraught MacDonagh, who disowned responsibility for the decision, unhelpfully adding that he did not believe the clerical assurances that none would be shot.[4] John MacBride eventually restored order, asking his men 'did they think he would surrender if he thought there was any chance of success, adding, that we must now save the lives of our people'.[5] The inaction at Jacob's made the capitulation all the more difficult to accept: Thomas Slater recalled 'a lot of recrimination that we were surrendering without having been in action at all'.[6]

Other garrisons that had seen relatively little action were also reluctant to surrender. Volunteers at Marrowbone Lane Distillery felt 'deeply humiliated' as a result of not being involved in any fighting.[7] The rumour that Pearse had surrendered 'was laughed at' in Boland's: 'we were holding our own, so fight on'.[8] Joseph O'Byrne was 'stunned' when the news, which he claimed met with 'general disapproval', was confirmed on Sunday: 'we could not conceive a collapse so quickly, believing that the rest of the country had risen'.[9] 'The excitement in Boland's was terrible. What did we want to surrender for?', Peadar O'Mara recalled: 'Volunteers were shouting themselves hoarse, denouncing everyone who had surrendered; others were singing songs and some were openly crying'.[10]

Volunteers who had been in the thick of action also saw little reason to surrender. In the narrow streets to the north of the Four Courts, where 16 soldiers had been killed and another 31 wounded in intense street-fighting on Friday and Saturday, the First Battalion outposts were notably reluctant to surrender. Cut off from the Four Courts garrison which had surrendered, many refused to capitulate on Saturday, agreeing only reluctantly to a temporary truce—brokered by priests—until Pearse's orders were confirmed the following morning. The news of the surrender provoked a similar response in the South Dublin Union: 'I felt kind of sick in my stomach', Robert Holland remembered, 'Colbert could hardly speak as he stood in the yard for a moment or two. He was completely stunned. The tears rolled down his cheeks'.[11] Others were angry, Lily Cooney recalled: 'they were saying "Was this what we were preparing for and living for all this time?" "Is this the end of all our hopes?" They were flinging their rifles around in temper and disgust'.[12]

There were numerous reasons for this highly charged response. Many Volunteers had a misleading impression of their position. 'I fainted at the news, it nearly broke my heart', a Cumann na mBan member recalled, 'After a week in which Tom MacDonagh kept us up by telling: "We are a great success"'.[13] When Piaras Beaslai, the vice-commandant of the Four Courts garrison, heard that a surrender had been ordered, he 'scoffed at the idea, pointing out that the position was "impregnable and could be held for a month"'.[14] One Volunteer in Boland's even assumed that the order meant that they had won: 'By heavens we have beaten the hell out of them and Pearse has ordered an unconditional surrender'.[15] Some rebels continued to believe that they could fight their way from the city to the mountains. Others were reluctant to surrender because of the likely consequences: 'surrender never crossed my mind', Joseph O'Connor stated, 'I knew perfectly well that surrender would mean hanging'.[16] At Jacob's, Seamus Hughes argued that it would be 'better to die with guns in our hands than to face the firing squad'.[17] In the Four Courts, one Volunteer recalled, 'we all thought that we were going to be shot'.[18] In contrast, Connolly, MacDermott, Clarke, and Plunkett assured their followers that although the signatories of the Proclamation would be executed, senior officers and the rank-and-file would be eventually allowed to return home. Ceannt told his men: 'You men will get a double journey, but we, the leaders, will get a single journey'.[19]

Like the leaders, many ordinary Volunteers appear to have accepted that they would die in the Rising, and some even preferred the idea to surrender. Recalling the 'heart-rending' scenes in the College of Surgeons, Frank Robbins claimed: 'The act of surrender was to each a greater calamity than death itself at that moment'.[20] Attempting to console a youth 'leaning on a shotgun and in floods of tears' in Jacob's, Thomas Meldon was surprised when he was 'turned on with the bitter retort: "I came out to fight, not to surrender"'.[21] That the surrender was unconditional made it all the more painful, as some leaders had previously made much of the possibility of forcing the British authorities to concede terms. Hearing an officer describe them as 'a lot of bloody rebels', it dawned on Charles Saurin 'that perhaps there was not going to be so much of the prisoner of war business for us'.[22] Joseph O'Byrne was angered by 'the thought of having to deliver ourselves as prisoners to an enemy who, we knew, would not acknowledge us as combatants in war, but as outlaws without any of the rights of enemy prisoners'.[23]

The reluctance to surrender was also linked to a sense of humiliation, reflecting the Volunteers' militaristic ethos. Many found it difficult to relinquish their weapons, smashing or burying them rather than handing them over.[24] Patrick Kelly recalled: 'After parting with my rifle I felt sad as if I had lost a very dear comrade'.[25] 'I dumped my gun with the rest', a Fianna captain stated, 'and it was the saddest parting I can remember'.[26] In north Dublin, as Ashe's vanquished column awaited the arrival of police reinforcements, 'Men who were passing aimlessly back and forward and gazing lovingly at the rifles took one up now and then, to have the last feel of it as it were, which seemed to make the policemen more nervous'.[27] Others handed over their weapons only when told that it was 'not honourable' to destroy them.[28] For one Volunteer, their disarmament brought home 'the destruction for God knows how long of the movement, built up with such skill and sacrifice and in spite of tremendous opposition'.[29] Beyond Dublin, the surrender of guns by commandants in areas where the Volunteers had not risen was seen as particularly shameful: in Cork city, Donal Óg O'Callaghan's anger led him to unfairly denounce the leadership there as 'three incompetent men in a state of blue funk'. The recriminations that followed led to bitter tensions, formal inquiries, and greater radicalism: 'Tomás MacCurtain said to me later, "If I live I will redeem 1916"'.[30]

The fact that many Volunteers chose not to escape despite ample opportunities to do so reflected a similar preoccupation with military honour, which would come to form an important aspect of the insurrection's powerful impact on public and separatist opinion. At Boland's bakery, de Valera told his men that as they had gone into battle together, they should surrender together.[31] Volunteers in the South Dublin Union resolved 'to stand together to the end'.[32] In the College of Surgeons, when Michael Mallin advised those who wanted to leave to do so, most refused: 'we have fought together, and, if necessary, we will die together'.[33] There was no shortage of chivalry and self-sacrifice. Michael McDonnell recalled that when he urged John MacBride to leave before he was spotted by the G men, 'He slightly bowed his head as if in deep emotion and replied: "Oh Mac! I wouldn't leave the boys"'.[34] Not everyone behaved in such a gallant way: at Jacob's, and elsewhere, 'some of the boys just walked out in the crowd which lined the way to the point of surrender'. 'Toor-a-loo, boys, I'm off', Joe McGrath, a future government minister and successful businessman, cheerfully announced before strolling out of Marrowbone Lane Distillery.[35] But most stayed. They 'thought they were in honour bound by the agreement to surrender, and "the hit and run" technique of the Black-and-Tan days had not been developed', Padraig Ó Ceallaigh reflected: 'But, it was the gallant hopelessness of the fight, the executions and the subsequent jailings and repressions that brought about a revulsion of feeling in favour of the Volunteers'.[36]

The Rising ended with the same emphasis on dignified, conventional military behaviour that had characterized it throughout, a mindset that reflected their internalization of their opponents' cultural values. 'Ceannt and General Lowe marched at the head of the men', Thomas Doyle recalled, 'Eamon looked great; he had his shirt thrown open, his tunic thrown open and was swinging along at the head of his men. He looked a real soldier'.[37] Even in defeat, Volunteers took pride in their military bearing, noting with satisfaction the enemy's admiration of their conduct. Eamon Dore was impressed by the sight of the Four Courts men marching behind Ned Daly:

> Still the same quiet, calm, self-possessed Ned, unconquered and unconquerable as his men marching four deep behind him. He brought them up O'Connell St, dropped out when he came to his allotted position and then drilled his men leaving them two deep 'standing easy'...I heard a British sergeant say to another 'That's an officer and those fellows know their stuff'.[38]

Eamon Price felt 'really proud of my Volunteers' as they marched in formation, executing 'a series of parade-ground manoeuvres' before laying down their arms.[39] British observers were also impressed: MacDonagh, remarked one, 'came to the surrendering-place as coolly as if he were going for a stroll of a summer evening'.[40] Another admiringly observed that the rebels 'held themselves erect, and looked absolutely defiant'.[41] For the military council, one of the objectives of the Rising had been to restore dignity to the separatist movement and the nation by making a courageous and disciplined stand in the face of impossible odds. In terms of its impact on public opinion, the rebels' manly acceptance of defeat and punishment, carefully choreographed by their leaders, exerted a greater emotional charge than the six days of scrappy fighting that preceded it. Although few yet realized it, their power to engender public sympathy

was vastly greater as noble victims of British injustice than fanatical
perpetrators of violence.

The defeated Volunteers experienced a multitude of conflicting
emotions. Addressing them before the surrender, their leaders emphasized
their achievements: 'we have won what we fought for', Ceannt declared,
'You may not see it now but you will see it later'.[42] Although beaten, they
were not cowed, Daly insisted: 'we should carry ourselves with pride and
conduct ourselves as true soldiers of the Republic'. Nonetheless, many—
like Michael Knightly—felt crushed: 'I thought of what was likely to
happen, especially the shooting of our leaders and the humiliation of our
rank and file. I burst into tears. A Church St priest, who was standing
close by, said: "Ah, be a man". I felt very hurt but made no reply'.[43] John
Shouldice described 'a feeling of pride amongst us that we defied the
might of England for a whole week', tempered by the knowledge 'that we
could meet with very little mercy from our old enemy'.[44] As the surrender
got underway in the College of Surgeons, Frank Robbins recalled how
the depressing atmosphere lifted: 'We were satisfied that all things that
were possible had been done. There was nothing to be ashamed of'.[45]
Marching to the surrender point, some of the Four Courts garrison were
disheartened but others sang, whistled, and shouted slogans such as 'Long
live the Irish Republic'. Such defiance, as Joe Good noted, did not go
down well with their opponents:

> The bearing and behaviour of the Volunteers was that of men who had done
> something laudable and, as their behaviour had been chivalrous, they
> expected that military etiquette would be observed by the enemy. The
> British soldiers—officers and men—were obviously irritated and puzzled by
> the Volunteers. They were shocked at the small numbers that surrendered
> and at the variety and crudity of their arms. They regarded the Volunteers
> as shameless, impertinent traitors, and said so.[46]

Walking through the smoking ruins of the city, with corpses still littering
the streets, the Volunteers finally witnessed the destruction they had
unleashed: 'The heart of the city presented a picture of utter desolation'.[47]
After the artillery barrage of the previous days, many found the silence—
broken only by the sound of marching feet, intermittent sniper-fire, and
the shouts of hostile onlookers—eerie. The rebels were left in little doubt
about the continued anger of many ordinary Dubliners, which some felt
had changed little since Easter Monday. Rebels were hissed at, pelted with
refuse, and denounced as 'murderers' and 'starvers of the people'. On High

Street, Joe Good recalled, 'crowds of women were in the side streets and they shouted "Bayonet them" '.[48]

It is difficult to know how widespread such sentiments were. Fred McKenzie, a Canadian journalist, reported that poorer districts were more sympathetic towards the rebels than more affluent parts of the city, particularly after their defeat.[49] However, James Stephens felt that the 'best dressed' and 'worst dressed' tended to be the most hostile.[50] Many Volunteers also believed that the very poor were the most antagonistic: 'the rabble of the city and not the ordinary citizen'. Almost everyone agreed that the most vocal protestors were the women of the slums: 'They looked like a few who were around during the French Revolution', Patrick Rankin recalled, 'The women were allowed to follow our men to barracks, shouting to the soldiers "use your rifles on the German so and so's" '.[51]

Lily Cooney was thankful for the presence of British soldiers as they marched towards St Patrick's Cathedral: 'we would have been torn to pieces by the "separation" women who followed us shouting out abuse and obscene language'.[52] At Francis Street, Charles Saurin was shocked by the 'mass of howling, shrieking women from the back streets who called us filthy names and hurled curses at us': 'The mounted officer in charge of us showed faint amusement at all these women's hatred and excitement; the Staffords marched stolidly on'.[53] For Frank Robbins, it was a painfully disillusioning experience:

> remembering these scenes along the route, particularly at Inchicore, the cheering and waving of hats and Union Jacks for the Staffordshire Regiment as they marched us into Richmond Barracks, the cries of encouragement...to 'shoot the traitors' and 'bayonet the bastards', seems to be incredible and just one bad dream...were the British army to have withdrawn at that moment, there would have been no need for court-martials or prisons as the mob would have relieved them of such necessities.

There were dissenting voices, Robbins noted, but they formed a 'very small section of those assembled'.[54] A courageous fireman shouted 'I'm with you boys' as Joe Good walked down Sackville Street: 'the first word of approval I heard from Dubliners that week'.[55] Another Volunteer recalled a solitary woman on High Street shouting encouragement: 'She was absolutely fearless and her encouragement at that stage had the effect of a tonic'.[56] More significantly, the Third Battalion was consoled by the presence of a large crowd outside Boland's bakery: 'many weeping and expressing sympathy and sorrow, all of them friendly and kind'.[57]

Some onlookers were also cowed rather than hostile, and it was obvious to Volunteers that some of those who stood watching in silence were sympathetic. Rebel sympathizers had good reason for reticence. The authorities did not require much of a reason to arrest people in the aftermath of the rebellion. Áine Ceannt witnessed the arrest of one woman who had cheered as they passed.[58] Several drunks who jokingly fell in with marching Volunteers were not allowed to leave later; elsewhere, a Russian sailor was inexplicably forced to join the prisoners. Civilians with gunshot wounds, drunks, looters, and the overcurious were also arrested. People were even arrested for 'wearing anything unusual, like kilts', an officer of the Royal Dublin Fusiliers claimed, including a particularly unfortunate woman who had been 'dressed in green'.[59]

II

For the first time, British army soldiers and rebels came into close contact. As Dublin was a small city, some already knew each other. At Jacob's, 'as one brother left the factory in the republican ranks another marched into it in the uniform of the British army'.[60] Eamon Price, a legal clerk, knew his arresting officer, a barrister: 'our relations were friendly and courteous'.[61] It is difficult to generalize about military attitudes to the rebels. Some soldiers were friendly, others were hostile; many did their jobs professionally: 'my experience of British Tommies', Michael Knightly recalled, 'was that their conduct generally was considerate'.[62] 'Generally speaking the Tommy was not a bad fellow', Ignatius Callender stated, 'even if at times his language was not all that could be desired'. There was certainly much curiosity about the Volunteers on their part. Some army officers were surprised to encounter well-educated rebels, not 'the riff-raff they were represented by the English and Irish press'.[63] A priest recalled Lord Powerscourt and his officers paying fulsome tribute to the rebels: 'they are the cleanest and bravest lot of boys he had ever met'.[64] But many soldiers remained perplexed and angry about what had happened:

> The soldier on my right was a rather beefy red-faced sergeant, and his indig-
> nation at our preposterous attack on the Empire knew no bounds. Almost
> the whole way along he cursed us fervently and went into all the gory
> details of what he would like to do to us if he had his way. 'Here I am', said
> he, 'having come safely through two blankety years in the blankety trenches

in France, come here for a blankety rest, and then run the chances of getting a blankety bullet from a lot of blank-blank-blanks like you', and so on ad nauseum. I could understand how he felt even then.[65]

Curiously, though, many soldiers didn't take the rebellion too personally. Callender's escort spent more time complaining about his officers than the rebels, before discreetly releasing him down a quiet lane: 'I think you ought to bolt...but don't go down that street again or that so and so Captain will put a bullet through you'.[66] The Lancers who arrested another Volunteer 'were nice type of fellows and never passed any offensive remarks to us'.[67] When William Oman was attacked by a mob on Grafton Street, 'The British officer displayed great courage...he told the crowd that, if they did not get back, he would shoot them'.[68] As they waited on Sackville St, Volunteers received a friendly warning from a sympathetic officer: 'a very decent type...he told us if we had anything on us which we should not have, we were to drop it on the ground at our feet'.[69] William Daly's military doctor admonished him for destroying 'the good work that J. E. Redmond was doing' but hid his bullets and other incriminating evidence.[70] When one soldier threatened to bayonet John Kenny as he lay in a stretcher, 'another soldier angrily intervened between us and threatened his comrade in turn, telling him he ought to be ashamed of himself'.[71]

Many of these soldiers were Irish Catholics and, for at least some of these men, their loyalty to the army (or Crown) was strained by local, national, or religious sympathies. Many nationalists, after all, had enlisted in order to win Home Rule for Ireland rather than because of any particular sympathy for Britain. Even John Regan—a (Catholic) Royal Irish Regiment officer with firm unionist convictions—appears to have experienced a degree of ambivalence, recalling how there was

> something weird in the sound of marching at the dead of night as the prisoners were singing, *God Save Ireland*. I seemed to hear the words, 'What matter if for Erin's cause we fall', sung in deadly earnest for the first time. I was greatly impressed in spite of my antipathy towards them owing to the loss of some of my men.[72]

Many Irish soldiers openly expressed sympathy with the rebels' objectives. Patrick Colgan was guarded by a 'decent poor fellow' from a neighbouring county who spent the day getting 'very tight': 'He couldn't understand why we should start a rebellion until the lads returned from the Dardenelles'.[73] A friendly Irish officer complained 'that we started the "racket" too soon', while Charles Saurin witnessed an altercation between sympathetic Irish solders and British soldiers who were abusing the rebels outside the Rotunda.[74] Another officer, who initially denounced the rebels as traitors, reportedly broke down in tears: 'Why didn't you wait till the war was over, and we'd all be with you'.[75] Others admired the rebels' conduct, if not their actions. At Richmond Barracks, one Volunteer was plied with biscuits and cigarettes by a tipsy soldier: 'He was very friendly and said he was an Irishman and proud of it and that he admired the way we fought'.[76] Michael Newell witnessed a dramatic example of the ability of local loyalties to transcend other allegiances when his group of prisoners from Galway was attacked by a mob in Nottingham en route to Frongoch prison camp: 'One of the soldiers dropped his rifle to the trail position and struck three of the hostile crowd, knocking them out. He then shouted: "Up Carraroe, Up Connemara"'.[77] Such accounts highlight one of the underlying weaknesses of British rule in Ireland, its reliance on the pragmatic acquiescence—rather than affection or loyalty—of much of the nationalist population. The repression that followed would ultimately stretch this highly conditional acceptance of the legitimacy of British authority beyond breaking point.

Some Irish soldiers demonstrated, if not sympathy, an intriguing ambivalence towards their compatriots. When Jim Grace (one of the veterans of Mount Street) broke down in tears, he was rebuked by an Irish RAMC officer who 'told him not to let the British see how he felt. He could still serve his country by keeping a brave face'.[78] Confined in a cattle pen in the Royal Dublin Society, one Volunteer was struck by the reason offered by one army officer for his kindness: 'He said to me, "I'll get some tea, because the same blood is in my veins as is in yours"'.[79] Such ambivalence was shared by English soldiers with Irish backgrounds like Edward Casey, a Cockney from Canning Town: 'It was easy to see that all those Tommys who had (like me) joined Irish regiments were upset at the Rising'.[80] Catholicism constituted another common bond and potential source of conflicting allegiances, one that would subsequently be skilfully exploited by republican propagandists. Some of the Irish soldiers at Richmond barracks, Seán Duffy observed, 'expressed sympathy—or rather pity for us.' Later, as they said the rosary, an armed sentry 'at the door put in his head and said, "I am glad to hear you at that, for I'm a Catholic myself." '[81] Other soldiers requested the rosary for themselves or relatives who had died in the war.

Of course, some Irish soldiers demonstrated no such ambivalence, and many rebels were brutally treated by their compatriots. Patrick Colgan's amiable Irish guard reported to 'an ignorant thug' from Dublin who 'instructed them to shoot at the least sign of movement'.[82] Séamus Murphy complained that the Irish soldiers were the most brutal:

> We were brought over to Kilmainham Jail, where some drunken soldiery of the Dublin Fusiliers immediately set upon us, kicking us, beating us and threatening us with bayonets...my tunic was ripped off me with bayonets, and our shirts and other articles of clothing were saturated with blood. We looked at one another the next morning and we thought we were dead. The Dublin Fusiliers were the worst of the lot. The English soldiers were mostly decent.[83]

Some soldiers behaved as occupying armies do everywhere. Volunteers were humiliated, robbed, beaten, bayoneted, threatened with summary execution, and murdered in cold blood: inevitably, it was these experiences, rather than any acts of decency, which shaped contemporary perceptions and the subsequent social memory of the British response to the Rising. In reality, much of the mistreatment endured by many in the immediate aftermath of the insurrection was due to the authorities' inability to respond to the extraordinary circumstances. The four hundred rebels who surrendered on Saturday were forced to spend the night penned into a small garden in front of the Rotunda Hospital because there was nowhere else to put them: 'we got no food or water; nor were any arrangements made to segregate the sexes'.[84] Liam Tobin recalled: 'those of us who wanted to relieve ourselves had to do it lying on the grass alongside our own comrades'.[85] T. M. Healy, the barrister and nationalist politician, observed that although it had been impossible to make proper arrangements for the rebels, their humiliation at the Rotunda 'left a memory as bitter as that enkindled by the executions...Men gnashed their teeth at the shame to which both sexes were exposed'.[86]

But much of the abuse that occurred that night was avoidable. An officer who had been held hostage by the rebels walked among them to identify his captors: '"I know this one and that one". "Monkey face", "Beast face", "Ape face" were some of the expressions he used'.[87] The soldiers' 'filthy expressions' outraged Winifred Carney: 'many of the boys are so young and have been to Communion before the Rising. I whispered to Seán [MacDermott] what I would do if I had my revolver'.[88] Soldiers inevitably took the opportunity to exact revenge: 'These are the bastards who shot our men in North King St'.[89] Eamon Dore described how one deranged officer, Captain Lee-Wilson, drunkenly abused Tom Clarke and other leaders:

> he stripped all three to the skin in the presence of us and, being broad daylight, in the presence of those nurses looking out windows. A comrade of mine... who was lying beside me on the grass swore out "if that fellow lives through the war I will search for him and kill him for this." He and four others kept that promise.[90]

Prisoners were put wherever they could be accommodated, most ending up in Richmond barracks in Inchicore. The largest group of rebels, who arrived there on Sunday, received little better treatment than they had on the previous night outside the Rotunda: 'We stood for about two hours on the square in Richmond Barracks, men continually falling down from exhaustion'.[91] Some were told that they would be shot, while many were robbed. (Frank Burke, who put in a claim for ten shillings 'for fun', was amazed to receive the money a year later, testimony both to the efficiency and curious integrity of aspects of the imperial bureaucracy.[92]) Rations—bully beef and hard biscuits—were meagre (as they were for soldiers), and water was withheld or served in buckets 'without any means of getting a drink from them, unless you put your head into them'.[93] Prisoners were crammed into rooms without beds, and denied exercise for days at a time: 'it was an all too common sight to see prisoners falling in a faint from loss of food and being prevented for over twenty-four hours from performing the ordinary calls of nature'.[94] The barracks was cold—'We slept together on the floor of the room, huddled together for warmth'—and sanitary conditions 'revolting' ('a large boiler in the room served as a latrine').[95]

As they arrived, the rebels were finger-printed and scrutinized in the gymnasium by army officers, CID detectives, and G men who attempted to separate the leaders from followers. The G men were particularly resented: 'One would imagine that they were going to a wedding as they were all smiles'.[96] In contrast, DMP constables like Patrick Bermingham were generally more reluctant to identify rebels, whether due to their politics or instinct for self-preservation: 'We pretended we never saw the men before'.[97] The DMP men who stood guard over Charles Saurin and his comrades 'could not or would not look straight at us': 'I felt they were ashamed of the part they had to play'.[98] Some of the hostages also refused to identify their captors: the army officer who had so cheerfully offered his medical expertise in the

GPO insisted that 'he was a doctor not a policeman'.[99] An Irish soldier who had been held prisoner in the GPO proved equally sympathetic: 'When passing me he winked and passed on', Patrick Colgan recalled; 'although he knew all the Rathfarnham Volunteers he did not identify one person for the British'.[100] Despite the G men's familiarity with their prey, some of the rebels were so dishevelled they were barely recognizable. Uniforms were mistakenly considered a sign of seniority. One Volunteer described how Seán MacDermott, dressed in plain clothes, and overlooked until the last minute, almost succeeded in leaving the barracks with a large body of deportees: 'I heard a voice, that of Johnny Barton, the "G" man, saying: "Ah no, Johnny, you're not leaving us"'.[101]

In the nationalist mythology that developed after the Rising, the G men were a dangerous and despised elite. In reality, some were friendly enough but most appear to have performed their work dutifully on this occasion. The odd detective did turn a blind eye: 'Good enough of him, he passed me by although he knew me well'.[102] But inevitably it was the malicious attitude of a minority of G men including Daniel Hoey ('He appeared to be relishing the job') and Johnny Barton ('He did more than his duty') that became the stuff of bitter legend.[103] One Volunteer witnessed the latter taunt Joseph Connolly: 'he opened his conversation by saying, "What is your name" though he knew perfectly well beforehand that he was a brother of Seán Connolly's. The next observation was: "Seán is dead". Joe replied, "He died for his country", to which Johnny retorted, "He was a disgrace to his country"'.[104] The fact that the same names were repeatedly mentioned by Volunteers suggests that most G men did their job and no more: Barton and Hoey were subsequently assassinated by the IRA as a consequence of their excessive devotion to their work.

The eighty or so women taken into custody generally received more benign treatment. Although Countess Markievicz was singled out for ridicule by the Dublin Fusiliers, like all women she was treated more leniently than her male comrades by the authorities.[105] Rose McNamara's diary entry, describing the surrender at Marrowbone Lane, suggests that both male and female rebels assumed not only that the women would not be searched but that they would be allowed to go home:

> We all (22 of us) gave ourselves up and marched down between two lines of our brave men. We waited until all the arms were taken away. The men gave each of us their small arms to do as we liked with, thinking we were going to go home, but we were not going to leave the men we were with

all the week to their fate; we decided to go along with them and be with them to the end whatever our fate might be. Some of the girls had as many as three revolvers...The sergeant in Richmond barracks told us we would be searched in Kilmainham, so after a while we reluctantly gave them up to him.[106]

The Volunteers, Lily Cooney similarly recalled, 'tried to persuade us to go home, but we refused, saying that we would stick it out to the end. I certainly have the impression that we could have gone home if we wanted to'.[107] In order to be arrested, many women were compelled to insist—to Volunteers and British soldiers alike—that it was their right. Other women were forced to insist on their combatant status, as the arresting officers assumed that they had been abducted by the rebels: 'It would never occur to them, of course, that they were women soldiers'.[108]

Some army officers clearly had little desire to arrest women, particularly the younger ones, and many were held only briefly for questioning before being released.[109] A group of women who had travelled from Liverpool to participate in the Rising were given fares to return home by the authorities, despite offering the less than convincing explanation that they had travelled to Dublin for a holiday.[110] Some chivalrous (or patriarchal) officers 'tried to get the girls to say that they were only doing first-aid': Áine Ceannt unhelpfully made it clear that she 'would have done anything that she was asked to do'.[111] Women both resented and exploited their inferior status. Min Ryan recalled an amusing example of the former during the surrender at Jacob's: 'One of the officers said: "We are not taking women, are we?" The other said: "No". We went off. Louise [Gavan Duffy] said: "The cheek of him anyway—not taking women"'.[112] But women could also capitalize on their gender to behave more defiantly—singing, dancing, or giving their names in Gaelic—than men without the risk of a beating. When a military party raided her home, Bridget Foley demurely refused to climb into the lorry 'unless they got a ladder'.[113]

Although women prisoners were exposed to harsh conditions in the aftermath of the Rising this was primarily due to the inadequate provisions for their incarceration. Ship Street barracks, where some were held, was described by Bridget Foley as a 'terrible place' with 'no sanitary arrangements': 'A sergeant came with a bucket which he placed behind the door. We became infested with flies and lice'.[114] Kathleen Lynn's account of the sanitary arrangements at Ship Street demonstrated how, even among the Citizen Army revolutionaries, access to the sole basin of water for washing was governed by surprisingly conventional considerations of social status: 'I being the doctor used it first. Miss Ffrench Mullen second, and Miss Molony [an actor] was last'.[115] Conditions at Richmond barracks were judged 'not too bad' by female prisoners although they were initially not supplied with blankets or mattresses.[116] Most of the women were at first held in Kilmainham in basic conditions: 'The prison was filthy as it had not been used for 16 years. There were no chairs, or forms or tables. We had to sit on the dirty floors with our backs against the dirty walls'.[117] Sanitary arrangements were humiliating: 'we had to knock at the door and two soldiers with fixed bayonets brought us to the lavatory which was a dry closet that had no door', Bridget Foley recalled: 'The soldiers stood jeering at whatever girl was in the closet, with the result that for the eleven days I was in Kilmainham I never went to the lavatory... This horrible experience had a permanent effect on my constitution'.[118] The soldiers were often drunk, she claimed: 'two of the Church St priests thought it advisable one night to stay in the prison all night for the protection of the girls'.[119]

Rose McNamara's diary indicates that they made the best of the grim circumstances:

> Awakened very early by sounds of shots outside our windows... We then arranged a sixteen-hand reel which we danced and enjoyed much to the alarm of the five soldiers on guard of us and two wardresses.
> ... More shots during daybreak. Exercise as usual; not allowed to dance today. Singing in the cells since we came here. Some of the girls dancing in their cells.... More terrible sounds of shots this morning.[120]

A few positively enjoyed their time inside: 'Countess Markievicz was brought in one day. She was in uniform and shouted to us "penal servitude for me". She seemed delighted with herself'.[121] After a week or two in relatively harsh conditions, the dozen or so women who were not released were transferred to Mountjoy Jail: 'After Kilmainham it was like going into a hotel'.[122] As Kathleen Browne wrote to her mother, with a touch of regret, 'we are almost too well off now and do not feel a bit like martyrs'.[123]

Ultimately, only five women joined the male internees in Britain. The rest were released on the grounds that they had been misled into taking part in the Rising, or had joined in out of a desire for 'excitement' or sense that it was 'something to be in' rather than political conviction: General Maxwell was delighted to find himself rid of 'all those silly little girls'.[124]

Inevitably, some republicans held similar views about the motivations of their female comrades, as Helena Molony subsequently complained to Seán O'Faolain, Countess Markievicz's biographer:

> It is a curious thing that many men seem to be unable to believe that any woman can embrace an ideal—accept it intellectually, feel it as a profound emotion, and then calmly decide to make a vocation of working for its realisation. They give themselves endless pains to prove that every serious thing a woman does (outside nursing or washing pots) is the result of being in love with some man, or disappointed in love of some man, or looking for excitement, or limelight, or indulging their vanity.[125]

Teenage rebels, who were treated in much the same patronizing way as women, also resented the leniency they received. Some youths, such as William Stapleton, lied about their age to remain incarcerated with the men.[126] Seán Harling recalled how he lined up with his older comrades outside the Four Courts to be inspected by the arresting officer: 'he came along and he looks at me, you know, and he gives me a clip on the ear and tells me to get the hell home. I was very annoyed at not being arrested but that's what happened and I watched the others being taken off as prisoners'.[127] Seán McLoughlin, who bizarrely (considering his youth and obscurity) had been appointed commandant-general of the army of the Irish Republic during the chaos of the retreat, was unceremoniously demoted by his arresting officer who tore the tabs that Connolly had given him from his coat: 'You are too young to be an officer'.[128] Fifteen-year-old Vinny Byrne was arrested at home a week after the Rising: 'The sergeant sat in the back of the lorry with me. He passed the remark: "You little [bastard] you would shoot me!" I said: "Yes, it was either you or me for it." He was very friendly'. Several days later, Byrne (one of about seventeen youths held at Richmond barracks) received his distressing punishment:

> On Friday evening, we were told to 'come on, get ready', and we all thought we were going to be deported. We paraded on the square—about twelve or fourteen young lads. We were given the command: 'Right turn, quick march'. We kept marching until we came to a big gate; the gate was opened for us and closed behind us. Someone of the party remarked: 'Oh, God, lads, we are out'.[129]

At Richmond barracks, the rebels had the opportunity to contemplate the events of the past week in relative leisure. To pass the time, they prayed, told stories, composed poetry, sang songs, and debated the merits of the

Rising, with themselves and their guards. Despite the failure of the insurrection and the hostile public response, most of the leaders appeared confident of vindication. Tom Clarke spoke of 'a minimum loss, which will result in a maximum gain'.[130] Claiming that the 'only failure in Ireland is the failure to strike', MacDermott appeared equally optimistic: 'We hoped to push the ball up the hill high enough for others to push it up the whole way after us'.[131] They had achieved 'all that had been expected', the people would 'see the light'.[132] Joseph Plunkett told his brother 'we had now started a new advance'.[133] Joe Good, who thought that little had been achieved, observed that his officers were not disheartened: 'I made some cynical remark to Ned Morkan and he replied: "If they let you live six months you will see the reaction" '.[134] A few of the leaders, like Con Colbert, were also disillusioned:

> outside that barrack wall the people whom we have tried to emancipate have demonstrated nothing but hate and contempt for us. We would be better off dead as life would be a torture. We can thank the Mother of God for her kindness in her intercession for us that we have had the time to prepare ourselves to meet our Redeemer.[135]

Opinion remained divided as to the impact of MacNeill's countermand. MacDermott, according to one priest who spent much time with him in his final days, remained 'very bitter' about it:

> He said what a pity that it prevented the Rising being a respectable rising, that it would have been over a considerable part of the country, employing a lot of British troops, and that, as far as the Germans were concerned, it would have been a more valuable thing than the mere flash in the pan it was.[136]

However, the general feeling of the leaders, one Volunteer judged, was that it 'was all for the best as the country was not sufficiently organised at that time to engage in an insurrection with any reasonable prospect of success and that the protest made in Dublin would have the effect of rousing the nationalist spirit'.[137]

There was much uncertainty about their own future: 'We hadn't a notion what was going to happen to us', Patrick Colgan recalled, 'The most persistent rumour was we were being taken to France to dig trenches'.[138] Others feared that they would be interned, drafted, or executed. Despite this, most remained defiant. Joe Good, who shared an overcoat with Michael Collins on the cold floor of the gym, admired the future Big Fella's spirited response when questioned by a sergeant: '"What has you here, Collins?"...Mick replied: "England's difficulty". There was a long pause then'.[139] Morale remained intact, some Volunteers describing 'an air of devil-may-careness and good humour'.[140] Michael Knightly described his 'clean-minded, patriotic and unselfish' comrades as 'cheerful and uncomplaining'. Incarcerated under 'revolting conditions' and fearful of execution, he admired the sanguine outlook of one comrade: 'As we watched the rain from our window one day he remarked: "It is a grand thing to be in from the rain"'.[141]

Despite its hardships, the separatists would soon come to realize that imprisonment was not without its advantages. Eamon Morkan spent his first days of incarceration afraid 'that we were going to pay the extreme penalty', only to become increasingly concerned by the prospect that 'we were going to be returned ignominiously to our homes'.[142] When Richard Mulcahy realized that they were to be interned, he reportedly remarked: 'I am as happy as the day is long—everything is working out grand'; he felt certain that their imprisonment would ensure public support for their cause. Mass incarceration was a new experience for this generation of separatists, and it would prove an important and positive experience for most, strengthening the bonds between those who would subsequently become the elite of the revolutionary movement during the War of Independence. Imprisonment reinforced their political beliefs, while their identification with persecution saw them welcomed home as heroes when they were later released. It was the experience of political imprisonment, as well as participation in the rebellion (with all the credibility which that entailed), that saw Michael Collins and other previously insignificant separatists emerge into the front rank of the revolutionary movement.[143]

III

There is a consensus that the suppression of the rebellion was the key factor in the transformation of public opinion after the Rising. The executions of the leaders are frequently described as draconian, although this may be due more to the intense emotion they generated than their inherent injustice. The term more accurately describes the policy of widespread arrests that followed the Rising. 3,500 people were swept up, over 2,500 of whom were interned in Britain. Many of these had not been involved in the

Rising or even separatist politics: Irish-Ireland activists, advanced nationalists, and other supposed trouble-makers were rounded up in a frenzy of
raids. Although the rebellion had been largely confined to Dublin, the
entire country was placed under martial law for the next six months.
Many of the innocent were quickly released but the indiscriminate punishment of such a large number of people generated outrage, sympathy, and
protests from a wide circle of friends and family, and has probably been
underrated as a factor in the alienation of public opinion from the British
government and the growth of support for the republican movement.[144]

The raids and arrests which extended throughout the country provoked
much resentment. On 7 May, the town of Roscommon (which had a
population of less than 1,900 inhabitants) was occupied by 700 soldiers
who arrested 27 people despite the absence of violence there during the
Rising.[145] The predicable result of such over-reactions, widely repeated
elsewhere, 'was to shift the balance of sin until still greater indignation
was felt against the repressors than the insurgents'.[146] Previous advocates of
a hard line, such as Arthur Norway (the Post Office Secretary), grew
alarmed by the scale and clumsiness of the repression: 'discrimination was
impossible, and the arrests were wholesale'.[147] Although the authorities had
a fair idea of the identity of leading separatists, it had little reliable intelligence on the movement beyond this minority. Only three days after the
general surrender, senior British officers were warning their subordinates
not to confuse innocent 'strong nationalists' with guilty 'Sinn Feiners', a
revealing use of terminology given that Sinn Féin was a non-violent party
that had not been involved in the Rising. Only two weeks after the Rising,
many of those arrested in the country were being released as soon as they
arrived in Dublin, prompting the military authorities to insist that only
those whose presence 'is considered likely to lead to further bloodshed'
should be arrested.[148] British coercion combined a provocative heavy-
handedness with a counter-productive ineffectiveness.

The suppression of the insurrection presented the British authorities
with demanding logistical, administrative, legal, and political challenges.
The army had to find food and secure accommodation for hundreds of
suspected rebels, restore order and essential services to disturbed areas,
and decide what to do with the prisoners in their custody and the thousands more that would be arrested over the next weeks. The prosecution
of rebels by conventional legal means—even those who were obviously
guilty—proved surprisingly difficult, as the Deputy Judge Advocate

General explained: 'it was necessary in every case to prove that the accused had surrendered with arms from some place which had been held by the rebels and where fighting had taken place. In many cases lists of prisoners had been taken but no officer could identify the accused as the person who had actually surrendered'.[149]

In the end, these legal niceties were deemed unnecessary. Most of those arrested were interned in England rather than prosecuted, while 171 of the worst offenders were court-martialled. The latter proved a hasty and inept affair. One Volunteer recalled that his trial (which he did not contest) lasted fifteen minutes.[150] When Liam Tobin's prosecutor told him that the penalty for aiding the King's enemies was death,

> the President of the court contradicted him on this point and said that the wording of the act was 'maybe death'...They turned over the leaves of books and papers to see which was right, and I must say that while the trial went on it was not clear to me which way it had been decided.[151]

Jack Plunkett thought his court martial 'awfully funny', describing its presiding officer as 'a regular buffoon' due to his inability to define what he meant by King's enemies: 'His ignorance of the job was ludicrous'. Like many others, Plunkett did not take the process seriously: 'it was perfectly clear to me that anything I could say would not affect the issue in the slightest'.[152] However, many Volunteers did attempt to fight the charges or limit their culpability, denying that they had held positions of responsibility or had foreknowledge of the Rising. Molly Reynolds claimed that after she and her father had gone into the GPO to buy some stamps they had been held captive for the week.[153] The South Dublin Union rebels devised an ingenious but optimistic plea of self-defence: 'they had no knowledge on the Monday morning that there was going to be a rebellion until they were suddenly rushed in to the South Union...where they were told to barricade themselves as they were about to be attacked by the military'.[154]

Others welcomed their arrest. For advanced nationalists who had not participated in the Rising—including Arthur Griffith (who was described as behaving in prison 'like a man having a carefree holiday aboard a ship') and Eoin MacNeill—imprisonment offered a political lifeline.[155] Many Volunteers were unwilling to say anything that might tarnish their involvement in the Rising, ignoring the court or merely disputing evidence that cast their cause in a poor light. Diarmuid Lynch was concerned only to deny the allegation that he had mistreated prisoners.[156] Harry Boland's sister, Kathleen, described how he had rebuffed his mother's naïve attempt to exonerate him when she visited him in Mountjoy Jail:

'Wasn't it an extraordinary thing to arrest you, and you only coming from the races!' But Harry bluntly replied, 'Ah, no, mother. I was not coming from the races. I went out to strike a blow against the bloody British Empire'. I can still remember the expression on my mother's face when she realised the hopelessness of her effort to save him.[157]

Boland's testimony to the court was actually more circumspect: he claimed that he had been unaware of the rebellion and that he had not sought to cause disaffection.[158] His death sentence was, like most of those meted out, commuted to imprisonment. Several prisoners recorded similar descriptions of the manner in which this sentence was confirmed:

during the night I was awakened by a British officer and a couple of armed soldiers, who had a lantern. They got me off the floor and put me standing up. I was completely dazed with sleep...He said: 'You have been sentenced to death', reading from a document he held. With that he left, brought his soldiers with him, and closed the door. In a matter of minutes...he re-opened the door and said, 'and the sentence of the court has been commuted to ten years' penal servitude'.[159]

Most of those arrested were deported, a process that began the day after the general surrender. By 20 June, the number of internees had dropped to 1,846 as many of the innocent were weeded out.[160] Deportation was a dismal process. Civilian spectators lined the route outside Richmond barracks, sneering and spitting as the groups of prisoners were herded towards the docks. 'It was very depressing', Gary Holohan recalled, 'We had no idea where we were going. We had an idea that they might press us into the navy'.[161] The prisoners signalled their defiance by humming, whistling, and singing 'until orders came that any man singing would be shot. In the temper our guards were in just then, we knew they would not hesitate to carry out their threat'.[162] Volunteers remarked on the 'eerie graveyard feeling' and 'deathlike silence' of the devastated city which remained under curfew.[163]

Not a light was visible though it was now almost dark; no sign of any living soul could be glimpsed even at the windows of the houses. It seemed indeed a deserted city...The gaunt ruins of the GPO were outlined against the twilight sky, and still smoking heaps of masonry were all that remained of most of the shops and buildings on either side of that once proud thorough-fare, while the street itself was lined with debris.[164]

Simon Donnelly's column of prisoners, heartened by the destruction they had wrought, 'gave a great cheer and burst into patriotic songs' when they saw the ruins of Sackville Street.[165] There were some indications of the shift in public mood now underway. Some of those who were deported after the executions began on 3 May reported a more mixed than hostile public response. William Daly, who had been spat at by 'women in shawls' who used 'filthy expressions' when he surrendered, was delighted by the reaction as he marched down the quays on 5 May: 'girls and women rush to shake hands; some of them crying and the crowds getting larger as we neared the North Wall sheds'.[166] John O'Reilly, an Enniscorthy rebel who was among a large contingent deported on 8 May, was 'boohed and cheered through the streets of Dublin—different receptions in different places...the big majority of the people of Dublin cheered us'.[167] Deported in June, Liam Tannam was surprised to hear 'encouraging cries' as he had previously 'experienced some of the spitting through the windows of the GPO'.[168]

Conditions were grim at the North Wall: 'We were embarked on a cattle boat in filthy surroundings and tightly crammed; almost everyone vomiting under these conditions'.[169] Many made the crossing in cattle pens, without adequate food or water. Fergus Burke spent the journey preoccupied by submarines: 'It would have been so convenient to get rid of so many and blame the atrocity on the Germans! I fell asleep, not caring much at the time whether I was under or over the water'.[170] Dick Humphrey's account (compiled from notes written on toilet paper when the twenty year old was in solitary confinement in Wakefield Prison), conveyed a resilient tone more characteristic of the prison memoir genre:

> Down in the cattle stalls we have no shelter whatsoever, and every big wave sends tons of water and spray into the decks...Someone suggests the Rosary, and a Volunteer recites the Mysteries in a voice that rings high above the shriek of the wind and the beat of the lashing waters. The responses come in a sonorous murmur from all points of the vessel. Afterwards, *A Soldier's Song* and *God Save Ireland* are sung, and the men take heart and courage at the sound of the undaunted voices...England has triumphed once again, but the very fact that she has had to transport hundreds of Irishmen hundreds of miles from their native shores proves that this fight has shaken her as she has never been shaken before. Next time the whole country, and not Dublin alone will join the fray.[171]

IV

Between 3 and 12 May, fourteen of the most prominent rebels were executed in Dublin; Thomas Kent was executed in Cork on 9 May, and Roger Casement was hanged in Pentonville Prison in London on 3 August. Although these deaths remain the most controversial aspect of the suppression of the insurrection they were hardly an extreme response given the scale of the Rising and its wartime context. It is unlikely that any other European belligerent would have responded with more restraint faced by such a significant internal challenge in time of war. It is clear, moreover, that the leaders expected to be executed. However, the important point about the executions is how they were perceived at the time. For various reasons, including their timing, rationale, and emotional impact, the executions played a pivotal role in the transformation of nationalist opinion from hostility to the rebels to an emotional identification with their cause. Internationally, particularly in the United States, they provoked damaging criticism of the British Government.

The manner in which the rebels were tried and executed provoked disquiet, which extended to the Viceregal Lodge and Downing Street. The speed and secrecy of the process was unseemly: some defendants were tried and executed within twenty-four hours. In contrast to the rebels of 1848 and 1867, who were tried in open courts under civil law, the fate of the rebels was decided in secrecy: one observer conveyed something of the impact of this when he wrote of 'a stream of blood coming from beneath a closed door'.[172] There were also well-founded objections to the trials on legal grounds. William Wylie, one of the prosecutors, described them as 'drumhead courts martial' although historians have disputed whether they had any firm basis in military or martial law.[173] The rebels were tried by field general courts martial (which required few of the safeguards of a general court martial): the prisoners had no access to defence counsels, and the officers of the court did not require legal qualifications. As the Defence of the Realm Regulations did not actually proscribe insurrection, the rebels were charged with taking part 'in an armed rebellion . . . for the purpose of assisting the enemy'.[174] Some of the leaders objected to this, although Casement's arrest and the Proclamation's reference to 'gallant allies in Europe' did not help their case.

A more popular objection, albeit a moral rather than legal one, was that having fought a clean fight there was no more justification for shooting the leaders of the rebellion than a prisoner of war on the Western Front.

Inconveniently for the authorities, there was also little actual evidence against the leaders. Aside from the Proclamation and an order by Connolly naming various commandants, the Deputy Judge Advocate General conceded that there was 'hardly any of any value'; so little, in fact, that a reference to Germany in Pearse's letter to his mother was treated as a significant item of incriminating evidence.[175] Despite this, few of the leaders sought to exploit what were essentially technicalities at the cost of undermining their legacy. Although all but Willie Pearse pleaded not guilty, the records suggest that MacDermott, Clarke, Plunkett, and Colbert demonstrated either contempt or disinterest in the proceedings, while Connolly and Pearse merely used them as an opportunity to explain their actions to a more important court of appeal, the Irish people.[176] Seán Heuston, Ceannt, Daly, and Mallin made a determined attempt to escape the death sentence: Heuston and Ceannt by disputing the inaccurate evidence put forward against them, Daly by denying any contact with German forces, and Mallin by the ethically more dubious strategy of dishonestly portraying himself as an ordinary soldier under Markievicz's command.[177]

The arbitrary way in which the sentences were meted out also provoked resentment. Although he was second-in-command at Jacob's factory, the execution of John MacBride seemed harsh given that he had no foreknowledge of the rebellion and how few people were killed by that garrison. In contrast, Eamon de Valera, commandant of the battalion responsible for the Mount Street massacre, was not executed, nor were Thomas Ashe or Richard Mulcahy, who commanded the Volunteers at Ashbourne. Willie Pearse was killed because he was the brother of Patrick. The survival of Countess Markievicz, the only woman to face a court martial, can alternatively be attributed to concerns about the likely public response, chivalry, or—as some feminist historians would see it—'an unwillingness to undermine the foundations of a patriarchy that benefited all men'.[178] As with all wartime justice, the process was influenced by political as well as legal considerations: the number and timing of the executions reflected political concerns. As General Maxwell complained to his wife on 9 May: 'the government is getting very cold feet and afraid. They are at me every moment not to overdo the death sentences. I never intended to but some must suffer'.[179] Even the fate of Sir Roger Casement, the only rebel to receive a fair and open trial, was manipulated by the Government which circulated extracts from his 'Black Diaries' (which described his frequent sexual encounters with adolescent boys) in order to undermine the campaign for the commutation of his death sentence.

Despite the secrecy surrounding the trials, they offered a forum for the leaders to justify their actions, helping them to shape a more potent legacy than the death in battle which most had originally sought. Pearse's address (accurately described by one prosecutor as a 'Robert Emmet type' speech) was eloquent and powerful, a moving crystallization of his life's purpose:

> When I was a child of ten I went down on my bare knees by my bedside one night and promised God that I should devote my life to an effort to free my country...If you strike us down now, we shall rise again and renew the fight. You cannot reconquer Ireland. You cannot extinguish the Irish passion for freedom. If our deed has not been sufficient to win freedom, then our children will win it by a better deed.[180]

An impressed Brigadier-General Blackader, who presided over the court martial, reportedly regretted having 'to condemn to death one of the finest characters I have ever come across. There must be something very wrong in the state of things that makes a man like that a rebel'.[181] The more stirring 'speeches from the dock' were smuggled out or, as in MacDonagh's case, simply invented. The leaders were, to a certain extent, acting out a public role in their final days, the conventions of which had been defined by a line of republican martyrs stretching back to Wolfe Tone and were widely understood by Irish nationalists of all shades of opinion.

Conscious of the posthumous importance of their legacy, the condemned men composed a stream of letters, statements, and political testaments. Ceannt, like many of the leaders, left behind two letters: one for his family, another for the nation he knew his death would help to bring about.[182] Seán MacDermott's final statement expressed a serene patriotism which reflected only some of the mixed emotions he experienced in his final days: 'I go to my death for Ireland's cause as fearlessly as I have worked for that sacred cause during all my short life'.[183] The tone of these statements indicated a growing confidence that the rebellion would be vindicated. 'Let our present-day place-hunters condemn our action as they will', MacDermott wrote, 'posterity will judge us aright from the effects of our actions'.[184] When Ceannt's wife told him that the Rising had been 'an awful fiasco', he replied: 'No, it was the biggest thing since '98'.[185] Connolly's last testament, which he slipped into his daughter's hands during her final visit to his hospital bed, exulted in their achievement:

> We went out to break the connection between this country and the British Empire and to establish an Irish Republic...We succeeded in proving that Irishmen are ready to die endeavouring to win for Ireland their national

rights which the British government has been asking them to die to win for
Belgium. As long as that remains the case the cause of Irish freedom is
safe.[186]

The rebels' willingness to die for their beliefs, viewed by many contemporaries as an essential test of integrity, evoked far more admiration than it
would in our present-day society inured to the eagerness with which zealous
extremists embrace self-sacrifice. Perhaps the most powerful aspect of the
executions, in terms of their impact on public opinion, was the piety of the
condemned men. The Capuchin Friars who ministered to the leaders in
their final days, anointing them in the stonebreakers' yard at the moment
before death, provided vital spiritual succour to the rebels and their families:
'They saved the reason of many people whose sons and brothers were
executed'.[187] But they also bore witness to their suffering, and their testimony helped to shape the nationalist perception of the executions as a
latter-day Passion. As Ceannt's widow recorded: 'Father Augustine told me
that Eamonn had held his, Father Augustine's, crucifix in his hands, and the
last words he spoke were, "My Jesus Mercy" '.[188] Father Aloysius described a
beatific vision of Pearse on his knees in a cell, clasping a crucifix as a light
shone from the spy hole on to his face, one of several potent images that
were soon reproduced on commemorative postcards and pictures.[189] In time,
the identification of the rebels with Catholic martyrdom would, for reasons
of self-interested pragmatism as well as patriotism, receive the endorsement
of the Catholic Church in Ireland. Pearse's crucifix, for example, is preserved
as a relic in the Church Street Friary, while a mosaic of Pearse's iconic image
can be found beside one of Jesus Christ in Galway Cathedral.

The rebels were conscious of the powerful symbolism of their sacrifice
at Easter—from his prison cell Pearse wrote a poem explicitly comparing
his fate to that of the crucified Christ. Even the Marxist James Connolly
died as a good Catholic, receiving Communion before his death, and
requesting his wife to convert to Catholicism.[190] The Protestant patriot
Roger Casement also converted to Catholicism before his death. The way
in which the latter occasion came to form part of the propaganda of the
Rising illustrated how the secular ethos espoused by some of the leading
organizers was subsumed by the sacralization of 1916. 'He talked freely of
his death and was looking forward to his Confession', the priest who
ministered to him in the Tower of London enthused, 'It was like the last
hours of some glorious martyr'.[191] Casement himself reportedly made a

similar explicit connection between faith and nation, resolving to die in the religion of Kathleen Ni Houlihan.[192]

The willingness with which the rebels embraced death reflected both their religious and political convictions: for some, as Pearse's poetry illustrated, both sacred causes were intertwined, the rhetoric of martyrdom and resurrection providing a common language for both. Pearse, whose life had been shaped by an appreciation of the importance of myth, whether Christian notions of redemptive sacrifice, the masculine heroism of Cúchulainn, or the broader European romanticism of the generation of 1914, was conscious of the tremendous power their fate would exert: 'Our deeds of last week are the most splendid things in Ireland's history. People will say hard things of us now, but we shall be remembered by posterity and blessed by unborn generations'.[193] Even more traditional old-school IRB men, such as Seán MacDermott whose characteristically Fenian resentment of clerical opposition to republicanism had estranged him from the Church in the past, spoke in similar terms: 'We die that the Irish nation may live, our blood will rebaptise and reinvigorate the old land'.[194]

Such rhetoric should not be seen as evidence of some sort of religious mania; many separatists, as Patrick Maume has astutely observed, 'were not primarily religious in inspiration but used the emotional power of this familiar language to convey their own political message'.[195] Dying for their cause, and increasingly confident of its vindication, some of the leaders met their death in a near ecstatic condition. In a final letter to his family, MacDermott assured them that he felt 'a happiness the like of which I never experienced in my life before, and a feeling that I could not describe'.[196] Several leaders expressed a consolation derived from knowing that they would join the pantheon of martyrs who had devoted their lives to the same cause: 'Think of the long succession of the dead who have died for Ireland', Roger Casement wrote, 'It is a glorious death for Ireland's sake with Allen, Larkin and O'Brien, and Robert Emmet—and the men of '98 and William Orr—all for the same cause—all in the same way. Surely it is the most glorious cause in history'.[197]

Inevitably, the complexities and grim realities that characterized the tragic events at Kilmainham Jail, which would come to form a powerful foundation myth for the independent Irish State, were obscured by the heroic narrative that emerged. Tom Clarke's anti-clericalism, MacDonagh's religious scepticism, and MacDermott's bitter diatribe against the political influence of the Catholic Church would go unnoticed. Markievicz's allegedly undignified performance at her court martial—'you cannot shoot a woman, you must not shoot a woman'—was not reported.[198] Nor was the angry defiance of Michael Mallin, which conflicted with the more useful narrative of heroic self-sacrifice. Thomas Mallin vividly recalled his brother's rage when he asked him if it was worth it:

> It is worth it. Ireland is a grand country, but the people in it are rotters. The first Irishman to join the British army was a bastard. The British army is made up of them and gaolbirds and wasters. Some join through drink and some through lack of work. I will show my guards how an Irishman can die for his own country—in his own country. I can die praying. If these men are sent to France they will die cursing. They will die lying on the ground, moaning, and not able to see their mothers and sweethearts.[199]

The harsh and petty treatment of the prisoners in their final days, and the anguish of their families, resulted in some pitiful scenes. Conditions in Kilmainham Jail, which had been closed since 1910, were particularly grim. Alfred Bucknill, the Deputy Judge Advocate General, found the prisoners there in 'a deplorable state. Some of them had been wounded and they all looked dirty and unkempt'.[200] On his first night there, one Volunteer described how he was kept awake by 'the shouting and screaming of prisoners who were being beaten up in the cells through which the soldiers had run amok'. Prisoners were unnecessarily humiliated: 'a bucket was handed to us when we could appease our thirst like animals…We had to eat with our hands and by dipping our faces in the pans'.[201] Aside from being allowed visitors, the condemned men were treated little better. Eily O'Hanrahan described her brother's cell: 'There was nothing in it, no light even, but an old bag thrown in the corner, and a bucket, no bed, no chair, no table, a place you would not put a dog'.[202] The prisoners' final conversations with their families were timed, monitored, and censored. The tragic circumstances of the rebels' final days, accounts of which would soon be widely circulated in the *Catholic Bulletin* and in poems and ballads, would, in time, provoke sympathy, bitterness, and a desire for vengeance.

Michael O'Hanrahan left his only possessions, a few books, to his mother and sisters. In what Min Ryan described as 'the most pathetic scene', Seán MacDermott attempted to etch his name on some coins and buttons as mementoes.[203] John MacBride, who had been on his way to his brother's wedding where he was to be best man when the Rising broke out, asked his final visitor to return the ring and pay the bill for his wedding suit. Mallin, writing to his wife only hours before his execution, was overwhelmed by grief at the thought of his imminent separation from his family:

> My heartstrings are torn to pieces when I think of you and them of our manly James happy go lucky John shy warm Una dadys Girl and oh little Joseph my little man Wife dear Wife I cannot keep the tears back when I think of him he will rest in my arms no more... my little man my little man my little man, his name unnerves me again all your dear faces arise before me God bless you God bless you my darlings.[204]

On her final visit, Mallin told his wife what to name their unborn child, made her promise not to remarry, and dedicated two of his children to the service of the Catholic Church. He gave his two sons a different vocation: 'I want you to grow up to be big men, to work and keep your mother, and when the time comes, to do as I have done'.[205] Nora Connolly has left a moving description of her final visit with her father in Dublin Castle:

> We were brought into the room where Daddy was. He lifted his head, and said: 'I suppose you know what this means?'...Mama could hardly talk. I remember he said: 'Don't cry Lillie. You will unman me'. Mama said: 'But your beautiful life, James', she wept. 'Hasn't it been a full life? Isn't this a good end?', he said. Then they took us away.[206]

Some of the condemned chose to spare their family, or themselves, the grief of a final parting. Con Colbert sent his girlfriend a copy-book of his poems 'all about Ireland and its struggle for freedom and the sufferings it endured from the English'.[207] Grace Gifford's marriage to Joseph Plunkett added a poignant note of tragedy although the ceremony, as described by his bride, was less romantic than the popular ballads that would subsequently immortalize it:

> I was brought in, and was put in front of the altar; and he was brought down the steps; and the cuffs were taken off him; and the chaplain went on with the ceremony; then the cuffs were put on him again. I was not alone with him—not for a minute...I was just a few minutes there to get married, and then again a few minutes to say good-bye that night; and a man stood there, with his watch in his hand, and said: 'Ten Minutes'.[208]

Min Ryan's final visit with Seán MacDermott on the night of his execution was marred by a similar lack of intimacy, due to the unwanted presence of the latter's landlady and accountant: 'We were all there together, listening to each other's conversation. He was very anxious to have the others go. He was much more intimate with us, but there was no budge out of them.

"That is all now" Sean would say, but there was no budge at all'.[209] When she finally left him at 3 a.m., shortly before his execution, 'he said, just said: "We never thought that it would end like this, that this would be the end."'[210]

Their stoic acceptance of death won admiration from nationalists and British observers alike. Borrowing a razor from a soldier before his court martial, MacDermott quipped, 'I have to make a nice corpse, you know'.[211] Pearse appealed to General Maxwell to spare the lives of his followers in return for his.[212] Asked by his priest to forgive the men who were to kill him, Connolly's final words were: 'I respect every man who does his duty'.[213] The prisoners were killed in much the same way. Each was blindfolded, a piece of paper pinned over his heart, and led out to the stonebreakers' yard, where some (and possibly all) of them were seated on a wooden crate and shot by firing squad in the early hours of the morning.

Accounts of the executions (all at least second-hand) vary, but emphasize the bravery of the rebels. Alfred Bucknill, the Deputy Judge Advocate General, was told by the officer in charge of the firing squad that 'all who were executed died bravely. MacDonagh indeed came down the stairs whistling'.[214] The attending medical officer reportedly stated that 'they all died like lions', whereas the 'rifles of the firing party were waving like a field of corn'.[215] A DMP sergeant at Kilmainham heard something similar: 'On the morning of the first executions there was only one firing party for the three men executed and I was told that the soldiers displayed considerable nervousness when the third man was brought out to be executed'.[216] He claimed that the rebels were indifferent to whether they were blindfolded: 'Death did not seem to hold any terrors for them'.[217] John MacBride, stylish to the last, told his firing squad that 'he was not afraid as he had been looking down the barrels of rifles all his life'.[218] Connolly's execution brought the killings in Kilmainham Jail to an end. Robert Barton learned of some of the sordid details from the officer in charge of the firing party: 'Heathcote told me he was probably drugged and almost dead. They brought him in an ambulance and from that on a stretcher to the chair…They shot him through the chest and blew the back out of the chair'.[219] It was not the final indignity. Observing that 'Irish sentimentality will turn these graves into martyr's shrines', General Maxwell ordered that the corpses be buried in quicklime in a mass grave at Arbour Hill.[220] Still a lonely and comparatively neglected spot, the choice of location proved one of Maxwell's few far-sighted decisions.

8

The Beginning of Ireland

Aftermath

The process by which the centre of gravity of Irish nationalism shifted from hostility to the rebels, to sympathy for their fate, and ultimately to support for their objectives was a gradual one, culminating in Sinn Féin's remarkable electoral landslide in December 1918. There was nothing inevitable about this transformation. In the immediate aftermath of the Rising, even many of those separatists who believed that the Rising had been worthwhile assumed—as Eoin MacNeill had earlier warned—that the republican movement would be set back for years. The remarkable change in public opinion that rapidly followed was a consequence not only of the dramatic impact of the Easter Rising, which destroyed the assumptions that had long underpinned popular nationalist politics, but also of British security and political policy decisions in the eighteen months that followed.

I

Regardless of their political outlook, most people responded to the end of the rebellion with relief. The streets of Dublin remained dangerous, with snipers continuing to fire from rooftops well into the following week, as people struggled to purchase food, collect pensions or wages, and return to everyday life. Huge crowds flocked to the city centre to witness the devastation at first hand. 'Sackville Street and its neighbourhood is an appalling spectacle', wrote Lord Desart, 'it still haunts me'.[1] Fire and artillery had reduced much of this area to smouldering rubble: 'One had to walk warily because the ground was covered with hot ashes, and if one

was not careful, one sank into them and was burned'.[2] With understandable exaggeration, many observers, including Louisa Norway, compared
the city's fate to that of Louvain and Ypres, images of which had dominated the press before the rebellion:

> The streets were thronged with people, and threading their way among the
> crowd were all sorts of vehicles: carts carrying the bodies of dead horses that
> had been shot the first day and lain in the streets ever since; fire brigade
> ambulances, followed by Irish cars bringing priests and driven by fire
> brigade men. The motors with Red Cross emblems carrying white-jacketed
> doctors would dart along, followed by a trail of Red Cross nurses on bicy-
> cles, in their print dresses and white overalls...From time to time we came
> across on the unwashed pavement the large dark stain telling its own grim
> story, and in one place the blood had flowed along the pavement for some
> yards and down into the gutter; but enough of horrors. We came sadly back,
> and on the steps we met Mr O'B, returning from a similar walk. He could
> hardly speak of it, and said he stood in Sackville Street and cried, and many
> other men did the same.[3]

Public opinion remained opposed to the rebellion during its immediate
aftermath.[4] But the tone of the press was noticeably more scathing: the
rebels were branded as criminals, traitors, fanatics, or, at best, dangerously
misguided fools.[5] Condemning the 'crime, horror, and destruction' of
Easter week, the unionist *Irish Times* urged General Maxwell to exact a
punishment severe enough to deter further outbreaks for generations to
come: 'The surgeon's knife has been put to the corruption in the body of
Ireland, and its course must not be stayed until the whole malignant
growth has been removed'.[6] Even after twelve of the leaders had been
executed, the *Irish Independent*, the most popular nationalist newspaper in
the country, urged Maxwell not to weaken his resolve: 'Let the worst of the
ringleaders be singled out and dealt with as they deserve'.[7] Although the
Catholic hierarchy, the most important body of opinion in nationalist
Ireland, had become increasingly disillusioned with the Irish Party's failure
to secure Home Rule, some individual bishops were quick to denounce
the insurrection as irrational, sinful, and futile.[8]

Nonetheless, contemporary accounts suggest that nationalist opinion,
while generally negative, was more fluid and nuanced than was reflected by
the press. Most Irish newspapers were owned by Redmondites or unionists,
while many organs of public opinion, such as local government bodies,
were also controlled by the Irish Party. Even within the hierarchy—no

admirers of separatism—several bishops privately regarded the Rising as an inevitable reaction against what one described as 'the extreme Britishism of Redmond'.[9] Other observers (including some who were not nationalists) blamed Dublin Castle and Ulster's unionists for the part they played in bringing about the violence. Nor did public hostility to the rebellion equate to a hatred of the rebels, much less a desire to see (in a much-used phrase of the time) 'our own flesh and blood' shot in cold blood by English soldiers. Ordinary nationalists were shocked and confused by what had happened, but many were also ambivalent. 'The prevailing opinion was the unbelievable madness of the whole affair', one Newry republican recalled, 'I heard a great many people saying "Weren't they great men, it's a pity there were not more of them"—others saying—"Of course they were mad to attempt such a thing—if they were so keen on fighting why did they not join the Army"'.[10]

Just as the rebels had been blamed for the devastation of Easter week, the authorities would assume responsibility for the condition of Ireland over the next weeks and months. The military occupation and nightly curfews that followed provoked resentment, particularly from those predisposed to feel resentful: 'movement was impossible', one rebel complained, 'Any person who ventured away from his own door was held up, questioned and searched, almost every few hundred yards. It was almost courting disaster to be seen with hands in pockets. The officers adopted a general attitude of domineering arrogant authority over all'.[11] British army soldiers, understandably nervous, took few chances on patrol, ordering people to remain in their homes with the lights out, aggressively pointing their rifles at faces that appeared in the window. The presence of twenty thousand troops in the city centre, as one English clergyman noted on 7 May, was not as conducive to public order as might be imagined:

> The public-houses have been shut since Friday until to-day at 2 p.m. Result: in one district near the Quays, the soldiers, in common with the populace, got blind drunk and ran amok. The scene was terrible...Many of the military lurched through the crowd brandishing bayonets...officers were almost equally uncontrolled, and the human vermin round about were falling over each other, fighting, bleeding, mad. Of course, the soldiers feel themselves to be top dogs now, and with 'drink taken' (as they say here) are ready to play their part well, without much encouragement.[12]

In the absence of reliable information about prisoners, and the emergence of disturbing press revelations of actual atrocities by the army, rumours of widespread executions and mass burials spread like wildfire. At Westminster, the maverick nationalist MP Laurence Ginnell told the Commons that seventy-one prisoners had been shot without trial in Richmond Barracks, and even the Irish Party's deputy leader, John Dillon, feared there was 'very considerable foundation' for these allegations.[13]

Against the backdrop of such rumours, press reports of heavy-handed British repression, and the dramatic impact of the executions which added a dark new chapter to the old story, separatist opinion was inflamed. Imprisoned in Richmond barracks, Liam Tannam's rage was compounded by the malice of his captors: 'we were informed each morning by a red-haired Royal Irish Regiment Sergeant that our turn would come very soon, and he gloated over having been present at the executions, and in one instance described how he had seen the brains scattered over the wall'.[14] The radicalizing impact of the executions can be judged by the reaction of Arthur Griffith, hitherto Ireland's most persuasive advocate of non-violent advanced nationalism: 'Something of the primitive man awoke in me', he recalled, 'I clenched my fists with rage and I longed for vengeance'.[15]

The perceived contrast between the treatment of unionists in 1913 and republicans in 1916 sharpened this sense of grievance, a double standard exemplified by the role of erstwhile UVF gun-runner F. E. Smith in the prosecution of Roger Casement: 'It appeared that Rebellion entailed the extreme punishment in Dublin and was a means of preferment and elevation in Belfast'.[16] Like many others, Máire O'Brolchain felt 'contempt and rage for British hypocrisy'.[17] In those parts of the country where Volunteers had failed to rise, the executions provoked humiliation as well as bitterness: 'One felt ashamed to be free, to be walking around while comrades were dying'.[18] In Belfast and elsewhere, Volunteer and IRB leaders judged to have dithered during the fateful week were pushed aside with the same ruthlessness that they had purged the preceding generation of Fenians.

Many separatists would come to view the executions as the tipping point for broader nationalist opinion: 'the people, who before took the Volunteers with a smile, changed completely', claimed a Kerry Volunteer: 'They were magnificent when the Dublin leaders were executed. It was difficult to believe the change. A new Ireland had been born'.[19] Certainly, for some nationalists, the executions were sufficient to effect a conversion to republicanism. On 9 May, while the executions were continuing, the Cork separatist Liam de Roiste cautiously noted in his diary that 'We are too near the event to judge in proper perspective' but he believed that after 'the orgy of blood…Ireland can not be the same'.[20] Many of their critics agreed. On 8 May, a shaken W. B. Yeats described his sense of a once familiar 'world…suddenly overwhelmed': 'As yet one knows nothing of the future except that it must be very unlike the past'. Infuriated by the Government's inept execution of the 'foolish idealists' responsible for the 'childish madness' of the insurrection, his sister Lily speculated, as early as 16 May, that what had happened may prove 'the beginning of Ireland'.[21] More prosaically, a memorandum prepared for the Cabinet the previous day (only three days after the final execution in Dublin) reported that popular sympathy for the rebels was growing everywhere except Ulster.[22]

Others were converted to separatism by the coercion that followed. According to his grandmother, Liam Lynch was a fiercely committed Redmondite 'until the day the British attacked the Kents of Bawnard and he saw Thomas Kent being brought in bleeding through the town of Fermoy, and his poor mother dragging along after them'.[23] Lynch's conversion provides a striking illustration of the fatal ripples unleashed by Easter 1916. It was actually Irish policemen who had been attacked by the Kent brothers, when they raided their farm at 4 a.m. as part of the nationwide round-up of suspects. Moments after the raiding party knocked on the door, Constable Frank King heard a shout—'We will not surrender until we leave some of you dead'—followed by shots. Head Constable William Rowe died in the first moments of the gun battle that ensued: 'His head was almost completely blown off by a shotgun blast'.[24] Although the deaths that followed—two of the Kent brothers were shot that night (one fatally while trying to escape) and another was subsequently executed—were more tragic than heroic, perception was everything: British vengeance had created two more martyrs. Liam Lynch, a political moderate before the raid on the Kent family farm, was killed on the Knockmealdown Mountains in 1923, leading the anti-treaty IRA in a futile civil war in defence of the Republic proclaimed by Pearse.

As early as June 1916, the RIC inspector general reported that the separatists enjoyed the support of the majority of people in towns.[25] The hierarchy's public stance provided another indication of the shifting mood. By the time it met in June 1916, the impact of the executions and deportations had led the majority to reject an earlier proposal to condemn the Rising.[26] To the delight of republicans, the Bishop of Limerick had already denounced Maxwell's response as 'one of the worst and the blackest chapters in the history of the misgovernment of this country', while, in July, the Archbishop of Dublin publicly rebuked the Irish Party for its political alliance with the British Government.[27]

It was also through the medium of the Catholic Church that popular sympathy for the rebels was first publicly demonstrated, as crowds flocked to requiem Masses throughout the summer of 1916. Recalling how he walked among the ruins of the Rising 'with a feeling of sadness and at the same time of holiness and exultation', thirteen-year old Charlie Dalton was one of many boys drawn to the patriotic Masses: 'That was a day of great happiness for me. I had a wonderful, proud feeling, walking in the procession'. Just over three years later, Dalton would become the youngest assassin in Michael Collins' ruthless Squad, which perfected a very different form of republican violence than the sacrificial variety witnessed in 1916. The dead leaders were venerated in much the same way as traditional Catholic martyrs, as sympathizers like Dalton collected Mass cards, badges, flags, picture postcards, and other relics: 'whenever I could get a photograph of one of the dead leaders I treasured it with a kind of sacred interest'.[28] Just as Pearse had once fantasized, ballads and poems depicted the rebels as Christ-like saviours:

> What did they do, Oh Irishmen whose souls are dead...
> And walk the way that saints have led...
> You ask of me what did they do?
> I ask of you—What did Christ do?[29]

Despite the hierarchy's staunch opposition to both the IRB and political violence, it was not surprising that this politicization was expressed in a religious context given the lack of alternative outlets: the separatist movement had been suppressed, while newspapers remained unsympathetic to republicanism or vulnerable to wartime censorship. Although the *Catholic Bulletin*'s detailed descriptions of the piety of the rebels may have been partly intended as a means of evading this censorship, it also contributed to the emergence of a 'quasi-religious cult of 1916', as physical-force republicanism fused with the more populist faith and fatherland tradition.[30] The appeal of this romantic mode of thought to earnest young Catholics is illustrated by a letter from John Moynihan, a formerly moderate nationalist from Tralee, to his brother, Michael, a soldier in the British army, written a fortnight after the executions:

was the rebellion a blunder? No doubt, from a practical view, it was...It may cost us a decade of oppression. But Pearse and M[a]cDonagh, Plunkett and M[a]cDermott are not really dead; the men who sought to destroy them only succeeded in giving them a power over the hearts and minds of men greater than ever they had before. They shall live while Ireland lives...I believe that God has preserved us for this hour, that, in the reconstruction of the world, Ireland may be, once more, a light unto men that, as is my prayer, she may bear aloft a cross now in triumph, that cross which she has borne so long in agony.[31]

While W. B. Yeats' *Easter 1916* remains one of the most powerful literary responses to the Rising, his deeply ambivalent poem (which he chose not to publish until 1920) challenged rather than endorsed the growing public mood. Like others who could not identify with the separatist minority, his immediate response was one of despondency: 'I feel that all the work of years has been overturned'.[32] The poem's ambivalence also stemmed from the shock felt by Yeats and his circle at the transformation that had occurred as hitherto marginal political and intellectual antagonists, 'people they had known with familiarity, and even regarded with contempt, had joined, at a stroke, the mythic company of Emmet, Fitzgerald, Tone'.[33] While acknowledging its transformative effects, the poem questioned the necessity of the Rising and its leaders' fanaticism:

> Was it needless death after all?
> For England may keep faith
> For all that is done and said.
> We know their dream; enough
> To know they dreamed and are dead;
> And what if excess of love
> Bewildered them till they died?
> I write it out in a verse—
> MacDonagh and MacBride
> And Connolly and Pearse
> Now and in time to be,
> Wherever green is worn,
> Are changed, changed utterly:
> A terrible beauty is born.

Reflecting the outlook of those unable to commit to the new nationalism, and anticipating some of the questions that would come to dominate the revisionist controversy in later decades, Yeats characteristically swam against the tide of history. More representative and resonant of the popular cultural response (or, as the authorities complained, the 'stream of sedition') provoked by the Rising was *Vengeance 1916*, a rage-fuelled ballad found in the possession of a police suspect:

> In Dublin Town they murdered them.
> Like dogs they shot them down.
> God's curse be on you England now.
> God strike your London town.
> And cursed be every Irishman
> Alive or yet to live
> Who'll e'er forget the deaths they died
> Who'll ever dare forgive.[34]

Almost everything that followed in the weeks and months after the Rising reflected poorly on the Government, converting public sympathy for the rebels into something more tangible. 'Next came news of men killed in action, of soldiers shooting down our innocent people in their homes as occurred in North King Street, execution of the leaders, deportations, raids, arrests', recalled a Cumann na mBan activist involved in prisoner relief: 'It soon became apparent that a change had taken place, as people who refused to subscribe before now gave generously and sympathetically'.[35] Although there was as yet no political organization through which commitment to republicanism could be channelled, prisoner welfare associations provided a relatively safe outlet for public expressions of support (just as the amnesty associations that emerged after previous rebellions had done). These were mainly run by women; in a letter to Asquith, General Maxwell blamed young priests and radical women for the growing resentment of British coercion.[36] By drawing large numbers of people into political activism, the prisoner issue provided an important 'bridge between the wreckage of the 1916 Rising and the reorganised Sinn Féin of 1917'.[37]

British coercion created insurmountable challenges for the Irish Party. The prevalent rumour that Irish MPs had cheered when the executions were announced at Westminster was false, but they had cheered the news of Britain's suppression of the rebellion and were inevitably, if harshly, seen as complicit in the executions that followed. In reality, following Maxwell's appointment and Birrell's resignation, Redmond had little influence with the British authorities (although he did accept the necessity for some executions). Tom Kettle, a prominent Home Ruler, academic, and writer, was quick to realize the predicament of those, like himself, who had enlisted in the British army to fight for Irish freedom: 'These men will go down in history as heroes and martyrs, and I will go down—if I go down at all—as a bloody British officer'.[38] Kettle, who had been stationed in a British army barracks in County Kildare when the Rising broke out, went to his death on the Somme in September 1916 under few illusions as to its impact on the Home Rule project, bitterly complaining to his wife that 'they had spoiled it all—spoiled his dream of a free united Ireland in a free Europe'.[39]

Significantly, Irish Party leaders diverged in their response to the Rising. John Redmond denounced the rebels as traitors whose actions were inspired more by hatred of Home Rule than England. In a powerful speech at Westminster on 11 May, John Dillon also described them as 'our bitterest enemies' but struck a radically different note by expressing his pride for the 'misguided' rebels whose 'conduct was beyond reproach as fighting men' and his rage at the Government's stupidity in 'washing out our whole life work in a sea of blood': 'I say deliberately that in the whole of modern history, taking all circumstances into account, there has been no rebellion or insurrection put down with so much blood and so much savagery as the recent insurrection in Ireland'.[40]

Although police reports indicate that sympathy for the rebels quickly evolved into resentment of the Irish Party, emotion alone would not have swung public opinion from constitutional nationalism to republicanism. Before the Easter Rising, many nationalists opposed violence for pragmatic rather than principled reasons (while the anglophobic rhetoric of some Irish Party leaders had routinely eulogized the physical-force martyrs of the past).[41] Nationalists supported Home Rule not because a measure of devolved power which kept Ireland within the United Kingdom fulfilled their aspirations but because it seemed all that could realistically be achieved. In contrast, violence was seen as not only futile but counterproductive. The Easter Rising shattered both of these assumptions. Ironically, it was the British Government that first made this clear. Less than a month after the Rising, Asquith—conscious of the need to placate nationalist and Irish-American opinion given the urgent wartime context—announced his intention to secure agreement to introduce Home Rule as soon as possible. Many nationalists, as the RIC inspector general observed, concluded that six days of violence had achieved more than twenty-five years of constitutional agitation.[42] The consequent failure to achieve Home Rule following a summer of determined opposition from Conservative politicians and southern unionists further humiliated the Irish Party, although possibly not quite as much as Redmond's decision to concede partition without receiving anything in return.

Quite when the Irish Party passed the point of no return remains a matter of debate. Despite failing to unite within a single party until the Sinn Féin convention in October, separatists won four successive parliamentary by-elections between February and August 1917. Although the Irish Party countered with three by-election victories in 1918, the political landscape had clearly shifted. The failure of a second attempt to agree Home Rule (at the drawn-out Irish Convention of 1917–18) and the unpopularity of Redmond's pro-war position stripped the party of any credible strategy. The necessity for the Government to respond to the growing public support for republicanism only hastened the demise of their constitutional rivals, as events such as the spurious 'German plot' arrests and the death of hunger-striker Thomas Ashe stoked further resentment against the Government and its Irish Party collaborators. The Government's attempt to impose conscription in April 1918, yet another example of how the domestic wartime necessities of British politics had driven Irish policy since 1914, sealed the fate of the Irish Party. In December 1918, Sinn Féin won a landslide victory in the general election, securing 73 out of 105 seats and a democratic mandate for its demand for an Irish republic. The next two and a half years would see an increasingly violent struggle in pursuit of that objective.

II

Perhaps the most controversial aspect of the Easter Rising was its legacy. The War of Independence and the Civil War were profoundly shaped by the legacy of 1916. Violence against the British authorities may have occurred regardless of the Rising—the anti-insurrectionary Volunteer leadership had always been clear that conscription would justify an armed uprising—but the nature and objectives of that war would have differed from the one that did take place. When Irish separatists finally united, the party that emerged from the October 1917 convention was not a reinvigorated version of Arthur Griffith's Sinn Féin but a new revolutionary movement formally committed, in de Valera's words, to achieving an Irish republic as 'a monument to the brave dead'.[43] Had the insurrection not occurred, Irish nationalism would not have united under the banner of republicanism, the most extreme and least attainable of the various political outcomes advocated by militant nationalists. It was the Easter Rising that brought republicanism from the margins to the mainstream of Irish nationalism. The second important consequence of the Rising was, just as Clarke and MacDermott had calculated, to revive and legitimize the physical-force tradition. Although separatists avoided a divisive and potentially unpopular commitment to the use of physical force during the Sinn Féin convention and the election campaign of 1918, republicans such as Michael Collins were under no illusions as to what they saw as its necessity in the struggle that would follow.

The Irish Civil War of 1922–3 occurred as a direct result of Sinn Féin's commitment to the objective of the Easter Rising. An Irish republic, as Griffith had warned, was only attainable if separatists could defeat the British Government. By the time the leadership of Sinn Féin and the Irish Republican Army came to accept that military victory was not possible, the Republic had been elevated to more than a mere political objective. IRA members had sworn an oath, not to achieve an Irish republic but to defend the living Republic that had been proclaimed in 1916 and established by the Dáil government in 1919. As Yeats had recognized as early as 1917, the Easter Rising had undermined the possibility of compromise, the lifeblood of the Redmondite project: 'who can talk of give and take ... while those dead men are loitering there?'[44] Many IRA men considered the idea of abandoning the Republic for a compromise that kept an Irish dominion within the British Empire as much a betrayal of their beliefs as Home Rule. Opposition to the Treaty, as the Dáil debates illustrated, was based less on its political flaws than its moral and spiritual illegitimacy; as de Valera put it: 'the people had never a right to do wrong'.[45] Although its timing and scale were contingent on circumstances, the Civil War was an inevitable consequence of the legacy of the Rising.

Following the Civil War, the legacy of the Easter Rising—in southern Ireland at least—proved less dramatic. Although southern politicians remained committed to achieving a republic, which was finally proclaimed on Easter Monday 1949, the accusation that they had failed to live up to the ideals of the Proclamation was increasingly voiced. Independence did not deliver the objectives for which the rebels had sacrificed themselves: a united, Gaelic, republic. Consequently, the importance of the Rising stemmed more from its place in the fragmented political discourse of independent Ireland, its function as a marker of the identity of the State, and a symbol of its contested legitimacy (a legitimacy coveted by both sides of the Civil War divide). The Rising became an important date in the national calendar but its formal commemoration by the State, almost invariably boycotted by some of the relatives of the executed leaders, opposition parties, and die-hard republicans, was often characterized by discord and embarrassment.[46]

The gulf between the idealism of the revolution and the mundane realities of independence provided another persistent source of tension. In 1948 the republican Clann na Poblachta party entered government, committed to making the radical ideals of the Rising a reality, but left office having managed only to distribute commemorative copies of the Proclamation to national schools. The progressive rhetoric of that document was overshadowed by the political requirements of an insular, clericalist, and impoverished state, as was evidenced by the marginalization of the role of women and socialists in favour of a socially conservative Catholic nationalist vision of 1916 in state-sponsored textbooks, commemorative ceremonies, and popular historical accounts.[47] One unintended consequence of the appropriation of the Rising by the dead hand of the State was to render one of the most exciting episodes of Irish history, divested of its drama and radicalism by pious re-enactment, dull and unappealing to the successive generations of schoolchildren to whom it was taught as a sterile political catechism. By the fiftieth anniversary, modernizers such as the Taoiseach Seán Lemass were attempting to fashion the legacy of 1916 into a more constructive patriotism that would emphasize social and economic aspirations rather than nationalist grievances.[48]

Their efforts were derailed by the renewal of political violence in Northern Ireland in the late 1960s. The three decades of sectarian conflict that followed both intensified and complicated the re-evaluation of the Rising that had already begun. Northern violence raised difficult questions about the Easter Rising, which were sharpened by the Provisional IRA's desire to claim its legacy to legitimize its own struggle. Was the use of violence by a minority which lacked a democratic mandate legitimate? Southern politicians struggled to explain convincingly why elitist violence in pursuit of a united Irish republic was justified in 1916 but immoral after 1969, and the State's glorification of past republican violence was seen by some to conflict with the increasingly urgent imperative to prevent the Troubles from contaminating the south. An influential section of opinion—including some politicians, intellectuals, and historians—resolved this dilemma by repudiating the actions of the Easter rebels. Others responded, if not by disowning the Rising, then by marking it in an increasingly muted fashion.

The Irish Government suspended the annual military parade on O'Connell Street in the early 1970s, while Sinn Féin's attempt to mark the sixtieth anniversary outside the GPO was proscribed under the Offences against the State Act. The Easter Rising's stock reached a nadir on the seventy-fifth anniversary. Against a backdrop of relentless sectarian violence, press coverage of the event was dominated by an emotive debate as to whether the Rising should even be commemorated, the Government opting to do so in a notably half-hearted fashion.[49] Inevitably, the faltering success of the northern peace process brought with it a gradual rehabilitation of the Rising: the Government marked the 80th anniversary with a formal ceremony at the Garden of Remembrance in Dublin, the between-ceasefires Provisional IRA by planting a thirty-pound bomb on Hammersmith Bridge. The ninetieth commemoration witnessed the largest and most popular commemoration since 1966, its success a consequence not only of the Belfast Agreement but the confidence instilled by the prosperity of the Celtic Tiger. Despite some criticism of the reinstatement of the annual military parade (with an anachronistic North Korean-style display of military hardware), and a strained attempt by the head of state to depict 'the heroes of the Rising' as modern democrats, most observers and participants felt that the occasion was marked by a patriotism that was conciliatory and dignified rather than narrow and triumphalist.[50]

Throughout the long fall and rise of its legacy, the Easter Rising consistently evoked more affection among the general public than academics, intellectuals, and politicians. Although some commentators argue that the general election of 1918 or the establishment of the Dáil in 1919 would offer a more appropriate date to commemorate the struggle for national independence, recent events suggest that the Easter Rising will remain the pre-eminent symbol of Irish sovereignty. The ninetieth anniversary supplement produced by the *Irish Times* resulted in the largest ever circulation in the long history of that newspaper: in contrast, the recent ninetieth anniversary of the founding of Dáil Éireann provoked only modest public interest. One of the most effective posters in the recent successful campaign against the ratification of the Treaty of Lisbon (intended to reform the workings of the European Union) was an image of the Proclamation, accompanied by the slogan 'They died for our freedom'. In an unconscious echo of one of the first 'revisionist' assessments of the Rising, an appalled German politician expressed outrage that the project for European integration could be derailed by 'a minority of a minority'.[51] The legacy of the Rising will remain an important feature of Irish public life but, following the emergence of a more confident and tolerant sense of national identity and the success of the northern peace process, it is one that will be increasingly shaped by the present-day needs of the Irish nation rather than those of the dead generations.

In Northern Ireland, commemoration of 1916 could never have been mistaken for nostalgic re-enactment. For the IRA and other militant republicans, the excesses of the golden jubilee demonstrated how a complacent southern State had turned its back on the revolutionary ideals of the Rising, not least its anti-partitionism. Although the claim that 1966 was a significant factor in the outbreak of northern violence is not convincing, the jubilee proved as useful a mobilizing opportunity for republicans as the commemoration of earlier insurrections had for the rebels of 1916.[52] Among the colour party which led a ten-thousand-strong parade to Casement Park in west Belfast was a seventeen-year-old barman, Gerry Adams, who would rise to international prominence as the leader of the latest reincarnation of physical-force republicanism dedicated to completing the objectives of the Rising. Although the Provisional IRA's long campaign of violence failed to achieve that republic, the Rising continues to retain a political significance no longer a feature of southern Ireland. Election literature for the largest nationalist party, Sinn Féin, continues to urge voters to support it on the grounds of its adherence to the goals of 1916, while its objective of unification by 2016 has only recently, and very quietly, fallen by the wayside.

Despite the resilience of a popular heroic narrative of 1916 after several decades of efforts by academics to debunk it, the writing of history is widely assumed to have played an important role in shaping popular attitudes to the Rising.[53] Although much of the critical re-evaluation of the Rising that occurred during the 1970s and 1980s was based on objective scholarship, the public debates it gave rise to were fiercely contested. The shadow of the Troubles could be discerned in such controversies as whether the violence of the rebels had been justified, as well as the acrimonious tone in which these polarized debates were conducted. As the divergence between academic historians, whose research inevitably undermined some of the certainties of the traditional narrative, and the public widened, 'revisionist' historians were increasingly accused of seeking to rewrite the past for contemporary purposes (a view endorsed by at least one recent Taoiseach).

Some historians, or those who popularized their research, did condemn the Easter rebels not just for their own violence but for facilitating that of subsequent generations. The elitism of the rebels and the Pearsean preoccupation with blood sacrifice led some to polemically depict the founding fathers of the independent Irish State as proto-fascists. Recent commentators have drawn comparisons with Al-Qaeda—another conspiratorial minority willing to sacrifice their lives in a spectacular act of symbolic violence against a superpower in a fanatical attempt to awaken the apathetic masses.[54] Islamist extremists, who would be appalled by the egalitarianism of the Proclamation, would surely admire its vanguardist authors' claim to value their cause 'more than life', and their tremendous success in legitimizing the violence that their iconic act of self-sacrifice would subsequently inspire.[55]

Whether historians have succeeded in imparting a more complex view of Ireland's violent past, one that (intentionally or otherwise) undermines the certainties that prove so essential during periods of conflict, remains a matter of debate. In a much-quoted essay, 'We are all revisionists now', published in 1986, the historian Roy Foster observed that 'the last generation to learn Irish history only from the old nationalist textbooks will soon be middle-aged men and women'. It would no longer be possible to tell the story of Ireland as the struggle of 'a people coming out of captivity', a story 'with a beginning, a middle and what appeared (up to about 1968) to be a triumphant end'.[56] In this formulation, the emergence of the Northern Irish Troubles is given as much weight as historiographical advances in undermining simplistic attitudes to the past.

The subsequent post-ceasefire emergence of a more assertive and confident southern nationalism untarnished by Provisional violence—unthinkable during the car bombs and sectarian murders of the 1980s—brings into question this eirenic notion of an Irish public evolving towards post-nationalist enlightenment. Commenting on the successful military parade marking the ninetieth anniversary in 2006, Diarmaid Ferriter—the most prominent of the next generation of Irish historians—declared: 'The post-revisionists won the argument—the commemoration was about what happened, not about what some people believe should have happened or fervently wished did not happen'.[57] Accusing 'the revisionists' of 'living in the past—the same intellectual crime that had, of course, formed part of their indictment of unreconstructed nationalist historiography', the conclusion of a recent scholarly volume marking the ninetieth anniversary similarly celebrated the triumph of the 'valuable, noble and enduring' elements of the Irish republican tradition over 'the rhetorical assaults it had endured for over three decades'.[58] Despite all this, it would take a rash historian to predict the end of Irish history.[59]

Such controversies illuminate the different ways the Easter Rising has been interpreted at different times, but tell us more about the period when such opinions were formed than the motives of the rising generation. This book has sought to assess the rebels in the context of their own times, exploiting the records of the Bureau of Military History to enable them to explain their own actions in their own voices. Some of the criticisms of the rebels made by their contemporaries still seem valid: with the enactment of the Home Rule bill, a democratic path towards independence was available. They were also mistaken, as the post-war European political order demonstrated, in their belief that national identity was facing extinction by the forces of imperialism. They were wrong to believe that the Great War represented the final opportunity to resurrect the Irish nation (although as Garret Fitzgerald observed 'the very success of 1916 has weakened our understanding of why its leaders felt that the Rising was needed').[60] The rebels had no democratic mandate for their actions, and their violence further polarized Irish society, rendering partition and independence a bloodier process. Republicans ultimately did not have a better answer to unionism than constitutional nationalists. Despite previously condemning, and in some cases killing, their nationalist rivals as traitors for accepting partitionist settlements, republicans would do the same in 1921, 1927, and 1998.

But 1916 must also be seen as a response to Britain's frustration of democratic Irish demands for self-government, demands that had been peacefully expressed for over three decades. Moreover, as many contemporary critics of the rebels accepted, Ulster unionism's recourse to the threat of force in 1913 was an essential precondition for the republican violence that followed. The actions of the rebels should be assessed not only within the context of Irish nationalism (where they are often unfavourably compared to those of constitutional nationalists), but within the wider Irish and British context where they pursued their aims in competition with other groups who resorted to the threat of violence in pursuit of their own political objectives. Nor was the path to Home Rule, as James Connolly observed, free of violence: the Irish Party's support for Irish enlistment in the Great War was a prerequisite for the attainment of Home Rule, one which exacted a high cost in Irish lives: 'those mountains of Irish dead'.[61] Given the thousands of deaths and lives destroyed by political violence in Ireland since 1916, there is a tendency to emphasize the counter-productive effects of republican violence or to underestimate its effectiveness but partition was inevitable by 1914 and Home Rule represented a substantially more limited measure of independence than the dominion self-government achieved by the Treaty in 1921.

The complexities and uncertainties of this period of history, as illustrated by the conflicting views of those who experienced it, should defy the condescending certainty with which hindsight is deployed to endorse or condemn one side or another. Whatever criticisms might be made of them, what shines through many of the voices of those who lived through this era is the integrity and idealism of a generation of Irish men and women who struggled to realize a vision of an Ireland different to the one in which they had been born.

Guide to Further Reading

GENERAL HISTORIES

Recent surveys of Ireland since the Union include Paul Bew's *Ireland: The Politics of Enmity 1789–2006* (Oxford, 2007), which focuses on the conflict between nationalism and unionism; Diarmaid Ferriter's *The Transformation of Ireland 1900–2000* (London, 2005), which places particular emphasis on social history and the experiences of ordinary people; and Alvin Jackson's thoughtful political analysis, *Ireland 1798–1998: Politics and War* (Oxford, 1999). J. J. Lee's *Ireland 1912–1985: Politics and Society* (Cambridge, 1989) remains an important and occasionally provocative assessment. David Fitzpatrick's *The Two Irelands 1912–1939* (Oxford, 1998) offers the sharpest concise account of the demise of the union and formation of the two Irish states. Roy Foster's highly influential *Modern Ireland 1600–1972* (London, 1988) surveys Ireland from the early modern period, while Charles Townshend's *Ireland: The 20th Century* (London, 1999) provides a useful concise overview of the past century.

THEMATIC STUDIES

The most recent and accessible critical account of Irish nationalism is Richard English's *Irish Freedom: The History of Nationalism in Ireland* (London, 2006). Other important studies of aspects of nationalist political culture include R. V. Comerford's stimulating *Ireland* (London, 2003); D. George Boyce's *Nationalism in Ireland* (London, 1982); John Hutchinson's *The Dynamics of Cultural Nationalism: The Gaelic Revival and the Creation of the Irish Nation State* (London, 1987); and Tom Garvin's iconoclastic studies, *Nationalist Revolutionaries in Ireland, 1858–1928* (Dublin, 2005 edn.) and *The Evolution of Irish Nationalist Politics* (Dublin, 2005 edn.).

Valuable—and contrasting—treatments of the Irish Republican Brotherhood in the decades before the Rising are provided by M. J. Kelly's *The Fenian Ideal and Irish Nationalism: 1882–1916* (Woodbridge, 2006) and Owen

McGee's *The IRB: The Irish Republican Brotherhood from the Land League to Sinn Féin* (Dublin, 2005). R. V. Comerford's *The Fenians in Context: Irish Politics and Society 1848–1882* (Dublin, 1998 edn.) remains the standard history for the mid-Victorian IRB. New research on the Brotherhood can be found in *The Black Hand of Republicanism: Fenianism in Modern Ireland* (Dublin, 2009), edited by Fearghal McGarry and James McConnel. Much of the still limited historiography on female republicans in this period—including Margaret Ward's *Unmanageable Revolutionaries: Women and Irish Nationalism* (London, 1983) and Ruth Taillon's *When History Was Made: The Women of 1916* (Belfast, 1999)—is written from a left-wing, feminist, and republican perspective. The most recent account of Cumann na mBan is Cal McCarthy's *Cumann na mBan and the Irish Revolution* (Cork, 2007).

Important studies of the constitutional nationalist and unionist political traditions include Paul Bew's *Ideology and the Irish Question: Ulster Unionism and Irish Nationalism, 1912–1916* (Oxford, 1994); Alvin Jackson's *Home Rule: An Irish History, 1800–2000* (London, 2003); Patrick Maume's *The Long Gestation: Irish Nationalist Life 1891–1918* (Dublin, 1999); and Michael Wheatley's *Nationalism and the Irish Party: Provincial Ireland 1910–1916* (Oxford, 2005).

For political and institutional aspects of British rule in Ireland, see Leon Ó Broin's *Dublin Castle and the 1916 Rising* (London, 1966) and Eunan O'Halpin's *The Decline of the Union: British Government in Ireland, 1892–1920* (Dublin, 1987). Aspects of the Anglo-Irish relationship are addressed in Sheila Lawlor's *Britain and Ireland, 1914–23* (Dublin, 1983) and D. George Boyce's *Englishmen and Irish Troubles: British Public Opinion and the Making of Irish Policy, 1918–22* (London, 1972).

THE GREAT WAR AND THE IRISH REVOLUTION

While the Easter Rising was long neglected by historians, its wider wartime (1914–18) and revolutionary (1913–23) context has formed the subject of more extensive research. Keith Jeffery's *Ireland and the Great War* (Cambridge, 2000) and *Our War: Ireland and the Great War* (Dublin, 2008), edited by John Horne, provide accessible introductions to the Irish experience of war. Since David Fitzpatrick's classic study, *Politics and Irish Life 1913–21: Provincial Experience of War and Revolution* (Dublin, 1977), the Irish revolution has most often been approached at a local level. The most important and controversial of these studies is Peter Hart's *The IRA and its Enemies: Violence and Community in Cork, 1916–23* (Oxford, 1998); also valuable are Marie Coleman's *County Longford and the Irish Revolution, 1910–1923* (Dublin, 2003); Joost Augusteijn's *From Public Defiance to Guerrilla Warfare: The Experience of Ordinary Volunteers in the Irish War of Independence, 1916–1921* (Dublin, 1996); and Fergus Campbell's *Land and Revolution: Nationalist Politics in the West of Ireland 1891–1921* (Oxford, 2005).

Hart's collection *The IRA at War 1916–1923* (Oxford, 2003) includes valuable essays on the Irish revolution, as does Augusteijn's edited collection *The Irish Revolution, 1913–23* (London, 2002). The Irish Volunteers lack a scholarly study of the sort recently devoted to the UVF by Tim Bowman's *Carson's Army: The Ulster Volunteer Force, 1910–22* (Manchester, 2007). *The Ulster Crisis* (Basingstoke, 2006), edited by D. George Boyce and Alan O'Day, contains useful articles spanning the broader revolutionary period. Michael Laffan's *The Resurrection of Ireland: The Sinn Féin Party 1916–1923* outlines the revolutionary politics of republicanism, while his *The Partition of Ireland, 1911–1925* (Dundalk, 1983) provides a usefully concise analysis of a complex issue. For accessible overviews of the War of Independence and Civil War, see Michael Hopkinson's *The Irish War of Independence* (Dublin, 2002) and his *Green against Green: The Irish Civil War* (Dublin, 1988). Other important studies of aspects of the Civil War include Anne Dolan's *Commemorating the Irish Civil War: History and Memory, 1923–2000* (Cambridge, 2003) and Bill Kissane's *The Politics of the Irish Civil War* (Oxford, 2005).

THE EASTER RISING

Prior to the mid-1960s, most historical accounts of the Rising were either journalistic—despite the absence of footnotes and its cheesy dialogue Max Caulfield's *The Easter Rebellion* (London, 1963) is the most valuable—or written from an uncritical 'faith and fatherland' perspective, such as Brian O'Higgins' popular *The Soldier's Story of Easter Week* (Dublin, 1925). Many of these, such as Desmond Ryan's *The Rising: The Complete Story of Easter Week* (Dublin, 1949), were written by participants.

The fiftieth anniversary of the Rising inspired the publication of several important collections of essays, including (the revealingly titled) *Leaders and Men of the Easter Rising: Dublin 1916* (London, 1967), edited by F. X. Martin; *1916: The Easter Rising* (London, 1968), edited by Owen Dudley Edwards and Fergus Pyle; and *The Making of 1916: Studies in the History of the Rising* (Dublin, 1969), edited by Kevin Nowlan. An early assessment of the importance of literary and cultural aspects of the Rising, William Irwin Thompson's

Imagination of an Insurrection (New York, 1967), was also published during this period and would prove the first of many such studies.

The most recent significant anniversary has produced another splurge of publications. Remarkably, it was not until the eve of the ninetieth anniversary, with the publication of Charles Townshend's *Easter 1916: The Irish Rebellion* (London, 2005), that the first authoritative account of the rebellion in its wider military and political context appeared. Prior to this, the only scholarly account of the rebellion was *The Easter Rising* (Stroud, 1999) by Michael Foy and Brian Barton, which, although useful, focused rather narrowly on military aspects of the Rising. The Irish Times *Book of the 1916 Rising* (Dublin, 2006) by Shane Hegarty and Fintan O'Toole is an attractively illustrated and expanded version of the anniversary supplement which first appeared in the *Irish Times*. Annie Ryan's *Witnesses: Inside the Easter Rising* (Dublin, 2005) was the first publication to mine the Bureau of Military History's witness statements, which are now filtering into wider scholarly research. Edited by Gabriel Doherty and Dermot Keogh, *1916: The Long Revolution* (Cork, 2007), features essays on a wide range of themes: particularly useful are Owen McGee's assessment of the role of the IRB and Michael Wheatley's analysis of Irish Party responses to the rebellion. Ruán O'Donnell's more uneven edited collection, *The Impact of the 1916 Rising: Among the Nations* (Dublin, 2008), includes new research on 1916 alongside some decidedly stale socialist republican musings. James Moran's *Staging the Easter Rising: 1916 as Theatre* (Cork, 2005) addresses an important dimension of the rebellion and its afterlife.

MEMOIRS AND CONTEMPORARY ACCOUNTS

Published by the *Weekly Irish Times* in 1916, the *Sinn Fein Rebellion Handbook* (republished as the *1916 Rebellion Handbook* (Mourne River Press) in 1998) is a valuable compendium of contemporary records and accounts. Breandán MacGiolla Choille's *Intelligence Notes, 1913–16* (Dublin, 1966) brings together RIC police reports, arranged by county, in the years leading up to the rebellion. Keith Jeffery's *The GPO and the Easter Rising* (Dublin, 2006) features a well-chosen selection of narrative accounts by combatants and observers. Interesting accounts by participants include Seán MacEntee's *Episode at Easter* (Dublin, 1966) and Desmond FitzGerald's *Desmond's Rising: Memoirs 1913 to Easter 1916* (Dublin, 2006 edn.). *The Moynihan Brothers in Peace and War 1909–1918* (Dublin, 2004), edited by Deirdre McMahon, brings to light a remarkable collection of correspondence to illustrate the complex and poignant impact of war and rebellion on a single Irish family.

BIOGRAPHIES

Biographical accounts published before the 1970s, such as Louis Le Roux's *Patrick. H. Pearse* (Dublin, 1932), were generally uncritical. Ruth Dudley Edwards' iconoclastic biography *Patrick Pearse: The Triumph of Failure* (London, 1977) marked the beginning of a more critical approach. Pearsean cultural studies have subsequently proliferated. Elaine Sisson's *Pearse's Patriots: St Enda's and the Cult of Boyhood* (Cork, 2004) provides a thoughtful account of a complex and oversensationalized subject, and the role of masculinity and gender within Irish republicanism more broadly requires further study. Sean Farrell Moran's biography *Patrick Pearse and the Politics of Redemption* (Washington DC, 1994) delves deep into Pearse's psyche, attributing his motives to failure, personal inadequacy, and a generational revolt against reason. It was characteristic of a broader critical approach to Pearse which prompted Brian P. Murphy's thoughtful *Patrick Pearse and the Lost Republican Ideal* (Dublin, 1991), which outlines the legitimist republican case for seeing Pearse's actions as a rational response to the behaviour of unionists and their British supporters.

The output of publications on Connolly is too vast to summarize: the most recent and comprehensive, Donal Nevin's methodical *James Connolly: 'A Full Life'* (Dublin, 2005), provides a useful starting point. Although Connolly lacked popular political support and Pearse was, in some respects, more the mouthpiece than leader of the rebellion, both men have proven a never-ending source of fascination for historians, political scientists, and literary theorists, partly due to the inherent appeal of their writings, but also because they conveniently left many of them behind. In contrast, the actual organizers of the rebellion—who left fewer records—have attracted little scholarly interest. Remarkably, the most recent biography of Tom Clarke remains Louis Le Roux's *Tom Clarke and the Irish Freedom Movement* (Dublin, 1936), while his co-conspirator only recently received a biography with the publication of Gerard MacAtasney's sympathetic *Seán MacDiarmada. The Mind of the Revolution* (Nure, 2004).

Aspects of the rebellion are addressed in many biographies of revolutionaries—such as Peter Hart's *Mick: The Real Michael Collins* (London, 2005) and David Fitpatrick's *Harry Boland's Irish Revolution* (Cork,

2003)—and those of other figures who were deeply affected by it despite playing more peripheral roles, such as Roy Foster's *W. B. Yeats: A Life. II: The Arch-Poet 1915–1939* (Oxford, 2003) and Richard English's *Ernie O'Malley: IRA Intellectual* (Oxford, 1999).

HISTORIOGRAPHY AND COMMEMORATION

Two collections of documents edited by F. X. Martin—'Eoin MacNeill on 1916', *Irish Historical Studies* 12/47 (Mar. 1961) and *The Irish Volunteers 1913–1915. Recollections and Documents* (Dublin, 1963)—heralded a more scholarly approach to the Rising. Fr Francis Shaw's polemical essay 'The Canon of Irish History—A Challenge' (*Studies*, 61, Summer 1972) marked one of the first explicit criticisms of Pearsean nationalism from a Catholic perspective. Although written in 1966 it did not appear until six years later, when it was published in a very different political climate. Mary Daly and Margaret O'Callaghan's edited collection, *1916 in 1966: Commemorating the Easter Rising* (Dublin, 2007), provides a valuable snapshot of the Rising's legacy on the eve of the Troubles and the 'revisionist' controversy. The publications marking the seventy-fifth anniversary—including *Revising the Rising* (Derry, 1991), edited by Máirín ni Dhonnchadha and Theo Dorgan, and *16 on 16* (Dublin, 1989), edited by Dermot Bolger—are the products of a bleaker and more contentious commemoration. The more ebullient atmosphere of the ninetieth anniversary, a consequence of both Southern prosperity and Northern peace, can be discerned in some of the essays in *1916: The Long Revolution* (Cork, 2007), edited by Gabriel Doherty and Dermot Keogh. Other useful articles on the historiography of the Rising include D. George Boyce's '1916, Interpreting the Rising', in D. George Boyce and Alan O'Day (eds), *Modern Irish History: Revisionism and the Revisionist Controversy* (London, 1996), and Michael Laffan's essay, 'Easter Week and the Historians', in *1916 in 1966*.

A version of the ballad featured at the beginning of this book, 'Who is Ireland's Enemy?', is included on Various Artists, *Songs of Ireland's 1916 Rising* (Derry, 1998). Recent novels (which appear to reflect revisionist rather than post-revisionist concerns) featuring the Rising include Roddy Doyle's *A Star Called Henry* (London, 1999) and Sebastian Barry's *A Long Long Way* (London, 2005). *The Easter Rising: A Guide to Dublin in 1916* (Dublin, 2009) by Conor Kostick and Lorcan Collins provides a useful guide for visiting the main locations of the rebellion in Dublin.

Notes

INTRODUCTION

1. B[ureau of] M[ilitary] H[istory] W[itness] S[tatement] 1746 (Matthew Connolly). The Bureau's witness statements can be consulted at the Military Archives (Dublin) and The National Archives of Ireland.

2. Michael Foy and Brian Barton, *The Easter Rising* (Stroud, 1999), 54. For the attack on the Castle, see also *1916 Rebellion Handbook* (Dublin, 1998 edn.); Charles Townshend, *Easter 1916: The Irish Rebellion* (London, 2005); Max Caulfield, *The Easter Rebellion: Dublin 1916* (London, 1963).

3. Foy and Barton, *Easter Rising*, 54–5.

4. BMH WS 316 (Peter Folan).

5. *1916 Rebellion Handbook*, 11.

6. Keith Jeffery, *The GPO and the Easter Rising* (Dublin, 2006), 127–8.

7. BMH WS 391 (Helena Molony).

8. Jeffery, *The GPO*, 33, 42–3. The individual referred to as the Attorney General, James O'Connor, was actually Solicitor General at the time.

9. BMH WS 316 (Peter Folan); BMH WS 398 (Bridget Foley).

10. On the Bureau, see Jennifer Doyle, Frances Clarke, Eibhlis Connaughton, and Orna Somerville, *An Introduction to the Bureau of Military History, 1913–21* (Dublin, 2002); Gerard O'Brien, *Irish Governments and the Guardianship of Historical Records, 1922–1972* (Dublin, 2004), 130–53; Diarmaid Ferriter, 'In Such Deadly Earnest', *Dublin Review* 12 (2003); Eve Morrison, 'The Bureau of Military History and Female Republican Activism, 1913–23', in Maryann Gialanella Valiulis (ed.), *Gender and Power in Irish History* (Dublin, 2008).

11. O'Brien, *Irish Governments*, 142.

12. Doyle et al., *Bureau of Military History*, 1.

13. On the use of oral sources in Irish historiography, see Guy Beiner, '*Bodhaire Uí Laoire*: Oral History and Contemporary Irish Historiography', available at http://www.ucd.ie/pages/99/articles/beiner.html.

CHAPTER 1: THE RISING GENERATION

1. Richard English, *Irish Freedom: The History of Nationalism in Ireland* (London, 2006), 37.

2. *Wolfe Tone Annual, 1950* (Dublin, 1950), 55–6. I am grateful to Patrick Maume for bringing this ballad to my attention.

3. English, *Irish Freedom*, 46–65.

4. Pádraig Lenihan, 'War and Population, 1649–52', *Irish Economic and Social History* 24 (1997).

5. S. J. Connolly (ed.), *The Oxford Companion to Irish History* (Oxford, 1998), 128.

6. Ibid. 593.

7. Thomas Bartlett, *Theobald Wolfe Tone* (Dublin, 1997), 7.

8. English, *Irish Freedom*, 107.

9. S. J. Connolly, *Divided Kingdom: Ireland 1630–1800* (Oxford, 2008).

10. Patrick Geoghegan, *King Dan: The Rise of Daniel O'Connell, 1775–1829* (Dublin, 2008); Patrick Maume, 'Parnell and the IRB Oath', *Irish Historical Studies* 29/115 (1995).

11. I. R. McBride, *Scripture Politics: Ulster Presbyterians and Irish Radicalism in the Late Eighteenth Century* (Oxford, 1998), 215.

12. Charles Townshend, *Ireland: The Twentieth Century* (London, 1999), 26.

13. Oliver MacDonagh, 'Ambiguity in Nationalism: The Case of Ireland', in Ciaran Brady (ed.), *Interpreting Irish History: The Debate on Historical Revisionism* (Dublin, 1994), 106.

14. David Fitzpatrick, 'Ireland and the Empire', in Andrew Porter (ed.), *The Oxford History of the British Empire: The Nineteenth Century* (Oxford, 1999). See also Kevin Kenny (ed.), *Ireland and the British Empire* (Oxford, 2004).

15. The controversy which accompanies popular films on the War of Independence, such as *Michael Collins*, usually focuses on the accuracy of colonial depictions of Ireland, as the existence of free elections, a relatively free press, and constitutional nationalist and unionist opposition to separatism is often not indicated to audiences; see, for example, Brian P. Murphy, '*The Wind that Shakes the Barley*: Reflections on the Writing of Irish History in the Period of the Easter Rising and the Irish War of Independence', in Ruán O'Donnell (ed.), *The Impact of the 1916 Rising: Among the Nations* (Dublin, 2008).

16. Peter Hart, *The IRA and Its Enemies* (Oxford, 1998), 44.

17. David Fitzpatrick, *The Two Irelands 1912–1939* (Oxford, 1998), 58; English, *Irish Freedom*, 327.

18. T. W. Moody and Leon Ó Broin, 'The IRB Supreme Council', *Irish Historical Studies* 19/75 (1975), 314.

19. For a recent account of the IRB in this period, see Owen McGee, *The IRB: The Irish Republican Brotherhood from the Land League to Sinn Féin* (Dublin, 2005).

20. B[ureau of] M[ilitary] H[istory] W[itness] S[tatement] 116 (Dan Dennehy).

21. BMH WS 167 (Christopher Byrne).

22. BMH WS 338 (Francis McQuillan); BMH WS 848 (Harry Phibbs).

23. BMH WS 4 (Diarmuid Lynch).

24. BMH WS 93 (Dan Corkery).

25. BMH WS 181 (Robert Kelly).

26. BMH WS 1005 (Liam Walsh).

27. BMH WS 976 (Seamus Connelly).

28. BMH WS 4 (Diarmuid Lynch).

29. Fergus Campbell, *Land and Revolution: Nationalist Politics in the West of Ireland 1891–1921* (Oxford, 2005), 185–9.

30. R.V. Comerford, 'Patriotism as Pastime: The Appeal of Fenianism in the Mid-1860s', *Irish Historical Studies* 22/86 (1980), 244.

31. BMH WS 914 (Denis McCullough).

32. BMH WS 1770 (Kevin O'Shiel).

33. BMH WS 581 (Augustine Ingoldsby).

34. Owen McGee, 'Who were the "Fenian Dead"? The IRB and the Background to the 1916 Rising', in Gabriel Doherty and Dermot Keogh (eds), *1916: The Long Revolution* (Cork, 2007), 109.

35. For the most recent account, see Timothy McMahon, *Grand Opportunity: The Gaelic Revival and Irish Society, 1893–1910* (Syracuse, 2008).

36. R.V. Comerford, *Ireland* (London, 2003), 212.

37. Diarmaid Ferriter, The *Transformation of Ireland 1900–2000* (London, 2004), 36.

38. BMH WS 151 (James Ryan).

39. BMH WS 320 (Tom Harris).

40. BMH WS 410 (Thomas McNally).

41. BMH WS 582 (Augustine Ingoldsby). Temperance, a popular movement at the time, was not exclusive to Gaels.

42. BMH WS 909 (Sidney Gifford).

43. BMH WS 376 (Padraig O'Kelly).

44. BMH WS 82 (Bulmer Hobson).

45. BMH WS 99 (Patrick McCartan).

46. BMH WS 939 (Ernest Blythe).

47. BMH WS 1103 (Denis Madden).

48. BMH WS 82 (Bulmer Hobson).

49. BMH WS 1770 (Kevin O'Shiel).

50. BMH WS 677 (Patrick McHugh).

51. Fitzpatrick, *Two Irelands*, 16.

52. BMH WS 391 (Helena Molony).

53. Ibid.

54. BMH WS 273 (Margaret Keogh).

55. Senia Pašeta, 'Nationalist Responses to Two Royal Visits to Ireland, 1900 and 1903', *Irish Historical Studies* 31/124 (1999).

56. BMH WS 755 (Sean Prendergast).

57. Ibid.

58. Marnie Hay, 'The Foundation and Development of Na Fianna Éireann, 1909–1916', *Irish Historical Studies* 36/141 (2008), 60.

59. BMH WS 328 (Gary Holohan).

60. BMH WS 676 (Liam Brady).

61. BMH WS 755 (Sean Prendergast).

62. BMH WS 856 (Elizabeth Colbert).

63. BMH WS 739 (Felix O'Doherty).

64. BMH WS 391 (Helena Molony).

65. BMH WS 627 (Seamus Reader).

66. BMH WS 755 (Sean Prendergast).

67. BMH WS 328 (Gary Holohan).

68. BMH WS 1198 (Thomas Dwyer).

69. BMH WS 389 (Roger McCorley).

70. Pádraic [Patrick] Pearse, 'To the Boys of Ireland', in *Political Writings and Speeches* (Dublin, 1924), 112–23.

71. BMH WS 140 (Michael Lonergan).

72. BMH WS 328 (Gary Holohan).

73. BMH WS 510 (Frank Thornton); BMH WS 1693 (John Kenny); BMH WS 203 (Edward O'Neill).

74. BMH WS 972 (Tomas O Cleirigh).

75. BMH WS 212 (Sean Boylan).

76. BMH WS 692 (James Quigley).

77. See Tom Garvin, *Nationalist Revolutionaries in Ireland 1858–1928* (Dublin, 2005 edn.), 116–20 for generational tensions.

78. BMH WS 30 (Denis McCullough).

79. BMH WS 246 (Marie Perolz); BMH WS 656 (Richard O'Connell); BMH WS 335 (Joseph Furlong).

80. BMH WS 927 (Sean Gibbons); BMH WS 995 (Eamon Price).

81. Peter Hart, *The IRA at War 1916–1923* (Oxford, 2003), 57; Barry Coldrey, *Faith and Fatherland: The Christian Brothers and the Development of Irish Nationalism 1838–1921* (Dublin, 1988).

82. BMH WS 399 (Mrs Richard Mulcahy [née Mary Ryan]).

83. BMH WS 1103 (Denis Madden).

84. Garvin, *Nationalist Revolutionaries*, 24–9.

85. BMH WS 645 (Nora Aghas [Ashe]).

86. BMH WS 361 (Peadar Bracken).

87. BMH WS 781 (Patrick Kelly). Published in 1903, *Croppies Lie Down* was written by the Cork writer William Buckley.

88. BMH WS 632 (Elizabeth Bloxham).

89. BMH WS 627 (Seamus Reader). Despite his recollection of the traditional 'good national background', neither of Reader's parents was Irish. See Máirtín Seán Ó Catháin, 'A Land beyond the Sea: Irish and Scottish Republicans in Dublin, 1916', in O'Donnell (ed.), *The Impact of the 1916 Rising*, 37.

90. BMH WS 328 (Gary Holohan).

91. BMH WS 1294 (Sean Whelan).

92. BMH WS 995 (Eamon Price). For an innovative study of social memory, see Guy Beiner, *Remembering the Year of the French: Irish Folk History and Social Memory* (Madison, 2007).

93. BMH WS 1555 (Thomas Reidy).

94. Lawrence McBride, 'Young Readers and the learning and teaching of Irish history, 1870–1922', in *idem* (ed.), *Reading Irish History: Texts, Contexts and Meaning in Modern Ireland* (Dublin, 2003), 80–117.

95. BMH WS 157 (Joseph O'Connor).

96. BMH WS 246 (Marie Perolz).

97. BMH WS 582 (Augustine Ingoldsby).

98. BMH WS 869 (P. J. Murphy).

99. BMH WS 1103 (Denis Madden).

100. BMH WS 447 (Thomas Courtney).

101. BMH WS 404 (Linda McWhinney [née Kearns]); BMH WS 637 (Mrs Terence MacSwiney [née Muriel Frances Murphy]).

102. BMH WS 687 (Fr Michael Curran).

103. Some Sinn Féiners, such as Eamonn Ceannt, did support the striking workers. Sinn Féin's opposition to the labour movement also reflected competition for urban working-class votes, and its suspicions of its pan-British organizational basis.

104. BMH WS 156 (Seamus Robinson).

105. Hart, *IRA at War*, 30–61.

106. Comerford, *Ireland*, 176–8.

107. For discussion of these themes, see Joost Augusteijn, 'Motivation: Why Did They Fight for Ireland? The Motivation of Volunteers in the Revolution', in *idem* (ed.), *The Irish Revolution, 1913–1923* (Basingstoke, 2002); English, *Irish Freedom*.

108. Patrick Maume, *The Long Gestation: Irish Nationalist Life 1891–1918* (Dublin, 1999), 2.

109. Michael Wheatley, *Nationalism and the Irish Party: Provincial Ireland 1910–1916* (Oxford, 2005), 266.

110. M. J. Kelly, *The Fenian Ideal and Irish Nationalism, 1882–1916* (Woodbridge, 2006), 239.

111. Garvin, *Nationalist Revolutionaries*, 12–32.

112. Gerard MacAtasney, *Seán MacDiarmada* (Nure, 2004), 17.

113. Kelly, *Fenian Ideal*, 223.

CHAPTER 2: ARMS IN IRISH HANDS

1. Alvin Jackson, *Home Rule: An Irish History, 1800–2000* (London, 2003), 119.

2. B[ureau of] M[ilitary] H[istory] W[itness] S[tatement] 368 (Sean McGarry).

3. BMH WS 4 (Diarmuid Lynch).

4. BMH WS 143 (Garry Byrne).

5. BMH WS 170 (Paul Galligan).

6. BMH WS 25 (Patrick Higgins).

7. BMH WS 19 (Liam Murphy).

8. BMH WS 24 (Cornelius Murphy).

9. BMH WS 15 (Fred Murray).
10. BMH WS 176 (Thomas Wilson).
11. BMH WS 184 (Alfred Cotton).
12. BMH WS 221 (Arthur McElvogue).
13. BMH WS 702 (Frank Drohan).
14. BMH WS 114 (Eamon O'Connor).
15. BMH WS 130 (Sean Fitzgibbon).
16. Joseph Connell, *Where's Where in Dublin: A Directory of Historical Locations* (Dublin, 2006), 158.
17. On Volunteering rhetoric, see Matthew Kelly, 'The Irish Volunteers: A Machiavellian Moment?', in D. George Boyce and Alan O'Day (eds), *The Ulster Crisis* (Basingstoke, 2006).
18. P. S. O'Hegarty, *A History of Ireland under the Union 1801 to 1922* (London, 1952), 671.
19. Fergus Campbell, *Land and Revolution: Nationalist Politics in the West of Ireland 1891–1921* (Oxford, 2005), 193.
20. BMH WS 51 (Bulmer Hobson).
21. BMH WS 651 (Diarmuid Lynch).
22. BMH WS 155 (Peadar Doyle).
23. Memorandum by Eoin MacNeill, Nov. 1913, NLI, Hobson papers, MS 13,174.
24. BMH WS 1770 (Kevin O'Shiel).
25. Ibid.
26. BMH WS 632 (Elizabeth Bloxham).
27. Timothy Bowman, *Carson's Army: The Ulster Volunteer Force, 1910–22* (Manchester, 2007), 16, 23.
28. Ibid. 204.
29. Ibid. 34.
30. David Fitzpatrick, *The Two Irelands 1912–1939* (Oxford, 1998), 44.
31. *New York Times*, 11 Aug. 1912.
32. Jackson, *Home Rule*, 117.
33. Ibid.
34. BMH WS 155 (Peadar Doyle).
35. BMH WS 143 (Garry Byrne).
36. Ruth Dudley Edwards, *Patrick Pearse: The Triumph of Failure* (London, 1979 edn.), 179.
37. BMH WS 25 (Patrick Higgins).
38. BMH WS 89 (Micheal O Cuill).
39. BMH WS 25 (Patrick Higgins).
40. BMH WS 24 (Cornelius Murphy).
41. BMH WS 34 (Patrick O'Sullivan).
42. BMH WS 248 (Liam O'Flaherty).
43. BMH WS 1563 (Michael Dineen).
44. BMH WS 388 (Joe Good).

45. BMH WS 162 (John Shouldice).

46. BMH WS 89 (Micheal O Cuill).

47. BMH WS 24 (Cornelius Murphy).

48. BMH WS 34 (Patrick O'Sullivan).

49. BMH WS 38 (Patrick McCarthy).

50. Conor McNamara, 'Politics and Society in East Galway, 1914−21', PhD thesis, St Patrick's College, Drumcondra, 2008, 66.

51. BMH WS 19 (Liam Murphy).

52. BMH WS 91 (J. J. Walsh).

53. Ibid.

54. BMH WS 94 (Michael Leahy).

55. BMH WS 62 (Patrick Looney).

56. Jerome aan de Wiel, *The Catholic Church in Ireland* (Dublin, 2003), 8.

57. BMH WS 57 (Thomas O'Donovan).

58. BMH WS 74 (Paud O'Donoghue).

59. BMH WS 46 (Patrick Twomey).

60. BMH WS 739 (Felix O'Doherty).

61. BMH WS 164 (Charles Wall).

62. BMH WS 325 (Eugene Coyle).

63. BMH WS 203 (Edward O'Neill).

64. BMH WS 1562 (Martin Newell).

65. BMH WS 1173 (Michael Hynes).

66. BMH WS 1346 (Bob Kinsella).

67. BMH WS 129 (Sean O'Shea).

68. Wiel, *Catholic Church*, 2.

69. BMH WS 20 (Tom Hales).

70. BMH WS 1399 (Thomas Peppard).

71. BMH WS 56 (Matthew Murphy).

72. BMH WS 20 (Tom Hales).

73. [RIC] I[nspector] G[eneral's monthly report], May 1914, T[he] N[ational] A[rchive], C[olonial] O[ffice] 904/93.

74. Campbell, *Land and Revolution*, 173.

75. McNamara, 'East Galway, 1914−21', 67. See also BMH WS 1138 (Gilbert Morrissey).

76. Peter Hart, *The IRA and Its Enemies* (Oxford, 1998), 188.

77. BMH WS 58 (Patrick O'Brien).

78. BMH WS 34 (Patrick O'Sullivan).

79. BMH WS 203 (Edward O'Neill).

80. BMH WS 136 (Patrick Crowley).

81. BMH WS 20 (Tom Hales).

82. BMH WS 88 (Kathleen McDonnell [née Healy]).

83. Campbell, *Land and Revolution*, 218−19.

84. Fitzpatrick, *Two Irelands*, 50.

85. BMH WS 740 (John McGahey).

86. BMH WS 325 (Eugene Coyle).

87. BMH WS 242 (Liam Tannam).

88. BMH WS 6 (Liam Ó Briain).

89. Campbell, *Land and Revolution*, 218–19.

90. Hart, *IRA and Its Enemies*, 188.

91. IG, May, Sept, Oct. 1914, TNA, CO 904/94–5.

92. Joost Augusteijn (ed.), *The Memoirs of John M. Regan: a Catholic Officer in the RIC and RUC, 1909–48* (Dublin, 2007).

93. BMH WS 25 (Patrick Higgins).

94. BMH WS 333 (Aine O'Rahilly).

95. Margaret Ward, *Unmanageable Revolutionaries: Women and Irish Nationalism* (London, 1983), 93.

96. BMH WS 541 (Nancy Wyse-Power).

97. BMH WS 399 (Mrs Richard Mulcahy).

98. BMH WS 122 (Elizabeth O'Brien).

99. BMH WS 333 (Aine O'Rahilly).

100. BMH WS 1344 (Máire Fitzpatrick).

101. Hart, *IRA and its Enemies*, 188.

102. Fitzpatrick, *Two Irelands*, 49.

103. BMH WS 300 (Henry Murray).

104. BMH WS 411 (Eamon Morkan).

105. BMH WS 676 (Liam Brady).

106. BMH WS 179 (Elizabeth Corr).

107. BMH WS 147 (Bernard McAllister).

108. BMH WS 148 (James Crenegan).

109. M. J. Kelly, *The Fenian Ideal and Irish Nationalism, 1882–1916* (Woodbridge, 2006), 217–18.

110. David Fitzpatrick, 'Militarism in Ireland, 1900–1922', in Tom Bartlett and Keith Jeffery (eds), *A Military History of Ireland* (Cambridge, 1996).

111. BMH WS 907 (Laurence Nugent).

112. BMH WS 676 (Liam Brady).

113. BMH WS 198 (James Walsh).

114. BMH WS 242 (Liam Tannam).

115. BMH WS 91 (J. J. Walsh).

116. BMH WS 318 (John Scollan).

117. BMH WS 842 (Seán Kennedy).

118. Kelly, *Fenian Ideal*, 219–20.

119. Ibid. 219.

120. BMH WS 1294 (Sean Whelan). Whelan's reference alludes to a popular 1798 ballad (in which a rebel caresses his pike).

121. BMH WS 694 (Frank Burke).

122. BMH WS 46 (Patrick Twomey).

123. BMH WS 116 (Dan Dennehy).
124. BMH WS 195 (Molly Reynolds).
125. BMH WS 179 (Elizabeth Corr).
126. BMH WS 258 (Maeve McDowell [née Cavanagh]).
127. Ruth Taillon, *When History was Made: The Women of 1916* (Belfast, 1999), pp. xviii, 6–7.
128. BMH WS 195 (Molly Reynolds); BMH WS 180 (Kathleen O'Kelly [née Murphy]).
129. BMH WS 259 (Bridget Thornton [née Lyons]).
130. BMH WS 805 (Lily Curran [née Cooney]).
131. BMH WS 246 (Marie Perolz).
132. Hart, *IRA and its Enemies*, 203; Joost Augusteijn, 'Motivation: Why Did They Fight for Ireland? The Motivation of Volunteers in the Revolution', in *idem* (ed.), *The Irish Revolution, 1913–1923* (Basingstoke, 2002), 103.
133. Hart, *IRA and its Enemies*, 188.
134. BMH WS 157 (Joseph O'Connor).
135. BMH WS 158 (Seamus Kenny). Owned by the Plunkett family, Larkfield was a disused stone mill on farmland near Harold's Cross, where many of the Volunteers who returned from Britain during the war lived.
136. BMH WS 80 (Patrick Harris).
137. BMH WS 79 (Diarmuid O'Donneabhain).
138. BMH WS 251 (Richard Balfe).
139. BMH WS 1041 (Thomas Doyle).
140. BMH WS 175 (John Styles).
141. BMH WS 734 (Thomas Meldon).
142. BMH WS 242 (Liam Tannam).
143. BMH WS 1043 (Joseph Lawless).
144. BMH WS 239 (Frank Necy).
145. BMH WS 282 (Charles O'Grady).
146. BMH WS 734 (Thomas Meldon).
147. BMH WS 909 (Sidney Gifford).
148. Richard English, *Irish Freedom: The History of Nationalism in Ireland* (London, 2006), 269.
149. BMH WS 291 (William Daly).
150. BMH WS 591 (Eamon Martin).
151. Ibid.
152. BMH WS 755 (Sean Prendelgast).
153. BMH WS 259 (Bridget Thornton).
154. BMH WS 739 (Felix O'Doherty).
155. BMH WS 25 (Patrick Higgins).
156. BMH WS 492 (John McCoy).
157. BMH WS 907 (Laurence Nugent).
158. BMH WS 79 (Diarmuid O'Donneabhain).

159. BMH WS 1587 (Daniel O'Keefe).
160. BMH WS 532 (John MacDonagh).
161. BMH WS 1043 (Joseph Lawless).
162. BMH WS 62 (Patrick Looney).
163. BMH WS 328 (Gary Holohan).
164. BMH WS 132 (Michael O'Sullivan).
165. BMH WS 258 (Maeve McDowell).
166. Hart, *IRA and its Enemies*, 205–7.
167. Sean Cronin, *The McGarrity Papers* (Kerry, 1972), 37–8.
168. BMH WS 18 (Denis Lordan).
169. Kelly, *Fenian Ideal*, 238.
170. Owen McGee, *The IRB: The Irish Republican Brotherhood from the Land League to Sinn Féin* (Dublin, 2005), 355.
171. Fitzpatrick, *Two Irelands*, 46–7.
172. BMH WS 1770 (Kevin O'Shiel).
173. BMH WS 25 (Patrick Higgins).
174. BMH WS 124 (Joseph Connolly).
175. BMH WS 19 (Liam Murphy).
176. BMH WS 76 (Seamus Hickey).
177. BMH WS 368 (Sean McGarry).
178. BMH WS 130 (Sean Fitzgibbon).
179. BMH WS 328 (Gary Holohan).
180. BMH WS 591 (Eamon Martin).
181. BMH WS 50 (Bulmer Hobson).
182. BMH WS 907 (Laurence Nugent).
183. IG, May 1914, TNA, CO 904/93.
184. BMH WS 176 (Thomas Wilson).
185. BMH WS 907 (Laurence Nugent).
186. BMH WS 91 (J. J. Walsh).
187. BMH WS 328 (Gary Holohan).
188. BMH WS 729 (Seamus Dobbyn); *Irish Volunteer*, 7 Nov. 1914.
189. Michael Wheatley, *Nationalism and the Irish Party: Provincial Ireland 1910–1916* (Oxford, 2005).
190. BMH WS 53 (Bulmer Hobson).
191. BMH WS 130 (Sean Fitzgibbon).
192. BMH WS 697 (Patrick Bermingham).
193. BMH WS 509 (J. J. McConnell).
194. BMH WS 53 (Bulmer Hobson).
195. BMH WS 755 (Sean Prendergast).
196. BMH WS 739 (Felix O'Doherty).
197. BMH WS 155 (Peadar Doyle).
198. BMH WS 1753 (Liam Tobin).
199. BMH WS 340 (Oscar Traynor).

200. BMH WS 232 (Joseph Kenny).
201. BMH WS 971 (George Berkeley).
202. BMH WS 6 (Liam O'Briain).
203. BMH WS 155 (Peadar Doyle).
204. IG, May 1914, TNA, CO 904/93.

CHAPTER 3: THE SOUL OF THE NATION

1. B[ureau of] M[ilitary] H[istory] W[itness] S[tatement] 157 (Joseph O'Connor).
2. BMH WS 1770 (Kevin O'Shiel); BMH WS 1700 (Alphonsus O'Halloran).
3. BMH WS 447 (Thomas Courtney).
4. BMH WS 328 (Gary Holohan).
5. BMH WS 733 (James O'Shea).
6. BMH WS 1770 (Kevin O'Shiel).
7. BMH WS 739 (Felix O'Doherty).
8. BMH WS 417 (David McGuinness).
9. BMH WS 1770 (Kevin O'Shiel).
10. BMH WS 115 (Matthew McMahon).
11. BMH WS 971 (George Berkeley).
12. [RIC] C[ounty] I[nspector's monthly report], Tyrone, Aug. 1914, TNA, CO 904/94.
13. Ibid.
14. BMH WS 714 (Thomas Hynes).
15. BMH WS 1737 (Seamus Fitzgerald).
16. BMH WS 492 (John McCoy).
17. BMH WS 155 (Peadar Doyle).
18. BMH WS 1041 (Thomas Doyle).
19. BMH WS 889 (James Kavanagh).
20. BMH WS 50 (Bulmer Hobson).
21. Joseph Finnan, *John Redmond and Irish Unity, 1912–1918* (Syracuse, 2004), 89.
22. R. F. Foster, *Modern Ireland 1600–1972* (London, 1989 edn.), 472–3.
23. Finnan, *Redmond*, 88.
24. Ibid. 86.
25. BMH WS 907 (Laurence Nugent).
26. BMH WS 733 (James O'Shea).
27. BMH WS 1043 (Joseph Lawless).
28. BMH WS 242 (Liam Tannam).
29. BMH WS 590 (Thomas Treacy).
30. BMH WS 64 (Cornelius Meany).
31. IG, Dec. 1914, TNA, CO 904/95.
32. BMH WS 176 (Thomas Wilson).
33. BMH WS 94 (Michael Leahy).

34. BMH WS 176 (Thomas Wilson).

35. BMH WS 1344 (Máire Fitzpatrick).

36. BMH WS 198 (James Walsh); BMH WS 6 (Liam Ó Briain).

37. BMH WS 328 (Thomas Courtney).

38. BMH WS 368 (Sean McGarry).

39. BMH WS 4 (Diarmuid Lynch).

40. BMH WS 242 (Liam Tannam).

41. BMH WS 819 (Liam Archer).

42. BMH WS 242 (Liam Tannam).

43. BMH WS 804 (Mortimer O'Connell); BMH WS 192 (Fionan Lynch); BMH WS 234 (James Smyth); BMH WS 223 (Robert Haskin).

44. BMH WS 118 (Patrick O'Mahony).

45. BMH WS 739 (Felix O'Doherty); BMH WS 114 (Eamon O'Connor).

46. BMH WS 279 (Seamus Dobbyn).

47. BMH WS 373 (John Hosty).

48. BMH WS 24 (Cornelius Murphy).

49. BMH WS 32 (Florence Begley).

50. BMH WS 57 (Thomas O'Donovan).

51. BMH WS 1770 (Kevin O'Shiel).

52. David Fitzpatrick, *The Two Irelands 1912–1939* (Oxford, 1998), 55–6.

53. BMH WS 1770 (Kevin O'Shiel).

54. IG, Aug. 1915, TNA, CO 904/97.

55. Peter Hart, *The IRA and Its Enemies* (Oxford, 1998), 189.

56. BMH WS 1770 (Kevin O'Shiel).

57. BMH WS 1041 (Peadar Doyle).

58. BMH WS 132 (Michael O'Sullivan). See James McConnel, 'Recruiting Sergeants for John Bull? Irish Nationalist MPs and Enlistment during the Early Months of the Great War', *War in History* 14/4 (2007).

59. BMH WS 896 (Edward Moane).

60. BMH WS 76 (Seamus Hickey).

61. BMH WS 1344 (Maire Fitzpatrick).

62. BMH WS 39 (Eamon Ahern).

63. BMH WS 119 (Eithne [Annie] MacSwiney).

64. BMH WS 585 (Frank Robbins).

65. BMH WS 1043 (Joseph Lawless).

66. BMH WS 132 (Michael O'Sullivan).

67. BMH WS 1700 (Alphonsus O'Halloran).

68. BMH WS 597 (Edmond O'Brien).

69. BMH WS 1700 (Alphonsus O'Halloran); BMH WS 1043 (Joseph Lawless).

70. BMH WS 300 (Henry Murray).

71. Ruth Dudley Edwards, *Patrick Pearse: The Triumph of Failure* (London, 1979 edn.), 236–7.

72. BMH WS 687 (Fr Michael Curran).

73. BMH WS 1754 (Mrs Tom Barry [née Leslie Price]).
74. BMH WS 62 (Patrick Looney).
75. BMH WS 1035 (Sean Cody).
76. BMH WS 291 (William Daly).
77. Keith Jeffery, *The GPO and the Easter Rising* (Dublin, 2006), 164.
78. BMH WS 874 (Gilbert Morrisey).
79. BMH WS 242 (Liam Tannam).
80. BMH WS 161 (Donal O'Hannigan).
81. BMH WS 391 (Helena Molony).
82. BMH WS 705 (Christopher Brady).
83. BMH WS 733 (James O'Shea).
84. Ibid.
85. Ibid.
86. BMH WS 79 (Diarmuid O'Donneabhain); BMH WS 1598 (Thomas Barry).
87. BMH WS 368 (Sean McGarry).
88. BMH WS 915 (Denis McCullough).
89. Michael Foy and Brian Barton, *The Easter Rising* (Stroud, 1999), 18.
90. BMH WS 6 (Liam Ó Briain).
91. BMH WS 328 (Thomas Courtney).
92. BMH WS 268 (W. T. Cosgrave).
93. BMH WS 939 (Ernest Blythe).
94. BMH WS 915 (Denis McCullough).
95. BMH WS 733 (James O'Shea).
96. BMH WS 167 (Christopher Byrne).
97. BMH WS 523 (Richard Connolly).
98. BMH WS 1052 (Sean MacEntee).
99. BMH WS 219 (John MacDonagh).
100. M. J. Kelly, *The Fenian Ideal and Irish Nationalism, 1882–1916* (Woodbridge, 2006), 240.
101. BMH WS 264 (Aine Ceannt [née O'Brennan]).
102. BMH WS 724 (Desmond Ryan).
103. BMH WS 155 (Peadar Doyle).
104. BMH WS 183 (Liam Gaynor).
105. Patrick Maume, *The Long Gestation: Irish Nationalist Life 1891–1918* (Dublin, 1999), 177.
106. Kelly, *Fenian Ideal*, 202; BMH WS 157 (Joseph O'Connor).
107. BMH WS 82 (Bulmer Hobson).
108. Sean Farrell Moran, *Patrick Pearse and the Politics of Redemption* (Washington, 1994).
109. BMH WS 81 (Bulmer Hobson).
110. F. X. Martin, 'Eoin MacNeill on the 1916 Rising', *Irish Historical Studies* 12/47 (1961), 236.
111. BMH WS 722 (Dan McCarthy).

112. BMH WS 591 (Eamon Martin).

113. Maume, *Long Gestation*, 151, 177.

114. Gerard MacAtasney, *Seán MacDiarmada* (Nure, 2004), 147.

115. Donal Nevin, *James Connolly: 'A Full Life'* (Dublin, 2006 edn.), 600.

116. Ibid. 632.

117. BMH WS 532 (John MacDonagh).

118. BMH WS 26 (P. S. O'Hegarty).

119. BMH WS 81 (Bulmer Hobson).

120. BMH WS 528 (Augustine Ingoldsby).

121. BMH WS 268 (W. T. Cosgrave). Cosgrave's recollection may have been influenced by his later experiences of contending with unmandated republican violence after the Treaty split.

122. BMH WS 25 (Patrick Higgins).

123. BMH WS 368 (Sean McGarry).

124. BMH WS 523 (Richard Connolly).

125. Charles Townshend, *Easter 1916: The Irish Rebellion* (London, 2005), 16.

126. BMH WS 727 (Michael Lawless).

127. BMH WS 175 (John Styles).

128. BMH WS 1043 (Joseph Lawless).

129. BMH WS 804 (Mortimer O'Connell).

130. Foy and Barton, *Easter Rising*, 36; Max Caulfield, *The Easter Rebellion: Dublin 1916* (London, 1963), 23.

131. Peter Hart, *Mick: The Real Michael Collins* (London, 2005), 84.

132. BMH WS 257 (Grace Gifford).

133. BMH WS 488 (Jack Plunkett).

134. BMH WS 735 (Charles MacAuley).

135. BMH WS 7 (Liam Ó Briain).

136. BMH WS 209 (Madge Daly). For Connolly's approval, see BMH WS 258 (Maeve McDowell).

137. C. D. Greaves, *1916 as History: The Myth of the Blood Sacrifice* (Dublin, 1991 edn.).

138. BMH WS 368 (Sean McGarry).

139. Foy and Barton, *Easter Rising*, 12—20.

140. BMH WS 81 (Bulmer Hobson).

141. BMH WS 161 (Donal O'Hannigan).

142. BMH WS 340 (Oscar Traynor).

143. BMH WS 264 (Aine Ceannt).

144. BMH WS 521 (Jerry Golden).

145. BMH WS 155 (Peadar Doyle).

146. BMH WS 203 (Edward O'Neill).

147. BMH WS 340 (Oscar Traynor).

148. BMH WS 419 (Mrs Martin Conlon).

149. BMH WS 497 (Eamon Bulfin).

150. BMH WS 139 (Michael Walker).

151. BMH WS 1687 (Harry Colley).

152. BMH WS 564 (Tom Byrne).

153. BMH WS 733 (James O'Shea).

154. BMH WS 156 (Seamus Robinson).

155. BMH WS 291 (William Daly).

156. Máirtín Seán Ó Catháin, 'A Land beyond the Sea: Irish and Scottish Republicans in Dublin, 1916', in Ruán O'Donnell (ed.), *The Impact of the 1916 Rising: Among the Nations* (Dublin, 2008), 37–48.

157. BMH WS 291 (William Daly).

158. BMH WS 244 (John McGallogly).

159. BMH WS 222 (William Stapleton).

160. BMH WS 215 (Michael Hayes).

161. Ben Novick, 'The Arming of Ireland: Gun-Running and the Great War', in Adrian Gregory and Senia Pašeta (eds), *Ireland and the Great War: 'A War to Unite Us All'*? (Manchester, 2002), 98–100.

162. BMH WS 188 (Sean O'Keefe).

163. BMH WS 1628 (James Busby).

164. BMH WS 328 (Thomas Courtney).

165. BMH WS 624 (Edward Handley).

166. BMH WS 388 (Joe Good).

167. BMH WS 694 (Frank Burke).

168. BMH WS 724 (Desmond Ryan).

169. BMH WS 1746 (Matthew Connolly).

170. BMH WS 185 (Margaret Kennedy); BMH WS 399 (Mrs Richard Mulcahy).

171. Novick, 'The Arming of Ireland', 94.

172. BMH WS 511 (Michael Lynch).

173. BMH WS 242 (Liam Tannam).

174. BMH WS 511 (Michael Lynch).

175. BMH WS 219 (John MacDonagh).

176. Owen McGee, *The IRB: The Irish Republican Brotherhood from the Land League to Sinn Féin* (Dublin, 2005), 356.

177. BMH WS 804 (Mortimer O'Connell).

178. BMH WS 734 (Thomas Meldon).

179. BMH WS 1687 (Harry Colley).

180. BMH WS 391 (Helena Molony).

181. Ibid.

182. BMH WS 1666 (Thomas O'Donoghue).

183. BMH WS 246 (Marie Perolz).

184. BMH WS 1754 (Mrs Tom Barry).

185. BMH WS 1152 (Miko O'Dea).

186. BMH WS 733 (James O'Shea).

187. BMH WS 119 (Eithne MacSwiney).

188. Ibid.
189. BMH WS 521 (Jerry Golden).
190. BMH WS 915 (Denis McCullough); BMH WS 258 (Maeve McDowell).
191. BMH WS 157 (Joseph O'Connor).
192. BMH WS 751 (Colm O'Lochlainn).
193. BMH WS 1043 (Joseph Lawless).
194. BMH WS 157 (Joseph O'Connor).
195. BMH WS 722 (Dan McCarthy).
196. BMH WS 833 (Michael Knightly).
197. BMH WS 1754 (Mrs Tom Barry).
198. Foy and Barton, *Easter Rising*, 37.
199. Eunan O'Halpin, 'British Intelligence in Ireland, 1914–1921', in Christopher
     Andrew and David Dilks (eds), *The Missing Dimension: Governments and Intel-
     ligence Communities in the Twentieth Century* (London, 1984).
200. Michael Laffan, *The Resurrection of Ireland. The Sinn Féin Party 1916–1923*
     (Cambridge, 1999), 37.
201. Foy and Barton, *Easter Rising*, 36. For MacDonagh's indiscretion, see BMH WS
     284 (Michael Staines).
202. BMH WS 4 (Diarmuid Lynch); BMH WS 585 (Frank Robbins).
203. Laffan, *The Resurrection*, 37.
204. BMH WS 246 (Marie Perolz); BMH WS 804 (Mortimer O'Connell);
     BMH WS 4 (Diarmuid Lynch).
205. Eunan O'Halpin, *The Decline of the Union—British Government in Ireland 1892–
     1920* (Dublin 1987), 102.
206. *1916 Rebellion Handbook* (Dublin, 1998 edn.), 209–11.
207. Fitzpatrick, *Two Irelands*, 55.
208. Ibid. 58.
209. BMH WS 81 (Bulmer Hobson).
210. Desmond FitzGerald, *Desmond's Rising: Memoirs, 1913 to Easter 1916* (Dublin,
     2006 edn.), 120.
211. BMH WS 915 (Denis McCullough).
212. BMH WS 724 (Desmond Ryan).
213. BMH WS 334 (Eugene Smith).
214. BMH WS 81 (Bulmer Hobson).
215. BMH WS 7 (Liam Ó Briain).
216. BMH WS 192 (Fionan Lynch).
217. BMH WS 286 (Nora O'Brien [née Connolly]).
218. Ibid.
219. BMH WS 154 (Nora Dore [née Daly]).
220. BMH WS 368 (Sean McGarry).
221. BMH WS 724 (Desmond Ryan).
222. BMH WS 246 (Marie Perolz).
223. BMH WS 733 (James O'Shea).

224. BMH WS 246 (Marie Perolz).
225. BMH WS 200 (Fr Aloysius OFM Cap).
226. BMH WS 568 (Eilis Ui Chonnaill [née Ryan]).
227. BMH WS 733 (James O'Shea).

CHAPTER 4: WALKING ON AIR

1. Owen McGee, *The IRB: The Irish Republican Brotherhood from the Land League to Sinn Féin* (Dublin, 2005), 355–6.
2. Peter Hart, 'The Fenians and the International Revolutionary Tradition', in Fearghal McGarry and James McConnel (eds), *The Black Hand of Republicanism: Fenianism in Modern Ireland* (Dublin, 2009), 199.
3. Charles Townshend, *Easter 1916: The Irish Rebellion* (London, 2005), 354.
4. David Fitzpatrick, *The Two Irelands 1912–1939* (Oxford, 1998), 59–60.
5. Michael Foy and Brian Barton, *The Easter Rising* (Stroud, 1999); Townshend, *Easter 1916*.
6. B[ureau of] M[ilitary] H[istory] W[itness] S[statement] 819 (Liam Archer).
7. BMH WS 842 (Sean Kennedy).
8. BMH WS 1693 (John Kenny).
9. BMH WS 208 (Seamus Kavanagh).
10. BMH WS 805 (Mrs Denis O'Brien [née Annie Cooney]).
11. BMH WS 585 (Frank Robbins).
12. BMH WS 532 (John MacDonagh).
13. BMH WS 1693 (John Kenny).
14. BMH WS 585 (Frank Robbins).
15. BMH WS 733 (Jim O'Shea).
16. BMH WS 1043 (Joseph Lawless).
17. BMH WS 781 (Patrick Kelly).
18. BMH WS 889 (James Kavanagh).
19. BMH WS 461 (Joseph Byrne).
20. BMH WS 423 (Vincent Byrne).
21. BMH WS 243 (James Foran).
22. BMH WS 258 (Maeve McDowell).
23. BMH WS 264 (Aine Ceannt).
24. BMH WS 1753 (Liam Tobin).
25. BMH WS 722 (Dan McCarthy).
26. BMH WS 155 (Peadar Doyle).
27. BMH WS 1766 (William O'Brien); Donal Nevin, *James Connolly: 'A Full Life'* (Dublin, 2006 edn.), 731.
28. BMH WS 186 (Thomas Doyle).
29. BMH WS 781 (Patrick Kelly).
30. BMH WS 192 (Fionan Lynch).
31. BMH WS 157 (Joseph O'Connor).

32. BMH WS 215 (Michael Hayes).

33. BMH WS 216 (Louise Gavan Duffy).

34. BMH WS 81 (Bulmer Hobson).

35. BMH WS 532 (John MacDonagh); BMH WS 150 (Gregory Murphy).

36. BMH WS 724 (Desmond Ryan).

37. BMH WS 409 (Valentine Jackson).

38. Ibid.

39. BMH WS 6 (Liam Ó Briain).

40. BMH WS 157 (Joseph O'Connor). Townshend (*Easter 1916*, 175) gives a figure of less than 130 men; Foy and Barton state that 173 Volunteers in total served in the Boland's area (*Easter Rising*, 73).

41. Townshend, *Easter 1916*, 157.

42. BMH WS 157 (Joseph O'Connor).

43. BMH WS 131 (George O'Flanagan).

44. BMH WS 201 (Nicholas Laffan).

45. BMH WS 388 (Joe Good).

46. BMH WS 621 (Patrick Mullen).

47. BMH WS 282 (Charles O'Grady).

48. BMH WS 722 (Dan McCarthy).

49. BMH WS 152 (Arthur Agnew).

50. BMH WS 694 (Frank Burke).

51. BMH WS 388 (Joe Good).

52. BMH WS 648 (Catherine Rooney [née Byrne]).

53. BMH WS 585 (Frank Robbins); BMH WS 541 (Nancy Wyse-Power); BMH WS 180 (Kathleen O'Kelly).

54. BMH WS 724 (Desmond Ryan).

55. BMH WS 755 (Sean Prendergast).

56. BMH WS 156 (Seamus Robinson).

57. BMH WS 6 (Liam Ó Briain).

58. BMH WS 733 (James O'Shea).

59. Ibid.

60. BMH WS 532 (John MacDonagh).

61. BMH WS 733 (James O'Shea).

62. BMH WS 476 (Joseph Kinsella).

63. BMH WS 733 (James O'Shea).

64. Keith Jeffery, *The GPO and the Easter Rising* (Dublin, 2006), 170.

65. Joost Augusteijn (ed.), *The Memoirs of John M. Regan: a Catholic Officer in the RIC and RUC, 1909–48* (Dublin, 2007), 92.

66. *1916 Rebellion Handbook* (Dublin, 1998 edn.), 9.

67. BMH WS 488 (Jack Plunkett).

68. BMH WS 724 (Desmond Ryan).

69. BMH WS 255 (Thomas Smart).

70. BMH WS 724 (Desmond Ryan).

71. BMH WS 724 (Desmond Ryan).

72. Jeffery, *The GPO*, 143.

73. Townshend, *Easter 1916*, 160; Foy and Barton, *Easter Rising*, 128.

74. Owen McGee, 'Who were the "Fenian Dead"? The IRB and the Background to the 1916 Rising', in Gabriel Doherty and Dermot Keogh (eds), *1916: The Long Revolution* (Cork, 2007).

75. Jeffery, *The GPO*, 142.

76. James Moran, *Staging the Easter Rising: 1916 as Theatre* (Cork, 2005).

77. BMH WS 687 (Fr Michael Curran).

78. BMH WS 694 (Frank Burke).

79. BMH WS 288 (Charles Saurin).

80. BMH WS 724 (Desmond Ryan).

81. BMH WS 1691 (Ernest Jordison).

82. Jeffery, *The GPO*, 171.

83. BMH WS 152 (Arthur Agnew).

84. BMH WS 1721 (Seumas Robinson).

85. BMH WS 532 (John MacDonagh).

86. BMH WS 755 (Sean Prendergast).

87. Max Caulfield, *The Easter Rebellion* (Colorado, 1995 edn.), 66.

88. BMH WS 189 (Michael Soughley).

89. *Rebellion Handbook*, 203. The DMP, it should be noted, was an unarmed force.

90. BMH WS 328 (Gary Holohan).

91. Jeffery, *The GPO*, 172.

92. Michael Laffan, *The Resurrection of Ireland. The Sinn Féin Party 1916–1923* (Cambridge, 1999), 44.

93. James Stephens, *The Insurrection in Dublin* (Gloucester, 2008 edn.), 10.

94. Jeffery, *The GPO*, 180. In his account, originally published in 1917, Ervine described himself as an 'Irish Home Ruler'. The Belfast-born Protestant became a staunch unionist in later life.

95. Maurice Headlam, *Irish Reminiscences* (London, 1947), 166.

96. BMH WS 376 (Padraig O'Kelly).

97. BMH WS 195 (Molly Reynolds); BMH WS 497 (Eamon Bulfin).

98. BMH WS 219 (John MacDonagh).

99. BMH WS 370 (Fintan Murphy).

100. BMH WS 255 (Thomas Smart).

101. BMH WS 251 (Richard Balfe).

102. BMH WS 242 (Liam Tannam).

103. Jeffery, *The GPO*, 88.

104. BMH WS 1766 (William O'Brien).

105. BMH WS 391 (Helena Molony).

106. BMH WS 316 (Peter Folan).

107. Jeffery, *The GPO*, 41–2.

108. BMH WS 316 (Peter Folan).

109. Augusteijn, *John M. Regan*, 93.

110. BMH WS 842 (Sean Kennedy).

111. BMH WS 819 (Liam Archer).

112. BMH WS 335 (Joseph Furlong).

113. Foy and Barton, *Easter Rising*, 167.

114. BMH WS 423 (Vincent Byrne).

115. BMH WS 822 (William Stapleton).

116. BMH WS 307 (Thomas McCarthy).

117. BMH WS 327 (Patrick Egan).

118. BMH WS 531 (Thomas Young).

119. BMH WS 733 (James O'Shea).

120. BMH WS 585 (Frank Robbins).

121. BMH WS 397 (Thomas Pugh).

122. Stephens, *The Insurrection*, 14.

123. BMH WS 1766 (William O'Brien).

124. BMH WS 724 (Desmond Ryan).

125. BMH WS 1766 (William O'Brien).

126. BMH WS 1108 (Jeremiah O'Leary).

127. BMH WS 152 (Arthur Agnew).

128. BMH WS 687 (Fr Michael Curran).

129. Bertram Carter, *Another Part of the Platform* (London, 1931), 28–9.

130. BMH WS 800 (Michael O'Flanagan).

131. Jeffery, *The GPO*, 79.

132. BMH WS 398 (Bridget Martin [née Foley]).

133. BMH WS 497 (Eamon Bulfin).

134. BMH WS 163 (Patrick Rankin); *Rebellion Handbook*, 8.

135. BMH WS 110 (Denis Daly).

136. BMH WS 293 (Aine Heron).

137. BMH WS 687 (Fr Michael Curran).

138. Carter, *Another Part*, 31.

139. Ibid. 32–4.

140. Jeffery, *The GPO*, 78.

141. BMH WS 1184 (Eileen Costello [née Drury]).

142. Jeffery, *The GPO*, 179.

143. BMH WS 660 (Thomas Leahy).

144. Desmond FitzGerald, *Desmond's Rising: Memoirs, 1913 to Easter 1916* (Dublin, 2006 edn.), 139.

145. BMH WS 81 (Bulmer Hobson).

146. Jeffery, *The GPO*, 175; see also Stephens, *Insurrection*, 7.

147. BMH WS 687 (Fr Michael Curran).

148. Headlam, *Irish Reminiscences*, 168.

149. BMH WS 850 (Patrick Colgan).

150. Jeffery, *The GPO*, 87.

151. Tim Pat Coogan, *1916: The Easter Rising* (London, 2005), 118.

152. Jeffery, *The GPO*, 145.

153. BMH WS 907 (Laurence Nugent).

154. Headlam, *Irish Reminiscences*, 166.

155. BMH WS 399 (Mrs Richard Mulcahy).

156. BMH WS 850 (Patrick Colgan).

157. BMH WS 807 (Fr Patrick Doyle).

158. BMH WS 422 (Sean Byrne).

159. BMH WS 340 (Oscar Traynor).

160. BMH WS 824 (Charles Donnelly).

161. BMH WS 242 (Liam Tannam); BMH WS 824 (Charles Donnelly).

162. Jeffery, *The GPO*, 144.

163. Peter Hart, *Mick: The Real Michael Collins* (London, 2005), 93.

164. BMH WS 889 (James Kavanagh).

165. BMH WS 369 (William Whelan).

166. BMH WS 399 (Mrs Richard Mulcahy).

167. BMH WS 1693 (John Kenny).

168. BMH WS 368 (Sean McGarry).

169. BMH WS 270 (Eily O'Reilly [née O'Hanrahan]).

170. BMH WS 920 (Fr Augustine OFM Cap).

171. BMH WS 685 (Claire Hobson [née Gregan]).

172. BMH WS 340 (Oscar Traynor).

173. BMH WS 850 (Patrick Colgan).

174. BMH WS 398 (Bridget Martin).

175. BMH WS 186 (Thomas Doyle).

176. *Rebellion Handbook*, 45.

177. BMH WS 399 (Mrs Richard Mulcahy).

178. BMH WS 310 (Seumas Grace).

179. BMH WS 376 (Padraig O'Kelly).

180. BMH WS 215 (Michael Hayes).

181. BMH WS 833 (Michael Knightly).

182. BMH WS 388 (Joe Good).

183. FitzGerald, *Desmond's Rising*, 136–7, 140.

184. BMH WS 320 (Tom Harris).

185. BMH WS 153 (Eamon Dore); *Rebellion Handbook*, 47.

186. BMH WS 850 (Patrick Colgan).

187. BMH WS 370 (Fintan Murphy).

188. BMH WS 923 (Ignatius Callender).

189. BMH WS 157 (Joseph O'Connor).

190. BMH WS 819 (Liam Archer).

191. BMH WS 201 (Nicholas Laffan).

192. BMH WS 646 (William Christian).

193. BMH WS 724 (Desmond Ryan).

194. BMH WS 4 (Diarmuid Lynch).
195. Foy and Barton, *Easter Rising*, 128.
196. BMH WS 219 (John MacDonagh); BMH WS 267 (Seamus Pounch).
197. BMH WS 312 (Seosamh de Brun).
198. BMH WS 889 (James Kavanagh); BMH WS 291 (William Daly).
199. BMH WS 694 (Frank Burke).
200. BMH WS 199 (Joseph Doolan).
201. BMH WS 302 (Maire O'Brolchain); BMH WS 532 (John MacDonagh).
202. BMH WS 648 (Catherine Rooney).
203. BMH WS 198 (James Walsh).
204. BMH WS 920 (Fr Augustine OFM Cap).
205. Dermot Keogh, 'The Catholic Church, the Holy See and the 1916 Rising', in Doherty and Keogh, *1916*, 280.
206. BMH WS 210 (Phyllis Morkan).
207. BMH WS 781 (Patrick Kelly).
208. BMH WS 568 (Eilis Ui Chonnaill).
209. BMH WS 335 (Joseph Furlong).
210. BMH WS 129 (Sean O'Shea).
211. BMH WS 432 (Pauline Keating).
212. BMH WS 1754 (Mrs Tom Barry). For Flanagan's (differing) account, see Jeffery, *The GPO*, 157–62.
213. BMH WS 733 (James O'Shea).
214. BMH WS 199 (Joseph Doolan).
215. BMH WS 388 (Joe Good).
216. BMH WS 158 (Seamus Kenny).
217. BMH WS 399 (Mrs Richard Mulcahy).
218. BMH WS 923 (Ignatius Callender).
219. BMH WS 288 (Charles Saurin).
220. BMH WS 687 (Fr Michael Curran).
221. BMH WS 186 (Thomas Doyle).
222. BMH WS 7 (Liam Ó Briain).
223. BMH WS 242 (Liam Tannam).
224. BMH WS 833 (Michael Knightly).
225. BMH WS 199 (Joseph Doolan).
226. Earl of Longford and Thomas O'Neill, *Eamon De Valera* (Dublin, 1970), 298.
227. BMH WS 1754 (Mrs Tom Barry).
228. BMH WS 258 (Maeve McDowell).
229. William Murphy, 'Political Imprisonment and the Irish, 1910–21', PhD thesis, University College Dublin, 2007, 106.
230. Ruth Taillon, *When History Was Made: The Women of 1916* (Belfast, 1999), 49.
231. BMH WS 1754 (Mrs Tom Barry).
232. BMH WS 399 (Mrs Richard Mulcahy).
233. BMH WS 648 (Catherine Rooney).

234. Townshend, *Easter 1916*, 261.
235. Margaret Ward, 'Gender: Gendering the Irish Revolution', in Joost Augusteijn (ed.), *The Irish Revolution, 1913–1923* (Basingstoke, 2002), 173.
236. BMH WS 919 (Ina Heron [née Connolly]).
237. BMH WS 432 (Pauline Keating).
238. BMH WS 805 (Lily Curran).
239. BMH WS 259 (Bridget Thornton).
240. BMH WS 195 (Molly Reynolds).
241. BMH WS 259 (Bridget Thornton).
242. BMH WS 925 (Mairead O'Kelly).
243. BMH WS 246 (Marie Perolz).
244. Beth McKillen, 'Irish Feminism and Nationalist Separatism', *Éire-Ireland* 17 (1982), 62; Ward, 'Gender', 173; BMH WS 585 (Frank Robbins); Margaret Skinnider, *Doing My Bit for Ireland* (New York, 1917).
245. BMH WS 539 (Maire Foley [née Smart]).
246. BMH WS 923 (Ignatius Callender).
247. BMH WS 398 (Bridget Martin).
248. BMH WS 246 (Marie Perolz).
249. BMH WS 1754 (Mrs Tom Barry).
250. BMH WS 419 (Mrs Martin Conlon). Jack Hurley was a cousin (and mentor) of Michael Collins.
251. BMH WS 398 (Bridget Martin).
252. BMH WS 399 (Mrs Richard Mulcahy).
253. *Rebellion Handbook*, 10–11.
254. Jeffery, *The GPO*, 47, 180.
255. Taillon, *Women of 1916*, 99.
256. BMH WS 399 (Mrs Richard Mulcahy).
257. Cal McCarthy, *Cumann na mBan and the Irish Revolution* (Cork, 2006), 70.
258. BMH WS 391 (Helena Molony).
259. Ibid.
260. BMH WS 216 (Louise Gavan Duffy).

CHAPTER 5: GLORIOUS FOREVER

1. Keith Jeffery, *The GPO and the Easter Rising* (Dublin, 2006), 18.
2. Charles Townshend, *Easter 1916: The Irish Rebellion* (London, 2005), 184–6.
3. Ibid. 187.
4. Jeffery, *The GPO*, 44.
5. Townshend, *Easter 1916*, 187–8.
6. Ibid. 189.
7. Jeffery, *The GPO*, 72.
8. B[ureau of] M[ilitary] H[istory] W[itness] S[statement] 807 (Fr Patrick Doyle).

9. BMH WS 196 (Albert Mitchell).

10. BMH WS 907 (Laurence Nugent).

11. BMH WS 157 (Joseph O'Connor).

12. Michael Foy and Brian Barton, *The Easter Rising* (Stroud, 1999), 77.

13. BMH WS 310 (Seumas Grace); BMH WS 646 (William Christian).

14. BMH WS 646 (William Christian).

15. BMH WS 198 (James Walsh).

16. BMH WS 208 (Seamus Kavanagh).

17. BMH WS 198 (James Walsh).

18. BMH WS 310 (Seumas Grace).

19. BMH WS 198 (James Walsh).

20. Ibid.

21. Foy and Barton, *Easter Rising*, 80.

22. BMH WS 309 (James Doyle).

23. Foy and Barton, *Easter Rising*, 78; Townshend, *Easter 1916*, 197.

24. BMH WS 309 (James Doyle).

25. Foy and Barton, *Easter Rising*, 81; Townshend, *Easter 1916*, 198.

26. BMH WS 198 (James Walsh).

27. BMH WS 813 (Padraig O'Connor).

28. Foy and Barton, *Easter Rising*, 82.

29. Townshend, *Easter 1916*, 197.

30. Ibid. 195.

31. BMH WS 348 (E. Gerrard).

32. BMH WS 907 (Laurence Nugent).

33. BMH WS 1756 (Seamus Murphy).

34. Foy and Barton, *Easter Rising*, 79.

35. Max Caulfield, *The Easter Rebellion* (Colorado, 1995 edn.), 197–8.

36. Townshend, *Easter 1916*, 199.

37. Foy and Barton, *Easter Rising*, 221.

38. BMH WS 131 (George O'Flanagan).

39. BMH WS 926 (Kevin McCabe).

40. Joost Augusteijn (ed.), *The Memoirs of John M. Regan: a Catholic Officer in the RIC and RUC, 1909–48* (Dublin, 2007), 95.

41. BMH WS 1693 (John Kenny).

42. BMH WS 280 (Robert Holland).

43. BMH WS 157 (Joseph O'Connor).

44. *1916 Rebellion Handbook* (Dublin, 1998 edn.), 45.

45. BMH WS 724 (Desmond Ryan).

46. BMH WS 687 (Fr Michael Curran).

47. Jeffery, *The GPO*, 158.

48. BMH WS 824 (Charles Donnelly).

49. BMH WS 497 (Eamon Bulfin).

50. BMH WS 1744 (Seán Nunan).

51. BMH WS 1687 (Harry Colley).
52. Conor Kostick and Lorcan Collins, *The Easter Rising: A Guide to Dublin in 1916* (Dublin, 2009 edn.), 79.
53. BMH WS 822 (William Stapleton).
54. BMH WS 585 (Frank Robbins).
55. BMH WS 781 (Patrick Kelly).
56. BMH WS 585 (Frank Robbins).
57. BMH WS 733 (James O'Shea).
58. F. X. Martin, 'Eoin MacNeill on the 1916 Rising', *Irish Historical Studies* 12/47 (1961), 226–71. For a recent discussion, see Séamus Murphy, 'Easter Ethics', in Gabriel Doherty and Dermot Keogh (eds), *1916: The Long Revolution* (Cork, 2007), 329–52.
59. BMH WS 1666 (Thomas O'Donoghue).
60. Foy and Barton, *Easter Rising*, 167.
61. BMH WS 1750 (Con O'Donovan).
62. BMH WS 333 (Aine O'Rahilly).
63. BMH WS 310 (Seumas Grace); BMH WS 157 (Joseph O'Connor).
64. Foy and Barton, *Easter Rising*, 76. David Fitzpatrick (*The Two Irelands 1912–1939* (Oxford, 1998), 62), for example, refers to 'the casual murder of five unarmed reservists'.
65. Maurice Headlam, *Irish Reminiscences* (London, 1947), 168; Townshend, *Easter 1916*, 259.
66. BMH WS 724 (Desmond Ryan).
67. BMH WS 388 (Joe Good).
68. BMH WS 748 (John Doyle); BMH WS 201 (Nicholas Laffan).
69. BMH WS 585 (Frank Robbins).
70. BMH WS 242 (Liam Tannam).
71. BMH WS 824 (Charles Donnelly).
72. BMH WS 833 (Michael Knightly).
73. BMH WS 685 (Claire Hobson).
74. BMH WS 423 (Vincent Byrne).
75. BMH WS 312 (Seosamh de Brun).
76. BMH WS 648 (Catherine Rooney).
77. BMH WS 889 (James Kavanagh).
78. Lord Dunsany, *Patches of Sunlight* (New York, 1938), 280–1.
79. BMH WS 399 (Mrs Richard Mulcahy).
80. *Rebellion Handbook*, 10–11.
81. BMH WS 388 (Joe Good).
82. BMH WS 201 (Nicholas Laffan).
83. Headlam, *Irish Reminiscences*, 171.
84. Jeffery, *The GPO*, 97.
85. Headlam, *Irish Reminiscences*, 174.
86. Jeffery, *The GPO*, 94.
87. BMH WS 889 (James Kavanagh).

88. Headlam, *Irish Reminiscences*, 174.
89. Jeffery, *The GPO*, 83.
90. BMH WS 1019 (Alfred Bucknill).
91. Headlam, *Irish Reminiscences*, 175.
92. Dunsany, *Sunlight*, 278.
93. Augusteijn, *John M. Regan*, 95.
94. BMH WS 348 (E. Gerrard).
95. BMH WS 258 (Maeve McDowell).
96. BMH WS 333 (Aine O'Rahilly); *Rebellion Handbook*, 58.
97. *Rebellion Handbook*, 45.
98. BMH WS 920 (Fr Augustine OFM Cap).
99. BMH WS 196 (Albert Mitchell).
100. BMH WS 979 (Robert Barton).
101. BMH WS 196 (Albert Mitchell).
102. Augusteijn, *John M. Regan*, 96.
103. BMH WS 697 (Patrick Bermingham).
104. BMH WS 1071 (George Duggan).
105. BMH WS 310 (Seumas Grace); BMH WS 722 (Dan McCarthy).
106. BMH WS 850 (Patrick Colgan).
107. BMH WS 193 (Seamus O'Farrell).
108. *Rebellion Handbook*, 216.
109. Townshend, *Easter 1916*, 294.
110. Foy and Barton, *Easter Rising*, 188.
111. *Rebellion Handbook*, 23–5.
112. Jeffery, *The GPO*, 81.
113. *Rebellion Handbook*, 23.
114. Tim Pat Coogan, *1916: The Easter Rising* (London, 2005), 152–3.
115. Foy and Barton, *Easter Rising*, 188.
116. Fitzpatrick, *Two Irelands*, 61.
117. BM WS 850 (Patrick Colgan).
118. BMH WS 1035 (Sean Cody).
119. BMH WS 934 (Mary McLoughlin).
120. Dunsany, *Sunlight*, 289.
121. BMH WS 242 (Liam Tannam).
122. BMH WS 423 (Vincent Byrne); BMH WS 397 (Thomas Pugh).
123. BMH WS 397 (Thomas Pugh).
124. BMH WS 734 (Thomas Meldon).
125. BMH WS 398 (Bridget Martin).
126. BMH WS 157 (Joseph O'Connor).
127. BMH WS 198 (James Walsh).
128. BMH WS 158 (Seamus Kenny).
129. BMH WS 531 (Thomas Young).
130. BMH WS 482 (Rose McNamara).

131. BMH WS 889 (James Kavanagh).
132. BMH WS 850 (Patrick Colgan). Jeyes fluid is a brand of disinfectant.
133. BMH WS 1722 (Seamus Robinson).
134. BMH WS 694 (Frank Burke).
135. BMH WS 648 (Catherine Rooney).
136. BMH WS 242 (Liam Tannam).
137. BMH WS 186 (Thomas Doyle).
138. BMH WS 320 (Tom Harris).
139. BMH WS 1722 (Seamus Robinson).
140. BMH WS 148 (James Crenegan); BMH WS 165 (Luke Kennedy).
141. BMH WS 113 (Simon Donnelly).
142. Foy and Barton, *Easter Rising*, 85–6.
143. *Rebellion Handbook*, 122–7.
144. BMH WS 155 (Peadar Doyle).
145. BMH WS 148 (James Crenegan).
146. BMH WS 398 (Bridget Martin).
147. Foy and Barton, *Easter Rising*, 140.
148. BMH WS 340 (Oscar Traynor).
149. BMH WS 724 (Desmond Ryan); BMH WS 195 (Molly Reynolds).
150. BMH WS 660 (Thomas Leahy).
151. BMH WS 216 (Louise Gavan Duffy).
152. BMH WS 724 (Desmond Ryan).
153. Jeffery, *The GPO*, 149–50.
154. Ibid. 76.
155. Bertram Carter, *Another Part of the Platform* (London, 1931), 30.
156. BMH WS 340 (Oscar Traynor).
157. BMH WS 850 (Patrick Colgan).
158. BMH WS 724 (Desmond Ryan).
159. BMH WS 497 (Eamon Bulfin).
160. BMH WS 889 (James Kavanagh).
161. BMH WS 926 (Kevin McCabe).
162. BMH WS 724 (Desmond Ryan).
163. Foy and Barton, *Easter Rising*, 168.
164. BMH WS 532 (John MacDonagh).
165. BMH WS 724 (Desmond Ryan).
166. Desmond FitzGerald, *Desmond's Rising: Memoirs, 1913 to Easter 1916* (Dublin, 2006 edn.), 146.
167. Jeffery, *The GPO*, 181.
168. Ibid. 91.
169. Brian Barton, *From Behind a Closed Door: Secret Court Martial Records of the Easter Rising* (Belfast, 2002), 18.
170. Jeffery, *The GPO*, 181.
171. Ibid. 177.

172. Ibid. 86.

173. BMH WS 196 (Albert Mitchell).

174. BMH WS 157 (Joseph O'Connor).

175. James Stephens, *The Insurrection in Dublin* (Gloucester, 2008 edn.), 32; Jeffery, *The GPO*, 178.

176. BMH WS 463 (Anonymous Sister of Mercy, Mater Hospital).

177. Ruth Taillon, *When History Was Made: The Women of 1916* (Belfast, 1999), 88; for Dublin's hospitals, see *Rebellion Handbook*, 240–5.

178. BMH WS 660 (Thomas Leahy).

179. BMH WS 333 (Aine O'Rahilly).

180. BMH WS 311 (Fr James Doyle).

181. BMH WS 687 (Fr Michael Curran). Curran's recollections may have been influenced by his (subsequent) strong separatist sympathies.

182. Jeffery, *The GPO*, 137.

183. BMH WS 1071 (George Duggan).

184. Jeffery, *The GPO*, 91.

185. Stephens, *Insurrection*, 20.

186. Jeffery, *The GPO*, 79

187. Dunsany, *Sunlight*, 283.

188. Jeffery, *The GPO*, 159.

189. BMH WS 541 (Nancy Wyse-Power).

190. BMH WS 388 (Joe Good).

191. BMH WS 311 (Fr James Doyle).

192. Jeffery, *The GPO*, 93.

193. Shane Hegarty and Fintan O'Toole, *The Irish Times Book of the 1916 Rising* (Dublin, 2006), 93.

194. BMH WS 687 (Fr Michael Curran).

195. BMH WS 160 (Joseph Byrne).

196. BMH WS 925 (Mairead O'Kelly).

197. BMH WS 259 (Bridget Thornton).

198. Hegarty and O'Toole, *Irish Times Book*, 97.

199. Stephens, *Insurrection*, 19.

200. BMH WS 1184 (Eileen Costello).

201. Jeffery, *The GPO*, 174.

202. Headlam, *Irish Reminiscences*, 168.

203. Stephens, *Insurrection*, 19–20, 30–1.

204. Jeffery, *The GPO*, 174.

205. BMH WS 420 (Charles Wyse-Power).

206. Ernie O'Malley, *On Another Man's Wound* (Dublin, 1990 edn.), 28–34.

207. BMH WS 492 (John McCoy).

208. BMH WS 162 (John Shouldice).

209. BMH WS 263 (Thomas Slater). See also BMH WS 312 (Seosamh de Brun).

210. Stephens, *Insurrection*, 22.

211. David Foxton, *Revolutionary Lawyers, Sinn Féin and Crown Courts in Ireland and Britain, 1916–1923* (Dublin, 2008), 65–7.
212. Foy and Barton, *Easter Rising*, 220.
213. Townshend, *Easter 1916*, 208.
214. BMH WS 320 (Tom Harris).
215. BMH WS 724 (Desmond Ryan).
216. BMH WS 242 (Liam Tannam).
217. Foy and Barton, *Easter Rising*, 150.
218. BMH WS 153 (Eamon Dore).
219. BMH WS 110 (Denis Daly).
220. BMH WS 1693 (John Kenny).
221. BMH WS 242 (Liam Tannam).
222. BMH WS 388 (Joe Good).
223. BMH WS 694 (Frank Burke); BMH WS 242 (Liam Tannam).
224. BMH WS 694 (Frank Burke).
225. BMH WS 340 (Oscar Traynor).
226. BMH WS 388 (Joe Good).
227. BMH WS 290 (Sean McLoughlin).
228. BMH WS 497 (Eamon Bulfin).
229. BMH WS 290 (Sean McLoughlin); BMH WS 388 (Joe Good).
230. BMH WS 370 (Fintan Murphy).
231. BMH WS 156 (Seamus Robinson).
232. BMH WS 694 (Frank Burke).
233. BMH WS 889 (James Kavanagh).
234. BMH WS 388 (Joe Good).
235. Ibid.
236. BMH WS 660 (Thomas Leahy).
237. BMH WS 889 (James Kavanagh).
238. Ibid.
239. BMH WS 497 (Eamon Bulfin).
240. BMH WS 660 (Thomas Leahy).
241. BMH WS 340 (Oscar Traynor).
242. BMH WS 694 (Frank Burke).
243. BMH WS 290 (Sean McLoughlin).
244. BMH WS 388 (Joe Good).
245. BMH WS 290 (Sean McLoughlin); BMH WS 388 (Joe Good).
246. BMH WS 694 (Frank Burke).
247. BMH WS 242 (Liam Tannam).
248. BMH WS 370 (Fintan Murphy).
249. BMH WS 288 (Charles Saurin).
250. BMH WS 244 (John McGallogly).
251. Townshend, *Easter 1916*, 247.
252. Gerard MacAtasney, *Seán MacDiarmada* (Nure, 2004), 123.

CHAPTER 6: CHARLIE WESTON, ARE YOU GONE MAD?

1. Charles Townshend, *Easter 1916: The Irish Rebellion* (London, 2005), 102, 110.
2. B[ureau of] M[ilitary] H[istory] W[itness] S[tatement] 26 (P. S. O'Hegarty).
3. BMH WS 24 (Cornelius Murphy).
4. BMH WS 161 (Donal O'Hannigan).
5. Ibid.
6. Michael Foy and Brian Barton, *The Easter Rising* (Stroud, 1999), 41; Townshend, *Easter 1916*, 125–31.
7. Gerry White and Brendan O'Shea, 'Easter 1916 in Cork—Order, Counter-Order, and Disorder', in Gabriel Doherty and Dermot Keogh (eds), *1916: The Long Revolution* (Cork, 2007), 169–98.
8. David Fitzpatrick, 'Militarism in Ireland, 1900–1922', in Tom Bartlett and Keith Jeffery (eds), *A Military History of Ireland* (Cambridge, 1996), 394.
9. BMH 6 (Liam Ó Briain).
10. Foy and Barton, *Easter Rising*, 14.
11. BMH 733 (James O'Shea); Foy and Barton, *Easter Rising*, 27; White and O'Shea, 'Easter 1916 in Cork'.
12. BMH WS 25 (Patrick Higgins).
13. BMH WS 119 (Eithne MacSwiney).
14. Ibid.
15. BMH WS 1598 (Thomas Barry).
16. BMH WS 70 (Jim Ryan).
17. BMH WS 47 (Liam O'Callaghan).
18. White and O'Shea, 'Easter 1916 in Cork', 181; Peter Hart, *The IRA and Its Enemies* (Oxford, 1998), 202.
19. BMH WS 19 (Liam Murphy). See also BMH WS 90 (Con Collins). 'Der Tag', the German expression meaning an expected day of national vengeance, was adopted by some Irish separatists.
20. BMH WS 74 (Paud O'Donoghue).
21. BMH WS 20 (Tom Hales).
22. BMH WS 138 (Timothy Riordan).
23. BMH WS 706 (Jeremiah O'Carroll).
24. BMH WS 73 (Denis Lyons).
25. BMH WS 20 (Tom Hales).
26. BMH WS 35 (Michael Lynch).
27. BMH WS 54 (Sean O'Hegarty).
28. BMH WS 1521 (Michael Walsh).
29. BMH WS 103 (Sean O'Hegarty).
30. BMH WS 80 (Patrick Harris).
31. BMH WS 345 (Brian Molloy).
32. BMH WS 16 (Riobard Langford).

33. BMH WS 343 (James Barrett).
34. BMH WS 39 (Eamon Ahern).
35. BMH WS 446 (Frank Hynes).
36. BMH WS 138 (Timothy Riordan).
37. BMH WS 34 (Patrick O'Sullivan).
38. BMH WS 24 (Cornelius Murphy).
39. Ibid.
40. BMH WS 54 (Sean O'Hegarty).
41. BMH WS 170 (Paul Galligan).
42. BMH WS 25 (Patrick Higgins).
43. BMH WS 279 (Seamus Dobbyn).
44. BMH WS 20 (Tom Hales); BMH WS 161 (Donal O'Hannigan).
45. BMH WS 24 (Cornelius Murphy).
46. BMH WS 1720 (John Manning).
47. BMH WS 447 (Thomas Courtney).
48. BMH WS 76 (Seamus Hickey).
49. BMH WS 24 (Cornelius Murphy).
50. BMH WS 869 (P. J. Murphy).
51. BMH WS 57 (Thomas O'Donovan).
52. BMH WS 21 (Joseph O'Shea).
53. BMH WS 35 (Michael Lynch).
54. BMH WS 90 (Con Collins).
55. BMH WS 39 (Eamon Ahern).
56. BMH WS 57 (Thomas O'Donovan).
57. BMH WS 20 (Tom Hales).
58. BMH WS 15 (Fred Murray).
59. BMH WS 62 (Patrick Looney).
60. BMH WS 21 (Joseph O'Shea).
61. BMH WS 950 (David O'Callaghan).
62. Maurice Headlam, *Irish Reminiscences* (London, 1947), 179.
63. BMH WS 24 (Cornelius Murphy).
64. BMH WS 915 (Denis McCullough).
65. BMH WS 235 (Fr James O'Daly).
66. BMH WS 325 (Fr Eugene Coyle).
67. Ibid.
68. Ibid.; BMH WS 915 (Denis McCullough).
69. BMH WS 402 (Sean Cusack).
70. BMH WS 915 (Denis McCullough).
71. BMH WS 124 (Joseph Connolly).
72. BMH WS 915 (Denis McCullough).
73. Ibid.
74. Ibid.

75. Fergal McCluskey, 'The Development of Republican Politics in East Tyrone, 1898–1918', PhD thesis, Queen's University Belfast, 2007, 209.
76. Ibid.
77. BMH WS 915 (Denis McCullough).
78. BMH WS 919 (Ina Connolly); BMH WS 179.
79. BMH WS 915 (Denis McCullough).
80. Ibid.
81. BMH WS 173 (Cathal McDowell); BMH WS 915 (Denis McCullough).
82. BMH WS 227 (Henry Corr).
83. BMH WS 221 (Arthur McElvogue).
84. BMH WS 176 (Thomas Wilson).
85. BMH WS 919 (Ina Connolly).
86. BMH WS 169 (James Tomney).
87. BMH WS 223 (Robert Haskin).
88. BMH WS 105 (Frank Burke).
89. BMH WS 1598 (Thomas Barry).
90. BMH WS 246 (Marie Perolz).
91. BMH WS 16 (Riobard Langford).
92. BMH WS 398 (Bridget Martin).
93. BMH WS 16 (Riobard Langford).
94. BMH WS 25 (Patrick Higgins).
95. Situated in a river valley, the city would have been particularly vulnerable to artillery from the surrounding hills.
96. BMH WS 20 (Tom Hales).
97. BMH WS 1598 (Thomas Barry).
98. BMH WS 16 (Riobard Langford).
99. BMH WS 15 (Fred Murray).
100. BMH WS 89 (Michael O Cuill).
101. BMH WS 739 (Felix O'Doherty).
102. BMH WS 959 (Patrick Houlihan).
103. Hart, *IRA and Its Enemies*, 191.
104. BMH WS 153 (Eamon Dore).
105. BMH WS 154 (Nora Dore).
106. BMH WS 79 (Diarmuid O'Donneabhain).
107. BMH WS 154 (Nora Dore).
108. Hart, *IRA and Its Enemies*, 48.
109. BMH WS 337 (Daniel Tuite).
110. BMH WS 122 (Elizabeth O'Brien).
111. BMH WS 1344 (Maire Fitzpatrick).
112. BMH WS 119 (Eithne MacSwiney).
113. BMH WS 286 (Nora O'Brien).
114. Ibid.

115. BMH WS 286 (Nora O'Brien).

116. BMH WS 258 (Maeve McDowell).

117. John O'Callaghan, 'The Limerick Volunteers and 1916', in Ruán O'Donnell, *The Impact of the 1916 Rising: Among the Nations* (Dublin, 2008), 9.

118. BMH WS 1700 (Alphonsus O'Halloran).

119. BMH WS 910 (Alphonsus O'Halloran).

120. BMH WS 258 (Maeve McDowell).

121. BMH WS 597 (Edmond O'Brien).

122. BMH WS 1110 (Peter Browne); *1916 Rebellion Handbook* (Dublin, 1998 edn.), 185.

123. Headlam, *Irish Reminiscences*, 178.

124. BMH WS 19 (Liam Murphy).

125. BMH WS 1110 (Peter Browne).

126. BMH WS 374 (Michael O'Droighneain).

127. BMH WS 7 (Liam Ó Briain).

128. BMH WS 446 (Frank Hynes).

129. BMH WS 374 (Michael O'Droighneain).

130. BMH WS 714 (Thomas Hynes).

131. BMH WS 406 (Frank Hardiman).

132. *Rebellion Handbook*, 183.

133. BMH WS 298 (Ailbhe O Manachain).

134. Fergus Campbell, *Land and Revolution: Nationalist Politics in the West of Ireland 1891–1921* (Oxford, 2005), 155–64; BMH WS 7 (Liam Ó Briain).

135. BMH WS 617 (Bridget Malone [née Breathnach]).

136. BMH WS 298 (Ailbhe O Manachain). C. D. Greaves (*1916 as History: The Myth of the Blood Sacrifice* (Dublin, 1991 edn.)) described the Rising in Galway as 'a kind of peasant war accompanying the national revolution in Dublin'.

137. BMH WS 373 (John Hosty).

138. BMH WS 572 (Thomas Newell).

139. BMH WS 1173 (Michael Hynes).

140. BMH WS 383 (Fr Thomas Fahy). O'Dea was more likely to have been influenced by pastoral concerns than political sympathies in approving of the role of these priests.

141. BMH WS 617 (Bridget Malone). Other accounts state that this clerical intervention did not deter the attack.

142. Townshend, *Easter 1916*, 231.

143. *Rebellion Handbook*, 182–3.

144. Campbell, *Land and Revolution*, 219.

145. Fergus Campbell, 'The Easter Rising in Galway', *History Ireland*, 14/2 (2006), 22.

146. BMH WS 342 (Michael Newell).

147. *Rebellion Handbook*, 35.

148. BMH WS 373 (John Hosty).

149. Campbell, 'Easter Rising', 23–4.

150. BMH WS 298 (Ailbhe O Manachain); BMH WS 383 (Fr Tom Fahy); BMH WS 446 (Frank Hynes).

151. BMH WS 1043 (Joseph Lawless).

152. BMH WS 1494 (Michael McAllister).

153. BMH WS 149 (Charlie Weston).

154. BMH WS 521 (Jerry Golden); BMH WS 149 (Charlie Weston).

155. BMH WS 142 (James O'Connor).

156. BMH WS 1494 (Michael McAllister).

157. BMH WS 147 (Bernard McAllister).

158. BMH WS 177 (Jerry Golden).

159. Ibid.

160. BMH WS 278 (Francis Daly).

161. BMH WS 177 (Jerry Golden).

162. BMH WS 904 (John Austin).

163. Terence Dooley, 'Alexander "Baby" Gray (1858–1916) and the Battle at Ashbourne, 28 April 1916', *Riocht na Midhe* 14 (2003), 222.

164. *Rebellion Handbook*, 35; BMH WS 147 (Bernard McAllister).

165. Townshend, *Easter 1916*, 219; see Dooley, 'Alexander "Baby" Gray', for a detailed account of the battle.

166. BMH WS 521 (Jerry Golden).

167. BMH WS 1494 (Michael McAllister).

168. BMH WS 904 (John Austin).

169. BMH WS 147 (Bernard McAllister).

170. BMH WS 1043 (Joseph Lawless).

171. BMH WS 467 (Eugene Bratton).

172. BMH WS 147 (Bernard McAllister); BMH WS 904 (John Austin).

173. BMH WS 383 (Fr Tom Fahy); BMH WS 298 (Ailbhe O Manachain).

174. BMH WS 1298 (Patrick Doyle).

175. BMH WS 147 (Bernard McAllister).

176. BMH WS 142 (James O'Connor).

177. BMH WS 149 (Charlie Weston).

178. BMH WS 904 (John Austin).

179. BMH WS 1043 (Joseph Lawless).

180. BMH WS 1343 (James Cullen).

181. BMH WS 170 (Paul Galligan).

182. Ibid.

183. BMH WS 1031 (John O'Reilly).

184. BMH WS 1175 (Michael Kirwin).

185. BMH WS 1031 (John O'Reilly).

186. BMH WS 1216 (Fr Patrick Murphy).

187. BMH WS 1373 (Ed Balfe).

188. BMH WS 170 (Paul Galligan).

189. BMH WS 299 (Patrick Ronan); BMH WS 1041 (Thomas Doyle).

190. BMH WS 1343 (James Cullen).
191. BMH WS 1158 (Michael O'Brien).
192. BMH WS 170 (Paul Galligan); *Rebellion Handbook*, 186.
193. BMH WS 1298 (Patrick Doyle).
194. BMH WS 1216 (Patrick Murphy).
195. BMH WS 1344 (Maire Fitzpatrick).
196. BMH WS 159 (Alexander Nowlan).
197. BMH WS 170 (Paul Galligan).
198. BMH WS 1343 (James Cullen); BMH WS 988 (Martin Dunbar).
199. H. C. Lyster, *An Irish Parish in Changing Days* (London, 1933), 117–18. The details of Lyster's account suggest that the term 'exodus' may be overdramatic.
200. *Rebellion Handbook*, 185
201. Ibid. 186.
202. BMH WS 1344 (Maire Fitzpatrick).
203. BMH WS 929 (Daniel O'Shaughnessy).
204. Campbell, *Land and Revolution*, 298.
205. Ibid. 299.
206. Gerard MacAtasney, *Seán MacDiarmada* (Nure, 2004), 128.
207. Peter Hart, 'The Fenians and the International Revolutionary Tradition', in Fearghal McGarry and James McConnel (eds), *The Black Hand of Republicanism: Fenianism in Modern Ireland* (Dublin, 2009), 200.
208. Conor McNamara, 'Politics and Society in East Galway, 1914–21', PhD thesis, St Patrick's College, Drumcondra, 2008, 95–6, 110.
209. Foy and Barton, *Easter Rising*, 18–19.
210. See, for example, White and O'Shea, 'Easter 1916 in Cork'; O'Callaghan, 'Limerick Volunteers'; McNamara, 'East Galway, 1914–21', 110.
211. J. J. Lee, *The Modernisation of Irish Society, 1848–1918* (Dublin, 1973), 156.

CHAPTER 7: A GOOD END

1. B[ureau of] M[ilitary] H[istory] W[itness] S[statement] 1730 (Peadar McMahon).
2. Ibid.; BMH WS 200 (Father Aloysius).
3. BMH WS 995 (Eamon [Bob] Price).
4. BMH 139 (Michael Walker).
5. BMH WS 335 (Joseph Furlong).
6. BMH WS 263 (Thomas Slater).
7. BMH WS 300 (Henry Murray).
8. BMH WS 377 (Peadar O'Mara).
9. BMH WS 160 (Joseph O'Byrne); BMH WS 208 (Seamus Kavanagh).
10. BMH WS 377 (Peadar O'Mara).
11. BMH WS 280 (Robert Holland).
12. BMH WS 805 (Lily Curran).
13. BMH WS 302 (Maire O'Brolchain).

14. BMH WS 800 (Michael O'Flanagan).
15. Michael Foy and Brian Barton, *The Easter Rising* (Stroud, 1999), 87.
16. BMH WS 157 (Joseph O'Connor).
17. BMH WS 995 (Eamon Price).
18. BMH WS 618 (Sean O'Duffy).
19. BMH WS 199 (Joseph Doolan).
20. BMH WS 585 (Frank Robbins).
21. BMH WS 734 (Thomas Meldon).
22. BMH WS 288 (Charles Saurin).
23. BMH WS 160 (Joseph O'Byrne).
24. BMH WS 411 (Eamon Morkan).
25. BMH WS 781 (Patrick Kelly).
26. BMH WS 267 (Seamus Pounch).
27. BMH WS 1043 (Joseph Lawless).
28. BMH WS 842 (Sean Kennedy).
29. BMH WS 160 (Joseph O'Byrne).
30. BMH WS 119 (Eithne MacSwiney); BMH WS 20 (Tom Hales).
31. BMH WS 1140 (Patrick Ward).
32. BMH WS 155 (Peadar Doyle).
33. BMH WS 585 (Frank Robbins).
34. BMH WS 225 (Michael McDonnell).
35. BMH WS 280 (Robert Holland).
36. BMH WS 376 (Padraig Ó Ceallaigh).
37. BMH WS 186 (Thomas Doyle).
38. BMH WS 153 (Eamon Dore).
39. BMH WS 995 (Eamon Price).
40. Keith Jeffery, *The GPO and the Easter Rising* (Dublin, 2006), 183.
41. Ibid. 87.
42. BMH WS 199 (Joseph Doolan).
43. BMH WS 833 (Michael Knightly).
44. BMH WS 162 (John Shouldice).
45. BMH WS 585 (Frank Robbins).
46. BMH WS 388 (Joe Good).
47. BMH WS 162 (John Shouldice).
48. BMH WS 340 (Oscar Traynor); BMH WS 388 (Joe Good).
49. Charles Townshend, *Easter 1916: The Irish Rebellion* (London, 2005), 306.
50. James Stephens, *The Insurrection in Dublin* (Gloucester, 2008 edn.), 20.
51. BMH WS 147 (Bernard McAllister); BMH WS 163 (Patrick Rankin).
52. BMH WS 805 (Lily Curran).
53. BMH WS 288 (Charles Saurin).
54. BMH WS 585 (Frank Robbins).
55. BMH WS 388 (Joe Good).
56. BMH WS 833 (Michael Knightly).

57. BMH WS 160 (Joseph O'Byrne).
58. BMH WS 264 (Aine Ceannt).
59. BMH WS 979 (Robert Barton).
60. BMH WS 312 (Seosamh de Brun).
61. BMH 995 (Eamon Price).
62. BMH WS 923 (Ignatius Callender); 833 (Michael Knightly).
63. BMH WS 303 (Josephine O'Neill).
64. BMH WS 200 (Fr Aloysius).
65. BMH WS 1043 (Joseph Lawless).
66. BMH WS 923 (Ignatius Callender).
67. BMH WS 149 (Charlie Weston).
68. BMH WS 421 (William Oman).
69. BMH WS 842 (Sean Kennedy).
70. BMH WS 291 (William Daly).
71. BMH WS 1693 (John Kenny).
72. Joost Augusteijn (ed.), *The Memoirs of John M. Regan: a Catholic Officer in the RIC and RUC, 1909–48* (Dublin, 2007), 95.
73. BMH WS 850 (Patrick Colgan).
74. BMH WS 155 (Peadar Doyle); BMH WS 288 (Charles Saurin).
75. BMH WS 532 (John MacDonagh).
76. BMH WS 781 (Patrick Kelly).
77. BMH WS 342 (Michael Newell).
78. BMH WS 646 (William Christian).
79. BMH WS 422 (Sean Byrne).
80. Joanna Bourke, *The Misfit Soldier: Edward Casey's War Story, 1914–1918* (Cork, 1999), 56.
81. BMH WS 618 (Sean O'Duffy).
82. BMH WS 850 (Patrick Colgan).
83. BMH WS 1756 (Seamus Murphy).
84. BMH WS 800 (Michael O'Flanagan).
85. BMH WS 1753 (Liam Tobin).
86. Gerard MacAtasney, *Seán MacDiarmada* (Nure, 2004), 130.
87. BMH WS 388 (Joe Good).
88. Ruth Taillon, *When History Was Made: The Women of 1916* (Belfast, 1999), 92–3.
89. BMH WS 804 (Mortimer O'Connell).
90. BMH WS 153 (Eamon Dore).
91. BMH WS 186 (Thomas Doyle).
92. BMH WS 694 (Frank Burke).
93. BMH WS 660 (Thomas Leahy).
94. BMH WS 152 (Arthur Agnew).
95. BMH WS 833 (Michael Knightly).
96. BMH WS 163 (Patrick Rankin).
97. BMH WS 697 (Patrick Bermingham).

98. BMH WS 288 (Charles Saurin).

99. BMH WS 865 (Jack Plunkett).

100. BMH WS 850 (Patrick Colgan).

101. BMH WS 1244 (Joseph O'Rourke).

102. BMH WS 550 (Maurice Collins).

103. BMH WS 850 (Patrick Colgan); WS 585 (Frank Robbins).

104. BMH WS 585 (Frank Robbins).

105. BMH WS 733 (James O'Shea).

106. BMH WS 482 (Rose McNamara).

107. BMH WS 805 (Lily Curran).

108. BMH WS 391 (Helena Molony).

109. BMH WS 887 (Aine Ryan).

110. BMH WS 655 (Nora Thornton).

111. BMH WS 264 (Aine Ceannt).

112. BMH WS 399 (Mrs Richard Mulcahy).

113. BMH WS 398 (Bridget Martin).

114. Ibid.

115. Ann Matthews, 'Vanguard of the Revolution? The Citizen Army, 1916', in Ruán O'Donnell (ed.), *The Impact of the 1916 Rising: Among the Nations* (Dublin, 2008), 33.

116. BMH WS 482 (Rose McNamara).

117. BMH WS 398 (Bridget Martin). Kilmainham prison had only been closed since 1910.

118. Ibid.

119. Ibid.

120. BMH WS 482 (Rose McNamara).

121. BMH WS 398 (Bridget Martin).

122. Ibid.

123. William Murphy, 'Political Imprisonment and the Irish, 1910–21', PhD thesis, University College Dublin, 2007, 99.

124. Foy and Barton, *Easter Rising*, 225–6.

125. BMH WS 391 (Helena Molony).

126. BMH WS 822 (William Stapleton).

127. Foy and Barton, *Easter Rising*, 122–3.

128. BMH WS 290 (Sean McLoughlin).

129. BMH WS 423 (Vincent Byrne).

130. BMH WS 367 (Joseph Gleeson).

131. BMH WS 6 (Liam Ó Briain).

132. MacAtasney, *MacDiarmada*, 123.

133. BMH WS 865 (Jack Plunkett).

134. BMH WS 388 (Joe Good).

135. BMH WS 280 (Robert Holland).

136. BMH WS 729 (Patrick Browne).

137. BMH WS 683 (Hugh Hehir).
138. BMH WS 850 (Patrick Colgan).
139. BMH WS 388 (Joe Good).
140. BMH WS 376 (Padraig O'Kelly).
141. BMH WS 833 (Michael Knightly).
142. BMH WS 411 (Eamon Morkan).
143. Peter Hart, *Mick: The Real Michael Collins* (London, 2005), 100–11.
144. David Fitzpatrick, 'Militarism in Ireland, 1900–1922', in Tom Bartlett and Keith Jeffery (eds), *A Military History of Ireland* (Cambridge, 1996), 396; Murphy, 'Political Imprisonment'.
145. Michael Wheatley, '"Irreconcilable Enemies" or "Flesh and Blood"? The Irish Party and the Easter Rebels, 1914–16', in Gabriel Doherty and Dermot Keogh (eds), *1916: The Long Revolution* (Cork, 2007), 74.
146. David Fitzpatrick, *The Two Irelands 1912–1939* (Oxford, 1998), 63.
147. Jeffery, *The GPO*, 49.
148. Murphy, 'Political Imprisonment', 88.
149. BMH WS 1019 (Alfred Bucknill).
150. BMH WS 244 (John McGallogly).
151. BMH WS 1753 (Liam Tobin).
152. BMH WS 865 (Jack Plunkett).
153. BMH WS 195 (Molly Reynolds).
154. BMH WS 1019 (Alfred Bucknill).
155. BMH WS 939 (Ernest Blythe).
156. BMH WS 4 (Diarmuid Lynch).
157. BMH WS 586 (Kathleen O'Donovan [née Boland]).
158. David Fitzpatrick, *Harry Boland's Irish Revolution* (Cork, 2003), 46.
159. BMH WS 1753 (Liam Tobin).
160. Murphy, 'Political Imprisonment', 111.
161. BMH WS 328 (Gary Holohan).
162. BMH WS 532 (John MacDonagh).
163. BMH WS 886 (Michael O'Reilly).
164. BMH WS 1043 (Joseph Lawless).
165. BMH WS 481 (Simon Donnelly).
166. BMH WS 291 (William Daly).
167. BMH WS 1031 (John O'Reilly).
168. BMH WS 242 (Liam Tannam).
169. Ibid.
170. BMH WS 694 (Frank Burke).
171. Jeffery, *The GPO*, 155.
172. Elizabeth Plunkett Fingall, *Seventy Years Young: Memories of Elizabeth, Countess of Fingall* (Dublin, 1991 edn.), 375.
173. BMH WS 864 (W. E. Wylie); Townshend, *Easter 1916*, 279. The legal consensus is that the trials were unlawful (Adrian Hardiman, '"Shot in Cold Blood",

Military Law and Irish Perceptions in the Suppression of the 1916 Rebellion',
in Doherty and Keogh, *1916*, 225). David Foxton concludes that there was no
justification for the use of field (as opposed to ordinary) general courts martial
(*Revolutionary Lawyers, Sinn Féin and Crown Courts in Ireland and Britain, 1916–
1923* (Dublin, 2008), 70–5).

174. Foy and Barton, *Easter Rising*, 227.
175. BMH WS 1019 (Alfred Bucknill).
176. Foy and Barton, *Easter Rising*, 228. See also Brian Barton, *From Behind a Closed
Door: Secret Court Martial Records of the Easter Rising* (Belfast, 2002).
177. Foy and Barton, *Easter Rising*, 227–9.
178. Margaret Ward, 'Gender: Gendering the Irish Revolution', in Joost Augusteijn
(ed.), *The Irish Revolution, 1913–1923* (Basingstoke, 2002), 174.
179. Foy and Barton, *Easter Rising*, 239.
180. Tim Pat Coogan, *1916: The Easter Rising* (London, 2005), 164.
181. Foy and Barton, *Easter Rising*, 231–2.
182. BMH WS 264 (Aine Ceannt). See Piaras Mac Lochlainn, *Last Words: Letters and
Statements of the Leaders Executed after the Rising at Easter 1916* (Dublin, 1990).
183. MacAtasney, *MacDiarmada*, 142.
184. Ibid. 137.
185. BMH WS 264 (Aine Ceannt).
186. Foy and Barton, *Easter Rising*, 230–1.
187. BMH WS 270 (Eily O'Reilly).
188. BMH WS 264 (Aine Ceannt).
189. *Catholic Standard*, 29 April 1966. See also BMH WS 200 (Fr Aloysius).
190. Some discern an element of opportunism in Connolly's embrace of Catholicism (Donal Nevin, *James Connolly: 'A Full Life'* (Dublin, 2006 edn.), 684–8).
191. BMH WS 381 (George Gavan Duffy).
192. BMH WS 588 (Fr J. M. Cronin); Richard English, *Irish Freedom: The History of
Nationalism in Ireland* (London, 2006), 274.
193. Ruth Dudley Edwards, *Patrick Pearse: The Triumph of Failure* (London, 1979
edn.), 314. As elsewhere in his writings, Pearse is deliberately echoing religious
texts, in this case the Magnificat, Mary's hymn of praise on learning that she is
to be the mother of Jesus.
194. MacAtasney, *MacDiarmada*, 137.
195. Patrick Maume, *The Long Gestation: Irish Nationalist Life 1891–1918* (Dublin,
1999), 166.
196. MacAtasney, *MacDiarmada*, 137.
197. English, *Irish Freedom*, 268.
198. Foy and Barton, *Easter Rising*, 232.
199. BMW WS 382 (Thomas Mallin). This sentiment is echoed in one of the best-
known 1916 ballads, *The Foggy Dew*: ' 'Twas better to die 'neath an Irish sky
than at Suvla or Sud el Bar'.
200. BMH WS 1019 (Alfred Bucknill).

201. Murphy, 'Political Imprisonment', 97.
202. BMH WS 270 (Eily O'Reilly).
203. BMH WS 399 (Mrs Richard Mulcahy).
204. Shane Hegarty and Fintan O'Toole, *The Irish Times Book of the 1916 Rising* (Dublin, 2006), 157.
205. BMH WS 382 (Thomas Mallin).
206. BMH WS 286 (Nora O'Brien).
207. BMH WS 856 (Elizabeth Colbert).
208. BMH WS 257 (Grace Gifford).
209. BMH WS 399 (Mrs Richard Mulcahy).
210. MacAtasney, *MacDiarmada*, 140.
211. Ibid. 133.
212. BMH WS 1019 (Alfred Bucknill).
213. BMH WS 200 (Father Aloysius).
214. BMH WS 1019 (Alfred Bucknill).
215. BMH WS 348 (E. Gerrard).
216. BMH WS 189 (Michael Soughley).
217. Ibid.
218. BMH WS 208 (Seamus Kavanagh).
219. BMH WS 979 (Robert Barton).
220. MacAtasney, *MacDiarmada*, 142.

CHAPTER 8: THE BEGINNING OF IREAND

1. Maurice Headlam, *Irish Reminiscences* (London, 1947), 177.
2. Keith Jeffery, *The GPO and the Easter Rising* (Dublin, 2006), 185.
3. Ibid. 89–91.
4. For a nuanced analysis, see Charles Townshend, *Easter 1916: The Irish Rebellion* (London, 2005), 301–10.
5. Michael Wheatley, '"Irreconcilable Enemies" or "Flesh and Blood"? The Irish Party and the Easter Rebels, 1914–16', in Gabriel Doherty and Dermot Keogh (eds), *1916: The Long Revolution* (Cork, 2007), 63–4.
6. *Irish Times*, 28, 29 April, 1 May 1916.
7. *Irish Independent*, 10 May 1916.
8. Dermot Keogh, 'The Catholic Church, the Holy See and the 1916 Rising', in Doherty and Keogh (eds), *1916*, 283.
9. Ibid. 287.
10. B[ureau of] M[ilitary] H[istory] W[itness] S[tatement] 492 (John McCoy).
11. BMH WS 923 (Ignatius Callender).
12. Bertram Carter, *Another Part of the Platform* (London, 1931), 36.
13. Patrick Maume, *The Long Gestation: Irish Nationalist Life 1891–1918* (Dublin, 1999), 180; F. S. L. Lyons, *John Dillon: A Biography* (London, 1968), 384.
14. BMH WS 242 (Liam Tannam).

15. BMH WS 707 (Michael Noyk).

16. BMH WS 492 (John McCoy).

17. BMH WS 321 (Maire O'Brolchain).

18. BMH WS 739 (Felix O'Doherty).

19. BMH WS 1110 (Peter Browne).

20. BMH WS 1703 (Liam de Roiste).

21. R. F. Foster, *W. B. Yeats: A Life. II: The Arch-Poet 1915–1939* (Oxford, 2003), 45–50.

22. Richard English, *Irish Freedom: The History of Nationalism in Ireland* (London, 2006), 275.

23. Peter Hart, *The IRA and Its Enemies* (Oxford, 1998), 205.

24. BMH WS 635 (Frank King).

25. Maume, *Long Gestation*, 181.

26. Keogh, 'Catholic Church', 306–7.

27. Ibid. 288, 295.

28. Hart, *IRA and its Enemies*, 204.

29. Joost Augusteijn, 'Motivation: Why Did They Fight for Ireland? The Motivation of Volunteers in the Revolution', in *idem* (ed.), *The Irish Revolution, 1913–1923* (Basingstoke, 2002), 110.

30. Maume, *Long Gestation*, 180.

31. Deirdre McMahon, *The Moynihan Brothers in Peace and War, 1909–1918* (Dublin, 2004), 122–3.

32. Foster, *Yeats*, 51.

33. Ibid. 49, 58–64.

34. Dublin Castle Special Branch files, TNA, CO 904/213/366B.

35. BMH WS 568 (Eilis Ui Chonnaill).

36. Townshend, *Easter 1916*, 302.

37. William Murphy, 'Political Imprisonment and the Irish, 1910–21', PhD thesis, University College Dublin, 2007, 437.

38. Fran Brearton, *The Great War in Irish Poetry: W.B. Yeats to Michael Longley* (Oxford, 2000), 20.

39. T. M. Kettle, *The Ways of War* (London, 1917), 31–2. See also Senia Pašeta, *Thomas Kettle* (Dublin, 2008).

40. Hansard, H.C. Debates, 5th series, vol. 82, cols 935–51. In reality, British repression was mild compared to earlier insurrections such as 1798.

41. Michael Wheatley, *Nationalism and the Irish Party: Provincial Ireland 1910–1916* (Oxford, 2005).

42. IG, Sept. 1916, TNA, CO 904/101.

43. Maurice Moynihan (ed.), *Speeches and Statements by Eamon de Valera, 1917–73* (Dublin, 1980), 217–18; Earl of Longford and Thomas O'Neill, *Eamon de Valera* (Dublin, 1970), 298.

44. Townshend, *Easter 1916*, 348.

45. Michael Laffan, *The Resurrection of Ireland. The Sinn Féin Party 1916–1923* (Cambridge, 1999), 381.

46. David Fitzpatrick, 'Commemoration in the Irish Free State: A Chronicle of Embarrassment', in Ian McBride (ed.), *History and Memory in Modern Ireland* (Cambridge, 2001), 184–203.

47. James Moran, *Staging the Easter Rising: 1916 as Theatre* (Cork, 2005), 68–83; Eve Morrison, 'The Bureau of Military History and Female Republican Activism, 1913–23', in Maryann Gialanella Valiulis (ed.), *Gender and Power in Irish History* (Dublin, 2008), 65.

48. Mary E. Daly, 'Less a Commemoration of the Actual Achievements and More a Commemoration of the Hopes of the Men of 1916', in Mary Daly and Margaret O'Callaghan (eds), *1916 in 1966: Commemorating the Easter Rising* (Dublin, 2007), 18–85.

49. *Irish Times*, 30 March 1991; *Sunday Press*, 31 March 1991.

50. Mary McAleese, '1916—A View from 2006', in Doherty and Keogh (eds), *1916*, 24–9.

51. *Irish Times*, 14 June 2008. This result was reversed by a subsequent referendum on 2 October 2009.

52. Daly and O'Callaghan, *1916 in 1966*; Gerry Adams, *Before the Dawn* (London, 1996); Matt Treacy, 'Rethinking the Republic: The Republican Movement and 1966', in Ruán O'Donnell (ed.), *The Impact of the 1916 Rising: Among the Nations* (Dublin, 2008), 221–40.

53. For historiographical criticisms of the Rising, see Townshend, *Easter 1916*, 349–54.

54. The ninetieth anniversary was marked by strident columns in even liberal British newspapers such as the *Guardian* and *Independent* comparing the rebels to Nazis and Islamist suicide bombers (Gabriel Doherty, 'The Commemoration of the Ninetieth Anniversary of the Easter Rising', in Doherty and Keogh (eds), *1916*, 403).

55. Donal Nevin, *James Connolly: 'A Full Life'* (Dublin, 2006 edn.), 600.

56. R. F. Foster, 'We are all Revisionists now', *Irish Review* 1 (1986); see also Colm Tobín, 'New Ways of Killing Your Father', *London Review of Books*, 18 Nov. 1993.

57. *Irish Independent*, 18 April 2006.

58. Doherty, 'Commemoration', 407.

59. This book is completed in 2009, a year which has seen the Celtic Tiger economy succumb to financial crisis, and dissident republicans claim the lives of the first policeman and soldiers in Northern Ireland since the Belfast Agreement of 1998.

60. Townshend, *Easter 1916*, 350. Fitzgerald, Taoiseach during the 1980s, was the son of Desmond, 1916 leader and government minister during the interwar period.

61. Nevin, *Connolly*, 598.

Index